Fundamentals of Educational Research:

A Guide to Completing a Master's Thesis

Fundamentals of Educational Research:

A Guide to Completing a Master's Thesis

Jeffrey Glanz
Wagner College

Christopher-Gordon Publishers, Inc.
Norwood, Massachusetts

Copyright Acknowledgments

Every effort has been made to contact copyright holders for permission to reproduce borrowed material where necessary. We apologize for any oversights and would be happy to rectify them in future printings.

Material from Desimore, L., Payne, B., Fedoravicius, N., et al., "Appendix" from Comprehensive School Reform: An Implementation Study of Preschool Programs in Elementary Schools Elementary School Journal 105:5 (2004) pp. 369–426, copyright © 2004 by The University of Chicago Press. Reprinted by permission of The University of Chicago Press.

Sullivan, S., Shulman, V., and Glanz, J., Education & Urban Society (34:4) pp. 451–467, copyright © 2002 by Sage Publications. Reprinted by permission of Sage Publications, Inc.

Thesis proposal by Evelyn Schachner reprinted with her permission.

Material from the Website http://www.bartleby.com/141/ used by permission of Bartleby.com, Inc.

Christopher~Gordon Publishers, Inc.
Bridging Theory and Practice

1502 Providence Highway, Suite 12
Norwood, MA 02062

800-934-8322
781-762-5577
www.Christopher-Gordon.com

Printed in the United State of America
10 9 8 7 6 5 4 3 2 1   09 08 07 06 05

ISBN: 1-929024-90-8
Library of Congress Catalogue Number: 2005907501

Contents

Note to the Student viii

Preface xi

Part One: **Preparing to Conduct Research for a Thesis Project** 1
       Module 1: The Stress of Undertaking a Master's Thesis 2
       Module 2: Time Management 10
       Module 3: Writing Suggestions 14
       Module 4: Ethics of Research 19
       Module 5: Preliminary Review of the Literature in Search
       of a Topic 27

Part Two: **Overview of Research in Education** 39
       Module 1: A Paradigm for Research 40
       Module 2: The Steps of Educational Research 55
       Module 3: Steps in Writing the Proposal 59
       Module 4: Steps in Writing the Thesis 68

Part Three: **Thesis Overview—Chapter 1 of Thesis: Introduction** 75
       Module 1: Selecting a Topic/Title 76
       Module 2: Identifying Research Questions 88
       Module 3: Formulating Hypotheses 94

Part Four: **Thesis Overview—Chapter 2 of Thesis: Literature Review** ... 101
       Module 1: Understanding Published Research Articles 102
       Module 2: Writing the Literature Review 117

Part Five: **Thesis Overview—Chapter 3 of Thesis, Section 1: Research Design I** ... 123
       Module 1: Choosing a Research Design and Research Plan 124

Part Six: **Thesis Overview—Chapter 3 of Thesis, Section 2: Research Design 2—**
       Quantitative Approaches 151
       Module 1: Descriptive Research 152
       Module 2: Correlation Research 156
       Module 3: Group Comparison Research 160

Part Seven: **Thesis Overview—Chapter 3 of Thesis, Section 3: Research Design 3—**
       Qualitative Approaches 167
       Module 1: Historical Research 168
       Module 2: Ethnographic Research 171
       Module 3: Case Study Research 174

Part Eight: Thesis Overview—Chapter 3 of Thesis, Section 4: Research Design 4—
                   Data Collection 181
                   Module 1: Writing Questionnaires... 182
                   Module 2: Conducting Observations... 188
                   Module 3: Conducting Interviews and Group Focuses.................... 205
                   Module 4: Examining Test Data 210
                   Module 5: Other Means to Collect Data 212
                   Module 6: Validity and Reliability of Instruments............................ 214

Part Nine: Thesis Overview—Chapter 3 of Thesis, Section 5: Research Design 5—
                   Quantitative Data Analysis 221
                   Module 1: Statistical Analyses..................................... 222
                   Module 2: The t-Test 234
                   Module 3: The Sign Test 238
                   Module 4: The Mann-Whitney U-Test 242
                   Module 5: The Chi Square Test and Other Statistics 246
                   Module 6: Using SPSS or STATPAK 252

Part Ten: Thesis Overview—Chapter 3 of Thesis, Section 6: Research Design 6—
                   Qualitative Data Analysis 257
                   Module 1: Analytic Procedures....................................... 258

Part Eleven: Thesis Overview—Chapter 3 of Thesis, Section 7: Research
                   Design 7—Results 265
                   Module 1: Presenting Results 266

Part Twelve: Thesis Overview—Chapter 4 of Thesis—Implications for
                   Practice/Research 281
                   Module 1: Specifying Limitations 282
                   Module 2: Interpreting Data 285
                   Module 3: Drawing Conclusions/Discussion 289
                   Module 4: Implications for Practice............................... 293
                   Module 5: Implications for Further Research 295

Part Thirteen: Putting It All Together 297
                   Module 1: Writing the Thesis 298
                   Module 2: Incorporating APA 300
                   Module 3: Writing the Abstract 308
                   Module 4: Advice and Suggestions 313
                   Module 5: Evaluating the Thesis.................................... 319
                   Module 6: Becoming an Intelligent Consumer of Research............. 321

References 325

Glossary 329

Test Bank 353

Appendix A: Sample IRB Application 381

Appendix B: Sample Parental Consent Form 385

Appendix C: Sample Research Proposal 387

Appendix D: Sample Thesis 407

Index 441

About the Author 443

Note to the Student

> *Helen [to her fellow graduate student]: "Ugh . . . I'm dreading this next sequence of courses we gotta take."*
>
> *Sarah: "I know what you mean. I've always cringed whenever anyone mentioned the word 'research,' especially in regards to completing a thesis."*
>
> *Helen: "I know I'm goin' to have big trouble with this research seminar. I hate statistics and I can't imagine myself ever writing, let alone completing a thesis."*
>
> *Sarah: "You know what makes it worse? I have a friend, at another college, who told me that the research textbook they used was so long, boring, and dry that it made doing the thesis almost unbearable."*
>
> *Helen [resigned to her fate]: "Oh well, let's grin and bear it. On an optimistic note, after we finish this course sequence we'll never have to use this research stuff again."*

Sound familiar? Do you anticipate taking a thesis seminar, usually one year long in duration, with trepidation and dismay? Well, you're not alone. Most graduate students approach the research seminar that culminates in a thesis project/paper with anxiety and, in the words of Helen, "dread." In fact, I too felt that way many years ago when I completed my master's degree. Go figure, not only would I complete that master's degree, but I would earn another one at another institution and then go on to complete a dissertation. I completed not one, not two, but three theses! Now, as I have been doing for many years, I'm teaching the research sequence to graduate students. I guess I feel like that math teacher, who became "teacher of the year" in her district, who told me that as a student she hated math more than any subject she ever took. "It's amazing how fate plays tricks on us," she said, "now I'm the math teacher of the year."

One of my graduate students once conducted her research for a thesis on a topic most timely and relevant to her classmates that semester. She titled her project, "Stress Levels among Master Degree Students Completing a Thesis." Here's what she discovered, in part. First, and not surprisingly, 92% of students enrolled in master degree research courses that culminate in a written and formally bound thesis experience tension, nervousness and, even for some, pangs of fear resembling being "approached by a stranger in an alley at night." Funny as it may sound, respondents to her initial questionnaire explained that their nervousness was intense. A second finding was that several factors influenced the degree to which stress levels remained constant, higher, or lessened. Among these factors included the professor's approach to presenting research, and the textbook used in the course. Students who reported that the textbook was written in a "boring style" and that the book included "mathematical formulae for computing statistical procedures," experienced constant or even higher levels of stress.

I remain sensitive to your needs because I too felt the way many of you do, and I have not forgotten that feeling. I have field-tested the contents of this book and have found that students appreciate its reader-friendly and practical approach to undertaking master's degree research for a thesis, devoid of much statistical computations. One of the chief benefits of this volume is that I did not include an exhaustive list or description of everything one can possibly know about a given research term or concept. I provided you with what I felt you needed to know for completing your thesis, based on my many years of teaching experience. Therefore, my descriptions and discussion of some concepts may not be entirely complete but I am certain your professor, if so desired, can fill in the gaps he or she would like to emphasize. The book is not written to satisfy research scholars; it was written for you, the student, enrolled in a master's degree program who may have little research background and who will not likely undertake extended research projects in the future. Now, that's not to say that what you will learn cannot be used as a foundation for further work.

Many books on educational research flood the market. Many of these texts are used in college courses for preparing teachers and other educators to undertake a master's thesis project. Most if not all of these books, in my view, are too wordy, and cover many topics that are not critical for completing a master's thesis. Usually, these books are intimidating, especially for students who rarely, if ever, undertook a research study of any significant length. Moreover, many of these works do not deal exclusively with the task of planning, writing, and completing a master's degree, nor do they address the concerns and needs of master degree students enrolled in graduate programs leading to a master's in education.

A new book is needed that culls the essential principles and ideas about educational research in an easy-to-read, yet comprehensive manner. *Fundamentals of Educational Research: A Guide to Completing a Master's Thesis* is such a text. The book is designed to help you understand and apply basic research principles so that you can more successfully complete a master's thesis and, more importantly, become an intelligent consumer of research (refer to Module 6 of Part Thirteen). Recall Helen's optimistic note above when she confidently proclaimed *"Oh well, let's grin and bear it . . . , after we finish this course sequence we'll never have to use this research stuff again."* Such an approach to research is lamentable and unnecessary. Research, as I'll try to convince you, is an invaluable tool to assist you in becoming an even better teacher or educator. Educational research will promote reflection, self-assessment, and a commitment to continuous learning and improvement.

Fundamentals of Educational Research: A Guide to Completing a Master's Thesis is written in workbook format to facilitate easy reading and use. Charts, blocked text, and practice exercises make for easier reading.

My approach, most importantly, is to present the material using the chunking method of learning. Rather than present text in extremely long chapters that may be tedious for some of you and does not facilitate learning of material, I will present the material in "chunks." For example, rather than learning about the general steps of writing a research proposal, how to select a topic, how to tend to the **ethics** of research, and how to review the literature in one continuous chapter, I'll break down various components of educational research into "modules." Each module will cover one fundamental research topic (e.g., "Formulating Hypotheses").

Please note that your professor may prefer a slightly different arrangement of thesis sections or topics than the order in which I present them. That's okay. Simply view each module as you would a selection on a music CD. Simply click, if you will, or skip to the module that you need. Since a Glossary is provided to assist you in concept understanding you'll likely be able to read many of the modules out of sequence.

The book is divided into thirteen (13) different "Parts." Each "Part" includes several modules, not formal chapters (see contents page). Such an approach is meant to facilitate easier learning of the material. Interactive review and reflective exercises will be included to further reinforce your learning. Also, I will not inundate your visual senses by packing pages with side-bars, boxed vignettes, and other material not directly related to the topic at hand. Have you ever walked into a classroom that is so overly decorated that it's hard to focus? Well, many ed research texts are written in a way that taxes one's senses; not this one. I have field-tested this approach with much student success and satisfaction. Please let me know if your stress levels are reduced after using this text.

Again, realize that you can begin with almost any module. You can, of course, read the modules in the order I've laid out. However, if you feel, for instance, that you don't need advice about stress or time management, or even writing suggestions, I suggest you begin with an overview of research possibilities that can be found in Module 1 of Part Two followed by Module 2 in the same part. Then, search for a topic by reading Module 5 of Part One, Module 1 of Part Three followed by Module 1 of Part Four. With the topic approved by your professor, proceed with identifying research questions or hypotheses in Modules 2 and 3 of Part Three. At this time you might want to really get started on writing the literature review, which is the most time consuming and possibly arduous, stressful part of thesis writing. So, read Module 2 of Part Four. Decide, then, on a research design in Module 1 of Part Five followed by an understanding of mixed methodological approaches that can be found in Parts Six and Seven. Next, learn the steps of writing a proposal in Module 3 of Part Two. You can then begin to collect data (Part Eight), and learn how to analyze data (Parts Nine and Ten). Parts Eleven and Twelve follow as you near the completion of your project. Brush up on requirements for writing a thesis (Module 4 of Part Two) and read Part Thirteen to place finishing touches on the project along with more suggestions, although you might want to read Module 4 of Part Thirteen, Advice and Suggestions, near the start of the semester. Actually, why not try doing so now? . . .

Learning to use the APA manual of style for some of you can also be tedious, time consuming, and even difficult. Learning to do so early is suggested. Also, I've placed a discussion of the ethics of research early on in Part One of the book because I want you to begin thinking about the ethical implications of undertaking research before you get so entrenched with your project that these concerns may not receive adequate attention. You could always skip this module, of course, until after you have a broader understanding of the research process dealt with in Parts Two, Three, and so on.

I hope you experience the satisfaction and sense of accomplishment in completing your thesis, as I did so many years ago. My expectation is that you'll develop an appreciation of research as a professional responsibility and useful tool to improve your teaching, promote student learning, or just to improve your practice as a professional educator. You'll realize that research is not all that complicated and will, perhaps, encourage you to continue exploring your practice systematically by conducting further studies that may take the form of dissertation work on the doctoral level or action research for classroom and school improvement. Continued success in all that you do . . .

Jeffrey Glanz
Personal email (tora.dojo@verizon.net)

Preface

Fundamentals of Educational Research: A Guide to Completing a Master's Thesis is not your typical book. So why should I write the Preface in typical fashion? I rarely if ever read a preface since all it usually contains is an overview and chapter-by-chapter description of topics and ideas covered. You are a graduate student. You can figure out easily what this book will cover by perusing the Contents page. You already know my purpose is to write a book on educational research that is reader and user friendly. Two chief purposes are: 1) to give you just enough information so that you can successfully complete your master's thesis project, and 2) to encourage you to become a reflective practitioner who uses research strategies to improve teaching, promote student learning, and/or professional practice.

Oh, a few more points should be noted. First, words bolded throughout the book are usually discussed within the context in which they appear but are defined in more detail in the Glossary. In fact, I highly recommend that you flip to the Glossary each time you come across a bolded word. Realizing some of you might not follow this suggestion, I have tried to explain the term where it appears as long as the flow of textual meaning is not seriously compromised. You can still find them, though, in the Glossary. Second, a preface usually contains a litany of acknowledgments to various individuals who have assisted in writing the book. The only acknowledgment I'd like to make is to you, my reader. This work is dedicated to your successful completion of a master's thesis. And, yes, I certainly acknowledge all my former and current students who taught me so much about how to present information in as easy a way as possible. I also thank them for some of the excerpted material throughout the book. Specific acknowledgments will be made where they occur. If I inadvertently omitted someone, please let me know so I can make the correction.

One point is in order about the use of *Self-Test Check*s that are included at the end of most modules. These are comprised of sample test questions. I am not encouraging your professor to actually administer a multiple choice exam. In fact, I do not think that administering a test to students is warranted since it only increases anxiety for a project that in and of itself can be overwhelming for some students. Rather, I've used the test questions as a way for you, the student, to assess your knowledge of material covered at your own pace and preference. Some professors are completely against the use of testing in a course like the one you are taking. Others, especially if the thesis project is comprised of two or three courses over a year or more, might opt to test your knowledge at some point. Many other professors avoid such tests because they want students to show their mastery of how well they were able to operationalize the steps of the research process itself. Although at one point in my teaching career I did administer a test to my students, I have now found it more useful not to do so. Regardless of which approach your professor takes, I have found that students appreciate the test questions as a guide to check their own understanding. In my case, any apprehensions my students might have about testing in general is alleviated when I inform them that the course does not require the passing of a multiple choice test. They use the test questions, therefore, as a study and review guide. Feel free to do likewise.

Finally, I'd like to start an email conversation group of users of this text. Feel free to write me at tora.dojo@verizon.net to share experiences, pose questions, offer suggestions, etc. I will likely develop a rather large email list of users of the text. I will then forward your email to others on the list for their reading and/or response. This format allows me to control the flow of email traffic and to decide which email messages are worthy of distribution. All incoming and outgoing emails are controlled by me. Don't worry about troubling me. I'm email addicted and use it everyday, for most of the day. If you join this email group you will receive emails from students and from me. Simply send me your email address. I do not need to know your name, so anonymity at all levels can be assured. You can request to have your email address removed at any time.

* * * * * * * * * * * * * * *

My purpose in this Preface is to now set the tone for the remainder of the book by stimulating your curiosity about research in, perhaps, some unusual ways.

I begin my course on educational research by relating a famous story told at Harvard Law School in which 175 eager, albeit anxious, first-year law students await their first professor in their first course.

> *A middle-aged, scholarly-looking gentleman dressed in a dapper suit enters the huge auditorium through one of the doors adjacent to the stage. As the professor approaches the podium he peers out at his students and selects his victim.*
>
> *"You," pointing to a male student in the rear of the auditorium, "state the facts in the case before you." Nervously and hurriedly, the 175 students read the case. The student selected by the professor offers no response. Once again the professor repeats his request. The student again freezes. Again the request is made. "State the facts in the case before you." The student gives an inadequate answer.*
>
> *The professor nonchalantly reaches into his pocket and takes out a dime and says "Take this dime, call your mother (it's an old story!), and tell her to pick you up because you'll never become a lawyer." Shocked, yet thankful they weren't called upon, the 174 other students anxiously await the student's reaction. No response.*
>
> *"You heard what I said. Take this dime and tell your mother to pick you up." The student rises and walks slowly towards the stage. Hushed silence pervades the auditorium. Suddenly the student stops, looks up and shouts "Sir, you are a bastard." Without batting an eyelash, the professor looks up and says "Go back to your seat, you're beginning to think like a lawyer."*

"This story," I inform my class, "epitomizes the purpose of law school, which is to instill habits of skepticism, verbal aggressiveness, and the readiness to challenge the authority of a lawyer." I continue by conveying my expectations and hopes for them this semester. "My purposes in teaching this course are very different from that professor at Harvard. I do, however, want to help you begin to *think and act* as researchers." This too is my purpose in this book; i.e., to help you understand that research is not something to be avoided but can, does, and will serve as an important vehicle for reflective practice that leads to improved teaching, student learning, and educational practice.

Ways of Knowing and Triangulation

So, let's begin to think as educational researchers. Walk over to the window. Yes, right now . . . with book in hand of course. As you peer through the window describe what you see. Trees, automobiles, the skyline, people walking, a sunny day, etc. Record your responses. Is there anything else you see? Is what you are seeing representative of what's out there? Is what you are describing an accurate assessment of what you've seen? You may assume that your responses are accurate, if not definitive, descriptions of "what's out there." Compare your notes with a fellow student . . . commonalities, differences? What does this all mean?

Before we answer that question, examine any chair in the classroom. Now trust me that on the underside of the chair the word "Taiwan" is imprinted. Write down what you know about this object and then compare your responses with a colleague. You may have written as follows: "a 4-legged object with a leather padding seat cover . . . that is made in Taiwan" or more simply, "a chair made in Taiwan." Nearly every student in my classes writes that the object is a chair made in Taiwan. After a brief, albeit intense, discussion it is apparent that the students have not thoroughly examined their assumptions and perceptions. Why did you assume that the object was made in Taiwan? All I said above is that the word "Taiwan" is imprinted on the underside of the object. Is this object a chair made in Taiwan or is it an object, we call a chair, that has the word "Taiwan" printed on it?

Our assumptions are lenses that affect what we see and how we interpret meaning. As researchers we should try to neutralize our assumptions, at least temporarily, in order to maintain a degree of objectivity. Doing research demands understanding that the chair may or may not have been made in Taiwan. Additional information is needed before a conclusive statement can be made about the origin of the object. Seeing things using multiple lenses or frames is a better way of ensuring a more accurate understanding of "what's out there."

Nietzsche once said that "all seeing is essentially perspective and so is all knowing." Read *It Looks Like This* (Webber, 1976) and *The True Story of the 3 Little Pigs* (Scieszka, 1996), and then you'll understand that there may be different ways of "seeing" or "knowing." How do we know anything about something? Is it possible to know everything about anything?

Reflection

Why are the latter two questions important to consider before undertaking a research project?

Although we may come to know something about anything by using our senses, past experiences, or seeking advice from an expert, researchers attempt to explain phenomena systematically through the application of the scientific method. To know something about anything necessitates a global or multidimensional perspective, in my view. One should acknowledge and consider a variety of perspectives or points of view before making a decision or reaching a conclusion.

Let's use the metaphor of "detective" to inform our work as educational researchers. If a detective arrived on the scene of an automobile accident and proceeded to interview the drivers without attending to bystanders and even the elderly gentleman peering through the window of his apartment located above the scene of the accident, s/he would certainly not adequately ascertain the facts. Moreover, if one of the drivers was an elderly woman and the other a forty-year-old man dressed in a neat blue suit, possibly the detective would infer that a detailed investigation was unwarranted. In this case, the detective's assumptions and conclusions may have been misleading and inaccurate without the benefit of a thorough investigation. Similarly, we as researchers, are detectives of sorts. We collect an array of data to inform the conclusions that we can justifiably make. To utilize a few **data collection** sources may lead to incomplete analyses, if not misevaluations.

The word *research* is derived, etymologically, from the French word, *rechercher*, meaning to travel through or to survey. As such, research can be thought of as some sort of investigation "to discover or establish facts and relationships" (Charles, 1997, p. 5). Research, at its most basic level, however, is a process of gathering information. All of us have conducted research in many ways. As educators we found ways of gathering information in order to assess our students' achievement and social development. Observing Sarah interact in a cooperative learning group, for instance, gave us much information about the degree to which she cooperated with her peers. As educators, we may informally observe a colleague working with a group of students during a reading lesson. As we observe, we collect information. We may note, for instance, that the teacher is asking her male students more thought-provoking questions than she is asking the female students. We also may note that she allows more wait-time for boys than for girls. As we continue to observe, we begin to better understand the nature of the interaction between this teacher and her students. As an aside, studies that involve first-hand observation of various phenomena are known as **empirical research**. Empirical research refers to methods of systematic investigation based on observations. In other words, any study you conduct that involves investigation by observation is considered empirical research. Observing Juan, who's been in special education classes, react when he's placed in an inclusive classroom for the first time, for instance, is an example of empirical research.

The credibility of research is enhanced by employing a technique known as **triangulation**. "Triangulation is the act of bringing more than one source of data to bear on a single point" (Marshall & Rossman, 1999, p. 146). As Marshall and Rossman continue to explain: "[D]esigning a study in which multiple cases are used, multiple informants or more than one data gathering technique can greatly strengthen the study's usefulness for other settings" (p. 146). Incorporating multiple sources of data is critical to ensuring a more accurate view of reality. Look at *Figure P.1* that reinforces this multidimensional framework underlying triangulation. Multiple uses of data collection methods will provide us with a more complete understanding of a given problem or **research question**.

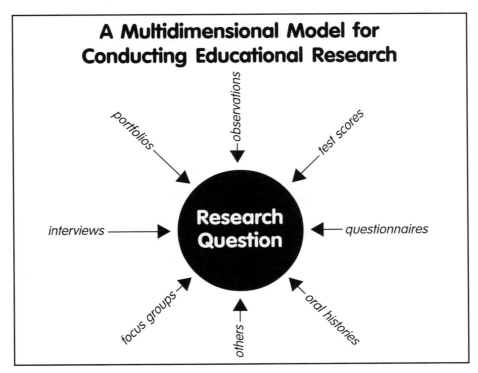

A Multidimensional Model for Conducting Educational Research

observations

portfolios

test scores

interviews ——→ **Research Question** ←—— *questionnaires*

focus groups

others

oral histories

Figure P-1.

To demonstrate the strength of **triangulation,** I'd like you to form groups of four individuals each. Collaboratively develop a simple problem and select a different **data collection** technique for each person in the group (e.g., **interview, questionnaire, historical analysis, unobtrusive measures,** etc.). [Don't forget to use the Glossary to help you!] For instance, a group might want to examine human behavior in the cafeteria. What are the discernible patterns of human behavior that make "life" in a cafeteria so unique? Confer on defining the problem your group selects and make sure each group member uses only one data collection technique. Spend an hour in the setting of your choice. Reconvene to share observations, findings, and tentative conclusions. Ask yourselves, "did my observations, findings, and conclusions coincide with those found by other members in my group?"; "in what way was my data collection limiting?"; "how can I more fully understand the problem?"; "how does the combination of techniques offer greater insights into the problem?" You will realize that triangulation rests on the assumption that the weakness in a single method will often be compensated by the strengths of another method.

Not surprisingly, therefore, I encourage you in undertaking your thesis project to use a **mixed methodology research design** incorporating both **qualitative** and **quantitative** approaches (Creswell, 1994). Using one modality is limiting and will not reveal all that can be known about the impact of a particular **treatment.** [Please note, that not all research designs utilize a treatment as there are other types of research that also may be appropriate (e.g., study replication, etc.)] Examine a specific issue or problem in your classroom or work situation. View the problem or topic from a multidimensional view. Realize the complexity of the "world of reality" and that, although everything cannot be known about anything, assuming a multiple framed perspective gives you a more realistic insight into a given educational problem.

I have two other (optional) assignments that will encourage you to use an array of data collection techniques that hopefully will preclude myopia and provincialism that often lead to unidimensional thinking about a given research topic. First, I want you to select a field site of some sort such as a health care facility, a restaurant, a faculty meeting, parent-teacher conference, or a college cafeteria. Describe the environment and interactions therein during a specified time frame using as many data collection techniques as is readily feasible. Report your findings and describe how each technique offers a unique dimension to the "reality" of your particular situation.

A second optional assignment is to rent Kurosawa's famous film "Rashomon," which recounts the same event through the eyes of several witnesses. Each witness tells a different story about how a murder took place. You are asked to write four different versions of what happened and are encouraged, through reflection, to realize and appreciate the social construction of reality and how "truth" depends on one's perspective.

Reflective Practice

"Reflective process is a powerful approach to professional development."
(Osterman & Kottkamp, 2001, p. 19)

You may ask, "Reflection? Who has the time?" "Certainly, we've learned about 'reflective practice' in graduate courses, but who has much time to really 'reflect' when you're on the job," complains a teacher in a suburban school in Long Island City, New York. Teaching is a challenging, complex art and science that demands not only knowledge and skill, but empathy, caring, and commitment. Frequently frustrating and exhausting, good teaching encourages, inspires, and arouses that latent spark within each student. Still, teachers are confronted with difficult, seemingly insurmountable obstacles that can be puzzling and exasperating. Student misbehavior, for instance, may drive a teacher to the very limits of his/her endurance. As an educator, you know what I mean. You face daunting tasks and inevitable challenges.

Anyone who has worked as an educator in a fairly large school setting realizes that teaching, counseling, or administering are "riddled (or blessed) with situations that demand quick action and almost immediate response" (Beck, 1994, p. 128). In spite of the fact that educators often have to make quick decisions, reflection is indeed possible. So, how can you find the time to reflect and what has this got to do with educational research?

Donald Schon (1983, 1984, 1987) advocates reflection in and on the practice of education. Schon maintains that "...the problems of real-world practice do not present themselves as problems at all but as messy, indeterminate situations" (1987, p. 4). Schon (1987) describes two types of reflective thinking: *reflection-in-action* and *reflection-on-action*. Reflection-in-action is the ability to "think on one's feet" when faced with the many surprises and challenges in our daily lives in schools. You are able to "think on their feet" as you face the multitude of crises that are all too common in almost any classroom/school. You must often decide quickly when confronted by an irate parent's demand that she be allowed "to whip" her child in front of the class. Even when challenged by less inflammatory situations, you must act decisively.

On the other hand, Schon also discusses reflection-on-action, which is most relevant to our discussion of educational research. Reflection-on-action occurs when educators look back upon their work and consider what practices were successful and what areas need improvement. Reflection-on-action is critical to understanding and thinking about events and phenomena as they unfold in the classroom/school. Special time must be set aside to allow for reflection-on-action.

Overwhelmed and sometimes incapable of dealing with increased demands, you think that reflection-on-action is impossible when, in fact, it is not only essential, but indeed possible (Whitaker, 1995). How then can you find the time to become a "reflective educator"? Here are some suggestions:

1. Set aside 15–30 minutes a day for reflective thinking. Build time into your schedule by closing your classroom door or office for 20 minutes so you are not disturbed. Do so at the start of a prep or during lunch. During this isolated time, deliberate on the overall structure of the day or on one specific issue. What do you wonder about your classroom or job situation? What issue is most disturbing? See the list of reflective questions below. Feel free to share your thoughts with a like-minded colleague.

2. Some of you may prefer to "reflect" early in the morning before school begins or after school. Time for reflection should be determined by your schedule and preference. Choose a time during which you are alert and can seriously contemplate the many issues that need attention. Personally, I'm a late night person and find that 1:00 a.m. suits me just fine. Don't cringe, I'm weird. But, I am most productive when the house is quiet and I am able to think undisturbed.

3. One principal I had the opportunity to work with held a "cabinet meeting" every day, from 7:30 a.m. until around 8:30 a.m., before students arrived. Such meetings allowed supervisory personnel to "reflect" and bring up important issues for general discussion. Anyone on the faculty or staff was allowed to attend these meetings to share their concerns or simply join in on "reflecting." If your principal encourages reflection, join in on the conversation. Join a grade-level or school-wide committee.

4. Find a colleague or "critical friend" who may share your educational concerns. Sometimes such a friend may be more helpful than a spouse or non-educator friend who can't really appreciate your concerns in the classroom or on the job. Discuss what bothers you or what you're interested in learning about a student or class/school situation.

5. Hey, why not go for a master's degree that requires a thesis project. Well, at least it's a way to "force," if not encourage you to engage in reflective practice.

Reflection

*What do you wonder about? What topic interests you so much that
you would like to spend some time conducting research?*

 One of the most important decisions you must make is whether or not to become a "reflective practitioner." A reflective educator is someone who takes the time to think about what has transpired or what steps should be taken tomorrow. A reflective educator thinks before s/he acts. S/he is proactive, not reactive. A reflective educator cares enough about her/his students to take the time to consider what works and what doesn't.

Reflection is the heart of professional practice. Robert Starratt (1995) explains that "practitioners who analyze the uniqueness of a problem confronting them, frame the problem in ways that structure its intelligibility, think about the results of their actions, and puzzle out why things worked and why they did not tend to build up a reservoir of insights and intuitions that they can call upon as they go about their work" (p. 66). Reflective practice is a process by which you take the time to contemplate and assess the efficacy of programs and practices in order to make judgments about the appropriateness or effectiveness of these aspects so that improvements or refinements might be achieved. Research-oriented educators are engaged in ongoing self-study in which they assess the needs of their classrooms/schools, identify problem areas, and develop strategies for becoming more effective.

Instilling habits of reflection, critical inquiry, and training in reflection is not always part of a preparatory program for educators. Educators should always submit their own practice to reflective scrutiny by posing some of these questions, among others:

1. What concerns me?

2. Why am I concerned?

3. Can I confirm my perceptions?

4. What mistakes have I made?

5. If I was able to do it again, what would I do differently?

6. What are my current options?

7. What evidence can I collect to confirm my feelings?

8. Who might be willing to share their ideas with me?

9. What have been my successes?

10. How might I replicate these successes?

11. In what other ways might I improve my classroom/school/job?

Preface Review

In this Preface you learned the following 3 major ideas:

✓ 1. ***Begin to think and act as researchers***—Recall the story I told at the outset of the Preface? Can you retell it? What does it tell you about undertaking research?

✓ 2. *Knowledge is multi-dimensional*—Recall the window and chair activities? What did these activities tell you about research?

- What did Nietzsche mean when he said that "all seeing is essentially perspective and so is all knowing"?

- Define the scientific method.

- What is triangulation? How can it help you understand a problem in your classroom?

- What is a treatment? (Are you checking out the Glossary for all bolded words?)

✓ 3. *Reflect on practice*—Recall a time when you were busy with no time to reflect? Ha, bet that wasn't difficult.

- Why is reflection so important for doing research?

- Who is Donald Schon? Which of his ideas encourage reflective practice?

- The Preface reviewed 5 suggestions for finding time to reflect. Which suggestion made the most sense for you? Do you have another strategy?

- How might the 11 questions to ponder, noted at the end of the Preface, help you find a topic for research?

Part One:

Preparing to Conduct Research for a Thesis Project

Focus Questions

1. What comes to mind when you think of the word "research," especially to complete a thesis?

2. Have you ever participated in a research project?

3. What stresses you most about undertaking a thesis?

4. How might you manage your time well so that you successfully complete your thesis?

5. What's one piece of advice you'd give a colleague in writing a thesis?

6. What are three most important ethical guidelines for conducting research?

7. How do you plan on going about finding a topic for your thesis project?

Module 1: The Stress of Undertaking a Master's Thesis

Does your thesis course cause you stress and anxiety? Do you want some general advice for dealing with stress? If not, skip the module. If yes, read on . . .

Let's begin this module with a brief questionnaire.

RESPOND

SA = Strongly Agree ("For the most part, yes")
A = Agree ("Yes, but . . .")
D = Disagree ("No, but . . .")
SD = Strongly Disagree ("For the most part, no")

SA A D SD   1. I believe I will have much difficulty completing a thesis project.

SA A D SD   2. In general, I handle stress well.

SA A D SD   3. I have difficulty expressing my emotions.

SA A D SD   4. I have a chronic sense of time urgency.

SA A D SD   5. I hate undertaking research.

SA A D SD   6. Completing my thesis won't bother me if the textbook is well written.

SA A D SD   7. My professor is the single greatest factor in determining how stressful I might become in this research seminar.

SA A D SD   8. I am under more stress than most of my colleagues.

SA A D SD   9. I consider myself an optimist.

SA A D SD   10. I chose to become a teacher or educator because I want to make a difference in the lives of my students not because I'll have summers off.

Let's briefly analyze your responses:

1. If you believe you'll have difficulty, you will indeed. Remember how the self-fulfilling prophecy works? The self-fulfilling prophecy functions whether or not we are aware of it. Becoming aware of how we react towards undertaking master's research is crucial.

2. You handle stress well; that's fine. But what kind of stress? Read the section that follows.

3. People who can't express their emotions, even their dislike of something, are in great jeopardy of experiencing increased levels of negative stress. Express your feelings about the course. Share them with a neighbor. If you're my student, we'll definitely devote some time in class to frank discussions. Stress is inevitable (read below), but the way you react to it is critical.

4. Having a sense of time urgency may be a good thing or a bad thing. Undertaking a thesis project does require one to organize time well. Procrastination can lead to increased levels of stress. Of course, being overly urgent with time can also be a negative. I like to think of myself as being "moderately compulsive." Hey, is that like being a "little pregnant?"

5. Don't forget, I did too.

6. Although probably not the most important factor for relieving stress, a well-written and user friendly text can't hurt. I hope you'll find this one useful.

7. Many people would agree with this statement. Ah, the influence of a good teacher!?!

8. Paranoia may be good or bad. Seriously, how does anyone really know that her/his stress is greater than someone else's stress? The point is to remain aware of your stress levels so that you can react appropriately.

9. Seeing the glass half-full is a plus. Cautious optimism avoids boastful overconfidence.

10. Dedicated and proud professionals will do very well in any course they take, even research.

Three Kinds of Stress

We must all learn how to deal with the 3 kinds of stress:

- distress (negative stress—like worry, anxiety, fear, disappointment, hate, and overload);

- stress (neutral stress—like change, noise, money, expectations, and people); and

- eustress (positive stress—like tenure, promotion, love, vacation, and success).

I define stress as a demand on our being, physically, emotionally, or mentally, that exceeds our ability to cope. Both neutral and positive stress can quickly turn into distress if uncontrolled. All three kinds of stress, however, may produce similar negative feelings in us. In that sense, stress is stress.

Stress is inevitable. As long as you are alive, stress will occur.

Accept stress for what it is. See stress as an opportunity to reach your potential.

Nothing in life that is worthwhile comes easy.

Don't give up.

Remaining Optimistic or at least Neutral

There is an apocryphal tale of a farmer who owned the only horse in town. One night, the horse broke loose and people asked him, "Isn't that terrible?"

He answered, "Perhaps."

The next day, the horse returned with wild mares following him.

"Isn't that wonderful?" they asked.

"Perhaps."

Two days later, the farmer's son fell off one of the wild horses

and fractured his leg.

"Isn't that terrible?"

"Perhaps."

A week later, the army recruiters came to town and drafted all the young men of the area, except for the farmer's son, because of his broken leg.

We all have setbacks. Frequently they are disguised blessings. I never realized before taking my first research course that I would love doing research, let alone teaching it one day! If you can't exude over the research course, at least remain neutral and see how it goes. Keep in mind that many other students before you have prevailed.

4 Ways to Relieve Stress

I have used the following four approaches with some of my students who had difficulty in dealing with the stress associated with the thesis experience.

- *Cognitive sophistication*
- *Positive affirmations*
- *Developing networks of support*
- *Humor*

1. Cognitive Sophistication
(framing the proper attitude)

I can't overemphasize the role that lifestyle and attitude play in relieving stress and enhancing general well being. Books have been written on these topics and I recommend you visit the "self-help" section of your local bookstore, or you may wish to read my own (Glanz, 2000).

Here, I want to present an 8-step approach for dealing with any stressor or problem that you may confront. This approach to attitude development involves cognitive sophistication; that is, confronting a stressful situation by verbally challenging the logic of its consequences. Below are 8 steps I have developed that have helped me and my students. I'll then provide one example of how I use them. Then it's up to you to practice the steps and see how they work for you.

Step 1:   Acknowledge Your Problem or Stressor [Consciousness]

> Sit down in a quiet place and verbalize the problem to yourself (e.g., "I won't be able to complete this thesis"). In this step, you state the problem clearly and forthrightly. This approach demonstrates that you are aware of the problem. You'd be surprised how often we really aren't aware of what is causing our tension.
>
> Although I'll later ask you to go through these 8 steps, consider this first step: what is bothering you —what is causing you stress? Verbalize the problem.

Step 2:   Affirm Your Feelings (Emotional)

> State how you feel about the situation (e.g., "When I even think of the word "research" I have chills all over my body"). Stress can wreak havoc on our emotions. We often conceal how we feel and, thus, more tension builds. In our culture, men, especially, do not express their emotions. This step encourages you to express how you feel to, at least yourself, if not to a confidant.

Step 3:   Control Your Reaction (intellect)

> Now that you are conscious of the problem and have expressed how you feel about it, you must now gain control over it intellectually by affirming ownership over the problem and acknowledging your ability to deal with it.
>
> Police officers are sometimes verbally abused, as are educators, by their clients, if you will. Such behavior is reprehensible. But do police officers have the right to confront such abuse by taking out their gun and shooting the person? Of course not. They are trained to remain stoic in such situations; they are, after all, professionals. They, as we educators, must realize our obligations to remain professional under all circumstances. In other words, they must control their reactions to the situation. One way of doing so would be to ask: "what will happen if I take this gun out and shoot this person?; what are the consequences of my actions?" Those individuals who are overcome by their emotions do not address these questions. This step encourages you to control

your reaction to the problem (e.g., "It's my problem. I will control my reaction. I realize the consequences of my actions. I take responsibility."). What have you done in the past to lose control? How can you in the future control your reaction?

Step 4: Consider Your Options

At this stage, you should consider what alternatives you have for dealing with the problem. You may, for example, do nothing and accept the situation. You may discuss the problem with someone. You may be able to do a number of things. Ask yourself at this step, "What are the options for dealing with my problem?" You will realize that *several* options exist. Whether you wish to pursue any of them is another matter. Options do exist. What are *your* options?

Step 5: Breathe and Relax

As you consider your options, simultaneously practice a breathing exercise or two. Simply take some deep breaths in and out. These exercises will allow you clear your mind and enable you to better confront your problem.

Step 6: Reconsider Consequences

You still, at this stage, have not done anything. Consider your options again and their consequences. Be deliberate and patient in your thinking.

Step 7: Act

Now it's time to act. Do something OR decide not to act (e.g., drop out of the course). Whatever you decide, you'll feel empowered, in control. Realize that whatever you now decide is not irrevocable (see the next step).

Step 8: Reconsider, Act, Reconsider, Act

Once you've decided on a course of action and some time has passed, you can now reconsider your options. You may decide that a new course of action is in order. The process I've described is cyclical. Apply these steps again and again as necessary.

Applying the 8 Steps

"I'm overcommitted with other projects and family responsibilities. I should have never signed up for the research seminar this semester. I'll never be able to complete my thesis. I feel overwhelmed, angry, and upset with myself. It was my responsibility for accepting these other projects and at the same time undertaking my thesis requirement. I realize the consequences for accepting them. I had the ability to say 'no.' I can say 'no' in the future. Now, what are my options? I can do my best to complete all these projects, after all I've never failed before. I could, however, give up two or three of them and focus on my thesis. I could, instead, also ask for assistance in completing them. Let me consider what I will do, but first I'll practice some breathing exercises. Let me now consider my options again and the consequences of each. Okay, I will now decide to fulfill my commitments, but I will ask the professor for assistance. At a later date, I can reconsider my decision."

2. Positive Affirmations—Thoughts

As educators, we are bound by our perspectives, our unique vantage points. Reality is perceived and understood by our belief systems that are, in turn, based on assumptions gleaned from our experiences. Reality is dependent on our thinking patterns, belief systems, and mindsets. Our belief systems are intimately connected to the language we use to articulate and communicate meanings that influence our actions and behaviors. How we think shapes the world in which we live. As Arthur Schopenhauer, German philosopher, once posited, "the world in which a man lives shapes itself chiefly by the way in which he [sic] looks at it."

How do you look at the world? What do you believe? Do you believe that your thoughts can influence not only how you look at things but how you feel? Belief that your thoughts can deeply affect you is essential to controlling stress.

"I think I can, I think I can . . . I know I can."

"They can do all because they think they can."
(Virgil, *Aeneid*, 19 B.C.)

Research on the use of positive affirmations indicates that positive thinking can have a powerful influence on how you react to stress. Try repeating several phrases in an almost mantra-like fashion. (Hint: I have found it very helpful to write my affirmation on a small index card. I keep it with me throughout the day and repeat the affirmation as needed.). This practice can condition your thought patterns in ways you wouldn't imagine. Try each of these affirmations over the course of the next week. What affect do they have on helping you relieve stress associated with completing your master's thesis?

- "I can complete this thesis."
- "Others before me did, why can't I?"
- "I can influence the way I feel."
- "I will not feel as if I have to meet everyone's expectations."
- "I will not run away from a problem. I will resolve the problem."

- "Take one step at a time and don't get overwhelmed."

- "It's ok to fail, to make a mistake."

- "I am responsible for my actions and reactions."

- "I think and know I can."

- "I will earn my master's degree."

3. Building Strong Professional and Personal Networks of Support

Finding an individual or individuals that could commiserate with your plight is very effective in allaying your apprehensions. Having someone you could speak to goes a long way towards helping you release your anxieties. For instance, one former student aptly put it: "Who else can I talk to? Who else will work this through with me? I find that talking to my spouse really helps. I have also found a colleague in class who shares my feelings. Together we'll make this work." Other ways that build strong professional and personal support mechanisms can help relieve stress:

- venting to other colleagues in my class

- forming a study group, much like is done in law school

- seeking assistance from someone who has already completed a thesis

- sustaining oneself through developing strong friendship bonds (inside and outside the workplace)

4. Humor

Evidence clearly demonstrates that humor or laughter can decrease anxiety and stress, improve self-esteem, and increase motivation and perceived quality of life. You must read (or reread) Norman Cousins's *Anatomy of an Illness* that tells the moving story of his successful fight against a crippling disease and demonstrates what the mind and body working together can do to overcome illness. The power of laughter and humor is emphasized.

What happens if you don't feel like laughing or you consider yourself not to be a very "humorous" person? Rent videos of your favorite funny movies or comedians. Watching these skits of the Marx Brothers, Abbott and Costello, or whomever for hours can relieve stress much more than you may realize. Try it today; visit a video store that carries these "old time movies." Don't like video stores? Share humorous anecdotes or situations with a spouse or colleague.

I also suggest that you skip the 10:00 or 11:00 nightly news and watch instead Jay Leno's "Headlines" or read a good book, for examples. Falling asleep with "happy" thoughts is more conducive to establishing a relaxed frame of mind. You'll sleep much better and awake energized.

AFTER HAVING READ THE ABOVE WAYS OF RELIEVING STRESS, TRY DOING THEM. SE-LECT ONE A DAY OVER THE NEXT WEEK OR SO. HOW DOES IT HELP YOU? WHAT WORKS BEST FOR YOU?

Module 1 Review

In this Module you learned the following 3 major ideas:

1. *Assess your stress levels*—Recall the questionnaire at the module? How did you do? Rate yourself on a scale of 1 to 10 (10 being the most stressed); how stressed are you about taking this course/about completing a master's thesis?

2. *Remain optimistic or at least cautiously optimistic*—Recall the story about the farmer? How would you have reacted to each event? Rate yourself on a scale of 1 to 10 (10 being the most optimistic); how optimistic are you about taking this course/completing a thesis?

3. *Review the 4 ways to relieve stress*—Recall each way? Name them. Too stressful? Check back then and relax. Which way makes most sense for you? Think of another strategy to "survive" this course and the thesis project. Share thoughts with a classmate, and even the professor. Doing so will relieve much stress; try it.

Self-Test Check

1. True or False: Undertaking a master's thesis project might be a stressful experience.

2. True or False: Handling stress successfully is possible.

Answers: True of course; reread module for specific strategies.

Study Question

1. Think about the way you usually handle stress. What would cause you stress and how do you usually handle it? Share thoughts with a colleague.

Activity

1. Explore strategies not discussed in this module for handling stress that would be particularly useful to you.

Module 2: Time Management

Are you generally late for project deadlines? Do you need some general time management advice? If not, skip the module. If yes, read on . . .

Let's also begin this module with a brief questionnaire.

RESPOND

SA = Strongly Agree ("For the most part, yes")
A = Agree ("Yes, but . . .")
D = Disagree ("No, but . . .")
SD = Strongly Disagree ("For the most part, no")

SA A D SD	1. I don't know where I'll find the time to complete this thesis project.
SA A D SD	2. In general, I manage time well.
SA A D SD	3. I am a natural procrastinator and I'm likely to procrastinate in this course.
SA A D SD	4. If given a plan or schedule by the professor, I'd more likely complete this project on time.
SA A D SD	5. I multi-task easily.

Let's briefly analyze your responses:

1. If you feel the pressure of time, I hope it's some comfort to know that you're not alone. Many of your classmates likely have many other obligations. Whether it's family, personal, job, or professional obligations, graduate students are busy people. You're not alone.

2. Well, then no sweat. But if you don't manage time well, you'll need to learn some time management strategies.

3. Procrastination may or may not be a bad thing. I know some people who are enormous procrastinators, but are very productive. They come through in the end. Knowing your natural tendencies is a good first step to getting things done in a timely fashion.

4. Many of my students inform me that giving them a detailed timetable helps organize their time. When I first taught the research course sequence, I felt I didn't want to stress

out my students by giving them a rigid schedule of due dates to adhere to. They later informed me that not having such a schedule caused them more stress. Ask your professor for such a schedule. If s/he doesn't provide one, read the information in this module to help develop your own timetable.

5. People who multi-task easily have little trouble completing their work. They enjoy the excitement of various responsibilities. If on the other hand, you don't multi-task well, then focus on the one task at hand and do the best you can; read on.

This module is not meant to provide you with all that you need to know about time management. A visit to any self-help section of your local library or bookstore will provide you with a plethora of resources. The suggestions that follow in this brief module are drawn from the author's personal experiences in working with hundreds of master's degree students who attempt to complete a thesis. Okay, I'll delete the words "attempt to"!

At the start of the semester the entire prospect of conducting research to write a thesis can seem daunting, if not impossible. When I first went mountain climbing, my instructor friend told me not to look down nor look up. Rather she said "just keep your eyes and attention on the next rock ahead of you." I'd give you that same sage advice as you approach this project. Take it one step at a time, which by the way reminds me about something I'd like to ask you.

Which would you choose: a million dollars in cash, or a penny that will double in value every day for thirty days? On first impulse, the average person would choose the million dollars. The far wiser choice, however, is the penny that would double itself daily. Although on day six you will have only thirty-two cents, by day 28 you will have accumulated $1,342,177. On day 29, you will have over $2.6 million.

This demonstrates the compound interest power of positive small steps. The snowball effect, over time, becomes immensely fruitful.

Reflection

*How does this "sage" advice help you in terms of approaching
managing time when completing your thesis project?*

What did George Washington, Martin Luther King, Jr., and Albert Einstein have in common? They all had 24 hours in a day. They accomplished much in their lifetime. Others had the same time but were not able to accomplish as much. Now, I don't really know what led to their success, but successful people do use their time wisely. How might you use your time most efficiently and effectively in order to complete this course project?

Here are a few suggestions I culled from observing some of my most successful students:

1. *Set a timetable*—Regardless of whether a professor provides one, set a timetable for yourself. When will you complete the first draft of the literature review? The professor might say the entire proposal is due one week before the end of the semester, but may not provide a

time for earlier drafts. So, at the outset of the semester, you should set a date when you want to "see" the first draft; say, March 15th. You may even want to ask the professor to look it over or if s/he prefers not, you can ask a fellow student to review/proofread it. Break up the major components of the proposal and establish pre-set dates for yourself.

2. *Reward yourself*—Here's an interesting suggestion offered by a number of my students. Using some behavior management theory, tell yourself (for some, actually writing it down on your calendar may be more powerful) that after the literature review is completed and submitted you will visit the local ice cream store for your favorite treat. Setting several rewards like this throughout the year just might give you some extra pounds, but some of my students say it also "does the trick." "I never missed one deadline . . . and it was lots of fun anticipating my reward."

3. *Set aside a time of day to work*—Trying to fit in work throughout the day may be difficult and stressful. Select one particular time of day to work. It's the time you know you'll devote to researching or writing. For some of you the best time might be 5:00 a.m. so you can have 90 minutes of uninterrupted work in your basement. For night-owls, it might be 11 p.m. Some students reported that they go to bed at 8:30 p.m. or so after an exhausting day, sleep for 7 hours and awake at 3:30 a.m., work for two "wonderfully productive hours" and then catch a nap for an hour or two. "After trying this twice, I was hooked. It works great for me. Not every day certainly, but twice a week. I find that the three or four hours spent this way is equivalent to fifteen hours spread out otherwise in which I'm harried and inattentive."

Module 2 Review

In this Module you learned the following 2 major ideas:

1. ***Time management is a crucial skill for successfully completing a thesis***—Recall the questionnaire at the module? How did you do? Rate yourself on a scale of 1 to 10 (10 being a dysfunctional procrastinator); how do you plan to manage your time during the semester?

2. ***Follow the suggestions offered in this brief module***—Recall the suggestions above. Which made the most or least sense? What other suggestions might you have to manage time better?

Self-Test Check

1. True or False: Undertaking a master's thesis project requires good time management skills.

2. True or False: Despite personal pressures, time management can help you greatly.

Answers: True of course; reread module for specific strategies.

Study Question

1. Think about the way you usually handle time pressures. What would cause you to possibly delay completing your thesis and how do you intend to avoid delay? Share any apprehension you might have about completing this project with a colleague and/or with your professor.

Activity

1. Explore strategies not discussed in this module for managing your time that would be particularly useful to you.

Module 3: Writing Suggestions

You might also want to refer to Module 4 in Part Thirteen for more advice, although some of the content of that module has not yet been covered. Read it anyway.

Might as well begin this module with a brief questionnaire . . .

RESPOND

Are You a Good Writer?

Good writing is an art and a craft. You can achieve clear communication by presenting ideas in an orderly manner and by expressing yourself smoothly and precisely. Are you a good writer?

Good writing takes practice. Three approaches to achieving effective communication are: (1) compose an outline and just write without regard to style, punctuation, and grammar; (2) put aside the first draft, then reread it after a delay; and (3) ask a colleague to critique the draft for you.

I suggest you consult some of the many excellent publications available on writing style. Try these for a start:

1. Strunk, W., Jr., & White, E. B. (2000). *The elements of style* (4th ed.). New York: Macmillan.—A classic and very inexpensive

2. Bates, J. D. (2000). *Writing with precision: How to write so that you cannot be misunderstood* (4th ed.). Washington, D.C.: Acropolis Books.—Students have recommended this one.

3. *Publication Manual of the American Psychological Association (APA)*, 5th ed., 2001 (ISBN: 1557987912).—This APA manual will be your "bible" for writing your thesis in terms of proper format accepted in the field of education as well as other social sciences (see Module 2 in Part Thirteen).

A visit to your local bookstore's writing section is also recommended.

Some of you might benefit from taking a course on writing style as well. I suggest you carefully assess your writing ability and take the necessary steps for improvement. Good writing skills are necessary for continued success in your professional endeavors. Good luck *and* good writing!

NOTE: These questions refer to writing for research purposes, not necessarily for general writing.

Circle the correct/acceptable/better sentence for each of the following pairs of examples:

1. a. Glanz (2000) designed the experiment.
   b. The experiment was designed by Glanz (2000).

2. a. Participants sat in comfortable chairs equipped with speakers that delivered the tone stimuli.
   b. The participants were sitting in comfortable chairs equipped with speakers that delivered the tone stimuli.

3. a. Glanz (2001) presented the same results.
   b. Glanz (2001) presents the same results.

4. a. Since that time investigators from several studies have used this method.
   b. Since that time investigators from several studies used this method.

5. a. The data are complete.
   b. The data is complete.

6. a. The percentage of correct responses as well as the speed of the responses increases with practice.
   b. The percentage of correct responses as well as the speed of the responses increase with practice.

7. a. The phenomena occur every 100 years.
   b. The phenomena occurs every 100 years.

8. a. Neither the participants nor the confederate was in the room.
   b. Neither the participants nor the confederate were in the room.

9. a. The positions in the sequence were changed, and the test was rerun.
   b. The positions in the sequence were changed, and the test rerun.

10. a. The group improved its scores 30 percent.
    b. The group improved their scores 30 percent.

11. a. The rats that completed the task successfully were rewarded.
    b. The rats who completed the task successfully were rewarded.

12. a. Name the participant who you found scored above the median.
    b. Name the participant whom you found scored above the median.

13. a. We had nothing to do with their being the winners.
    b. We had nothing to do with them being the winners.

14. a. Using this procedure, the investigator tested the subjects.
    b. The investigator tested the subjects using this procedure.

15. a. I hope this is not the case.
    b. Hopefully, this is not the case.

16. a. Brag (1999) found that participants performed well, whereas Bohr (2000) found hat participants did poorly.
    b. Brag (1999) found that participants performed well, while Bohr (2000) found that participants did poorly.

17. a. The names were difficult both to pronounce and to spell.
    b. The names were difficult both to pronounce and spell.

18. a. In regard to this matter,…
    b. In regards to this matter,…

19. a. Charles's friend
    b. Charles' friend

20. a. None of us is perfect.
    b. None of us are perfect.

How do you think you did? If you answered more than two incorrectly, my suggestion is to go out quickly and purchase one of the aforementioned writing resources. For the answers, see the end of this module.

Okay, now that you have some insight into your knowledge of some grammatical and sentence structure rules of writing, here are some other suggestions for actually writing your thesis or parts of it like the literature review:

1. *Write a little each day*—You'd be amazed how much accumulates when you just write a line or two a day.

2. *Write a lot at one sitting*—Well, some of you may not have the discipline to follow the suggestion above. Some of you may prefer to allot a few hours for intensive thinking and

writing. Setting aside one or two long sessions a week may work best for you. Also, the time of day should fit your style preference. One of my former students reported that he thinks and writes best late at night when everyone is asleep. Actually, at times, he goes to sleep early around 8:30 p.m. and wakes up at 3:30 a.m. Then he works for three uninterrupted hours and gets a lot accomplished. He quietly goes back to sleep for an hour or so, and then he's ready for his day knowing he accomplished a great deal.

3. *Write information to start on index cards (or your laptop) when conducting the literature review*—As you research you'll come across many sources including good articles or ideas that may come in handy later on. If you don't discipline yourself to record these references or bits of information as you come across them, you'll have much difficulty recalling them when you actually begin writing.

4. *Write without attention to grammar or spelling*—Just write . . . don't get bogged down by worrying about grammatical or spelling errors, sentence structure difficulties, or even paragraph development. At this stage all you want to do is get as many ideas down as possible. One of my former students said he tape records his ideas and then later transcribes them. "Although it takes me a long time, I feel more comfortable speaking rather than writing at this early stage in the process."

5. *Proofread*—After you've accumulated enough writing for a section, reread what you've written. Check for flow of ideas. Did you communicate what you meant to say? Did you leave anything out? Proofreading your material the next day or even a week later is advisable. You'll discover several errors you missed earlier.

6. *Invite a friend to proofread*—The more sets of eyes that peruse your writing the greater chance of finding errors and improving your manuscript. When someone says to you, "I don't understand what you wrote here." Your first reaction might be to defend yourself and explain what you meant. The person may respond, "Oh." But you shouldn't let it go at that. The reader's confusion is a hint that the passage might be confusing or unclear. Rewrite the section. Often, when I came across a passage that I can't understand, I ask "what do you mean." My student responds and then I say, "Well, say it exactly like that." In other words, "say what you mean or write what you say."

7. *Writing Center*—If your college or university offers writing workshops or free tutorials, you may want to take them. At my college we have an excellent Writing Center that offers one-on-one assistance in proofreading and other writing skills. Find out what resources exist at your institution.

8. *The 5 Easy Steps*—Skip to Module 4 in Part Thirteen for some "advice and suggestions" for writing a successful thesis.

By the way, the answers to the opening questionnaire: all were choice "a."

Module 3 Review

In this Module you learned the following 2 major ideas:

1. *Assess your writing skills*—Recall the questionnaire in the module? How did you do? Rate yourself on a scale of 1 to 10 (10 being an accomplished writer). What steps might you need to take to improve your writing skills? The more you write the better writer you'll become. My grammar school and even high school teachers would be astonished that I've written twelve previous books. I wasn't always a good writer. It's a skill that can be learned and improved.

2. *Seek suggestions to improve your writing*—Which of the writing suggestions above make sense? Let me know of any other suggestions that work well for you because I may want to include them in the next edition of this book, with your permission and acknowledgment of course.

Self-Test Check

1. Which statement is stated properly?

    a. Rodriguez (2005) maintained that stress levels among elementary school students have significantly increased over the last decade due to societal pressures to succeed academically.

    b. Rodriguez, 2005, accurately maintains that stress levels among elementary school students have significantly increased over the last decade due to societal pressures to succeed academically.

Answer: a

Study Question

1. Think about the way you write. What additional necessary skills might you need to successfully complete your thesis, and what other suggestions, not mentioned in this module, work best for you?

Activity

1. Explore writing strategies not discussed in this module that are particularly useful to you.

Module 4: Ethics of Research

I never think it's too early to think about the ethics of research. In fact, the earlier you do so you'll be in a much better position to avoid some pitfalls than if you waited.

Let's begin this module with a very brief questionnaire.

RESPOND

SA = Strongly Agree ("For the most part, yes")
A = Agree ("Yes, but . . .")
D = Disagree ("No, but . . .")
SD = Strongly Disagree ("For the most part, no")

SA A D SD	1.	"The ends justify the means" when it comes to undertaking research. If doing slight harm to a group means that a greater good is possible, then such a project would be sanctioned.
SA A D SD	2.	You should rather terminate a project than resort to misrepresenting data or results.
SA A D SD	3.	At times, students do not need to know that they are participating in a study.

Let's briefly analyze your responses:

1. "The ends should never justify the means" if it means that even one student may be harmed emotionally, psychologically, physically, academically, socially, etc. Your aim as a researcher is to further knowledge about a topic or issue; to help improve conditions in the classroom or in educational practice so that students learn in an atmosphere of trust. Operating unethically by "doing harm" is in violation of a principle known as **beneficence**. Therefore, your job is to always protect the participants of your study from harm.

2. Are there circumstances when you would alter your data to conform to your preconceived notions? Would you intentionally copy another's work without acknowledgment? Doing either of these would violate the principle of **honesty**. Remaining honest is a matter of personal integrity. Dishonesty is a character flaw. Educational researchers should always strive for integrity and strength of character.

3. Participant students, in my estimation, should always know the general parameters of your study. Always solicit permission to conduct a study. Permission should be sought from district/region officials and school administrators, parents, and even the students

themselves. Researchers should assure participants that their names will be kept confidential and that they will not be subject to any harm. I once had a student who refused to conduct a **group comparison** study because she knew one of the **treatments** (an approach to teaching spelling) was better than another. "I don't want to use an approach with some students that I know will definitely not help them improve their spelling skills just for purposes of completing my thesis." Frequently, however, in education we test instructional or curricular approaches that do not have definitive benefits or detriments; they might both be very good approaches. We investigate to determine which approach works best in a given situation with a particular group. Positive results with one approach, with one group, rarely mean that one may **generalize** to all **populations**. The ethical principle in this case is known as **accurate disclosure**. We are duty bound as educational researchers to inform participants about the general approach taken in a study. Accurate disclosure doesn't mean full disclosure. In sum, accurate disclosure is an ethical principle related to conducting research that assures that participants in research are informed accurately about the general topic under investigation as well as any unusual procedures that may be used in the study.

Reflection

Why do you think accurate disclosure does not mean full disclosure?
What would you tell participants if you were engaged in a
study to determine the impact of cooperative learning
activities on students' motivation to learn?

To disclose all information will likely corrupt the study because participants might react to the fact that they know they are expected to behave in a certain and may do so (and may try even harder) simply because they know they are participants in a study (see **Hawthorne Effect** and **John Henry Effect**). Consequently, our responsibility as researchers is merely to give them enough general information so as not to disclose information that might influence study results. Change in behavior or achievement, as examples, might not be attributed to the **treatment**, but to the fact that the participants knew they were being "studied." In the case in the reflective activity above you might say something like this: "We want to investigate two different instructional approaches (cooperative learning and computer-assisted instruction), both of which are considered by professional educators to be worthwhile) and to study their impact on student motivation. Students, over time, will experience both approaches. No unusual procedures are used in the study and participants under no circumstances will be harmed. Names and test scores will be kept strictly confidential.

Accurate disclosure ensures that participants are informed about the nature of the study; how it will not harm them and how it will be used. The agency that monitors research studies at a college or university is usually called the Institutional Review Board (IRB). The information that follows is generic, but check to see if your institution has an IRB. If they do, you must obtain and follow their guidelines precisely.

Usually, all master's degree thesis proposals have to undergo review by the IRB prior to initiation of a study. The primary purpose of an IRB is to ensure no ethical violations, intended or not, take place. Although guidelines and requirements may vary among IRBs, there are generally three types of IRB review: exempt, expedited, and full.

The least rigorous review (i.e., easiest to obtain approval) is the exempt status. Research studies fall under exempt status if these conditions, among others, are met:

- Study does not involve human subjects

- Study involves review of existing documents or records

The next kind of review is known as expedited. Research studies fall under expedited review if these conditions, among others, are met:

- Study does involve human subjects but potential risk of harm is minimal or negligible

- Study is conducted with subjects who are part of the researcher's class

- Study involves examination of human behavior in a natural setting in which observations may be conducted, surveys distributed, etc.

- Study involves use surveys but there is no way for subjects or respondents to be identified

Full review occurs when criteria above are not met.

Examine Appendix A, which illustrates a researcher's request for an expedited review. The form used is a modified from one used by Daemen College's Human Subjects Review Committee. Note that in Appendix A an expedited review is undertaken because

- Subjects will voluntarily participate in the study that involves minimal risk for harm and the subjects are students in the researcher's class.

- Individual participants in the study cannot be identified

As a researcher, you must attend to the following criteria, among others that your IRB may require:

- Informed consent—Parents of minors are requested to sign a form in advance of the study that describes the general nature of the study and the minimal risk of any harm. Parents should be given the option to withdraw their child from the study at any time; therefore, participation is voluntary. Parents need not complete all survey questions, although they will be requested to do so. A statement of confidentiality is provided to ensure parents that their child cannot be identified by name. Parents are also informed that results of the study will be available should they wish to receive them.

Check with your IRB to verify these requirements or any others that may be necessary.

More on Research Ethics

For information on research ethics every student should consult the American Educational Research Association (AERA) that provides very helpful information to guide ethical research practice. Visit http://www.aera.net/about/policy/ethics.htm for this information.

Reflection

List as many different principles or ideas about ethical research from the AERA guidelines above. Compare your list with a colleague. How might these guidelines assist you in planning, conducting, and reporting your study? Compose a brief list of guidelines you intend to follow. Place them on an index card so that they are easily accessible throughout your study. Again, compare your index card list with a colleague. Have you omitted an important ethical guideline?

Module 4 Review

In this Module you learned the following 2 major ideas:

1. *Three ethical principles*—Recall the questionnaire at the beginning of the module? How did you do? Rate yourself on a scale of 1 to 10 (10 being a extremely ethical); how do you plan to adhere to a thorough system of ethics when planning, conducting, and reporting your study?

2. *Other ethical guidelines*—Always keep ethics in mind when conducting research; Never misrepresent yourself or your study; Don't discriminate among participants by race, gender, etc.; Allow participants to freely withdraw at any time from study; Obtain informed consent from all participants; Don't coerce students to participate in your study; Avoid deception; Cause no harm; Avoid invasion of privacy; Maintain anonymity of participants; Risks to participants should never outweigh benefits; etc.

Self-Test Check
Ethical or Not? Explain.

1. You are a special education teacher in an elementary school and you want to help reduce stress levels of your students as they prepare for the forthcoming standardized reading test. You divide your class into two groups and teach one group stress-reduction techniques; while the other group receives no **treatment**. You begin your study in October by measuring student stress levels. You continue to monitor their stress levels as you implement your approach with one group of students. You conceal your intentions with the group not receiving the treatment. You urge participants in the experimental group not to inform the other students.

2. You are student completing a master's thesis and you are under a lot of stress. Family and school pressures seem almost too much to bear. You are about two months behind most students in your class. You know the final draft of the thesis is due in three weeks. You haven't begun even to collect data. You decide to make up results from survey data that you fraudulently create. You rationalize that you "must complete the project, . . . after all who am I harming; I never even conducted a study in my classroom?!"

3. Conducting a literature review, a thesis student reads a review of literature from an encyclopedia. S/he decides to extract a few paragraphs by changing a few words or sentences. S/he includes the extracted piece for her literature review saying, "I couldn't have said it better myself."

4. Fred is undertaking his master's degree thesis project. He requires his 9th grade freshmen to sign a form in which they agree to participate in his study.

5. Maria deletes participant responses to her survey that do not conform to her **hypothesis**.

6. Leonardo purposely teaches his unit to his 7th graders without use of instructional materials of any sort for a month to see what impact such a practice will have on their midterm grades.

7. Sarah asks special education teachers in her school to take a questionnaire to survey their knowledge of inclusion. She purposely reports that some respondents scored far below the national norm in terms of their knowledge of inclusive practice. Sarah really wants to study how teachers react to failure. Had she told them that in advance, it is unlikely that she would have been able to achieve her research objective.

8. A class taking their masters thesis is informed by the professor that they do not have to submit their studies for review by the **Institutional Review Board** (IRB) because "it's only a maser's thesis." See for example, www.irb.umn.edu/

Answers:
1. Clearly, not ethical because you are deceiving one group while providing what may turn out to be substantive assistance to one group of students. Furthermore, it's unethical to engage in the study without consent of participants and, in this case, notification of parents and school/district authorities.

2. Clearly, not ethical for obvious reasons. No amount of rationalization suffices for such fraudulent and unethical behavior. The student, acting ethically, should have consulted the professor in order to receive an extension or to take an incomplete grade in the course so that the study could be later carried out honestly.

3. Clearly, not ethical because s/he has plagiarized. Not providing a proper citation for the extracted material is plagiarism. A number of good web sites that discuss plagiarism and how to detect it can be found at: http://www.plagiarism.org/ , http://sja.ucdavis.edu/avoid.htm, etc. See vignette about plagiarism below.

4. Fred has in effect coerced his students to participate. I've seen others bribe students to participate, and even threaten them with lower grades for refusal.

5. Maria has acted dishonestly by not accurately reporting her findings regardless of her hypothesis. Some students new to research think that if their findings do not support their hypothesis or research question then they have unsuccessfully carried out their research. Nothing could be further from the truth. I always inform my students that as long as they have adhered to the rigors of the scientific method, their study is valid regardless of the results.

6. Leonardo has violated the "cause no harm" guideline to ethical practice.

7. Although such deception may be warranted on some occasions or in research that attempts to generate new theories or knowledge, most experts would agree that any use of deception that violates honesty should be avoided when conducting research for a master's thesis.

8. Many institutions of higher learning have **Institutional Review Boards** (IRBs) that serve to review research proposals of anyone (student and professor alike) who wish to undertake a formal research project. Members of the IRB make judgments regarding the ethical appropriateness of a particular project to ensure that no ethical standards of behavior are violated. See, for instance, the University of Minnesota's IRB documentation on http://www.irb.umn.edu/. Applications for all research projects should be submitted to the IRB before conducting a study. If your college or university does not have an IRB, then you need to clearly articulate the potential benefit of your study as well as any risks that might ensue. Assuring confidentiality must also be affirmed. Discussion with the professor or department chair/dean is recommended. See a sample IRB application in Appendix A (note, again, that applications of this sort will vary depending on college or university requirements).

Reflection

Examine the IRB application in Appendix A. What have you learned about the ethics of research? What specific guidelines should you follow? Why is doing so important?

Cases of Plagiarism from the Author's Experience

Plagiarism has probably always been a problem in schools across the world. According to recent reports, plagiarism at the college level is particularly rampant. Many high school and college students have reported that at one time or another they have plagiarized or cheated in some way connected to their academic study. My experience below with a student whom I caught cheating, although extreme, is meant to caution thesis students to remain vigilant and cautious about how they collect data and write their thesis.

Thesis projects were due. One student, Jerry, was particularly confident all semester, not ever once submitting requested drafts for my review. Parenthetically, early on in my teaching career at the college level, I did not require, as I do now, students to submit work for my review throughout the semester. Although most students did voluntarily submit their work for my reaction throughout the semester (and, by the way, they appreciated my willingness to review their work and offer constructive feedback. They felt, in the end, that they earned higher grades and completed a better project than had they not submitted their work to me), Jerry never did.

As I read Jerry's literature review on classroom management, I thought I had read something similar but could not really recall. In the old days, I could not conduct a Google search. Still, I was somewhat disturbed and very suspicious. Coincidently and amazingly, later that week I came across some faculty notes from I.S. XX, a local middle school, in which the principal included a packet reviewing the latest research on classroom management. I had only previously glanced at the material (excuse the pun—"glanced"…Glanz?!), but now discovered that this fellow had copied the faculty notes verbatim as his literature review. His accuracy was astounding so much so that at the end of one section in his paper he wrote. "a teacher must have sill and experience when dealing with misbehavior." Upon my first read, I corrected his typo for "sill" and inserted the missing "k." Well, when I read the faculty notes I noticed the exact same omission. Amazing, right?

Well, you might ask what happened next. What would you have done as the professor?

A. *Fail him in the course*

B. *Report his actions to the proper school administrators or committee*

C. *Give him a second chance after hearing an explanation*

D. *Something else?*

It was early in my career and I was much nicer than I am now… choice c.

On another occasion, I suspected a student plagiarized a paper on the "medical and social implications of ADHD." After having read her in-class midterm essay exam and was dismayed at her poor writing style, I was stunned to read her term paper that was professionally and flawlessly written. I noted this discrepancy to her and all she said was "I improved my writing didn't I?" Although I conducted a thorough web search, I could not definitely locate the source of plagiarism. I concluded that someone else had written the paper for her. I awarded her a "C" grade on the paper, although the paper deserved an "A+." My comments to her in writing were "although the paper is well written it did not cover the course objectives." She never complained.

These latter two cases are obvious, egregious instances of plagiarism. More often, inadvertent plagiarism occurs. Students claim they weren't aware of their indiscretion or state they forgot to include the source. Although college policies differ (and you should check well in advance the college policy toward any form of plagiarism), I do feel that sometimes errors are made that are unintentional. Still, it's important to remain vigilant and aware of various policies. One excellent source of information, and there are others, can be found at http://sja.ucdavis.edu/avoid.htm. This web site includes definitions of plagiarism, examples, how to cite sources correctly, and general guidelines on how to avoid it. The site is a must read; of course, policies established by your college supercede any other information. See a brief discussion of plagiarism in Module 1 of Part Thirteen.

Study Questions

1. Research famous cases in which human beings have been ill-treated in research settings. Examine particularly, the medical experiments carried out by Nazi Germany before and during World War II. Examine experiments with people with disabilities and with Jews in camps. Also, research the infamous Tuskegee Experiment that inflicted egregious psychological and

physical pain to research participants. Although these are extreme cases of unethical behavior, what might you learn from them?

2. Sometimes a dilemma presents itself that is not easily resolved. It's not very clear that a practice is unethical. Provide some examples of subtle ethical issues. Have you encountered or read about cases in which the resolution was not very clear? Explain. What guidelines would you follow in these cases?

3. Consider what ethical principles or guidelines relate to your study. How do you intend to conduct your study ethically? How can you assure that you do so?

Activity

1. Interview three other individuals who have already completed their thesis to ask, "what measures did you take to ensure ethical behavior on your part when conducting the study?"

2. What ethical dilemmas or situations do you think you may encounter?

Module 5: Preliminary Review of the Literature in Search of a Topic

Let's begin this module with, you guessed it, a very brief questionnaire.

RESPOND

SA = Strongly Agree ("For the most part, yes")
A = Agree ("Yes, but . . .")
D = Disagree ("No, but . . .")
SD = Strongly Disagree ("For the most part, no")

SA A D SD   1. Searching for a topic is one of the most difficult and important steps in thesis writing.

SA A D SD   2. Conducting a preliminary review of the literature can invaluably assist you in finding a topic.

SA A D SD   3. The following sources, among others, can be used to locate information for a topic: a textbook, a journal article, an encyclopedia, a handbook, an index, the Internet, and **ERIC**.

I hope you circled SA to each of the above questions.

Thus far in Part One, we have suggested ways of reducing the ill effects of stress associated with undertaking a master's thesis project, provided some guidelines for managing time so that you successfully complete your thesis, offered writing suggestions that are essential in thesis work, and identified critical ethical issues that must be confronted even before you undertake research. Concluding Part One, we will deal with an issue that is perhaps of foremost concern to you—assisting you in the initial stages of developing an idea or topic for research. Finding a topic is the most difficult part of doing a thesis. Once you have a topic, the rest is easy; trust me. The truth of the matter is that the key to a satisfying and gratifying master's thesis experience is selecting a topic that really interests and motivates you. So as you scan the literature described in this module, keep that admonition in mind. Module 1 in Part Three will deal in more detail with actually selecting an acceptable research topic. Also, in Module 1 in Part Four you'll learn how to best evaluate published articles as you review them. Here, as you just begin to prepare to frame a study, I want to introduce you to some ideas or strategies that will aid in topic formation. The thinking here is that the earlier you begin to think about a topic the easier it will become and the more likely you'll find an appropriate topic for research.

This module will, in large part, review how to conduct a preliminary review of the literature in order to gain some ideas about a suitable topic. Now, when I say find a "topic," I don't just mean "methods for teaching science," for instance. While that is a researchable topic (i.e., one that you can find much research on), it's simply too broad. Narrowing that general topic a bit is in order. You might, for instance, decide to study "methods for teaching science to English Language Learners." Even this topic can be narrowed. You might want to investigate "methods for teaching science to English Language Learners in grades 4 and 5 in public and private schools." Getting so specific, however, so early on in your study is inadvisable because it limits you to pursue other types of areas of investigation as you peruse the literature. A "suitable" topic is one, however, that is somewhat broad, but not too broad. "Academic performance of children in elementary school classrooms that incorporate instructional approaches that emphasize multiple intelligences" is a far better topic than simply "multiple intelligences." This module will guide you to scan the literature for such a suitable topic, one that is not too broad, but not too specific as well. Narrowing a suitable topic is important much later on as you more fully explore the literature to develop **research questions** and/or **hypotheses**.

Let me now suggest some alternate ways to garner good ideas, as you ask that fateful and important question, "How do I begin to find a 'suitable' topic?"

1) *Examine textbooks in courses* – The first and most logical source of information is a textbook. Gather all the textbooks you used in the courses you've taken related to your field of study. Peruse the Table of Contents and Index or topics that might interest you, and are related to your work experience. Reread portions of chapters and consult references cited at the end of chapters. You're not necessarily looking for research studies at this point, but are rather looking for major ideas, concepts, or theories that might stir some interest. For example, in looking through a text you might come across Gardner's Multiple Intelligence Theory that has attracted much attention. You might recall how intrigued you were about his theory, yet you were curious about its applicability in your particular school. You notice that one of the chapters in the textbook cites a few studies that have attempted to field-test Gardner's theory. You wonder if you might be able to replicate such a study in your classroom/school/district. You now have an idea that you can explore further by examining other research on the topic.

2) *Consider references from textbook* – Although I mentioned references in the suggestion above, I can't overemphasize how important it is to look up references cited by others. They are a tremendous source of ideas often overlooked by master's degree students.

3) *Review notes taken in classes* – As you dusted off old textbooks, do likewise for class notes. They are an invaluable source of good ideas for a research topic. Reread the notes and look for an idea or two that interests you. What did you record that might assist you?

4) *Visit the library and skim journal articles* – Flipping through relevant journals (considered as primary sources) that contain articles in your field of study might serve to stimulate your interest. Although such an approach, according to some, is like "looking for a needle in a haystack," you might be surprised that you come across a good idea. I'd suggest you

ask your professor what journals are most relevant to the research topic. Here are some journals, though, you may want to explore:

- *Action Research Journal*
- *American Annals of the Deaf*
- *American Educational Research Journal*
- *American Journal of Education*
- *Child Development*
- *Clearing House*
- *Cognition and Instruction*
- *Curriculum Studies*
- *Early Childhood Education Journal*
- *The Educational Forum*
- *Educational Leadership*
- *Educational Psychology Review*
- *Educational Researcher*
- *Educational Review*
- *Elementary School Journal*
- *Exceptional Children*
- *Harvard Educational Review*
- *Journal of Classroom Interaction*
- *Journal of Counseling Psychology*
- *Journal of Curriculum and Supervision*
- *Journal of Education*
- *Journal of Educational Research*
- *Journal of Information Technology for Teacher Education*
- *Journal of Learning Disabilities*
- *Journal of the Learning Sciences*
- *Journal of Research in Mathematics Education*
- *Journal of Special Education*
- *Journal of Teacher Education*
- *Kappa Delta Pi Record*
- *Kappan*
- *Learning Disabilities Research and Practice*

- *Personnel and Guidance Journal*
- *Reading Research Quarterly*
- *Reading Teacher*
- *Reading and Writing Quarterly*
- *Review of Educational Research*
- *School Review*
- *Social Education*
- *Teachers College Record*
- *Teaching and Teacher Education*
- *Theory into Practice*
- *Topics in Early Childhood Special Education*
- *Urban Education*
- *The Urban Review*

Plus journals specializing in early childhood, middle, and secondary levels, and literacy

5) *Look for review articles* – Several journals contain, from time to time, review articles. Articles that review current literature in the field are a proverbial goldmine of information and ideas. A journal to consult for instance might be *Review of Educational Research (RER)*. Some journal articles you may come across may include **meta-analyses**. Meta-analyses are quantitative reviews of previous studies that use some rather new and advanced statistical procedures (beyond the scope by the way of most master's thesis students) to systematically combine results from many previous studies on a particular topic in order to come up with some sort of conclusion of evidence. These reviews are useful to consult for literature reviews or simply to develop a possible topic of study for a thesis project.

6) *Refer to interesting references cited in the article* – Just as you referred to references cited in the textbook, so too you should consult relevant journal articles often cited in review articles mentioned above. Merely checking titles of the references might stimulate a topic idea.

7) *Refer to reference works such as encyclopedia, handbooks, or yearbooks* – These secondary works provide a wealth of information on a plethora of topics. For instance, the *Review of Research in Education (RRE)*, published yearly, provides in-depth scholarly coverage in specific areas such as mathematics and science instruction, English as a Second Language research, etc. As you consult these reference works, you'll find detailed literature reviews that contain extensive bibliographies from which you may cull many relevant sources. There is nothing unethical about using these handbooks or encyclopedias as long as you cite their use in assisting your literature review. Actually look up these sources and select ones that relate best to your topic. The point here is that these reference works are an

invaluable tool to help finding a research topic. Below you'll find sampling of some relevant reference works:

- *Handbook of Reading Research*
- *Handbook of Research on Catholic Education*
- *Handbook of Research on Curriculum*
- *Handbook of Research on Early Childhood Education*
- *Handbook of Research on Educational Administration*
- *Handbook of Research on Improving Student Achievement*
- *Handbook of Research on Mathematics Teaching and Learning*
- *Handbook of Research on Multicultural Education*
- *Handbook of Research on Music Teaching and Learning*
- *Handbook of Research on School Supervision*
- *Handbook of Research on Science Teaching and Learning*
- *Handbook of Research on Social Studies Teaching and Learning*
- *Handbook of Research on Teacher Education*
- *Handbook of Research on Teaching*
- *Handbook of Research on Teaching Literacy Through the Communicative and Visual Arts*
- *Handbook of Research on Teaching the English Language Arts*
- *Handbook of Research on the Education of Young Children*
- *Encyclopedia of African American Education*
- *Encyclopedia of Early Childhood Education*
- *Encyclopedia of Educational Research*
- *Encyclopedia of Special Education*
- *The International Encyclopedia of Educational Research*
- *National Society for the Study of Education Yearbooks*
- *Yearbook of Special Education*

8) *Magazines and newspaper articles* – Although not scholarly, these popular and widely read resources are a good source of information on perhaps the latest issues of the day that may peek your curiosity and lead you to more scholarly outlets. Although you may cite a magazine or newspaper in a literature review, you should be cautioned against their overuse.

9) *Refer to educational associations or organizations*—The following organizations provide a wealth of information ranging from full-text articles to journals to research summaries to professional standards. Each has an invaluable web site. The following is a short list of selected associations.

- American Educational Research Association (AERA) www.aera.net;
- American Federation of Teachers, Research Department (AFT) www.aft.org/research;
- Association for Supervision and Curriculum Development (ASCD) www.ascd.org;
- International Reading Association (IRA) www.reading.org;
- National Association for the Education of Young Children (NAEYC) www.naeyc.org;
- National Council of Teachers of English (NCTE) www.ncte.org;
- National Council of Teachers of Mathematics (NCTM) www.nctm.org;
- National Education Association (NEA) www.nea.org;
- National Middle School Association (NMSA) www.nmsa.org;
- National Science Teachers Association (NSTA) www.nsta.org;
- Phi Delta Kappa International (PDKI) www.pdkintl.org.

10) *Catalog and research databases from your college or university* – Every college nowadays provides free access to library databases from home or school. Ask your college librarian for information. Scan the databases for topic ideas. Below are directions from my institution that should be similar to yours:

> *You can access the Wagner catalog and research databases from the following address:*
>
> *http://www.wagner.edu/library/electres.html*
>
> *You can log in to the catalog from home without a password. However, if you wish to access the indexes or full-text databases from home, you'll be prompted to enter a username and password. Your username is the same as your Wagner email username (in your case it would be xxxxxx). Your password is the same as your email password.*
>
> *Feel free to contact me if you have any problems accessing the databases form home.*

Three other commonly used databases for research are ERIC, INGENTA, and EBSCO. Please note that ERIC at the time of this writing is undergoing some changes (see http://www.ed.gov/news/pressreleases/2004/03/03182004.html. The U.S. Department of Education has awarded a five-year, $34.6 million contract to Computer Sciences Corporation (CSC) of Rockville, Maryland, along with its subcontractors, to develop and operate a new database system for the Education Resources Information Center (ERIC). The ERIC database will use the latest search and retrieval methods to cull education literature and give high-quality access to educators, researchers, and the general public. The ERIC database is the world's largest education database. It is composed of more than one million bibliographic records. The goal of the new ERIC is to provide more education materials quicker, and more directly, to audiences through the Internet.

With the new ERIC, individuals will be able to go to one Web site to search a comprehensive database of journal articles and document abstracts and descriptions and, for the first time, directly access full text. The database will include as much free full text as possible, and links will be provided to commercial sources so that individuals can purchase journal articles and other full text immediately.

During the development and transition to the new ERIC, the ERIC database will continue to be available at http://www.eric.ed.gov. You should access the web page to obtain updated information about the transition. Visit http://eric.ed.gov/ and the Educator's Reference Desk (www.eduref.org). You can also continue to access the ERIC database at the Educator's Reference Desk. If you are looking for ERIC related information, please go to www.eric.ed.gov.

Again, during the transition period, continue to use this ERIC website to:

- Search the ERIC database – (http://edrs.com)

- Link to the ERIC Document Reproduction Service (EDRS) to purchase ERIC full-text documents.

- Stay up-to-date about the ERIC transition to a new ERIC database model.

Toll-free contact for general questions about ERIC: (800) LET-ERIC (538-3742).

ERIC is user-friendly. The best way to learn to use ERIC of course is to actually "use it." The time you spend doing so may seem tedious at first, but let me assure you that the time will be well spent in the long run. Do not avoid ERIC. Doing so will jeopardize your literature review.

Now, try www.ingenta.com. It's a United Kingdom web service that provides free online searches. The site is amazingly easy to use and you can peruse much information (abstracts and full-text articles) on many topics from many journals. It's worth spending 30 minutes web surfing this site. Go to the site to register. It'll take a day to receive approval once you register (you'll receive an email that you're ready to use the site). Go to the search box and type in for instance "multiple intelligences," then click search. You'll come across dozens of articles on the topic. Click "summary" to read the abstract. It's a fast and easy way to generate topic ideas as well as collect sources for the literature review. You can also scan journal articles directly by clicking on "browse publications" on the left bar. Click "choose a subject" and click on "social sciences." Then select "education" and you'll have an alphabetical listing of almost every research journal in the field. You can peruse contents for each journal, but you can't read an article unless you subscribe to it or are willing to pay a fee for a particular article. When actually collecting articles for a literature review it may be worth the expense if you come across a great article you need for the review.

Finally, try http://www.ebsco.com/home/. Many colleges and universities subscribe to this invaluable database. If they don't, you should look into an individual purchase because the time you save, trust me, will be more than worth the cost!

Sources to Consult in Conducting a Preliminary Review of the Literature in Search of a Topic:
Source 1: Textbooks and references
Source 2: Course notes
Source 3: Journal articles, especially review articles
Source 4: Reference works
Source 5: Magazines and newspapers
Source 6: Educational associations or organizations
Source 7: Database like ERIC
Source 8: Ingenta &/or Ebsco web site/college library on the web

At this point, identify some key terms or topic ideas and search for articles on that topic. Good luck. There's a lot out there. Consult McGuire, Stilborne, McAdams, and Hyatt's (2000) very useful work titled *The Internet handbook for writers, researchers, and journalists* and their web site at http://www.guilford.com/cgi-bin/cartscript.cgi?page=writernet/index.html&cart_id=. Don't rush yourself or feel compelled to select a topic quickly. Take your time; it's the most important decision you make in thesis writing. Learn to tolerate a degree of uncertainty during the first few weeks or so. I'm certain you'll find what you need. For now, spend time surfing ERIC from your local computer or go to the library to search the database and other related sources of information. Note that a growing trend is for students not to visit the library since they have Internet access. In my view, not visiting the library is a mistake. First, the librarian, as an experienced researcher, will likely be a great source of information and assistance. Second, you might come across many other valuable sources for ideas about a topic by browsing the stacks, reference sections, other databases (e.g., the *Education Index* that dates back to 1929 whereas ERIC only goes back to 1965), etc.

If you have not yet read Module 4 in Part Thirteen, I'd recommend you do so to obtain a few more guidelines that may assist you in this preliminary search for a topic.

Module 5 Review

In this Module you learned ways of searching the literature for topic ideas. Although there's more to do to actually have an acceptable topic (see Module 1 in Part Three) you can generate some good ideas at this preliminary stage. Complete the exercise that follows as a module review.

Sources I consulted:

_____

_____

_____

Topic ideas from each source:

_____

_____

_____

Possible topics (in step above you randomly listed topic ideas; here you organize them by group):

_____

_____

_____

Topic(s) I may be most interested in that has enough literature to conduct thesis research:

_____

_____

_____

Self-Test Check

1. One of the first steps in conducting a preliminary review of the literature might be to
   A. conduct an ERIC search
   B. scan through some textbooks in previous courses
   C. read someone else's thesis
   D. read the *Encyclopedia of Educational Research*

2. Which of the following is the best example of a suitable topic?
   A. Methods for teaching mathematics
   B. Mathematics performance of English Language Learners in elementary school
   C. 5th graders exposed to computer assisted instruction in mathematics will score higher on the State's standardized test than students taught using the textbook approach
   D. Is bilingual education a good approach?

3. Selecting a sufficiently broad topic at the outset is more advisable than selecting a narrower one because
   A. it allows for greater flexibility in shaping the study as you continue to explore the literature
   B. it is easier to do
   C. it is harder to do
   D. it allows the researcher to remain broad throughout the study

4. Which of the following is not an advisable way to search for a topic?
   A. Examine the *Encyclopedia of Educational Research*
   B. Examine notes from previous courses
   C. Scan ERIC
   D. Conduct a full-blown literature review

5. Which is the best advice for conducting preliminary review of the literature in search of a topic?
   A. Decide early on a topic so that you have enough time to complete the thesis with minimal stress
   B. Scan ERIC immediately
   C. Read literature reviews from a least three handbooks or yearbooks
   D. All of these
   E. None of these

Answers: 1) b; 2) b (not too specific and not too broad); 3) a; 4) d; 5) e (refer to page 34)

Study Questions and Activity

1. What is the purpose of a preliminary review of the literature?

2. How can conducting a review of the sources mentioned in this module help identify an initial research problem?

3. Why is previous research on a topic so critical in framing your own study?

4. Consult meta-analyses. What have you found that may of use in framing your own research problem?

5. List several possible topics and locate two or three studies that relate to them. Which are most interesting and researchable to you?

6. Team up with a class partner or two and share information gleaned from this preliminary review of the literature. What information did you glean that may be useful to you?

Part Two:

Overview of Research in Education

Focus Questions

1. What are the chief components of educational research?

2. What are the advantages of employing quantitative *and* qualitative approaches?

3. Which approach to research provides a more biased-free assessment of a situation: quantitative or qualitative?

4. What are the differences among experimental, quasi-experimental, and ex post facto designs?

5. What steps would you need to follow when conducting educational research?

6. How is writing a thesis proposal different from writing the actual thesis?

Module 1: A Paradigm for Research

While textbook authors of educational research have categorized types, methods, and forms of research differently (Best & Kahn, 1998), I have found the paradigm in Figure 2.1 a useful means to give my students an overall understanding of how educational research is situated in a broad context as well as highlight specific methods and research techniques that may be valuable to the master's degree student. Discussion here is meant as an introductory overview of research as subsequent modules will provide more in-depth coverage in each important area of research. **Be sure to consult the glossary for information as you read this module.** This "paradigm," then, is a lens from which to view all educational research.

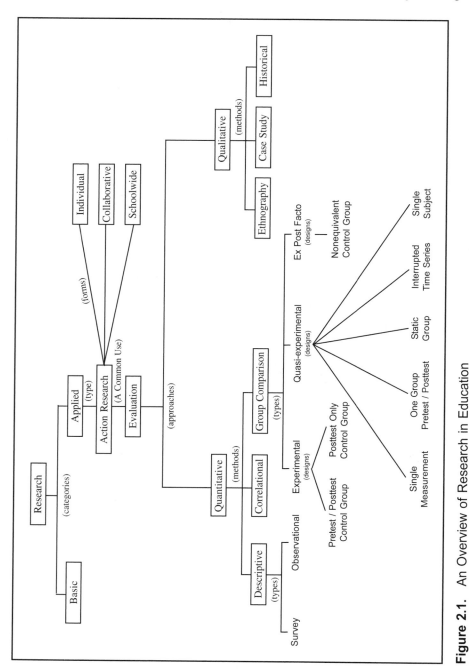

Figure 2.1. An Overview of Research in Education

Research is disciplined inquiry that utilizes a systematic approach by applying the **scientific method** to study educational problems. There are two *categories* of research: *basic* and *applied* (see Figure 2.2). They differ from one another in purpose.

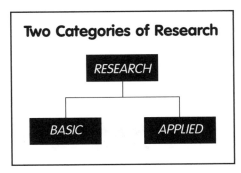

Figure 2.2.

Basic (also called pure or fundamental research) involves experiments that attempt to extend our knowledge in a given discipline or field of study. The goal of basic research is to develop **theory** through broad generalizations. Basic research has no immediate practical value, but is essential in furthering our understanding of important phenomena. Theories of learning, for example, are generated from basic research. Master's theses rarely, if ever, attempt to generate new theories at this basic research level. Master's work can indeed contribute toward theory development but generally does not in and of itself produce ground-breaking theory.

Applied research is conducted chiefly in order to improve practice by solving some sort of specific problem. Attempts at applying learning theory to solve practical problems that teachers face in the classroom are examples of this category of research (see, e.g., Hunter, 1967).

Action research is one *type* of applied research (see Figure 2.3). Teachers, administrators, and supervisors (and other educational leaders) conduct action research in order to address a specific problem by using the principles and methodologies of research. Although action research utilizes less rigorous designs and methodologies than other forms of applied research, its benefits are enormous not only for the professional development of those educational leaders who use action research, but for the school as a whole.

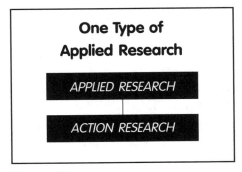

Figure 2.3.

Three forms of action research allow educators to investigate areas of concern in their classrooms and schools: individual, collaborative, and schoolwide (see Figure 2.4) (Calhoun, 1993). Individual teachers, counselors, and supervisors may conduct a research project that focuses on a specific class, program, or activity. The educator may define an area of investigation and then seek a solution or may simply collect data to determine a course of action. All action research projects, indeed, begin with an individual educator who has the necessary knowledge, skills, and desire to carry out such an enterprise.

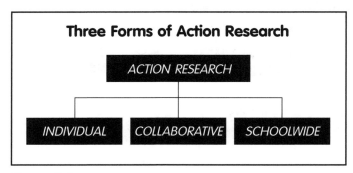

Figure 2.4.

Collaborative action research is a *form* of action research that is taken on by a group or team of individuals that can, for instance, focus on one classroom or several classrooms. A collaborative action research team may also conduct a districtwide investigation (Oja & Smulyan, 1989). Schoolwide action research, a third form of action research, is undertaken by a community of practitioners including teachers, guidance counselors, special education personnel, parents, students, and administrators to address schoolwide issues and solve common problems (see, e.g., Calhoun, 1994; Calhoun & Allen 1996; *Equity and Choice,* 1993; McNiff, 1995; Sagor, 1992; Stringer, 1999).

The distinction between collaborative and schoolwide research may be subtle and even arbitrary. Certainly a school faculty committee that involves parents and students, for instance, is collaborative in nature. Although collaborate and schoolwide action research are essential for school renewal (Glickman, 1998), educators must learn how to conduct individual research. This approach is justified by the belief that before teams of committed professionals can deal with complex schoolwide problems, training in research should be provided for dealing with classroom or gradewide projects. Action research projects are more likely to be encouraged and supported by educational leaders who have experienced firsthand the benefits of this type of research on a small scale. Furthermore, such training empowers educators to conduct action research themselves without reliance on "outside" experts.

Although action research is invaluable in school-based settings as a means of professional development and to assess practices and programs, educational research, more broadly addressed in this volume, is more applicable for students completing more traditional masters degree research. Research strategies learned through educational research, however, can benefit those who engage in action research work. For specific information on conducing action research, refer to Glanz (2003).

Evaluation research is one possible use of action research (see Figure 2.1). A goal of evaluation research is to assess the quality of a particular practice or program in a school. Evaluation research is very much involved in addressing a specific problem. From my experience, educational leaders as action researchers undertake evaluative studies quite often. Although, evaluation research is considered the most common use of action research, most students undertaking master's thesis work will not be involved in such research.

Educational research, in general, may utilize two *approaches* to inquiry: quantitative and qualitative (see Figure 2.1).

Three *methods* of **qualitative research,** among others, that may be useful to the educational researcher are **ethnography, case study,** and **historical** inquiry (see Figures 2.1 and 2.5). Qualitative approaches do not, of course, utilize statistical or mathematical expressions, as will be explained in Part Seven. Rather, they rely on detailed verbal descriptions of phenomena observed.

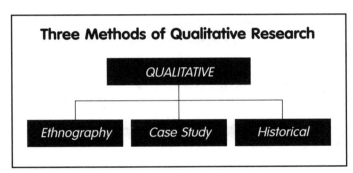

Figure 2.5.

Qualitative research approaches "are used to examine questions that can best be answered by *verbally* describing how participants in a study perceive and interpret various aspects of their environment" (Crowl, Kaminsky, & Podell, 1997, p. 499). A study involving how a principal, for instance, fostered shared decision making in her school could be reported qualitatively. By interviewing key participants in the school, observing decision-making committees in action and describing in detail how participants interrelate with one another, and analyzing written documents and other sources about site-based management, the researcher may reach certain conclusions about the impact of shared decision making in this particular school.

Qualitative approaches examine the "how" (process) and the "why" questions. The power of qualitative research is in its ability to enrich our understanding of a given phenomenon.

Although results cannot usually be generalized to other schools and populations in the same way that quantitative research can, qualitative research offers a unique opportunity to conduct an in-depth analysis into the intricate processes at work when attempting to study some aspect of the classroom or school. The value of qualitative approaches is that they provide rich detail and insight often missing from quantitative studies (see below). Also, qualitative research can indeed generate some theory (i.e., theory building). In other words, you undertake a number of ethnographic studies that may indicate a pattern of thought or behavior from which a theory might be developed that can then be explored further utilizing both qualitative and quantitative approaches.

Three *methods* of **quantitative research** that may be useful to the educational researcher are **descriptive, correlational,** and **group comparison** research (see Figures 2.1 and 2.6). **Descriptive research** can be broken down further into two *types:* **survey** and observational research (see Figures 2.1 and 2.7). **Correlational research** has no subdivisions, whereas **group comparison research** can be divided into three *types:* **experimental, quasi-experimental,** and **ex post facto research** (see Figures 2.1 and 2.7). Specific research designs are employed to conduct experimental, quasi-experimental, and ex post facto research (see bottom part of Figure 2.1 for designs related to each). Note that in Figure 2.1 there are six **designs** used in quasi-experimental studies (these will be explained in Part Six).

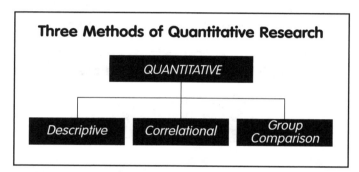

Figure 2.6.

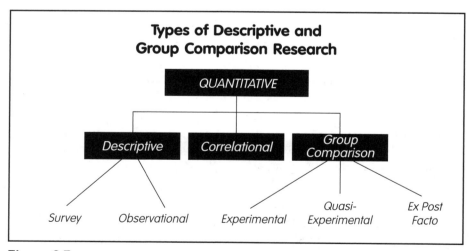

Figure 2.7.

Differences exist between qualitative and quantitative approaches. Qualitative research captures behavior occurring in naturalistic settings and does not involve purposeful manipulation of subjects for experimental purposes as do many quantitative studies. Qualitative research is not just another methodology (a set of data collection and analysis tools), but can be conceived as a paradigm or a way of thinking about how knowledge is created and best understood. A fundamental belief that qualitative researchers espouse is that events cannot be understood unless one understands how they are perceived and interpreted by the people who participated in them. Moreover, quantitative approaches assume that social facts, in the first place, have an objective reality that can be studied scientifically. Qualitative modes, in contrast, assume that reality is socially constructed and is best represented, if you will, by the subjective perceptions or observations of individuals. Qualitative research can occur naturally by simply walking into a classroom, for instance, and recording behavior objectively or anecdotally without any prescribed or predetermined criteria. Qualitative research, in this vein, is more flexible and inductive than quantitative research that, by definition, requires a more structured, prescribed, and deductive format.

The quantitative researcher tries to maintain a degree of objectivity and detachment from whatever is examined. In contrast, a qualitative researcher may be more actively involved by participating at the same time observation, for example, is undertaken. While quantitative researchers attempt to identify a problem in advance of a study, qualitative researchers feel comfortable in waiting for problems or issues to emerge. In essence, quantitative research attempts to establish facts, while qualitative research tries to develop understanding of a problem.

Qualitative Research in Action

Situation: Ms. Georgina Urbay, a lead-teacher in a suburban elementary school on the West Coast, just completed her master's degree at a local university. As a culminating project, she successfully completed her master's thesis on a topic relevant to her work situation.

For her project Ms. Urbay investigated gender influences on the quality of attention students receive in their class. Having reviewed the literature in this field, Ms. Urbay wondered whether gender biases existed in the classes she was responsible for supervising. When she observed some of the newer teachers, in the past, her observations focused on the quantity of thought-provoking questions asked during a lesson or identifying, numerically, which students were on- or off-task. In these previous visits, Ms. Urbay and the teachers predetermined the nature of each observation. This time she felt that she just wanted to get a general feeling about the classroom without previously established criteria for observation. She read about qualitative observation tools like the Wide Lens strategy (Acheson & Gall, 1997). With this procedure, the observer makes brief notes of events as they occur in the classroom. A favorite technique used by anthropologists, the wide lens strategy enables intensive, direct observations of behavior. No prearranged categories or questions are developed. The recorder may perceptively determine how wide a lens to make. The wider the lens, the more behaviors are observed. As narrow lenses are used, specific behaviors of individuals may be focused upon.

Anecdotal records usually consist of short descriptive sentences summarizing a particular event or situation. These recordings are usually made objectively and nonevaluatively. Rather than recording that "Susan was day-dreaming," Ms. Urbay might write "Susan was gazing out the rear window of the classroom." Ms. Urbay decides to reserve the right to make interpretive observations as well, but includes her interpretive comments in brackets. Although audio recordings would help capture the lesson, Ms. Urbay decides that such a recording would make the teacher feel uncomfortable and since she knows short-hand, recording data would not be a problem.

Ms. Urbay decides that rather than sitting in the back of the room as a detached observer, she would get a "better feel" for the classroom environment by participating to any extent possible in the lesson, at the same time she was recording observations. Ms. Urbay entered Mr. Jones' classroom. Eric Jones was a second-year teacher who was still receiving mentoring from Ms. Urbay. Ms. Urbay informed Mr. Jones that she would be observing and participating in his lesson. She informed Mr. Jones that this was not a formal observation, but merely an opportunity to just get a better sense of the classroom climate. She, in fact, spoke with Eric Jones about her research into gender-related issues in the classroom and suggested that she was curious about how gender might influence teacher behavior. It is important to note that Ms. Urbay is not responsible for personnel evaluation. She has established a good rapport with Eric Jones, as she has with the other teachers she mentors.

Ms. Urbay took the following notes during one segment of the lesson:

> *5th grade class; 13 boys and 12 girls; self-contained classroom; Eric Jones, teacher; 9:45 a.m.; I enter as Mr. Jones tells class to take out their readers; As Mr. Jones gives instructions for silent reading, three students (2 male and 1 female) are out of their seats hanging their clothing in the rear classroom closet; The girl is talking; Mr. Jones tells her to be quiet and sit down; During silent reading students are reading quietly; After about 3 minutes a monitor enters classroom and teacher is recording daily attendance; Noise level in class rises; Monitor leaves room; Teacher walks back and forth as students get quiet; At 9:49 a.m., Mr. Jones asks a boy to tell the class what the story was about; Student responds; Class attentive; Mr. Jones asks a girl, "Why do you think Billy in the story was so upset?"; Student responds; Teacher calls on a boy who also responds, albeit differently; Mr. Jones probes and asks boy to explain; Mr. Jones asks another thought-provoking question to a girl; Girl responds; Teacher asks another question to a boy and probes;...[10 minutes elapse and I note that it appears that Mr. Jones calls on boys and girls evenly, but that he consistently probes male responses, but rarely probes a female response,...curious, ask Mr. Jones about this!]; Time elapses; Teacher divides class into study groups; I join one of the groups with 2 boys and 1 girl; Teacher circulates; Students answer reading questions and discuss story; I ask them if they liked the story and to explain why or why not; Teacher requests attention from class; Mr. Jones continues asking many thought-provoking questions and follows the same pattern of probing more for boys than for girls; Interestingly, when the boy sitting to my right in the group was asked a question, he was probed, but the girl to my left was not; I could not discern any concern among the students.*

This situation is one in which the lead-teacher, Ms. Urbay, decided that a qualitative approach would be best suited for her observation of Mr. Jones' lesson. Her primary purpose was to obtain a better understanding of the lesson given by Mr. Jones. Although her observations focused on teacher questions and student responses, she had the flexibility to note any usual or unusual behavior in the classroom. Her format was flexible and unstructured. Her recordings occurred in the natural classroom environment without any manipulation of subjects or classes.

Reflection

What other features of the scenario above demonstrate its qualitative nature?
Can you create a scenario, different from the example above,
that illustrates a qualitative approach?

Please note that this description of qualitative research in action is meant as an example and one, in fact, not related to a research topic. Note that the field notes are also simply illustrative, but not very detailed as they would be in a full-blown qualitative research study. Ethnographers, for instance, would produce copious notes. Moreover, in qualitative research observations would, of course, take place numerous times over a longer period of time. Data analysis that would sometimes even occur simultaneous to data collection was similarly not highlighted in the previous example.

Quantitative Research in Action

Situation: Ms. Rhonda Minotti, a principal of an urban middle school in New York City, was assigned to her first principalship in a school where the average years of teaching experience was close to 20. Her teachers were more comfortable using traditional teaching methods than more innovative or progressive ones. She has tried to demonstrate to her teaching staff that under some circumstances non-traditional instructional approaches might have a greater effect on student achievement. Note that the name is fictitious but the study real (see Farkas, 2003).

Ms. Minotti conducting an experimental study that examined the effect of teaching through traditional versus learning-style instructional methods on an urban sample of 105 heterogeneously grouped 7th grade students' achievement, attitudes, empathic tendencies, and transfer skills in response to lessons on the Holocaust. She posed four hypotheses:

1. Students taught the Holocaust unit with the multisensory learning-styles instructional method would demonstrate significantly higher achievement gains than students taught the unit using traditional teaching methods (e.g., lecture, group discussion, visual resources).

2. Students taught the Holocaust unit with the multisensory learning-styles instructional method would demonstrate significantly higher attitudes towards toward learning than students taught the unit using traditional teaching methods.

3. Students taught the Holocaust unit with the multisensory learning-styles instructional method would demonstrate significantly higher empathy-toward-people tests scores than students taught the unit using traditional teaching methods.

4. Students taught the Holocaust unit with the multisensory learning-styles instructional method would demonstrate significantly higher student transfer test scores than students taught the unit using traditional teaching methods

After reviewing the extensive literature on learning styles and the positive effects of the multisensory approach, Ms. Minotti solicited participants for her study. The participants included 105 7th graders in an urban middle school who were in four separate classrooms but were comparable in terms of intellectual ability. The four classes were comparable to other classes in the school and represented a heterogeneous and inclusive sample of students that included gender, ethnicity, family's socioeconomic status, level of parental education, and prior achievement levels. Two classes were randomly designated as the experimental group and were instructed by a teacher using the multisensory approach, whereas the other two classes were taught using traditional methods.

Instruments were identified and administered. They included: the Learning Style Inventory, the Semantic Differential Scale measuring attitudes towards learning, the Balanced Emotional Empathy Scale, and the Moral Judgment Inventory measuring stages of moral development and transfer of knowledge. Participants were given pretests to ascertain that both groups were equivalent in terms of their knowledge of the Holocaust and post tests were administered to assess content mastery after the four-week unit.

Administration of **t-Tests** indicated positive and significant impacts on achievement scores ($p<.001$) for students taught using the multisensory approach. When students were taught through the multisensory method, gain scores on the empathy scale revealed significance ($p<.001$). Furthermore, students indicated significantly more positive attitudes when instructed with the multisensory approach ($p<.001$), and performance was higher ($p<.001$) on the transfer of skills when instructed with the multisensory approach rather than the traditional approach.

Reflection

What other features of the scenario above demonstrate its quantitative nature?
Can you create a scenario, different from the example above,
that illustrates a quantitative approach?

Note that a **mixed methodology** approach could have been used with each scenario above.

Reflection

How might Ms. Urbay in the first scenario have incorporated quantitative approaches and how might Ms. Minotti have used qualitative ones? What are the benefits of a mixed methodological approach?

While qualitative and quantitative procedures differ in purpose, orientation, and, essentially, how research is conducted (see Figure 2.8), other differences center on how data are collected and analyzed, and how conclusions are reached. Unlike quantitative research, few authorities in the field agree on precise methods for data collection, analysis, interpretation, and, even, the reporting of findings derived from qualitative procedures (Creswell, 1994). Notwithstanding these differences, patterns or similarities emerge among those individuals who conduct qualitative inquiry. Although data collection and analysis are described in separate modules later in this book, a brief overview of data collection and methods of analysis for qualitative and quantitative studies is in order.

Characteristics of Quantitative and Qualitative Research

Quantitative	Qualitative
numbers or statistics	verbal descriptions
generalization possible	specific to situation
describes the "what"	describes the "how"
positivistic	naturalistic
testable hypotheses	tentative hypotheses
structured	flexible
reality is objective	reality is constructed
detached	involved
deductive	inductive
predetermined	emergent
establishes facts	develops understanding

Figure 2.8.

Data collection in qualitative approaches depends on the purpose for the study and the type of information sought. If the researcher is interested, for instance, in understanding meanings given to certain events such as reactions to faculty meetings, then a combination of direct observation, participant observation, and interviewing may be used. On the other hand, if visual evidence of a particular situation is required (e.g., a student's behavior during a lesson), then a video recording may be more appropriate than distributing surveys. Although primary and secondary data collection techniques (such as observations, interviews, documents, and audiovisual materials) will be discussed in Part Eight, some of the following data collection approaches in qualitative research (culled from Creswell, 1994) are commonly used:

1. Gathering observational notes as a participant-observer

2. Gathering observational notes by an observer

3. Conducting unstructured, open-ended interviews

4. Keeping a journal during a research project

5. Collecting personal documents (e.g., letters and official records)

6. Analyzing public documents (e.g., memoranda and minutes)

7. Videotaping a social situation of an individual or group

8. Examining photographs or videotapes

9. Watching and recording non-verbal behaviors

Reflection

Can you think how you could use any of the data collection techniques above?

Data analysis in qualitative research, discussed in Part Ten, is also varied. According to Patton (1990), "sitting down to make sense out of pages of interviews and whole files of field notes can be overwhelming" (p. 297). While data analysis can certainly be overwhelming, certain basic principles can be applied:

Simultaneity—Data analysis and even interpretation can be conducted at the same time as data are collected. Sorting similar pieces of information into categories and attaching meaning to them is commonly used in qualitative projects.

Reduction—Seemingly disparate pieces of data can be reduced into categories, patterns, or themes. Reduction is often accomplished by a procedure known as coding. Coding involves attaching meaning to a particular scene, document, or event. For example, in viewing different types of leaders in films, one may categorize the different leaders by their style by first coding each leader with a given leadership style. Reduction also involves **content analysis.**

The distinction between data analysis and data reduction should be made. Data analysis in qualitative research refers to the process of categorizing, describing, and synthesizing data. Data reduction is used to better describe and interpret data under analysis.

Display—Data can be displayed in numerous ways (visually and otherwise) to aid analysis and interpretation.

Computer—Data can be easily analyzed using qualitative text software packages.

Suppose you had carefully conducted some interviews with teachers and collected some open-ended anonymous questionnaires that dealt with teachers' perceptions of effective or "good" principals. After spending several weeks collecting data, you now wonder how you can make sense of it all. "Qualitative data analysis is primarily an inductive process of organizing the data into categories and identifying patterns (relationships) among the categories. Unlike quantitative procedures, most categories and patterns emerge from the data, rather than being imposed on the data prior to data collection" (McMillan & Schumacher, 2000, p. 501).

Creswell (1994) describes qualitative data analysis as an inductive process this way:

> …*Treat the responses and documents like a giant inductive set: At the simplest level you are searching for categories and their attributes-figuring out what things go together (convergence). For responses to open-ended survey or interview questions, read the set quickly for a general impression. Then take each item, and list or group all responses together. Look at this list and decide if there are responses similar in content that appear frequently.*
>
> *For example, one team interviewed a sample of eighteen students…using four questions…As the team looked at these eighteen responses on the first pass, they noticed immediately that projects of various sorts were mentioned frequently. On the next pass, they looked more closely at the comments students made during their discussion of projects. They noticed that students gave descriptions of projects across subject areas in science, social studies, math, and reading. (p. 75)*

In contrast, **quantitative research** has for many years been the research of choice in the social sciences. The model of social research—the **scientific method**—and the logic that underpins it—positivism—have dominated educational and administrative theory. The predominance of this social science perspective has only recently undergone criticism in light of the emergence of qualitative, including ethnographic and biographical, analyses. The traditions of positivism and the scientific method in educational research, although still popular, have given way somewhat to alternative (qualitative) approaches for conducting research (Denzin & Lincoln, 2000).

Three *types* of qualitative methods that may be applied by the educational researcher are: **historical, ethnography,** and **case study** inquiry. While other qualitative methods exist, I have personally used and found these forms useful. Qualitative methods do not, for the most part, utilize statistical or mathematical expressions. Qualitative approaches rely on detailed verbal descriptions of observed phenomena. Educational researchers often find qualitative methods most suitable and more easily adapted for school settings.

No randomization is employed in nonexperimental qualitative studies. The researcher may select a particular individual to observe using "thick descriptions" (intensive, daily, observation over an extended period of time; see discussion in Module 2 of Part Eight). For example, the day in a life of a city superintendent may be investigated by following the superintendent around for a day. Observations are recorded anecdotally (verbatim). Since this form of research is qualitative and nonexperimental, findings are primarily based on the investigator's perceptions and interpretations. (See discussion, in the Glossary, of ways of enhancing **validity** and **reliability** in qualitative approaches.)

In terms of quantitative analyses, data derived from descriptive, correlational, and/or group comparison research can be analyzed mathematically. Some sort of statistical analyses are required to analyze quantitative studies. For a more complete discussion of quantitative data analysis explicating various statistical measures see Part Nine.

Keep in mind, as we conclude this module that as each *approach, method, type,* and *design* of research is explained in the text, Figure 2.1 and the other figures should be referred to in order to help place the concept within context. Key terms are explained in the Glossary; however, most terms are treated more fully where they naturally occur in the text.

Reflection

How does this paradigm overview of educational research help you think about your own study?

Module 1 Review

In this Module you learned the following major idea:

1. *An overview of educational research* – Given a paradigm or lens in which to consider various research possibilities will help those of you who are global learners. Global learners prefer to learn by considering the whole picture first and then breaking down the information into smaller parts. When they do so, they begin to recognize patterns and see relationships. For those of you who prefer the analytic learning style and seek the details, you may skip ahead if you'd like to Parts Six and Seven.

Self-Test Check

Part A

1. True or False: Basic and action research are two categories of research.

2. True or False: Action research strategies are sufficient by themselves to conduct traditional education research.

3. True or False: Using both quantitative and qualitative approaches to research helps you triangulate.

4. True or False: Ex post facto research is a type of group comparison study.

5. True or False: Case study research is synonymous with ethnography.

Answers:
1. False: Basic and *Applied* research
2. False
3. True: Refer back to "Ways of Knowing" in the Preface.
4. True
5. False

Part B: You may not be able to answer these questions by simply reading the previous module unless you also refer to the Glossary.

1. True or False: Ethnography is used to observe individuals or groups of individuals in natural settings. The ethnographic researcher takes many notes describing what was observed.

2. True or False: Case studies are one of three methods of qualitative research. Case studies involve in-depth investigations of an individual or group of individuals. Findings are stated verbally, not numerically.

3. True or False: Historical research uses written documents of the past (primary and secondary sources) and oral testimonies to provide insight into phenomena or events.

4. True or False: Descriptive studies may involve observational reports that use statistics or numbers (usually percentages) to describe data.

5. True or False: Correlation (synonymous with the word "relationship") is a statistical technique for evaluating the degree to which two variables relate to one another.

6. True or False: In Group Comparison research the researcher administers different treatments to groups and then compares the groups on a **dependent variable**.

7. True or False: Experimental research, as one type of Group Comparison study, involves randomization of individuals.

8. True or False: Quasi-experimental research, as one type of Group Comparison study, involves no randomization but just assigning of groups to either experimental or control conditions.

9. True or False: Ex Post Facto research, as one type of Group Comparison study, involves groups already formed because members of each group exhibit characteristics that the researcher has no control over (e.g., whether or not they had pre-school experience).

10. Experimental research, in contrast to non-experimental research, shows cause and effect relationships.

Answers:
1. True
2. True
3. True
4. True
5. True
6. True
7. True
8. False: There is random assignment of intact groups, but not individuals
9. True
10. True

Study Questions

1. How does this overview of educational research help you in undertaking a research project?

2. Most neophyte researchers hesitate to delve into the quantitative approach for fear of statistics. Consider your interest in quantitative research. Why or why not would you employ it? Would you prefer qualitative research? Why or why not? What factor or factors will determine which approach you use?

3. How might you incorporate a mixed methodological approach to research?

4. Why do you think having this overview of educational research will help you to develop a topic?

5. Study Figure 2.1 and then without referring to the figure, try to replicate it. Knowledge of the figure will help you more easily proceed as you begin your project.

Activity

1. Find an article in a journal or magazine that represents each method of quantitative and qualitative research mentioned in this module.

Module 2: The Steps of Educational Research

Steps in Research

Educational research is an ongoing process of examining problems in school settings. Five (5) guiding steps, as shown in Figure 2.9.

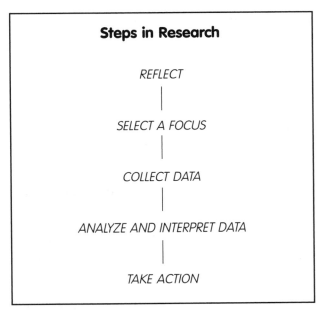

Figure 2.9.

1. Reflection

Reflective practice was previously introduced in the Preface. As reflective practitioners, you continually seek ways of improving your classroom/school/district/job. Undertaking a master's degree research project, you probably would like to conduct a study that somehow affects your professional practice (especially since master's degree work focuses on applied, not basic research). You ask yourself "what do I need to know to do a better job?"; "what concerns do faculty and staff raise?"; "what do I wonder about my job?; "what practices would enable me to do a better job?"; etc. During this initial phase, you might examine the literature for ideas about school/classroom renewal or improvement. You might explore "best practices" and find ways to implement innovative ideas that could work in your classroom/school/district/position. Before you engage in educational research you must always spend time in reflection. Simply spending an afternoon thinking about your professional practice is critically important in order to successfully conduct a meaningful thesis project.

Reflection

After spending some time in reflection,
what concerns and/or ideas come to mind?

As an aside, some master degree students may not be currently employed. Still, keeping in mind your area of interest will help *focus* your thesis project. Some of you, though, may not want to necessarily study something related to your area of specialty. Rather, you may want to investigate an educational issue that is simply intriguing or "hot" in the field such as retention or high stakes testing. Still, reflection is key.

2. **Select a focus**—includes three steps:

a. Know what you want to investigate (conduct a preliminary literature review, see Module 5 in Part One) and identify some needed area of concern such as:

- *Student Outcomes:* e.g., achievement, attitudes, etc.

- *Curriculum:* e.g., effectiveness of instructional materials, alignment with state content standards, etc.

- *Instruction:* e.g., teaching strategies, use of technology, etc.

- *School Climate:* e.g., teacher morale, relationships between teachers and supervisors, etc.

- *Parental Involvement:* e.g., participation on committees, attendance at school events, etc.

b. Develop some **research questions/hypotheses** about the area you've chosen based on the literature review. As you focus on a specific concern or problem, you need to begin to pose some questions that will serve to guide your research (refer to Module 2 in Part Three). If, for instance, low levels of parental involvement are a concern, you might ask: "How can I document these low levels of parent involvement?"; "What impact do these low levels of participation have on students' completion of science projects?"; "Will increased levels of involvement yield higher student achievement levels?"; and "How might parental involvement in school affairs be increased?" Developing these guiding questions will eventually lead to specifying **research questions** and/or **hypotheses**.

c. Establish a research plan to answer these questions. Plan includes:

-how many and what kinds of participants in the study (see **population** and **sample**)

-the **variables** under study

-how the variables will be studied

Reflection

If you have conducted a preliminary review of the literature,
see if you can jot some notes down on each of the aforementioned steps above.

3. *Collect data*—Once you have narrowed your focus, that is, have a specific area of concern, have developed some **research questions,** and know how you plan to answer them, you are now ready to gather information to answer your research questions. Let's say you're investigating the new science program adopted by the district. You've posed some research questions about achievement levels and students' attitudes toward science. You can now begin to collect data that will provide evidence for the effectiveness of this program in terms of achievement and attitudes.

    You may administer teacher-made and **standardized tests,** conduct **surveys** and **interviews,** and examine **portfolios.** What other kinds of evidence could you collect to help you understand the impact of this new science program? How would you collect such evidence? Discuss these questions with a classmate.

    Quite often educational researchers collect data, but do not organize them so that they can be shared with others. Raw data that just "sit around" in someone's file drawer are useless. Collected data must be transformed so that they can be used. Data that are counted, displayed, and organized by classroom, grade level, and school, for example, can then be used appropriately during the data analysis and interpretive phases. In order to present research in the most concise and useable way possible, data organization is included in the data analysis phase (see below).

4. *Analyze and interpret data*—Once you've collected relevant data, you need to begin the process of analysis and interpretation in order to arrive at some decision. Data analysis and interpretation of results will be major concerns of Parts Nine and Ten.

5. *Conclusions*—Finally, you've reached the stage at which you draw conclusions. You've answered your **research questions** and/or confirmed or rejected your **hypotheses.** The conclusions you draw result from the evidence that emerges from your data. At this point you also draw some implications from your findings and suggest avenues for further investigation. See Module 4 in this Part and Module 3 in Part Twelve for more details.

Module 2 Review

In this Module you learned the following major idea:

1. *The 5 main steps in conducting educational research* – Review the five steps and team up with a partner to help each other think through them based on any work you've accumulated so far on your topic. Some students at this point like to even sketch out a mock plan

with mock data. Global learners particularly enjoy this activity. Whether or not you want to do this is your own decision at this point.

Self-Test Check

1. Which is not an accurate statement regarding the five steps in educational research?

    a. Defining a problem is done after reflection
    b. Always state the hypothesis, when applicable
    c. In the research design you must state how the sample was formed and what statistical measures will be employed
    d. The final stage is to collect and analyze the data

2. Which is not a step in Selecting a Focus for a research topic?

    a. develop a research plan
    b. establish research questions/hypotheses
    c. define a problem is done after reflection
    d. have an idea of what you want to investigate

3. Topic: cooperative learning and science achievement. Which is best research question?

    a. is cooperative learning related to science achievement?
    b. is science achievement measurable?
    c. is cooperative learning a viable teaching strategy and can it promote science achievement?
    d. all of these are satisfactory

Answers: 1) d; 2) c; 3) a

Study Questions and Activities

1. How do these five steps assist in framing your study?

2. Concentrate on steps one and two. Brainstorm by yourself, or with a partner, ideas to help frame a topic.

Module 3: Steps in Writing the Proposal

A year-long research course sequence usually requires a research proposal due at the end of the first semester and a completed thesis project at the end of the academic year. The steps in proposal writing that follow are generic in that some professors may require other components, while others may not include some of the steps I include. As in lesson planning, components may vary but the guidelines that follow are the norm. Also, note that while I require students to specify each component and then provide the appropriate material, some professors do not require labeling of most components, as long as they are included in the proposal. One professor I know just includes a "Methods" section and a "Data Analysis" section; the rest of the proposal is in narrative form, very much like a published article in a journal.

Note that whatever is included in the proposal usually gets included in the final thesis. You have the right, however, to alter (delete or expand) components of the proposal as you write the thesis. For instance, you may add to the literature review as you discover new and relevant material during the second semester. You may also add material to other section such as study limitations.

One last caveat is in order. The reason I included this module that reviews steps for completing a research proposal so early in this book is that some of you who are global learners probably want to get an overview of the project. You probably often ask yourself, "So what's expected of me, or What will the project that I am about to undertake look like?" For those who might feel overwhelmed by the information that follows, simply skip the module and the next one on "Steps in Writing the Thesis" and continue with Part Three.

A proposal usually includes the following steps or components:

Proposed Title

Table of Contents

Statement of the Problem

Research Questions and/or Hypothesis (hypotheses)

Importance of the Study

Definitions of Terms

Limitations

Review of Literature (Literature Review or Related Research)

Research Design (or Methodology)

References

Appendixes

From my teaching experience, I find that students appreciate viewing portions of a completed sample proposal (see Appendix C for an actual complete proposal). I tell them, as I caution you my readers, that the sample that follows is a general guidepost and that your proposal may take a different form depending on the nature of the proposed topic. Still, a student can receive a fairly good idea of what is expected. The partial proposal below is basic but an acceptable one and can serve as a guide to preparing your own. Note that in order to assist you in learning about the proposal I have included some commentary indicated by underlined text in the proposal below, although not to overburden you at this early stage with too many details. More detailed explanations of material will be found in modules to follow. Also note that although the proposal below is based on a student's work, I have taken the liberty to amplify and delete certain portions for purposes of analysis in this module.

Proposed Title:

IMPACT OF GROUP WORK STRATEGIES ON PROBLEM-SOLVING IN MATHEMATICS AND ATTITUDES TOWARDS MATHEMATICS AMONG 10th GRADERS IN AN URBAN PUBLIC SCHOOL

*(Note that the student did not write "The Impact of . . ." I inform students to merely start the title off without the word "the" because the study is not "the" definitive statement on the subject. Also, note that page #s are not included in this sample but I require students to paginate using a **running head** that identifies some continuous key words in the title followed by the page number. Pages are numbered consecutively beginning with the title page. The running head for this sample proposal could be "Group Work Strategies 1." Running heads are usually placed in upper right hand corner of the page.)*

Reflection

Can you identify the main components of a title?

Answer: **independent variable**; **dependent variables**; relationship; **sample**

Can you identify each variable in the title? What word in the title indicates "relationship"? What's the sample referred to in the title?

Answers: independent variable-group work strategies; dependent variables-problem solving and attitudes towards mathematics. The word "impact" indicates relationship between the variables, i.e., what influence does group work strategies have on achievement in mathematics problem solving and student attitudes towards mathematics? The sample is 10th graders in an urban school. See Module 1 in Part Three.

Table of Contents: (sometimes simply called "Contents")

STATEMENT OF THE PROBLEM (purpose of study) (page #s included) ....

RESEARCH QUESTIONS (derived from purpose, reflecting title, poses
    questions to investigate; used in both quantitative and qualitative approaches;
    See Module 2 in Part Three) ....

HYPOTHESES (see Glossary and Module 3 in Part Three; generally used
    only for the quantitative approach) ....

IMPORTANCE OF THE STUDY (why problem is worthy of study) ....

DEFINITION OF TERMS (key terms defined, check Glossary) ....

LIMITATIONS OF THE STUDY (all studies are flawed in some way) (Or simply "Limitations") ....

REVIEW OF LITERATURE (literature background for study) (some call this Literature
    Review, Related Research, or Theoretical Frame; See Module 2 in Part Four) ....

RESEARCH DESIGN (the plan) (some call this Methodology; See Part Five) ....

SAMPLE (some call this "Participants") ....

INSTRUMENTATION (sometimes called "Materials"; See Part Eight) ....

PROCEDURE ....

TREATMENT OF DATA (some call this "Data Analysis"; See Parts Nine and Ten) ....

REFERENCES (see Module 2 in Part Thirteen) ....

APPENDIXES (Note that the word "appendices" is sometimes used, but not according to the
    APA manual of style) ....

Statement of the Problem:

Research has shown that group work strategies positively influence high school student achievement in mathematics (bring citation-Whenever you refer to "research" you must bring a citation or two to reinforce your statement; for APA use see Part Thirteen Module 2). Few, if any studies have been conducted to demonstrate academic benefits in specific areas of mathematics (e.g., computation or problem solving). This study will seek to replicate findings from the literature that confirm the benefits of group work strategies on mathematics achievement for high schools students. More specifically, however, this study will assess the impact of group work on problem-solving abilities of these students. Literature in the field of mathematics demonstrates the import of problem-solving abilities as fundamental to mathematics learning in general (bring citation). Research also indicates that problem-solving instructional activities in mathematics could be expanded at the high school level (bring citation). The main purpose of this study will be to ascertain the impact of group work strategies on problem solving in mathematics among 10th graders in a local public high school. A secondary purpose of this study is to survey of students' attitudes towards group work as a style of interactive learning to solve problems. The rationale is that if students are motivated by group work to solve mathematical problems then achievement will be affected positively. The study will explore the relationship between student motivation (i.e., attitudes towards mathematics) and problem solving achievement.

Research Questions:

1. What impact do group work strategies and techniques have on problem-solving achievement in mathematics among 10th graders?

2. What are the attitudes of 10th graders towards group work activities?

3. Is there a relationship between student motivation (i.e., attitudes towards mathematics) and problem-solving achievement?

Notice that the three research questions reflect both the study title and problem statement above.

Hypotheses:

10th grade students in an urban public school who are taught mathematics using a group work strategies exclusively will score significantly higher in problem-solving abilities on teacher-made tests and the City standardized mathematics examination than students taught math with strategies other than group work.

10th grade students in an urban public school who are taught mathematics using a group work strategies exclusively will exhibit significantly more positive attitudes towards mathematics than students taught math with strategies other than group work.

Key words in two hypotheses above are "will score significantly higher" -
indicates statistical use - see Part Nine

Favorable attitudes towards group work activities among 10th grade students in an urban public school will be positively correlated with achievement in problem-solving.

(inclusion of both research questions and hypotheses indicates that both qualitative
and quantitative approaches will be incorporated in the study)

Reflection

Referring to the Glossary, what types of hypotheses were stated above?

Importance of the Study:

According to surveys distributed to high school students, mathematics instruction remains traditional as teachers focus on lecture and use of chalkboard as primary instructional approaches (Entwistle, 1998). Mathematics teachers, according to this research, are pressured to teach to the test and consequently focus on memorization and test sophistication strategies. If presentation takes the form of lessons exclusively focused on a finished product ("getting the right answer"), students are unlikely to gain insight into the processes that underpin mathematics (Dreyfus 1991) and their learning remains shallow and temporary.

Considerable research has been carried out in the last half century on the relationship between the quality of students' learning and styles of teaching. Kember and Gow (1994), for example, identified two orientations in relation to teaching in secondary education: "knowledge transmission" and "learning facilitation." They linked these foci to the way in which students adopted "reproducing" and "meaning" orientations respectively in their approaches to studying. It is generally accepted that students who adopt a "meaning" orientation to studying are more likely to understand course content and, therefore, stand a better chance of doing well in mathematics (e.g., Entwistle & Ramsden, 1983).

In acknowledging that students' learning styles differ, it can be assumed that some will always find lessons - an engaging and useful style of teaching; many more, however, will not. It is by offering a range of teaching methods that a larger percentage of the students will engage with the course content and be more likely to adopt a "meaning" orientation in their approach to studying (MacBean & Graham, 2001).

Using group work strategies as a style of interactive learning is one of the traits of the "learning facilitation" orientation to teaching. In most subject disciplines, types of group work can involve communication, verbalization and the development of shared understanding. Many, however, and this includes both students and teachers, find it difficult to see how these processes can apply to the learning of mathematics.

The primary aim of this project is to gain a better understanding of students' attitudes towards the use of group-based learning. Its chief aim, however, is to investigate the impact of group work on problem-solving in mathematics among 10th graders. This research is important in order to add to the extant literature on methods for teaching mathematics to high school students that best promote student achievement.

<u>Good background information leading up to "importance" statement, then importance</u>
<u>is stated concisely and emphatically</u>

Definition of Terms:

Although you have been referred several times thus far to the Glossary for further information about definitions, it seems important in this context to provide some essential information. **Operational definitions** are one of two ways to define terms in a research study. Operational definitions involve observable, measurable, and quantifiable descriptions of key terms in a research study. Science achievement, for example, can be operationally defined as follows: a passing score of 70% on a teacher-made science test. A supervisor-made questionnaire could also be defined operationally by stating the nature of the survey (e.g., **Likert**), the design (e.g., designed by researcher, as opposed to using some commercially developed **instrument**), and how the questionnaire will be measured (e.g., a favorable attitudinal score would be 25 and above). Operational definitions do not merely define the terms conceptually (see below), but rather describe them and state how they will be measured.

Conceptual definitions are another way to define terms in a research study. A conceptual definition is a typical dictionary-type definition of a term or concept. Sources for conceptual definitions usually are authorities in the field. The following is an example of a conceptual definition:

> Cooperative Learning "involves positive interdependence among students, face to face interaction, individual accountability for mastery of material and the development of personal and small group skills." (Johnson & Johnson, [year and page number]).

Group Work—a teaching method that includes all activities in which students work in pairs or groups, literally whenever they work together (in contrast to "cooperative learning") (<u>bring citation</u>) (<u>This is a conceptual definition</u>)

Group Work Strategies—tasks which are specifically designed for, and assessed in, groups and when the students come together naturally to help each other with their mathematical work (<u>bring citation</u>) (<u>This is a conceptual definition</u>)

Mathematics achievement in problem-solving—measured by three unit teacher-made tests with a raw score of 50 considered passing and 1 state standardized test with a grade level score in problem solving considered passing (This is an operational definition)

Attitude—measured through use of researcher-developed Likert scale questionnaire instrument with a score of 40 or higher indicating positive attitudes (operational definition)

Notice that key terms in the title are defined. Other specialized terms brought in the literature review need not be defined here if they are explained in the review.

Limitations of the Study:

1. The sample of this study will be limited to four 10th grade math classes (each heterogeneously grouped including high-track, average, low-achievement students) totaling approximately 110 students at Howard High School in Staten Island, New York. Therefore, results of this study cannot be generalized to all high school students within this borough of New York and certainly not outside of New York City. Notice that limitation is stated along with its consequence

2. An ex post facto control group design will be utilized. Randomization is not feasible. Check Glossary for ex post facto and why randomization is not possible

3. Teachers volunteered to be part of the study. Years of teaching experience varied. Teachers utilized a preferred style of teaching. Therefore, it will be difficult to control for teacher quality during the instructional process.

4. The results of the math tests for 10-graders may not be a representation of the influence of group work technique only. Many other styles of teaching used by the teachers at the same time of the experiment could unintentionally affect the results of the study.

Recall that you can add to limitations as the study progresses

Review of Literature:

See Module 2 in Part Four

Research Design:

Sample:

The sample for this study will be notice the future tense ("will" not "was") since this is the proposal comprised of four 10th grade mathematics classes at Howard H.S., Staten Island, NY. The school was selected due to convenience as the researcher teaches in the school. Four intact classes were identified at the 10th grade during the start of the fall semester. Classes were heterogeneously grouped based on standardized test results from the previous year. The numbers of male and female students in all classes were not significantly different. The standardized test from the preceding year served as the pretest to ensure group equivalence.

Instrumentation:

The study will take place over the course of the first three months of the school year. Three teacher-made tests will be developed based on the 10th grade curriculum. Content and consensual validity will be achieved. Reliability will be assured as well. Each test will be administered approximately after three weeks of instruction.

The researcher will develop a Likert scale questionnaire to assess student attitudes towards mathematics. A split-half reliability coefficient, corrected for test length, will be computed for the questionnaire. Consensual validity will be achieved.

Refer to Glossary and Module 6 in Part Eight for details about validity
and reliability as well as discussions later in this volume

Procedure:

1. Obtain permission from the principal of Howard H.S. (and the New York City Department of Education, if necessary) to conduct the study. Consult Institutional Review Board (IRB) at college.
2. Inform the Head of the Math Department about this study and solicit assistance and cooperation.
3. Identify classes in conjunction with the Department Head.
4. Teachers volunteer to use group work strategies. Two others to use traditional methods.
5. Create test instruments and questionnaire (see Appendix X).
6. A four-month period of intensive use of group work strategies will ensue.
7. Students administered teacher-made tests to assess level of achievement.
8. Administer questionnaire to students near end of treatment.
9. Interviews with teachers and students conducted.
10. Analyze data

Treatment of Data:

A t-test for nonindependent means will be used to determine whether or not the mean achievement and attitudinal scores of each group differ significantly from each other. A Pearson-Product moment correlation coefficient test will be applied to ascertain relationship between variables identified in the third hypothesis. Data might also be analyzed qualitatively (especially data assessing student attitudes).

References:

References are cited in APA fashion. See discussion in Module 2 in Part Thirteen

Appendixes:

Copies of sample tests and questionnaires, if completed at this stage, included in Appendixes

I require, not merely encourage my students to thoroughly proofread their proposal before they submit it for my review. After they proofread the document, I inform them to share the proposal (or even parts of it) with at least one other classmate or colleague. I ask that that person's name be noted indicating s/he offered comments on the work. Certainly, any deficiencies with the proposal rests solely with the student.

The following is a rubric that I developed to provide feedback to students on their proposals (it also offers them a guide as to criteria I'm using to assess their work):

PROPOSAL RUBRIC

Components	1	2	3	SCORE= 1, 2, or 3 (add comments as needed)	Place score below
	Unacceptable	Acceptable	Target		
Selection of Research Topic	No topic selected; topic not significant nor related to course objectives; topic too broad; topic too specific; unresearchable; not feasible	Topic selected; topic relevant to course objectives; topic is specific but not minute; researchable; feasible	Topic selected; topic relevant to course objectives; topic is specific; significant; researchable; feasible; unique		
Title of Proposal	Too general; does not specify variables, relationships and/or sample	Specifies variables, relationships, and sample	Specifies, without extraneous words, variables, relationships, and sample		
Proposal components	Out of sequence; missing; erroneously framed	All components included	All components included with more than sufficient detail		
Format	Guidelines not followed; disorganized and sloppily arranged	Guidelines followed; organized and arranged in a logical, presentable order	Guidelines followed precisely; Well organized and arranged logically; aesthetically presented		
APA (citations)	APA not adhered to (3 or more errors)	APA generally adhered to (1 or 2 errors)	APA meticulously adhered to (no errors)		
Content	Insufficient; lack of information; superficial understanding of research	Acceptable; information provided; researched; Literature may be a "work in progress"	Substantial; detailed information; thorough and well researched; Literature completed or nearly so		
Control	Poor "technical control"; incomplete sentences, spelling errors, incorrect punctuation, improper use of grammar, poor paragraph development, etc.	Correct "technical control"; few, if any, incomplete sentences, few, if any, spelling errors, correct punctuation, proper use of grammar, correct paragraph development, etc.	Excellent "technical control"; complete sentences, no spelling errors, correct punctuation, proper use of grammar, excellent paragraph development, etc.		

OVERALL SCORE-_____

Qualitative comments: (on reverse side)

Module 3 Review

In this Module you learned the components of a thesis proposal:

1. Follow the outline below and jot some notes that will serve as your proposal.

STATEMENT OF THE PROBLEM ....

RESEARCH QUESTIONS ....

HYPOTHESES ....

IMPORTANCE OF THE STUDY

DEFINITION OF TERMS ....

LIMITATIONS OF THE STUDY ....

REVIEW OF LITERATURE ....

RESEARCH DESIGN ....

    SAMPLE ....

    INSTRUMENTATION ....

    PROCEDURE..

TREATMENT OF DATA ....

REFERENCES ....

APPENDIXES ....

REMINDER: SEE APPENDIX C FOR A COMPLETE SAMPLE PROPOSAL

Module 4: Steps in Writing the Thesis

Skip this module for now if reading about how to put together your final thesis may be too stressful at this early point in the course. Of course, you global learners (some even compulsive like me) appreciate its inclusion, even at this early time.

The following steps or components are included in your final thesis. I include this information here because students like to know in advance what is expected of them. Also, they can compare the components of a proposal with that of the finished product. Please note once again that the components included here are generic; some professors may include others and delete ones that I mention. Regardless, the guidelines below are generic and will serve you well, I hope. Always, of course, follow the guidelines set forth by your professor.

    After the components are listed, more detailed information is provided for key components. As before, in order to assist you in learning about the thesis and research in general I have included some underlined commentary throughout the descriptions below. Sample text illustrating various components in the thesis are found in subsequent modules in various parts of the book.

Generic components of a thesis

TITLE PAGE

ACKOWLEDGMENTS

ABSTRACT

LIST OF TABLES
LIST OF FIGURES

TABLE OF CONTENTS

CHAPTER 1: INTRODUCTION
    Background
    Importance of the Study
    Statement of the Problem
    Hypothesis and/or Research Question(s)
    Definition of Terms

CHAPTER 2: REVIEW OF LITERATURE/RELATED RESEARCH

CHAPTER 3: RESEARCH DESIGN/METHODOLOGY
    Sample
    Instrumentation
    Procedure
    Data Analysis
    Results

CHAPTER 4: IMPLICATIONS FOR PRACTICE AND RESEARCH

    Limitations of the Study
    Discussion/Conclusions
    Implications for Practice
    Implications for Further Research

REFERENCES

APPENDIXES

Detailed Description of Steps for Quantitative and/or Qualitative Studies

Note that your professor may require different components depending on which approach is used: quantitative or qualitative. Also note that you should consult university/college guidelines for end-of-the-semester guidelines for filing your master's thesis.

TITLE PAGE

[For example, "Impact of Technology on Sight Word Recognition and Sentence Structure on Kindergarten and First Grade Self-Contained Special Education Students"]

[Usually a statement like this appears: "This thesis submitted in partial fulfillment of the Masters Degree in Education"] *Follow format of your college professor*

[Your name, date, and other data are usually included as well] *Again, check with your college professor. See Module 1 in Part Three for more details.*

ACKNOWLEDGMENTS [1-2 paragraphs]

This section is optional but affords you to thank anyone you'd like who in some way contributed to helping you complete your thesis. One may even thank one's spouse for "staying out of the way"—ha!

LIST OF TABLES

A table is used to present a large amount of information in an easy to read and concise format. Tables usually present quantitative data such as statistical summaries. Word tables used in qualitative studies are also possible (see *Publication Manual of the American Psychological Association*, 2001). This section is optional, but if you have many tables you should list them in sequence as they appear along with title and page number.

LIST OF FIGURES

A figure includes any type of illustration other than a table such as charts, graphs, diagrams, maps, photographs, etc. (see *Publication Manual of the American Psychological Association*, 2001). This section is optional, but if you have many figures you should list them in sequence as they appear along with title and page number.

ABSTRACT

A summary (approximately 100–150 words) of the study that contains the following elements: purpose or problem statement, description of research methods used, brief description of sample and materials, results in concise form (including any statistical conclusions), and brief implications of study. See Module 3 in Part Thirteen for more details.

TABLE OF CONTENTS

CHAPTER 1: INTRODUCTION
Background [1–2 pp.] *This section is optional; follow guidelines of your professor*
Describes background information such as:
- A) where study was conducted;
- B) size of school, location, population, and other demographics;
- C) performance levels and other relevant instructional information;
- D) For qualitative approaches: include researcher's background, interests in study, potential biases, etc.;
- E) any other information that sets the stage for your study.

Importance of the Study [1–2 paragraphs]
Describes why you are undertaking this study, why it is significant, and what you hope to ascertain. *Note that sections that were completed at the proposal stage are simply transposed during the final thesis stage. You can, of course, alter statements and content at this stage if necessary.*

Statement of the Problem [1 paragraph]
States the purpose of the study and includes somewhere in the paragraph the following: "The purpose of this study was…" *Use past tense throughout to indicate this thesis was written after completion of the study. Includes variables and how they are related given the sample. Is the problem stated clearly so that the reader understands the purpose of the study?*

Hypothesis and/or Research Question(s)
If you triangulated, then hypothesis *and* research question(s) are likely. Are hypotheses and/or questions stated properly and clearly? Are they related to the literature review and testable? Refer to **hypothesis** and **research questions** in the Glossary for more details on definitions and types. *Whereas the previous sections were written in narrative form, this section (along with Definition of Terms, Procedure, and Limitations of the Study), is listed or numbered. See Modules 2 and 3 in Part Three for more details*

Definition of Terms [1–2 pp.]
Defines relevant words either conceptually or operationally. See **conceptual definitions** and **operational definitions** in the Glossary.

CHAPTER 2: REVIEW OF LITERATURE/RELATED RESEARCH [10–30 pp.]

Use the first term for quantitative studies and the latter term for qualitative studies. If you triangulate, either will do. You should, however, consult with your professor on the style or approach most desired. Some professors will tell you that Literature Review, Review of the Literature, and Related Research are all acceptable for both quantitative and qualitative work. The same applies for Research Design and Methodology, see the following section.

This chapter reviews relevant literature pertaining to your topic. What previous research, for instance, informs your study? Educational researchers should be aware of relevant and recent literature in the area they are investigating. Is the review comprehensive, up-to-date, well organized, and critical? *See Module 2 in Part Four for more details.* For qualitative approaches the review may be preliminary or exploratory.

CHAPTER 3: RESEARCH DESIGN/METHODOLOGY

Use the first term for quantitative studies and the latter term for qualitative studies. If you triangulate, either will do.

Sample *or called "Participants"* [1–2 paragraphs]

Describe your **sample** in terms of:

    A) who they are (including gender, ages, grade level data, ability levels, ethnicity, if relevant);

    B) where they are from, how many are participating, how they were selected and assigned; and

    C) any other relevant information the reader may need to know about the sample.

Refer to **sampling** in the Glossary for definition and discussion of different types.

Instrumentation *or called "Materials"* [2–5 paragraphs]
List and briefly describe any relevant materials (instruments) used in the study. For example, a researcher-developed survey should be described and a sample placed in an appendix. Reference appendix in this section by noting, for example, "See survey in Appendix B."

Also, include names and descriptions of any commercial tests, games, computers, children's literature, or other surveys.

Discussion of **validity** and **reliability** of testing instruments and/or surveys are discussed in this section.

Are instruments clearly described and how data were collected?

Procedure [1–2 pp.]
Describes, step-by-step, how you conducted your study, including a timeline. Anyone reading your report should be able to explain or, at least, understand the steps you took in conducting your study. In other words, they should be able to replicate your study from the information provided in this section. Include a description of the **treatment** and precisely how it was administered. *Note that the example below is not in list form, but in narrative form. No hard and fast rules apply. Always follow your professor's guidelines.*

Data Analysis [1 paragraph]
Brief statement as to how you analyzed your data. For some studies several paragraphs may be appropriate to detail data analysis. For example, your proferssor may ask you to detail the coding scheme used for your qualitative study. Follow your professors guidelines, as always. *See Parts Nine and Ten for more details.*

Results *or called "Findings"* [1–2 pp.]
State and describe the results of your study. State whether the hypotheses were confirmed or rejected. Restate the research questions and answer them. Just provide the raw data.
Reserve your conclusions and insights for the next chapter. Results should also be presented in table form using graphs, charts, or any other acceptable manner of presenting your findings. *See Part Eleven for more details.*

CHAPTER 4: IMPLICATIONS FOR PRACTICE AND RESEARCH

Limitations of the Study [1 page]

Every study is limited by factors beyond your control, such as mortality (see **internal validity**), **sample size**, time factor, etc. List and briefly explain each limitation. Refer to **confounding factors, internal validity,** and **external validity** in the Glossary. *See Module 1 in Part Twelve for more details.*

Discussion/Conclusions [4–10 pp.]

Describe your observations, opinions, and conclusions based on the results reported in the previous chapter. Provide possible explanations and note interesting, significant, and/or curious findings. *See Module 3 in Part Twelve for more details.*

Implications for Practice [2–5 pp.]

Describe the implications your study has for instructional improvement. Be specific about implications for practice and/or instructional improvement. *See Module 4 in Part Twelve for more details.*

Implications for Further Research [1 page]

Describe areas of further investigation that you might recommend others to undertake. Include areas of investigation you couldn't delve into, but were important nonetheless. *See Module 5 in Part Twelve for more details.*

REFERENCES

Lists all the works you cited in the text of the thesis, not ones you merely referred to in researching your topic. Start the "references" section on a new page labeled "References." I recommend use of the American Psychological Association's (APA) *Publication Manual,* the most recent edition. All documentation throughout the paper should conform to APA style. *See Module 2 in Part Thirteen for more details.*

APPENDIXES

APA prefers "appendixes" to "appendices." Any relevant materials such as copies of surveys, selected curriculum materials, photos, etc. should be placed in separate appendixes and labeled A, B, C, etc.

NOTE: See Module 5 in Part Thirteen for a rubric used to evaluate your thesis

Module 4 Review

In this Module you learned the steps/components of a thesis (why not jot some notes next to each component? Doing so, may assist you later on.):

TITLE PAGE

ABSTRACT

LIST OF TABLES

LIST OF FIGURES

TABLE OF CONTENTS

CHAPTER 1: INTRODUCTION

    Background
    Importance of the Study
    Statement of the Problem
    Hypothesis and/or Research Question(s)
    Definition of Terms

CHAPTER 2: REVIEW OF LITERATURE/RELATED RESEARCH

CHAPTER 3: RESEARCH DESIGN/METHODOLOGY

    Sample
    Instrumentation
    Procedure
    Data Analysis
    Results

CHAPTER 4: IMPLICATIONS FOR PRACTICE AND RESEARCH

    Limitations of the Study
    Discussion/Conclusions
    Implications for Practice
    Implications for Further Research

REFERENCES

APPENDIXES

SEE APPENDIX D FOR A COMPLETE SAMPLE THESIS

(Note that theses vary in type, length, quality, etc. The sample provided is merely one guide. Always consult your professor for other acceptable guidelines and types.)

Part Three:

Thesis Overview—
Chapter 1 of Thesis: Introduction

Focus Questions

1. What would help you most to find a topic?

2. How has the information in preceding modules helped you begin to select a topic?

3. Would you think that framing a title for your thesis sometime at the outset of your study is sensible?

4. What is the difference between a research question and a hypothesis?

Module 1: Selecting a Topic/Title

Let's begin this module with a brief questionnaire.

RESPOND

SA = Strongly Agree ("For the most part, yes")
A = Agree ("Yes, but . . .")
D = Disagree ("No, but . . .")
SD = Strongly Disagree ("For the most part, no")

SA A D SD   1. I believe I need to select a topic within the first two weeks of the course.

SA A D SD   2. I believe I should be interested in the topic I select rather than merely select a topic for convenience or ease.

SA A D SD   3. I believe I should select a topic that I am very familiar with.

SA A D SD   4. I believe I have adequate time to carry out my study.

SA A D SD   5. I believe that once I have a topic I'll be fine.

SA A D SD   6. I believe that a title for my thesis will naturally emerge once I get a handle on the basic components (e.g., preliminary literature review, problem statement, research questions, methodology, etc.)

Compare your responses to the information that follows:

Guidelines to finding a topic:

• Don't panic or rush when selecting a topic – Perhaps the biggest mistake students make is rushing to select a topic. Although it's important to find a topic early on, take your time. Follow the guidelines that follow so that you can be best assured of finding the right topic given your unique circumstances. Follow the 3 criteria for topic selection in the next bullet.

• Choose a topic that is of *interest* to you, is *researchable*, and is *feasible* to carry out – Do not select a topic that doesn't interest you. This caveat may sound silly but you'd be surprised how many students select a topic out of convenience. These students quickly get bored and lose interest. The quality of their work is dramatically affected. Don't forget that you are spending at least a year on this project. Choose a topic that will motivate you and keep your interest. Also, related to this idea is to select a topic that you have some knowledge about but need to explore much more. Sometimes students select a topic they have much knowledge about because they have written previous papers about the topic. Choosing a topic you are very familiar with will result in loss of interest and motivation. Besides, you will not really be expanding your knowledge very much, which is the essence of a thesis project.

Make certain your topic is researchable. You may be interested in a topic, but ask yourself, "Is there enough literature about it?" A master's thesis project doesn't require you to invent a new theory or create something never done before. In fact, replicating a study previously carried out is acceptable. You may want to alter portions of the study, but in effect you are carrying out the same study to ascertain whether or not the findings are relevant to your situation or educational setting. A good test to determine whether or not a topic is researchable is to conduct an ERIC search (see Module 5 in Part One). If you don't come up with at least 30 "hits" on the topic or related topic, then drop the topic in search of something more researchable.

You may very well be interested in a topic and the topic may indeed be researchable, but can it be feasibly carried out given your time constraints, school/classroom situation, etc.? If a study requires you to conduct, for instance, in-depth **ethnographic** interviews with participants, yet you do not really have time to spend interviewing dozens of people, then you might decide that although the topic is interesting and researchable, it is not feasible given your ability to carry it out. Ask, "do I have the time to carry out this study?" "What other obstacles might influence your ability to conduct a study?"

Reflection

If you have previously conducted a preliminary review of the literature and have a possible topic, ask yourself:

1) Am I really interested in this topic (be able to articulate 3 reasons)?

2) Are there enough references on the topic?

3) Given my unique situation, can I really carry out a study on this topic over the course of the year?

- *Other important considerations* – Besides interest, researchability, and feasibility, consider these criteria that I've phrased in form of questions to ask yourself:

   1. Is the topic important or significant? Not that a topic has to involve groundbreaking research (in fact, most master's theses do not), your topic should be of some educational

and theoretical value. Will the topic contribute to your knowledge of the subject under study? Will it make some impact on teaching, learning, or educational practice in general? If the topic doesn't add anything new at all (e.g., a study that merely rehashes generally accepted knowledge – "teachers must have some sort of classroom management plan"), then the topic should be reframed somehow (e.g., "comparing two or three different classroom management strategies or programs in different educational settings to determine which approach is more effective") or just dropped.

2. Is the topic timely? Not that your topic has to deal with an issue currently in vogue or "hot" (e.g., Charter schools, inclusion, or high-stakes testing), but your topic should have some relevance and usefulness to educators. For instance, if you want to research the use of programmed instruction or teaching machines that was perhaps timely back in the 1960s, then you need to consider the benefits of such study. To study the topic from a historical perspective might be insightful not merely to enlighten readers about its use and impact on learning in the 1960s and 1970s, but such study may suggest ways to improve teaching and learning via the use of technology in schools today.

Reflection

Think of a topic or two that you consider timely.
Think of one that is not so.

3. Can you remain objective? If the topic you've selected is one you are overly passionate about, ask yourself, "can I remain unbiased and present all sides of the issue?" If you work for a company that promotes a new literacy approach at the elementary school level, can you conduct an unbiased evaluation of the program? Will you rationalize data you collect by saying, "well, their responses to my survey are insignificant or don't really matter."

4. Are there ethical considerations that may influence your ability to conduct the study? If you want to study the impact of two approaches to teaching reading and you know all the literature indicates that one approach is clearly superior to the other, then can you justifiably expose a group of students to the approach that the literature says doesn't work? (See Module 4 in Part One for discussion of ethical issues). If so, you might want to consider another topic or alter your methodology by conducting a study that exposes all students to the "better" reading approach by conducting an **ethnographic** rather than a **group comparison** study.

- *Be ready to tolerate initial uncertainty* – Confusion, someone once told me, is the first step to progress. Of course, confusion that remains constant over a two month period is worrisome. As indicated earlier, it's okay if you really have no idea what you want to research at the outset of the course. Even after two weeks, you might just have a vague idea. As you work, however, a topic will crystallize soon enough. If you are naturally impatient or compulsive, you'll have much trouble with this suggestion. I suggest you write on your calendar after the first three weeks of the semester, "It's all right if I don't yet have a topic. One will come soon." For those of you who tend to procrastinate, then you need to jot this on your calendar after three weeks, "Better find a topic soon."

- *Brainstorm a list of things that you wonder about*:

  - Classroom practice—What interests you most about classroom practice? You might have always wanted to spend time studying some aspect classroom practice and now is the time. What interests you about your job in general?

  - Your school—How might the school function better to promote student learning? What about classroom and school climate?

  - Your profession—What is it about your profession that you might have always wanted to address in a scholarly way?

  - An instructional issue—What instructional strategies or approaches are currently in vogue? Are you curious about learning about their effectiveness to promote pupil interest, achievement, etc.?

  - A problem—What problems or challenges confront you? Behavior management, dealing with bureaucracy, parental concerns, supervision, etc.?

  - An educational issue—Is there a burning, current educational issue that intrigues you?

- *Replicate a study*—Master's degree students do not have to create new theories or proposals. Master's degree work implies that students build upon existing theories, concepts, and ideas in their field. They achieve "mastery" over them, and demonstrate such expertise by selecting and researching a topic by building on extant work in the field in a scholarly fashion. Master's degree students can even "replicate" a study that has been conducted in the past. Often my students seem surprised when I offer this as an option. Although study replication would add no new knowledge, it does have a positive influence in that it confirms and verifies initial findings. Actually, such work in educational research is needed to build more theories. As such, replication serves a noble and much needed function.

  Replication is possible to:

  A. Confirm or reject previous findings

  B. Broaden the study by working with a different or expanded sample (e.g., you might want to use Spanish-speaking individuals or increase the size of the sample).

  C. Using different methodologies on the same topic (e.g., instead of an experimental study you might decide to conduct a qualitative case study approach).

- *Find an article to build on*—Somewhat related to the previous suggestion, why not find an article that you find intriguing? Think about thekind of work you might be able to do that builds on the fundings or results of that article.

- *Discuss your choices with a colleague or two*—Networking and actually spending time sharing one's ideas is not only cathartic but will help crystallize an idea.

- *Skim your textbook for ideas*—See Module 5 in Part One

- *Go to the library or scan the web*—Locate articles, books, textbooks, and journals that interest you – look for studies on the general topic. Locate dictionaries (e.g., *Dictionary of Education* or *Dictionary of Multicultural Education*), encyclopedias (e.g., *Encyclopedia of Education* or *International Encyclopedia of Education, Encyclopedia of Educational Research*), handbooks (e.g., *Handbook of Educational Psychology, Handbook of Research on Curriculum,* or *Handbook of Research on School Supervision, Handbook of Reading Research,* or *Handbook of Research on Teaching*). See Module 5 in Part One

- *Discuss your ideas again with a colleague or two; even with your professor*—Then he may share his ideas. As you both ponder, you may come up with a general topic. With persistence though, you will, with his help, narrow the topic down into something much more manageable.

- *Select one broad topic, then try to narrow down your area* – Okay, let's start with an example:

  1. A broad topic might be "multiple intelligences." This topic is of interest to you and it's certainly researchable. You can't address feasibility yet because you don't know yet what you intend to do with it. (Another example of a broad topic would be: Social Problems of Youngsters). Don't rush at this point to narrow down the topic too soon as you can consider at this stage many questions to investigate. After some preliminary research, you come up with "multiple intelligences somehow linked with learning styles among high school students." Now you're less broad but not focused enough as you've not articulated a research oriented approach. So, after continued review of the literature and discussions with colleagues you come up with, "Assessing Multiple Intelligences and Learning Styles among 10th graders in Urban High Schools." You know this topic is feasible because you have access to 10th graders at several district high schools and you've discussed feasibility with local school administrators. Now the topic you've selected may be approached from several perspectives. You might undertake an exploratory or descriptive study that merely identifies intelligences and learning styles in these students to determine whether or not there might be a relationship.

Reflection

What other approach might you take?

Note that a topic may also be too narrow or vague as in, respectively: "Investigating the Amount of Time Students Take to Sit Down When they First Enter the Classroom" or "Investigating Ethnic Views towards Social Interaction." Narrow topics are so minute that one may question their significance. Vague or amorphous topics need much clarification.

The following topic ideas may be satisfactory at the beginning stages of a research project, however, they are too broad to use as a title once your study has been framed. Explain why they are too broad and offer a way to narrow them into a more suitable topic or title:

1. Involving parents to improve learning.

2. Developing a literacy program to improve achievement.

3. Using exercise to improve children's classroom behavior.

4. Using multicultural education to improve relations among ethnic groups.

5. Using mnemonic techniques with learning disabled students.

- *Refine topic by clarifying the problem and supplementing it with research questions or hypotheses* – If your topic is "Multiple Intelligences and Learning Styles" before you can transform it into a title (see below) you'll need to continue your preliminary review of the literature and come up with a problem concerning the topic and some questions you want answered. After reading articles, you might ask, "How are multiple intelligences and learning styles related?" or "How are they incorporated in middle school classrooms in the sciences?" Thinking carefully about the problem you want to investigate and some associated questions will help crystallize the topic.

- *Peruse the titles below* – Below you'll find a list of theses my students conducted. The list is meant to stimulate your curiosity. You might indeed find some topic of interest to you or one might provoke thought about a related topic. You might find some ideas in two or three theses that you can combine in some way. Or, you may actually want to select one for replication. The list is not exhaustive and is not meant to stifle your creativity. The list will merely demonstrate what others before you have done. Why not ask your professor for a similar list?

Forty-Two Pre-School Students' Gender Related Views of Careers

Regular Classroom Teachers' Attitudes towards Resource Room Students

Relationship Between Family Size and Academic Achievement

Relationship Between Birth Order and Academic Achievement

A Comparison of Community-Based Training and Constant Time Delay Procedures in Teaching the Mentally Retarded

Impact of a Token Economy System on Task Performance among Three Mentally Retarded Adolescents

A Day in the Life of a School Superintendent

Effects of the Whole Language Approach Versus Phonics Instruction and Attitudes towards School among 5th graders

Impact of Self-Questioning Techniques on Reading Comprehension

Teaching Decoding Skills Using a Linguistic Approach: A Case Study

Inclusion and Resource Room Intervention: A Comparative Analysis among Fifth Grade LD Students

Effects of Manipulatives on Math Achievement among Second Grade Elementary Students

Factors Affecting Levels of Stress among Graduate Students Undertaking Their Masters Degree Thesis

Impact of Using Instruction Based on Learning Styles on the Cognition Skills of Preschoolers

Teachers' Attitudes towards Bilingual Instruction in the Native Language Versus ESL

Impact of Television on Preschool Children's Social Behavior

Effects of Ability Grouping on Reading Comprehension among Sixth Grade Students

Gender Differences in Attitudes towards Math among Junior High School Students in a District

Impact of a Teacher Training Program on Student Teachers' Attitudes towards Inclusion

Peer Tutoring: Impact on the Social Acceptance of Developmentally Delayed Children among Regular Kindergarten Students

Effects of Explicit Notetaking Instruction on Social Studies Achievement among Sixth Grade Students

Relationships Between School Climate and Levels of Stress on Elementary School Teachers

Effects of Parental Involvement on Reading Readiness among Kindergarten Students in a Self-Contained Spanish Bilingual Classroom

Effects of Whole Language Instruction Versus the Phonics Approach on Reading Readiness of Kindergarten Students in a Self-Contained Spanish Bilingual Classroom

Non-Bilingual and Bilingual Teachers' Attitudes towards Haitian Students

Effects of Contingency Contracting on the Frequency of Aggressive Behavior of Three Neurologically-Impaired 8 Year Olds

Effects of Individualized Versus Group Instruction on Vocabulary Development of 8th Grade ESL Students

Effects of Daily Dialogue Journals on Attitudes towards Writing among Secondary Learning-Disabled ESL Students

Effects of Cooperative Versus Traditional Learning on Math Achievement among 3rd Grade Bilingual Students in a Self-Contained Classroom

Relationships Between Early Print Experience and Reading Readiness among Kindergarten Children

Effects of Cooperative Learning on Social Studies Achievement of 9th Grade Bilingual Students

Effects of Art Activities on Achievement in Science among Grade One Bilingual Students

Effects of Whole Language Instruction Versus Traditional Basal Instruction on Reading Comprehension Achievement among 2nd Grade Bilingual Students

Relationships between Ethnic Identity and Self-Concepts of Native Born and First Generation Portuguese Children

Grading Assessment and ESL Teachers' Need for Social Acceptance

Effects of Literacy Materials from School on Language Acquisition among Portuguese Children in a Self-Contained Bilingual Classroom

Gender Bias in the High School Mathematics Classroom

A Comparison of Sixth, Seventh, and Eighth Grade Students' Attitudes towards Science

Impact of Invented Spelling on Kindergartners' Ability to Spell

A Comparison of Computer Anxiety Attributable to Gender and SES Between Urban and Suburban Sixth Graders

Impact of Parents Reading Aloud on Promoting Literacy Development and Enjoyment among Kindergarten Students

Effects of Cooperative Learning on Interpersonal Skills and Science Academic Achievement among Eighth Grade Students

Effects of Cooperative Learning on Middle School Students in the Inclusive Classroom

High School Teachers' Knowledge of AIDS: A Descriptive Study

An Integrated Whole Language Approach to Teaching ESL to Second Grade Students

Literature-Based Instruction on Vocabulary Development among Limited English Proficient Students

An Analysis of the Reading Recovery Program in the Piscataway School District and Its Effect on First Graders' Reading Comprehension

An Analysis of a University School Partnership Program to Recruit, Train, and Develop Hispanic Teachers

Effects of Demonstrations and Laboratory Activities on High School Students' Misconceptions of the Nature of Gases

Teaching Multicultural Awareness and Prejudice Reduction to Third Graders: Development and Assessment of a Curriculum

Developing a Literature-Based Content-Integrated Curriculum for K-2 ESL Students

Impact of a Whole language Instructional Program on Reading Achievement and Attitudes towards Learning

Influence of Teachers' Attitudes on Students' Attitudes towards Math

Athletic Participation among Seniors in Two Local High Schools

Teachers' Attitudes towards ESL Students and ESL Students' Self-Perceptions

Factors that Promote Parental involvement and Its Influence on the LEP Students' Academic and Social Development

Impact of Mnemonic Devices on Knowledge Retention among Learning Disabled Students

Celebrating Diversity: Development and Assessment of a Multicultural Curriculum

Integrating Howard Gardner's Theory of Multiple Intelligences into Science Classes for the Deaf and Hard of Hearing

Effects of Brain Compatible Logic-Based Instruction on the Problem Solving Abilities of Eighth Grade Math Students

Effects of Homogeneous Vs. Heterogeneous Grouping on Selected Mapping Skills of 9th Grade Earth Science Students

Sensory Integration and Its Impact on an Attention Deficit Hyperactivity Disorder (ADHD) Child's Attentional Skills

Image-Making within the Writing Process and Its Impact on Reading Comprehension among 1st Graders

Relationships Between Gender and Attitudes towards Science & Science Achievement among College Preparatory Chemistry Classes

Using Holocaust Related Literature to Enhance Student Awareness of Genocide and Human Rights Violations

A Social Studies Integrated Art Curriculum Using Multiple Intelligence Theory for 6th Graders

A Handbook of Strategies to Encourage Parental Involvement

The Language Assessment Battery (LAB) as a Measure of the Communicative Competence

Skin Color and Acculturation among Hispanic Immigrants In New Jersey

Impact of an Assertive Discipline Classroom Management Strategy in Suburban and Urban Elementary School Settings

Attitudes and Anxieties towards Mathematics among Students in Grades 3 and 7

Impact of Heterogeneous Versus Homogeneous Grouping of a High Achieving Second Grade Student on Writing Achievement

Teachers' Views of the Impact of Inclusion on the NonDisabled Students

Impact of Tests on Three Fifth Grade Special Education Student's Long Term Retention of Knowledge of History Facts

Multiple Intelligences (M.I.) in Theory and Practice: Teachers' Knowledge and Use of M.I.

Impact of Chunking and Word Families on the Spelling Achievement of Student with Learning Disabilities

Impact of Behavior Modification Systems on Promoting Positive Classroom Climate in a Special Education Classroom

Impact of Planned Ignoring on Attention Maintained Problem Behavior with a School-Aged Student with Autism in a Special Education Self-Contained Classroom

Effects of Gender on Mathematics and Reading Achievement among Fourth and Seventh Grade Students

Extrinsic and Intrinsic Motivational Strategies for Promoting Interest in Mathematics among Learning Disabled Students

Mainstreamed Students' Attitudes towards Inclusion

Peer Acceptance of Middle School Students with Disabilities in an Inclusive Setting

A Cross Cultural Study on the Identification and Knowledge Base of Attention Deficit Hyperactive Disorders (ADHD) among Caucasian-American and African-Americans

Impact of Sugar on Children's Behavior

Impact of Teacher Expectations on Student Participation in Special Education Classrooms

Promoting Positive Classroom Climate: A Comparative Analysis of Four Classrooms

Relationship between Preschool Attendance and Social Development

A Case Study Examining a Preschool Child with Autism Receiving Training in Social Skills

Impact of Picture Exchange Communication System on Behavior with a Child with Autism

A Case Study Examining the Impact of Respite Care on a Family with Multiple Handicapped Children

Impact of Parent-Teacher Conferences on Parent/Teacher Communication

Impact of Sensory Integration Treatment on Behaviors in Adaptive Developmental Skills and Academic Achievement among Preschool and Elementary School Aged Students

Relationship between Antisocial Behavior and Cognitive Development in Preschool Children

A Case Study of the Impact of Brain Gym on Reading Achievement with a High School Aged Student with Dyslexi

Attitudes of Teachers and Students towards In-School Breakfast on Academic Achievement

Impact of Learning Disabilities on Social Competence among Elementary School Students

Teachers' Views on the Impact of the Special Education Itinerant Model of Inclusion on the Development of Preschoolers

Should one develop a title at the outset of a study? Generally not. Titles emerge inductively from the literature review and methodology employed. But for compulsive individuals like myself I can't seem to get on target unless I come up with at least a working title at the outset to help guide my research and work. I may of course change later but I do like to "at first, keep the end in mind."

Identifying a topic: One Case

"Reflecting on my classroom, I've read about cooperative learning in journals and magazines and wondered if this strategy might work for me. I think my instructional approach is too lecture, talk oriented. The literature appears to indicate that group work via cooperative learning might yield social and academic results. I am interested in this topic. I know it's researchable because there are many articles on the subject. I know I can easily implement such a strategy in my classroom because my supervisor encourages us to try out new instructional approaches. Now, I teach 8th grade geography. I can incorporate the approach with my 5th period class of heterogeneously-grouped learners to field test its use and then expand its use to other classes and ability levels. I want to see what impact cooperative learning has on the social development of my students and their achievement levels in the tests I administer in class."

• Refer to some of the suggestions in Module 4 of Part Thirteen as well.

Reflection

Can you come up with a few possible titles from the case above?

* * * * * * * * * * * * * * * *

Module 1 Review

In this Module you learned some ways to develop a topic and frame a title.

1. Which ways explained above seem most helpful?

Self-Test Check

1. Which topic is best?

   A. Fifth graders' feelings towards their teachers
   B. Charter Schools in Five States
   C. Relationship between television viewing habits and homework habits among fifth graders
   D. School Violence in America

2. Among the most important criteria for selecting a topic are

   A. creativity and importance
   B. rationale and design
   C. interest and researchability
   D. feasibility and convenience

3. Selecting a broad topic initially

   A. makes sense to allow for possible avenues for investigation
   B. is never a good idea
   C. is okay but develop a specific topic soon
   D. is not advisable

Answers: 1) c; 2) c; 3) a

Study Questions

I   Change these broad topics into acceptable titles:

1. Gender and Math Achievement
2. Kindergarten Readiness and Retention
3. Time-on-Task and Motivation
4. Computer-assisted Instruction
5. Gender Bias
6. Instructional Materials and Classroom Environment

II   Give two examples of a topic that is too narrow.

III   Give two examples of a topic that is too vague.

Activity

1. Explore 5 titles in research journals to determine how accurate they are in terms of the criteria explained in this module. Are they narrow or vague? Why or why not?

Module 2: Identifying Research Questions

Robert Slavin, in his 1992 volume titled *Research methods in education* published by Allyn and Bacon, tells a story of his two-year-old daughter who when asked by her older brother "what is fourteen minus seven?" immediately responds "seven." When asked, "eighty-eight minus 79" she responds "nine" and when asked the cube root of 125, she confidently answers "5." Someone listening to this apparent two-year-old genius would be amazed. In truth, she has only learned a trick that when asked those particular questions she should always respond by repeating the last number she heard. When asked "what's three plus zero?" She would incorrectly respond zero. Slavin explains that the message of the story is that "it's not only the answers you get but the questions you ask that determine the value of a study" (p. 1). Research is about finding answers to questions worth asking. Developing research questions is necessary in order to select an appropriate **research design** that serves as the basis to guide your complete study.

Pose Research Questions that Interest You

Simply ask yourself, "What do I want to learn from this investigation?" You might pose this question, for example: "What factors seem to account for differences among boys and girls in math and science achievement in my high school?" Your research would attempt to discover those critical factors that account for such presumed differences. Can you pose another research question that might interest you given a topic you have in mind?

What are Research Questions?

Research questions are generally questions posed by educational researchers as they undertake a non-experimental or qualitative study. In quantitative studies, research questions may be posed to guide initial stages in developing a research design, but are later supplanted with **hypotheses** (Note that some studies prefer research questions to hypotheses). Hypotheses differ from research questions in that they are tested statistically (see next module). Research questions guide the research and are answered as a result of conducting the study.

Research questions usually emerge from exploring the literature on a given topic, and in qualitative research emerges at times as the researcher begins to conduct the study (see **grounded theory**). Research questions reflect and relate to the problem statement and title of the study. Notice these relationships in the example below:

Title: "Impact of Technology on Sight Word Recognition and Sentence Structure on Kindergarten and First Grade Self Contained Special Education Students"

Statement of the Problem (in part): The purpose of this study is to determine the impact of technology on literacy development among kindergarten and first grade self contained special education students. (Note that Literacy Development will be defined conceptually in the Definition of Terms; see **conceptual definitions**).

Research Questions: What impact does technology use have on sight word recognition among K/1 special education students? What impact does technology use have on sentence structure ability among K/1 special education students?

Although research questions are more often used in qualitative studies, it is indeed possible to answer the questions by using quantitative evidence. If you asked, for instance, "What are the attitudes of parents, students, and teachers toward inclusion?" you might of course conduct interviews, often used in qualitative studies, to record various responses to the question. On the other hand, you might have distributed a **Likert Scale** questionnaire to parent, student, and teacher respondents and could report you findings using **descriptive statistics** such as percentages and means. Doing so indicates that you have used a **mixed methodological** approach incorporating, by definition, qualitative and quantitative measures. The point here is that although use of research questions generally indicate qualitative approaches, quantitative measures are also possible. When no qualitative approach is used, researchers employ only hypotheses (see next module).

Poorly Phrased Research Questions

Often, students beginning their first research project pose inconsequential or obvious questions. See the questions below and identify what is wrong with them:

1. What is meant by literacy development?

2. What is on the Internet that can give me some information on assessment?

3. What technological hardware exists in the school?

Each of these questions is not worthy for master's research. Question 1 requires a simple definition as an answer. Question 2 requires a quick and simple web search and question 3 requires someone to walk around to record the hardware. Although a question might be appropriate for a particular study, it might be considered poor if worded ambiguously or imprecisely as in: 1) What impact does two English reading tutoring programs have for Spanish-dominant English language learners? 2) What do successful primary school teachers do to develop self-regulation in students both in behavioral and academic applications that sheds light on the value of student engagement, teaching experience, and professional training? The former question is somewhat confusing in that an essential piece of information is missing? Know what it is? Answer: the dependent variable; i.e., students are presumably exposed to an English reading program but for what purpose? Well, you might say it's obvious, "on English reading development." That might be so, but it must be stated precisely. The latter question is ambiguous because too many terms are included without an apparent connection.

Here's another poorly worded question: "Are Hispanic students at Groverwood High School achieving better than African American students?" Clearly, the word "better" is vague and uninforming. "Better" can be transformed into something like, "significantly higher reading scores on standardized tests." Some questions are inappropriate for their unanswerability as in: "How can we ascertain the genetic predisposition of students from Asian descent and students of European American descent in regards to achievement in science?" I hope you need no explanation here.

Reflection

Think of a better way of rephrasing each question above.

Adequately Phrased Research Questions

Good research questions are more substantive, significant, considerably thought-provoking, simple, and precisely worded (see various rubrics in this text that help differentiate poorly worded research questions from better ones).

Now, see the list that follows and indicate why they are fairly good research questions:

1. What impact does technology have on sight word recognition among K/1 special education students?

2. Will using reading comprehension strategies improve students' understanding of text?

3. What is the effect of participating in football as an extracurricular activity on academic performance in science?

Each of these questions is concise, specific, researchable, and clearly stated.

Reflection

Having conducted a preliminary literature review, you probably have a topic in mind. If so, identify some research questions. Ask yourself, what questions intrigue me?

Research Questions Connected to Type of Study

The reflective activity above is really difficult if you don't consider the type or method of research you'll undertake. Recall that research questions can be framed for both qualitative and quantitative approaches. In qualitative studies, your research questions not only guide your study but form the basis for resolving the problem under investigation. In quantitative studies, you articulate research questions to help frame your hypotheses. Consider the following methods of research and note the sample questions that might be posed:

- Ethnography – What is a typical day in the life of an urban school superintendent?

- Case Study – How can we explain Ernest's social behavior over the course of the school year in relation to the varied approaches taken to assist him?

- Historical – What role did ghetto schools play in Jewish survival during the Holocaust?

- Descriptive – What are the social, academic, economic, and political factors that influence student achievement among minority students in School District X, and how successful are those groups academically?

- Correlational – What is the relationship between allocated instructional time and mathematics achievement among Broward County School District high school students?

- Experimental – Can structured relaxation strategies improve special education students' achievement on the Citywide Reading Test?

- Quasi-experimental – Will 5th graders who are taught vocabulary using the Manfried Teaching Method score higher on a vocabulary test than students taught by rote memorization?

- Ex post facto – Will mainstreamed (included) special education students have higher self-esteem levels than non-mainstreamed (not included) elementary school students?

Reflection

Based on your knowledge of the different research methods as described briefly in Module 1 of Part Two (and your reading of the Glossary), what are the chief characteristics of each research question above as they relate to the method of research? How do these questions help you better understand the role of research questions for your study?

Research Questions for Quantitative Studies

As stated earlier, research questions are posed for quantitative studies to help get a better handle on what it is exactly you want to accomplish. Ultimately, however, a hypothesis is stated. See example that follows but read the next module for more details on hypotheses:

Topic: Birth order; mathematics achievement and social acceptance

Research question: How do middle school students (grades 5–8) who have at least one sibling and were born first compare with those middle school students who were not born first regarding mathematics achievement and social acceptance among their peers?

Research Hypothesis: Middle school students who were born first will score higher in mathematics **achievement tests** and will demonstrate higher levels of social acceptance among their peers than middle school students not born first.

Module 2 Review

In this Module you learned some basics about research questions:

1. What are research questions?

2. Why are they important?

3. What are worthy and interesting questions?

4. How are they related to the problem statement and study title?

5. What are some examples of poorly worded questions? Adequate questions?

6. How do research questions differ depending on the type of investigation undertaken?

7. What is the role of the research question in quantitative studies?

Self-Test Check

For each research topic, identify the correct method (type) of research and note whether it is quantitative or qualitative:

1. Teachers, administrators, parents, and students relate their attitudes towards inclusion.

2. The School-Based Leadership Team examines leadership behaviors of principals ever since the school was founded in 1925.

3. You want to investigate patterns of student behavior during recess at one local middle school.

4. You want to discover whether or not there's a relationship between student achievement and number of hours of assigned homework.

5. You want to know which group is best prepared for reading readiness: 1st graders who had preschool versus 1st graders without preschool experiences.

6. You want to know whether the literature-based reading series promotes higher reading achievement than the current series in use.

Answers:

1. Descriptive (usually quantitative unless results are expressed non-mathematically)

2. Historical (usually quantitative unless results are expressed non-mathematically)

3. Ethnography (usually quantitative unless results are expressed non-mathematically). By the way, what makes this topic more ethnographic than descriptive? Answer: Although you are describing their behavior, you're not merely reporting but you are delving deeply into patterns of behavior providing explanations and offering insights that might not ordinarily be understood by simple observation.

4. Correlational – quantitative

5. Ex post facto – quantitative

6. Experimental – As long as randomization of individuals is feasible. If not, it would be quasi-experimental. What would a quasi-experimental study look like? Answer: You would randomly assign intact groups to a different reading series.

Indicate what is wrong with this research question:

1. What is the impact of participation in extracurricular school activities on academic performance?

Answer:

1. Not precise enough – What is meant by "extracurricular activities" – all of them? Which one? Same for "academic performance" – in all subjects?

Critique these research questions (note that some may have no problems):

1. What impact does behavior modification systems have on promoting positive classroom climate in a special education classroom?

2. What impact do teacher expectations have on student participation?

3. What impact does social skill training have on a child with autistic characteristics?

4. How can social and community support help reduce stress experienced by a family of children with special needs?

5. How does sensory integration treatment impact the behaviors of preschool and elementary school aged students in academic achievement?

Answers will vary. Share your responses with partner. Ask your professor what she or he thinks in order to get a better sense of what may be expected of your research question(s):

Study Question and Activity

1. Examine the research questions you have developed for your project and ask yourself, "Is this information important?" "How do I know it's important?" "What else might I want to know?" "Are there other questions I need to ask?"

2. Gather five research studies and identify the research questions. Note that in some studies the questions may not be stated directly, but must be inferred.

Module 3: Formulating Hypotheses

The word "hypothesis" is commonly used, often loosely, in everyday language but also in educational parlance. At best, someone will say that a hypothesis is an "educated guess." Left as such, it leaves an erroneous impression that anyone can posit a hypothesis as long as one has an opinion about some matter. For instance, one may "hypothesize" that the new literacy-based reading series purchased by the school district will likely fail since "all the other programs this district invested in have failed." Aside from the fact that such a generalization is probably inaccurate and biased, what is the basis on which this individual posed such a hypothesis, if indeed it is even a hypothesis?! Hypotheses in educational research are very important in that they form the basis which to guide and conduct a quantitative research study. Hypotheses are infrequently incorporated into qualitative studies.

What is a Hypothesis?

A **hypothesis** (**hypotheses**) is a researcher's educated or informed guess about the relationship between two or more **variables.** A hypothesis is a statement of prediction, an anticipated outcome. Hypotheses are utilized, for the most part, in quantitative studies. Importantly, in contrast to the opening paragraph of this module, a hypothesis is carefully derived from extant literature on the topic under investigation. A hypothesis is not made out of mere convenience or unresearched opinion. Hypotheses reflect current literature that may indicate the basis for the hypothesis. For instance, one may make a hypothesis that Method A for teaching language arts will yield significantly higher test scores than if Method B was used with a particular group of students. The basis for making such an assertion centers on current research that indicates that Method A has yielded positive results in particular situations with certain groups of students. It is, therefore, acceptable to hypothesize that a similar conclusion may be drawn under this new study.

Types of Hypotheses

There are three major types of hypotheses: *directional, non-directional*, and *null.*

Directional hypotheses indicate some direction between the variables under study, as in the following example: Teachers supervised by clinical supervision will have more favorable attitudes towards their supervisors than teachers supervised by traditional forms of supervision. Note that this hypothesis indicates that one group will demonstrate more favorable attitudes, thus, indicating that a particular variable will influence or *direct* the other. Can you construct your own directional hypothesis?

Non-directional hypotheses, in contrast, indicate, as in the previous example, that there will be a difference between teachers who are observed, but do not specify a direction between the two variables. "There will be a difference between self concept levels between mainstreamed and non-mainstreamed students" is an example of a non-directional hypothesis. Construct a non-directional hypothesis of your own.

Null hypotheses indicate that no relationship or difference between the two groups or variables is likely. "There will be no difference in self concept levels between mainstreamed and non-mainstreamed students" is an example of a null hypothesis. Null hypotheses are usually employed when statistical analyses are calculated.

In educational research, hypotheses are generated only after an extensive review of the literature on a given topic. When the literature indicates that one method or approach is clearly more effective than another, you can use a directional hypothesis. If the literature is uncertain as to which approach is more effective (in other words, some studies support one approach other studies support the next approach), use the non-directional hypothesis. Generally, frame your hypotheses in the null form, especially when some statistical work will be done. Thus, at the conclusion of the study, you'll either accept or reject the null hypothesis. For instance, if you in fact discovered that mainstreamed students exhibited significantly higher self-concepts than non-mainstreamed students, then you would reject the hypothesis that stated there would be "no difference."

Composing Hypotheses

Examine this hypothesis:

There will be no difference between teacher use of praise and student motivation.

Reflection

What are the main components of a hypothesis?
What are some essential points to keep in mind when framing hypotheses?

Essential ideas about hypotheses include:

1. A hypothesis should be expressed in a single, well-phrased and clearly worded declarative sentence.

2. A hypothesis should reflect extant research and literature in the field.

3. A hypothesis should flow from the problem statement.

4. The two or more variables are clearly stated.

5. The relationship between the variables is clearly stated (e.g., there will be one variable that is expected to yield more positive results, there will be a difference among the variables, or there will be no difference between or among them).

6. They'll be no repetitive phraseology. Notice how this poorly worded hypothesis contains repetitive phrases: "Among middle school students, who are in special advanced curricular programs will report having higher motivation than those middle school students not in special advanced curricular programs." Rather state as follows: "Middle school students who are in special advanced curricular programs will have higher motivation than those not in such programs."

7. Avoid using the term "prove" – Don't say, "This study will prove that one method is better than another, etc." First, use of the word "prove" is not appropriate for hypotheses. Second, as an educational researcher you never set out to "prove" anything. You merely conduct an objective investigation by posing some sound research questions and/or hypotheses and apply the scientific method in order to answer or address them.

8. Ensure that hypotheses are testable – Hypotheses cannot be tested if they contain unclear words such as "better" as in Students exposed to Method A will score better than students exposed to Method B. What does "better" mean? Too vague and unmeasurable. Also, hypotheses that are not clearly worded are difficult to test as in "Is there a relationship between reading and science achievement among boys and the kind of classes they are in?" The last phrase "and the kind of classes they are in" is nebulous and confusing. Finally, a hypothesis that is value-laden is problematic as in "The best teachers at Midwood School District are more interested in helping their students than teachers in Crawford School District." Such a hypothesis is clearly untestable. Remember that a hypothesis must be capable of being either rejected or accepted.

9. Match the hypothesis with the corresponding research method or type. As stated earlier, hypotheses are generally stated only for quantitative studies (although there are exceptions, but these go beyond the purposes of this volume). Examine the hypotheses below for each quantitative study:

    -   Correlational (recall that in correlation studies you are indicating some "relationship" between two variables) – There will be a significant positive correlation between fifth graders' performance in mathematics and their performance in science. A "positive" correlation indicates that as one variable goes higher or lower and so does the other. A "negative" correlation means that as one variable goes higher, the other one goes lower. A negative correlation does not always indicate something undesirable as in "Students who attend the After-School Mathematics Program will have fewer absences during the course of the regular school day." Therefore, students who do regularly attend the special after-school program (high attendance) will, states the hypothesis, demonstrate "lower" rates of absence during the regular school day over a period of time.

    -   Descriptive – Science achievement scores as measured by the City Science Examination among African-American, European-American, and Hispanic-American high school students will differ significantly. Notice that one purpose of descriptive research is to *describe*, as in this case, the performance levels of two or more groups.

- Group comparison research – Hypotheses are most common in this type of research. Note the example hypotheses below:

  A. Experimental – Elementary fifth grade special education students who are taught relaxation techniques and strategies will demonstrate lower levels of anxiety and higher achievement on the City-wide Reading test than fifth grade special education students not taught these techniques. Recall that in experimental studies random assignment of individuals occurs. In this case students at the outset of the year were randomly assigned to one class who would be taught relaxation techniques whereas the other students were randomly assigned to the class not using these techniques.

  B. Quasi-experimental – High school English classes taught using computer-assisted instruction will score significantly higher on essays than students in other classes that do not use computers to aid instruction in writing essays. Recall that in quasi-experimental studies groups are already formed. In this case, the researcher might have two intact groups to which s/he randomly assigns computer instruction.

  C. Ex post facto – Middle school students who have attended pre-school will exhibit significantly less social adjustment problems than middle school students who have not attended pre-school. Recall that in ex post facto studies we are dealing with groups already formed. In this case, either they have attended pre-school or they haven't. As an educational researcher you have no control over pre-school attendance.

Module 3 Review

In this Module you learned some basics in hypothesis development.

1. What are hypotheses?

2. Why are they important?

3. Why research approaches use hypotheses?

4. What are the three main types of hypotheses?

5. What are some essential ideas about hypotheses?

Self-Test Check

1. Which of the following is an identifying characteristic of a well-formulated research hypothesis?

    A. it is stated in question form

    B. it includes a detailed description of the population under study

    C. it includes references to educational theory

    D. it is always short

    E. it specifies the variables to be studied and the nature of the expected relationship between these variables

2. Which of the following is stated as a null hypothesis?

    A. 6th grade students who attend a literacy workshop after school will perform better academically than students who do not.

    B. No difference exists in academic achievement for 6th grade students who attend a literacy workshop as opposed to students who do attend.

    C. Is there a difference in 6th grade students who attend a literacy workshop after school than students who do not?

    D. All of these

3. True or False. A hypothesis is a statement that predicts an outcome.

4. True or False. Hypotheses should not contradict current research on a given topic.

5. True or False. Null hypotheses are used to tests statistical significance.

6. True or False. If a researcher believes that Method A will yield higher scores in student achievement than Method B, but the literature review indicates otherwise, s/he should state the hypothesis to show that Method B will yield higher score results than Method A.

7. True or False. Use a non-directional hypothesis when the literature review indicates conflicting evidence; i.e., no one approach is superior than the other.

8. True or False. This is an example of a null hypothesis: No differences exist in the average achievement levels in 12th grade science and English among African, Asian, and Hispanic American students.

9. True or False. "Teachers in schools with inclusive classrooms will have significantly more positive attitudes towards inclusion than teachers in schools without inclusive classrooms" is an example of a directional hypothesis.

10. Transform this question into a null hypothesis: Are children who attend pre-school more socially mature than students who did not attend pre-school?

11. Transform into a directional, non-directional, and null hypothesis: What is the effect of the differentiated instruction workshops on teachers' attitudes toward differentiated instruction?

12. Name the two variables, kind of hypothesis, and type of study in: Among elementary school teachers, years of teaching experience and numbers of disciplinary problems reported to the principal are directly related.

13. Which of the following hypotheses are stated correctly?

    A. Korean students will have better attitudes toward mathematics than students of Jewish descent.

    B. Students at Hartwood Middle School score higher than students at Foxwood Middle School.

    C. No difference will exist in standardized achievements scores in mathematics between fourth grade students at Hartwood Elementary School and Foxwood Elementary School.

    D. Mathematics achievement is positively related among students of African decent.

14. Which hypothesis is in the directional form?

    A. It is hypothesized that there will be no significant relationship between Variable A and Variable B.

    B. It is hypothesized that there will not be a significant relationship between Variable A and Variable B.

    C. It is hypothesized that there will be a significant negative relationship between Variable A and Variable B.

    D. It is hypothesized that there will be a significant relationship between Variable A and Variable B.

15. Which of the following variables are negatively correlated?

    A. height and weight

    B. teacher hair color and student achievement

    C. teacher use of praise and student motivation

    D. student achievement and absenteeism

Answers: 1) e; 2) b; 3) t; 4) t; 5) t; 6) t; 7) t; 8) t; 9) t; 10) There will be no difference in the maturity levels of the two groups of students; 11) Directional: Teachers attitudes towards differentiated instruction will improve as a result of attending the workshop. Non-directional: There will be a difference in teacher attitudes as a result of attending the workshop. Null: There will be no difference in teachers' attitudes towards differentiated instruction measured before a workshop compared to after the workshop; 12) variables: years of teaching experience and numbers of disciplinary problems. Kind of hypothesis: directional. Type of study: correlation; 13) c; 14) c; 15) d.

Critique these hypotheses (note that some may have no problems):

1. Teacher use of praise will have a positive impact on student attentiveness.

2. Students exposed to stress reduction training will demonstrate lower levels of stress than students who do not receive such training.

3. There is no relationship between antisocial behavior and cognitive development on pre-school children.

Answers will vary. Share your responses with partner. Ask your professor what she or he thinks in order to get a better sense of what may be expected of your research question(s).

Study Question and Activity

1. Gather five research studies and identify the hypotheses. Indicate the type of study for each.

2. Examine the hypotheses you may have already developed and ask yourself, "Have I addressed all the essential components as explained in this module?"

Part Four:

Thesis Overview— Chapter 2 of Thesis: Literature Review

Focus Questions

1. Have you read many research articles from academic journals?

2. What criteria would you use to assess the value or accuracy of an article?

3. How would you use the Internet to assist you with your thesis (other than using ERIC)?

4. Why is spending so much time reviewing the literature important?

5. What kinds of information would be useful to you for helping to write your literature review?

Module 1: Understanding Published Research Articles

Most of the research you will accumulate when you conduct a literature review will likely come from published articles in academic (peer reviewed) journals. Understanding the components of a research article will help you in several ways:

1. You will be able to read research literature intelligently

2. You will become a more critical consumer of research

3. You will be able to select more appropriate and relevant research for your project

The components of a research article are not unlike that of a thesis or even a proposal (see Modules 3 and 4 in Part Two). Most, not all, articles contain these features, although they may not be labeled as such:

- Title and author(s), including their affiliation

- Abstract (some journals do not include one)

- Introduction (background, significance, and need of study, etc.)

- Review of Literature (including theoretical rationale); note that a literature review for a published article is more concise than one for a thesis.

- Research question(s) and/or hypotheses

- Method or Design (including sample, procedures, instrumentation or materials, and data analysis)

- Results (or sometimes called Findings in qualitative studies)

- Discussion (includes limitations)

- Conclusions

- References

Reflection

Locate an article in one of the eight categories below in order to become aware of the style of research type articles. Besides giving you a flavor of research in the field, it will serve as a model as you write various components of your own proposal and/or thesis.

As you conduct a literature review you'll come across many different types of articles. Many articles won't be research articles. They may be summaries of research on a topic; they may be field-based articles that summarize how a particular school or district implements a given strategy. Although these non-research type articles may be useful in a literature review, please note that for more scholarly projects such as thesis writing or writing an article for publication in a research journal, research type articles are preferable. Depending on the topic you select, at least 50–60% of the articles you cite should be research-based.

Eight Categories of Articles

Article 1:   Ethnographic

Article 2:   Historical

Article 3:   Case Study

Article 4:   Descriptive/Correlation

Article 5:   Experimental

Article 6:   Quasi-Experimental

Article 7:   Ex post facto study

Article 8:   Mixed methodology

In order to guide you to search for articles related to your topic, undertake the following activity:

Assess the quality of the research articles you are reading and eventually citing. You need to become familiar with the format of journal articles and learn to critique them so that you are an educated consumer who doesn't believe everything s/he reads. See the rubric #1 below to guide you in evaluating research articles. In the course I teach, I require students early on in the semester to select three articles on a given topic and have them complete the rubric below and write a one-page summary and critique of each article. These initial articles may or may not serve later on as part of their study. But this educational activity will teach them to critically read journal articles and other literature. For a Sample Critique that one of my star students, Evelyn Schachner, submitted see page 106. Afterward, select an article or two on your own and use Rubric #1 to guide you.

RUBRIC 1: EVALUATING RESEARCH ARTICLES

Components	1 Unacceptable	2 Acceptable	3 Target	SCORE= 1, 2, or 3 (add comments as needed)	Place score below
Nature of research	Abstract (if provided) fuzzy; Topic unclear; Title doesn't reflect abstract or contents; Introduction too brief or unclear; Unclear problem statement; Unclear about quantitative or qualitative nature of study; Research questions/hypotheses not stated precisely or emerging from literature; import/need of study omitted or insignificant	Abstract (if provided) stated; Topic clear; Title reflects abstract and contents; Introduction clear; Clear problem statement; Clear about quantitative or qualitative nature of study; Research questions/hypotheses stated precisely and emerging from literature; import/need of study discussed	Abstract (if provided) clear; Topic clear; Title precisely reflects abstract or contents; Introduction clear and insightful; Clear and precise problem statement; Clear about quantitative or qualitative nature of study; Research questions/hypotheses stated precisely and emerging from literature; import/need of study discussed in detail		
Variables and terms	Not identified or defined; Identified but defined improperly; No distinction between conceptual/operational definitions	Identified and defined; Identified and defined properly; Distinction between conceptual/operational definitions	Precisely identified and defined; Identified and defined properly; Clear and appropriate distinction between conceptual/operational definitions		
Literature review	Insufficient (e.g., too brief, shallow, not comprehensive, doesn't establish link between variables; etc.); Inadequate (e.g., doesn't cover prior research or does so scantily, not up-to-date, disorganized, no background or theoretical framework/rationale, not critical, etc.); Inappropriate given research design (i.e., quantitative or qualitative)	Sufficient (e.g., not too brief or shallow, comprehensive, Establishes link between variables; etc.); Adequate (e.g., covers prior research, up-to-date, organized, adequate background or theoretical framework/rationale, critical, etc.); Appropriate given research design (i.e., quantitative or qualitative)	Comprehensive, Establishes strong link between variables; etc.); Highly adequate (e.g., covers prior research, up-to-date, very organized, sound background or theoretical framework/rationale, critical, etc.); Appropriate given research design (i.e., quantitative or qualitative)		

Methodology (e.g., participants, instruments, procedure, data analysis, results)	Methods section not identified; Doesn't describe treatments; No or insufficient details about study participants (key info missing); No description of materials (instruments) provided; Data collection inadequately described; No mention of validity or reliability; Insufficient detail for study replication; Research design inappropriate or confusing; No indication how data were analyzed; Data analyzed incorrectly (e.g., incorrect statistics, choice of analysis inappropriate); Results scanty, confusing, or omitted; &/or Tables or figures not provided or not clearly presented	Methods section identified; Treatments described; Sufficient details about study participants; Description of materials (instruments) provided; Data collection adequately described; Validity and reliability addressed; Sufficient detail for study replication; Research design appropriate; Data analysis provided; Data analyzed correctly (e.g., correct statistics, choice of analysis appropriate; Results provided; &/or Tables or figures provided and clearly presented	Methods section identified; Treatments described well; Sufficient details about study participants; Description of materials (instruments) provided in detail; Data collection adequately described; Validity and reliability addressed; Superior detail for study replication; Research design appropriate; Data analysis appropriate; Data analyzed correctly (e.g., correct statistics, choice of analysis appropriate); Results provided in detail; &/or Tables or figures provided and clearly presented	
Discussion/conclusion	Omitted; Scanty; Doesn't adequately answer research questions/hypotheses (i.e., findings not presented adequately); Limitations not addressed; Conclusions inappropriate (e.g., doesn't follow from results, biased, erroneous, etc.); Future directions omitted or insufficient; Implications unclear	Included and detailed; Adequately answered research questions/hypotheses (i.e., findings presented adequately); Limitations addressed; Conclusions appropriate (e.g., follows from results, unbiased, accurate, etc.); Future directions included and sufficient; Implications clear	Included and richly detailed; Adequately answered research questions/hypotheses (i.e., findings presented adequately); Limitations addressed with reasons; Conclusions appropriate (e.g., follows from results, unbiased, accurate, detailed, etc.); Future directions included and with great detail; Implications clear	
Citations/references	Manual of style (e.g., APA) inconsistently applied; Works cited but not referenced; Incomplete; Not up-to-date	Manual of style (e.g., APA) consistently applied; Works cited and referenced; Complete; Up-to-date	Manual of style (e.g., APA) rigorously and accurately applied; Works cited and referenced; Complete; Up-to-date	**OVERALL SCORE-** ___

Qualitative comments: (on reverse side)

SAMPLE CRITIQUE

Kaplan, B.J., McNicol, J., Conte, R.A., & Moghadam, H.K. (1989). Dietary replacement in preschool-aged hyperactive boys. *Pediatrics, 83*(1), 7–17.

Summary of Article

Authors: Bonnie J. Kaplan, PhD, Jane McNicol, RD, Richard A. Conte, PhD, & H.K. Moghadam, MD

Purpose of Study

This study was designed to determine the impact of dietary replacement on the behavior and physical symptoms of preschool-aged hyperactive boys. Previous investigations studied challenge diets, which target an individual substance or class of substances. This experiment focused on a broader range of substances, including not only artificial colors and flavors, but also simple sugars, chocolate, monosodium glutamate, preservatives, and caffeine.

Hypothesis

Preschool-aged hyperactive boys will exhibit improved behavior and decreased physical discomfort while receiving the experimental dietary replacement diet.

Design

In this study researchers used a within-subject crossover design. A placebo- controlled period was included so that placebo effects could be observed. The study consisted of 3 weeks of a baseline diet, 3 weeks of a placebo-controlled diet, and 4 weeks of a replacement diet. In order to test treatment order effects, 12 of the 24 participants received the diets in baseline-placebo-replacement order and the remaining 12 received the diets in baseline-replacement-placebo order.

The results of the study are expressed in quantitative measures.

Findings

A majority of parental reports indicated behavioral improvement while the children were on the replacement diet. Ten of the 24 children showed significant behavioral improvement, while 4 of the children showed mild improvement. The remaining 10 children were unresponsive to dietary intervention.

Parental responses were similar during the baseline and placebo periods, indicating the lack of a placebo effect.

Treatment effects were significant for 2 of 7 sleep variables tested. Children experienced shorter sleep latency and less night awakenings during the replacement phase than during the baseline and placebo phases. Of 9 physical variables tested, treatment effects were significant only for halitosis and rhinitis.

There was a lack of data available from statistical tests since the hyperactive children were not able to be tested during many of the sessions.

Critique of Article

The article is precise and detailed. The problem is stated clearly and emerges from the existing literature. The methods section is superior; the descriptions allow for easy study replication. The results are explained well with appropriate charts. A richly detailed discussion is provided which adequately presents the findings of the study. The implications of the study for further research, as well as for practitioners and educators, are included.

Several elements, however, are omitted or insufficient. The title of the article does not identify the dependent variables in the study. The hypothesis is not stated explicitly, and the limitations of the study are not addressed.

Questions Answered

This article answered some preliminary questions I had about the nutrition-behavior connection, including:

- Do more children respond to replacement diets than to challenge diets?
- What are the behaviors that tend to change in children on replacement diets?
- Can physical symptoms in children improve with dietary replacement?

Questions Remaining

The following questions remain unanswered:

- How will a challenge diet which eliminates only simple sugars impact on a child's behavior?
- Can elimination or challenge diets impact on the cognition of hyperactive children?
- How long must a child avoid a substance to which he/she is sensitive before behavioral improvement is noticeable?
- Do hyperactive children show more significant behavioral improvement when on elimination diets than children who are not hyperactive?
- Is age a factor in responsiveness to dietary manipulation?

Relevance to My Study

The study I plan to carry out would include fewer participants than the experiment discussed above. As opposed to dietary replacement, my study would involve a challenge diet which would target simple sugars.

Though my study will differ from the one discussed above, I would use the same design as well as some of the same methods of data collection. I would probably use a within subject crossover design. I could not, however, include a placebo phase since I would not provide the participants with the food. Like the aforementioned study, I would distribute behavioral checklists to the students' parents and teachers during the baseline and treatment phases.

Crook, W.G. (1980). Can what a child eats make him dull, stupid, or hyperactive? *Journal of Learning Disabilities, 13*(5), 281–285.

Summary of Article

Author: William G. Crook, MD

Purpose of Study

This study was designed to determine whether a relationship exists between allergic reactions to food or food additives and hyperactivity and behavioral and learning problems.

Research Question

Is there a relationship between allergic reactions to food or food additives and hyperactivity and behavioral and learning problems?

Method

In this study a within-subject crossover design was used. The participants included 182 of the researcher's patients. Sublingual food and food dye tests were conducted to identify suspect food substances. These food substances were then eliminated from the patients' diets for 7-10 days or until significant improvement in the patients' symptoms was observed. The eliminated foods were then individually reintroduced to the patients' diets to confirm the suspicion that the foods caused adverse reactions.

After 5 years of testing patients with hyperactivity and associated emotional, behavioral, and learning problems, the researcher gathered additional information about the patients via a questionnaire that was distributed to the parents.

Findings of the study are described qualitatively.

Findings

The researcher concluded that adverse or allergic reactions played a major role in causing hyperactivity and associated behavioral and learning problems in patients studied.

Critique of Article

The researcher accounts for the brief and seemingly shallow literature review. He points out that the lack of scientific evidence of a relationship between diet and behavior should not cause professionals to dismiss the belief that dietary manipulation can impact a child's behavior. Because elimination diets are safe, until scientific reports establish a link between diet and behavior, anecdotal data should be sufficient to convince parents and practitioners to try diet therapy.

The author touches on important points regarding diet-behavior studies in the discussion section. The limitations of the study are addressed. The conclusion is stated emphatically and adequately answers the research question. Overall, the article is clear and flows well.

Questions Answered

The article answered several questions I had regarding the link between diet and behavior:

- How long must a child avoid an offending food before behavioral changes are noticed?
- Can a child's ability to learn be affected by his/her diet?
- How do parents describe behavioral changes in their children that result from dietary manipulation?
- Do some children experience dramatic physical or behavioral improvement when sugar is eliminated from their diets?

Questions Remaining

The following questions remain unanswered:

- Why is it that allergists have found that food affects children's behavior while scientific studies have failed to confirm those results? (The author of the article attempted to answer this question. However, I feel it still needs further explanation.)
- What is the organic explanation for the effect of sugar on behavior in children?
- What are parents' initial reactions to recommendations for diet therapy for their children?

Relevance to My Study

The study I plan to carry out will include a sample much smaller than the one in this study. The method that will be used in my study will also differ in a number of ways. I did, however, find some aspects of this study helpful. The author of the article mentioned that parents of his patients filled out a behavioral inventory prior to dietary treatment. If I could access the behavioral inventory, I would use it in my study as well.

The author cited comments made by parents regarding their children's positive reactions to dietary manipulation. A few parents described the dramatic behavioral improvements they noticed in their children when sugar was eliminated from their diets. Since my study will target simple sugars, I found this information relevant and fascinating.

Rapp, D.J. (1978). Does diet affect hyperactivity? *Journal of Learning Disabilities, 11*(6), 383–389.

Summary of Article

Author: Doris J. Rapp, MD

Purpose of Study

This study was designed to:

1) Determine if dyes, foods, or allergy relate to increased activity in some children.
2) Determine if sublingual food or food coloring tests may be of diagnostic value.
3) Evaluate the benefit of a diet that omits major suspect foods and food coloring.

Research Questions

1) Do dyes, foods, or allergy relate to increased activity in some children?

2) Of what diagnostic value are sublingual food or food coloring tests?

3) Of what benefit is a diet that eliminates major suspect foods and food coloring?

Method

The researcher in this study used a within subject crossover design. Twenty-four children, aged 5–16, were initially tested using sublingual dye and food tests to determine if changes in activity levels could be observed immediately following the ingestion of individual dyes and foods. The children were then put on 7-day restricted diets which excluded milk, wheat, egg, cocoa, corn, sugar, and artificial food colors.

At the conclusion of the 7-day period, each excluded food was individually reintroduced into the diet. For the next 12 weeks, each child maintained an individual diet which excluded substances that caused adverse symptoms when reintroduced to the diet.

Results of the study were reported in both quantitative and qualitative measures.

Findings

The researcher found that 12 of 23 patients showed marked improvement in activity within one week. This improvement continued for at least 12 weeks in 11 of the 17 children who continued to adhere to the restricted diet.

Fifteen of 23 children showed moderate to marked improvement in chronic symptoms, including gastrointestinal discomfort, headaches, and muscle aches after one week on the elimination diets. This improvement persisted for at least 12 weeks in 15 of the 17 patients who continued selected dietary restriction. Nasal symptoms decreased from 71% to 52%, gastrointestinal symptoms and muscle aches from 54% to 10%, and headaches decreased from 50% to 0% within 6 weeks of the initial diet.

Fourteen of 24 patients exhibited an increase in activity after the sublingual dye tests. 11 of 24 patients exhibited an increase in activity following the sublingual food tests. A single sugar ingestion challenge test consistently caused hyperactivity in 7 of the 24 patients, irritability in 2 of the patients, and stomachache in 1 patient.

Critique of Article

The article is clear and easily comprehensible. The problem statement is stated and emerges from the existing literature. Conflicting reports about the effect of diet on behavior is given as the need of the study. The conclusions drawn are appropriate, and the implications for future study as well as for parents of allergy-sensitive children are listed.

The title of the article, however, does not name the population to which the findings of the study will be generalized. The research questions are not stated, and the author is unclear about the quantitative or qualitative nature of the study.

Questions Answered

The article answered several questions I had regarding the nutrition-behavior connection:

- Is there a relationship between allergy and hyperactivity?
- Do the short-term effects of dietary manipulation persist when the diets are prolonged?
- Can diet affect the behavior of school-aged students?
- What are the physical symptoms that are related to the ingestion of offending foods?
- What percentage of hyperactive children are sensitive to sugar?

Questions Remaining

The following questions remain unanswered:

- Is there a relationship between sugar ingestion and inattentiveness in school-aged children who are not diagnosed with Attention Deficit Disorder?
- Do children who are not hyperactive tend to be more sensitive to sugar than to other allergic foods?

Relevance to My Study

The method I would use in my study would be similar to the one used in this study. Like the researcher did in this study, I would probably conduct the elimination diet in my study for 7 days. I would not, however, use sublingual dye or food tests since my study will target an individual food substance. Also, I would report the findings of my study using only qualitative measures.

Reflection

What did you learn from examining the Sample Critique? How can such an effort be useful to your work? Did you find the rubric helpful in evaluating your research article(s)? Explain.

RESEARCH TOPIC WITH CRITIQUE OF 3 ARTICLES RUBRIC

Components	1 Unacceptable	2 Acceptable	3 Target	SCORE= 1, 2, or 3	Place
Selection of Research Topic	No topic selected; topic not significant nor related to course objectives; topic too broad; topic too specific; unresearchable; not feasible	Topic selected; topic relevant to course objectives; topic is specific but not minute; researchable; feasible	Topic selected; topic relevant to course objectives; topic is specific; significant; researchable; feasible; unique		
Selection of Research Articles	Less than 3 articles selected; one or more unrelated to topic; two or more unscholarly or not research-oriented; two or more from popular magazines	3 articles selected; all related to topic; two or more scholarly and research-oriented	3 articles selected; all related to topic; all scholarly and research-oriented		
Critique of Articles	Reviewed, not critiqued; omits two or more of following: summary, hypotheses/research questions; variables; research designs utilized; strengths and weaknesses; indicating relevance of articles to study	Reviewed, somewhat critiqued; Includes all of following: summary, hypotheses/research questions; variables; research designs utilized; strengths and weaknesses; indicating relevance of articles to study	Reviewed and sufficiently critiqued; Includes all of following in detail: summary, hypotheses/research questions; variables; research designs utilized; strengths and weaknesses; indicating relevance of articles to study		
Format	Guidelines not followed; disorganized and sloppily arranged	Guidelines followed; organized and arranged in a logical, presentable order	Guidelines followed precisely; Well organized and arranged logically; aesthetically presented		

Qualitative comments: (on reverse side)

OVERALL SCORE- _____

Module 1 Review

In this Module you learned to apply the rubric for evaluating articles.

Compose a list of insights gained from perusing and evaluating academic research articles. For instance, you may write the following ideas:

- The review of literature in academic journal articles is much briefer than in a thesis.

- The statement of the problem may be stated without calling it such (it may just state, for instance, "in the present study, we examine the causes of . . . .").

- The word "subjects" is used under "Method or Methodology" for "participants."

- Etc.

Self-Test Check

1. Which of the following is an accurate statement regarding qualitative research published in academic journals?

    A. All qualitative articles are similar in format

    B. Qualitative and quantitative research studies are quite similar in format

    C. Qualitative research is more amenable to a mixed methodology than quantitative research

    D. Qualitative research is more inductive in its approach than quantitative research

2. Which is not a useful guideline for reviewing articles in academic journals?

    A. Don't bother to critique an article since if it wasn't high quality it wouldn't be published

    B. Articles in peer-reviewed journals vary greatly in quality

    C. Skim articles of interest before you read them in detail

    D. Reading an abstract is helpful to obtain a sense of the relevance of a particular article

3. Which is not an appropriate question to pose when examining the problem statement of a quantitative research article?

    A. What are the independent and dependent variables?

    B. Is the problem stated clearly and precisely?

    C. Are primary sources emphasized?

    D. Is the problem researchable?

4. Which is an appropriate question to pose when examining the literature review of a quantitative research article?

    A. Is the review up to date?

    B. Is the review similar to the review of a qualitative study?

    C. Are the participants identified?

    D. Are response rates noted?

5. Which is an appropriate question to pose when examining the methods section of a qualitative study?

    A. Is the review up to date?

    B. How does the researcher deal with potential bias when collecting data?

    C. Is the purpose clearly stated?

    D. Are appropriate conclusions offered?

Answers: 1) d; 2) a; 3) c; 4) a; 5) b

Study Questions

1. Answer the following questions for each of the qualitative articles you locate:

Introduction and Problem:

    A. Is background information adequately provided?

    B. Are potential biases evident?

    C. Does the article provide an adequate introduction?

    D. Does the article provide an adequate problem statement?

Related Research:

    A. Is the researcher knowledgeable about the literature on the topic?

    B. Is the review well organized?

    C. Is a theoretical framework provided?

Methodology:

    A. Is triangulation achieved?

    B. Are potential biases presented and explained?

    C. Is the method appropriate to the study?

    D. Are methods used to analyze data explained?

Findings:

    A. Are findings stated explicitly?

    B. Is sufficient detail provided?

    C. Are all research questions answered?

Discussion:

    A. Are interpretations appropriate?

    B. Are implications of results discussed thoroughly?

    C. Are limitations indicated?

2. *Answer the following questions for each of the quantitative articles you locate:*

Statement of Problem:

    A. Are variables explicitly stated?

    B. Is problem stated clearly and precisely?

Review of Literature:

    A. Is the review comprehensive and inclusive of alternative views, if appropriate?

    B. Is review detailed and well organized?

    C. Does the review cite sources relevant to the purpose of the study?

Research Hypotheses or questions:

    A. Are they explicitly stated?

    B. Are they testable?

    C. Are they clear and written properly

Research Design:

    A. Is sample clearly defined and described?

    B. Is sample adequate to derive meaning from the study?

    C. Is method of sampling identified?

    D. Are instruments sufficiently described?

    E. Is evidence for validity and reliability stated?

    F. Has triangulation been achieved?

    G. Is procedure clear and logical?

    H. Has data analysis been presented?

    I. Has type of study been explicitly stated (e.g., experimental, correlational, etc.)?

Results:

    A. Are hypotheses and/or research questions restated and answered or addressed?

    B. Are results stated clearly and accurately?

    C. Are tables or charts easy to understand?

    D. Are appropriate statistical tests offered?

Discussion:

    A. Does article discuss the results in a thorough and clear manner?

    B. Does the discussion reflect results obtained?

    C. Are limitations reasonable?

    D. Are conclusions or implications provided?

Activity

1. Locate eight articles, each representing the types mentioned in this module.

Module 2: Writing the Literature Review

Writing the literature review, for students, seems the most cumbersome activity of the thesis project. The literature serves, though, as the foundation for your entire thesis. It provides substantive background information for the topic you've selected. It familiarizes you with key aspects of your research. The literature review indicates to readers that you are cognizant of the extant research in your chosen topic and that you acknowledge this work and intend to build on it in some meaningful way. Some master's degree students, by the way, think they have to create something anew while undertaking this project. Although perhaps a novel approach to a particular topic might be in order, there is no expectation that you need to create new theories or major ideas. You can simply build on past research and even replicate a study done in the past, as long as you add something just a bit different, e.g., conducting the study with a new or different **sample**.

Writing a literature review is not very different from writing an in depth research or term paper. The same components of good writing apply. This module will provide you with some key guidelines for writing your lit review. Still, these principles will become more meaningful when you actually start writing. As John Dewey once simply yet profoundly quipped, there is, and I paraphrase, nothin' like learnin' by doin'. So, good luck!

Key Guidelines for Writing a Literature Review

- Spend the first week or so, just scanning the literature and reading. No need to start taking notes at this initial stage.

- Once you've gotten a handle on a topic you can begin to read articles more in depth and take careful notes. Record the complete reference carefully right away. You'd be surprised how many people, when they begin to write their review, discover a great quote in their notes, but cannot locate its original source. If you find a good article or quote, record the complete reference, including page numbers. Doing so, will save you much aggravation and extra work in the end.

- As you read some more, at first scan the articles. Group various articles by categories (e.g., quantitative or qualitative studies or studies conducted with elementary school students versus high schoolers, etc.). Group also by major sub-divisions (e.g., pro articles, con articles, articles that demonstrate a positive effect, articles that do not, etc.) These various categories might serve later on to organize your paper into sub-divisions or categories.

- Copy articles that seem relevant and then read each article in detail. Take notes as you read articles. Keep an index card (or use a data base program or some other kind of software, e.g., Endnote) that includes the following information: 1) Title; 2) Author(s); 3) Journal, volume, year, pages, etc. (I suggest you record the complete citation in APA form- see Module 2 in Part Thirteen); 4) Type of study; 5) Purpose of study; 6) Research questions/hypotheses; 7) Methodology or Research Design including sample, instrumentation (materials), procedure, and data analysis; 8) Results; 9) Major findings; 10) Your own comments or observations. Number the card and the article. That way you can refer to the article later. If you decide to include quotations on the card, make sure you include accurate quotes and correct page numbers. Label cards by topic e.g., Pros of Cooperative Learning, Cons, Research Studies at the High School Level, etc.

- Include pro *and* con perspectives. Present a balanced, fair review. Look for articles that contradict your own opinion. For instance, if you are reviewing the use of phonics, you should include the work of those who support *and* oppose its use. You should also review the literature on whole language instruction to place the subject in proper perspective.

- Ask yourself: What are the study findings? Is my selection of studies balanced? Have I missed alternate views? Have I read works by noteworthy researchers, theorists, or authors. Have I considered the preponderance of evidence? Is there consensus? Are there contradictions?

- Point out any gaps in the literature. For instance, you might discover that no work has been done with English Language Learners in a particular subject area at a particular grade level. State this apparent omission and such information may serve to form a niche for your own work. You can indicate how your research will build upon or be different from others.

- Summarize minor studies but detail major studies.

- Point out trends and themes. Don't merely quote study after study in list form. Compose a thoughtful and interesting narrative that highlights these studies, but also point out common ideas and trends in the field.

- Feel free to cite peripheral research studies even though they do not directly or immediately bear upon your own. You might not find much research in a given topic for your particular grade level. But you may find research conducted with other populations. Keep in mind that you need not just find identical research studies on your topic. Finding conceptually related articles is acceptable and good research practice.

- Refer to current research but don't forget the classics in the field. Always include references to them.

- Your literature review does not have to be exhaustive. You don't have to locate every study completed on your topic. The purpose of a literature review is to find out and acknowledge what work has been done on the topic. Your literature review, then, merely has to represent accurately what the experts have to say about it.

- Refer to encyclopedias or reviews of literature in journals. These extensive reviews are a great source of information. Select citations and references in the review so that you may refer to them. If you paraphrase or quote from these reviews make certain you cite them so that readers know the source of the information.

- Divide your literature review as you would any story into: a beginning, middle, and end. The beginning includes a one- or two-paragraph introduction that states the purpose of the literature review and what will be included. The middle may include several subsections. Use the various topics you noted on the cards above to guide development of the middle subsection. The end is just a concluding statement summarizing what you found.

- When is "enough too much?" How do you know when you've exhausted all the information on a given topic? When study after study appears to be saying the same thing. Once you've cited a number of these studies, you no longer have to discuss them at any length in the review. You may just want to include some of these others in a citation and/or in the reference section. Be sure to only include works cited in the text of your review in the reference section. Do not include works that are merely referred to, but you never cited or quoted them.

- Create and use an outline before you begin writing. The outline will contain major and minor sub-divisions.

- Use of first person is acceptable but only when referring to your personal observations, experiences, etc.

- Avoid these common errors:
    a. Don't simply summarize one study after another on a topic. In the end, the literature review will appear nothing more than a series or a list of studies.
    b. Don't remain uncritical. Feel free to criticize research if you can document omissions or errors. Point out gaps in the literature, as stated earlier.
    c. Not receiving feedback from at least two other colleagues before you submit your work to the professor is a big error!
    d. The literature review does not provide support for either the hypothesis or research question.
    e. Starting from past research to more current work. Rather, start from current and work backwards.
    f. Not following APA
    g. Not attending to inadvertent plagiarism
    h. Not proofreading your manuscript repeatedly. Not having colleagues assist you.

- Adhere "religiously" to APA (see Module 2 in Part Thirteen)

- Consult if you must a very good work on writing literature reviews: Ling Pan, M. (2004). *Preparing literature reviews* (2nd ed.). Glendale, CA: Pyrczak Publishing.

Below you will find a rubric to help guide your literature review. I ask my students to use it to critique their own literature review when complete. I inform my students that I will use this same rubric to evaluate their work.

LITERATURE REVIEW RUBRIC

Components	1 Unacceptable	2 Acceptable	3 Target	SCORE= 1, 2, or 3 (add comments as needed)	Place score below
Introduction	Nonexistent; Weak beginning; Confusing; Doesn't get to the point; Little or no background information provided; No connection made to importance of topic; &/or overview of review not provided	Sound and sensible; Adequate beginning; Not confusing; Gets to the point; Sufficient background information provided; Connection made to importance of topic; &/or Overview of review provided	Sound, sensible, and enticing; Strong beginning; Clear and precise; Superior background information provided; Strong connection made to importance of topic; &/or Overview of review provided in detail		
Body of Review	Variables not identified or defined correctly; Doesn't establish link between variables; Inadequately paraphrased and summarized previous research; Inadequate background and theoretical framework/rationale established; Not comprehensive; Citations disorganized (doesn't proceed from general to specific and old to new); Doesn't cite actual findings of studies; Portions unclear; &/or Basis for research questions/hypotheses not established	Variables identified and defined correctly; Establishes link between variables; Adequately paraphrased and summarized previous research; Adequate background and theoretical framework/rationale established; Although not comprehensive, sufficient; Proceeds from general to specific and old to new; Cites actual findings of studies; Clear; &/or Basis for research questions/hypotheses established	Variables identified and defined correctly; Establishes strong link between variables More than adequately paraphrased and summarized previous research; Excellent background and theoretical framework/rationale established; Comprehensive; Proceeds from general to specific and old to new; Clearly cites actual findings of studies; Very clear; &/or Basis for research questions/hypotheses established		
Conclusion/Discussion/ Summary	Nonexistent; Weak; Incomplete; Confusing; Biased; Not related to body of review; &/or No summary or conclusion provided	Existent; Adequate; Complete; Not confusing; Not biased; Related to body of review; &/or Summary or conclusion provided	Existent; Superior; Very complete; Not confusing at all; Related to body of review; Not biased and extremely well balanced and fair; &/or Summary or conclusion comprehensive		
Citations/References	Irrelevant studies; Not critically reviewed and analyzed pointing to strengths and weaknesses of studies; Not up-to-date; Poor quality (e.g., too many non-refereed articles); Cited but not referenced; &/or APA not adhered to	Relevant studies; Critically reviewed and analyzed pointing to strengths and weaknesses of studies; Up-to-date; Adequate quality (e.g., not too many non-refereed articles); Few, if any, cited but not referenced; &/or APA adhered to	Relevant studies; Critically reviewed and analyzed pointing to strengths and weaknesses of studies; Up-to-date; High quality (e.g., few non-refereed articles); All citations referenced; &/or APA strictly adhered to		
Organization	Material unorganized; Inappropriate headings and sub-headings; illogical; Inappropriate given research design (i.e., quantitative or qualitative)	Material organized; Appropriate headings and sub-headings; Logical	Material very well organized; Very appropriate headings and sub-headings; Logical		
Control	Writing reflects poor "technical control," i.e., incomplete sentences, spelling errors, &/or incorrect punctuation, grammar, paragraph development, etc.	Writing reflects adequate "technical control," i.e., complete sentences, few spelling errors, &/or correct punctuation, grammar, paragraph development, etc.	Writing reflects superior "technical control," i.e., complete sentences, no spelling errors, &/or correct punctuation, grammar, paragraph development, etc.		

Qualitative comments: (on reverse side)

OVERALL   **SCORE-**   _____

Reflection

Use the Literature Review rubric to assess the literature reviews for articles you locate in the process of undertaking your own study. Reflect upon what comprises a good review. The more experience you have using this rubric the more adept you'll become at writing your own literature review.

In this Module you learned some guidelines for writing a literature review.

1. *Which guidelines made most sense to you?*

2. *Were the rubrics useful?*

3. *How might you improve them? Please let me know.*

Self-Test Check

1. Which of the following rationales for a literature review is most sound?

   A. provides a context or background for your investigation

   B. ensures that all research on a topic is covered

   C. provides a list of research questions and/or hypotheses

   D. presents contradictory research for the chosen topic

2. Which is not a useful guideline for writing a literature review?

   A. Take notes as you read articles

   B. Refer to APA

   C. Proofread review

   D. Use of an outline is not helpful

Answers: 1) a; 2) d

Study Questions

1. Examine literature reviews in various articles and assess their quality using the rubric in this module. What differentiates an adequate literature review from an inadequate one?

2. In what ways can writing a literature review be made easier?

Activity

1. Examine three literature reviews from articles in an academic journal and note three similarities and differences among them.

ADVICE TO INSTRUCTORS (AND STUDENTS):

Students often have difficulty writing scholarly literature reviews. For many of them, it's the first time they've undertaken such a project. I've found the following strategies useful, so much so that I require my students to follow these guidelines:

1. Always proofread your work before you show it to anyone. Re-read what you've written after a few hours or even the next day. Does what you've written make sense to you? Write precisely what you mean to say. Instructor: Never accept work from a student that has not been proofread in advance of submission.

2. Have a friend or colleague proofread your work too. If they ask for clarification of anything you've written that's a clue that you need to re-state what you've written. Don't simply explain to them what you meant to say. Odds are that if they had difficulty, other readers will as well. So, instructors: Never accept work from a student that has not been proofread by at least one other person.

3. Finally, provide your students sample drafts of literature reviews of past students (simply ensure you have permission and that any way of identifying them is eliminated). Have your current students critique them. Use class time to work in small groups at first, then as a whole class to review revisions made. Categorize errors from simple typos, to ambiguously or awkwardly worded phrases or sentences, to leaps or disconnects in logical flow of ideas. All of which you'll find in the sample paragraph below:

> "Research has showed taht the impact of phonics instuction in early elementary literacy classrooms os quite remarkable. Findings from research suggests taht students who enter first gradde with little exposure to phonologicval awareness experience less success than peers that enter with a sound background (Citation #1). The latest trend in the educational world has placed an emphasis on Whole Language learning. While in no way should this method of instructiopn be discredoited, it is not as effectove as phonics instruction. The litearture on language acquisition is vast. This debate of phonics vs. whole language acquisition is one of the most heated in the world of literacy. Proponents of phonics instruction find it to be of value because of it's direct relation with the ability to read unfamiliar words with a greater level of ease. The purpose of thsi literaure review will be to . . . ."

I am certain you and your students will have a "field day" with this passage. My pint (I mean, "point") is that spending class time on such activities will save you, the instructor, and you the student, much time and frustration.

Part Five:

Thesis Overview— Chapter 3 of Thesis, Section 1: Research Design I

Focus Questions

1. What comes to mind when you think of the words "research design," especially in order to complete a thesis?

2. How do you plan on handling all the logistics of carrying out a thesis project?

3. What logistical challenges are you likely to confront in designing your thesis?

4. How do you plan on selecting your sample?

5. Recall our previous discussion of ethics and research. How do you plan to handle the selection of your sample ethically?

Module 1: Choosing a Research Design and Research Plan

Thus far, you have selected a topic or area of investigation, have clarified your purposes in undertaking this research venture, and undertaken a literature review (preliminary or otherwise) by scrutinizing extant research articles and other types of works. At your disposal are quantitative and qualitative approaches to research. Within each approach, different methods (e.g., surveys, group comparison studies, or case study analyses) may be selected. Selection of a particular method depends on a variety of factors such as the nature of the study, the kinds of questions asked, and the resources available. In this module, in order to assist you in getting started, I will discuss another aspect of **research design** that is of utmost importance.

Why is a design necessary? As an educator, you'll likely have to implement various programs, establish certain procedures, and/or institute specific practices. Evaluating the efficacy of these instructional concerns will be a challenging, yet urgent task. Any such evaluation requires attention to design as the foundation for setting up a research project. Without attention to design, it would be like building a home without a blueprint.

Before you can choose a sound research design, you'll need to know what designs are readily available and when and how they should be used. Then, you can select the appropriate design to suit your objectives.

This module will discuss eight frequently used **research designs** that may or may not be appropriate for educational research, depending upon the purpose. These research designs are generally suitable for quantitative approaches, although the single measurement design may be used for qualitative research. Note that the first four designs, although used, are not as powerful as the latter four. As you learn about these designs, think of ways you might easily implement some of them in your own research.

Research Designs

There is really only one inadequate or unacceptable research design and that is called the unassessed treatment design (Popham, 1972). Unfortunately, this approach is often used by practitioners in school settings. A program may be implemented or practice established without thorough and thoughtful consideration of its efficacy. The program or practice is continued or discarded without undertaking any sort of evaluative measure. Sound familiar?!

Unassessed Treatment Design $T \rightarrow$

An unassessed treatment design is characterized by an educator's inaction. The educational leader, for example, makes no effort whatsoever to assess whether the **treatment** (T) is effective. Popham (1972) characterizes this design as T = nothing; i.e., no **assessment** is conducted to determine the impact of a given treatment. I knew a supervisor who once introduced a new procedure requiring teachers to more closely monitor student progress. At the end of the semester, he "felt" that the program was a good idea. He decided to expand the program to the entire grade. When I asked him why he decided to take this action, he replied "It sounds good, doesn't it?!"

Popham (1972) describes the unassessed treatment design as follows:

> *In this approach, the instructional treatment developer simply implements a new instructional treatment or alters the existing instructional treatment without making any kind of systematic effort to measure whether the treatment is effective. Usually, of course, judgments have been made regarding whether the treatments are likely to prove worthwhile, but these evaluations are often made without any evidence whatsoever. A school administrator, for example, may introduce a new procedure requiring pupils to spend more time in the school library. At the end of the semester, he may "feel" it was a good idea and should be continued. Or a teacher may decide to alter the nature of his homework assignments so that students do half their assigned work during class sessions. Intuitively, he may decide that this new treatment worked out well, but he makes no attempt to measure the results produced by the innovation. (p. 140)*

Popham concludes by cautioning against such an approach. "It is preferable for educators to remain open-minded, postponing all decisions about treatment until such time as appropriate measurements can be collected" (p. 142).

Reflection

Can you think of a situation in which such an approach was taken? Explain.

A **treatment** (synonymous with intervention or independent variable) is any specific instructional practice, program, or procedure that is implemented by a researcher in order to investigate its impact on the behavior or achievement of an individual or a group. A treatment might include, for example, a reading series recently adopted by P.S. X, use of computers to assist problem solving, or a behavioral contract system implemented to positively influence behavior of three seventh graders. As a researcher, you want to understand the impact these treatments have on various outcomes (e.g., achievement or attitudes). The following research designs allow you to gather evidence to demonstrate the efficacy of the treatment. Below, seven research designs are discussed that might prove useful for educational research projects.

Single Measurement Design   *T → M*

The "T" stands for treatment and the "M" indicates the measurement, i.e., the impact that the treatment has on the sample.

Although single measurement designs do not necessarily consider factors that may have influenced a particular outcome, these designs are frequently employed in educational research projects because they are relatively easy to use. When single measurement designs are employed, the educator introduces a treatment and, at least, attempts to measure its impact. Often the measurements take the form of some sort of traditional test. Note also that single measurement designs are commonly employed in qualitative approaches (see Part Seven for three different qualitative approaches).

Let's say you were writing a case study to indicate the positive influence that behavior contracting had on the behavior of John, a fifth grader. A case study would involve detailed descriptions of John's behavior over time as a result of several observations. The researcher would provide anecdotal evidence demonstrating how, for instance, John's behavior has changed since the introduction of behavior contracting. Observations are recorded anecdotally in the sense that explicit descriptions of observable acts are recorded without interpretation. Note the following statements that are made anecdotally:

> Jerry got out of his seat at 9:15 a.m. and walked over to Susan and took her pen without permission.
>
> Juanita dropped her pen on the floor.
>
> There are 40 students in this class.

Note the difference between anecdotal annotations and inferences:

> He is a trouble maker.
>
> The information on this test may be too difficult for Susan.
>
> She is hyperactive.
>
> Fred behaves very nicely.
>
> She appears neurotic at times.

As you learn about case study research in Module 3 of Part Seven you will see that anecdotal records and interpretations of them are considered "measurements," albeit qualitative. Single measurement designs may be used in quantitative research, too.

One-Group Pretest/Posttest Design $M \rightarrow T \rightarrow M$

A second design commonly used is known as the **one-group pretest/post test design**. In this design, one group is selected and is pretested on some **variable**. A **treatment** is then introduced and its impact is assessed by a post test of some sort.

This research design is not as powerful as the following designs, yet it is commonly used by educational researchers because very often only one group is available for study. Growth from pretest to post test can be assessed. The serious weakness, of course, of the one-group pretest/post test design is that one can't be certain that an increase in achievement, for example, is a consequence of the treatment itself. No control is provided for intervening variables that might have influenced post-treatment findings. Suppose you find an increase from pretest to post test, how confident can you be that the gain was attributable solely to your treatment and not due to some other factor? Learners could have gained due to maturation or experiences not associated with the intervention or treatment. Too many other plausible explanations exist.

Some people maintain that pretest-posttest comparisons may be effectively used to ascertain achievement gains. Yet, most researchers caution against such a procedure because it may be possible for one group with very low initial scores to make large gains as compared to another group that starts off with a high average and may make smaller gains. Groups who score higher on pretests will not always make as significant improvements as groups who start with lower averages. This fact is known as the "test ceiling factor."

Nevertheless, despite this serious flaw, use of this design is feasible if two conditions are met: (a) you don't rely only on this design but rather you *triangulate* (see **triangulation**) to every extent possible; and (b) you analyze data using the **Sign Test**, which will be explained in detail in Module 3, Part Nine.

Static-Group Comparison Design $T \rightarrow M \rightarrow M$

This is a **research design** used in **quasi-experimental research** involving two groups in which only one group, the **experimental group**, receives a treatment. Although a post test is administered to each group (experimental and control), no pretest is usually administered. Individuals are not randomly assigned to groups.

Let's say you want to conduct a study with one class. This design is often used by educational researchers who have only one class in which a study can be conducted. You divide the class into two groups. No pretest is used to accomplish this division. Rather, you merely estimate two equivalent or comparable groups. Then, one treatment (e.g., use of stickers as positive reinforcement for math achievement) is administered to the group designated as experimental. The control group is intentionally not offered this form of positive reinforcement for their math work. At the end of a period of time (perhaps after a unit of instruction), you administer an **achievement test**. Achievement tests commonly used measures or **assessment** tools in educational research. As an aside, an achievement test is a kind of **standardized test** in which an individual's knowledge or proficiency in a given content area is assessed. The Stanford Achievement Test and the Iowa Test of Basic Skills are examples of standardized achievement tests. You would then use a statistical test (the **Mann-**

Whitney U-Test; see Module 4 in Part Nine) to determine whether or not there is a significant difference between the two groups.

Non-equivalent Control Group Design $M \rightarrow T1 \rightarrow M$
$M \rightarrow T2 \rightarrow M$

The next four designs are among the most powerful designs that can be used by educational researchers (Popham, 1972). They include classic group comparison studies that, as you recall, involve two contrasting groups: the experimental group might receive one treatment, while the control group receives another.

The **non-equivalent control group design** is useful for educational researchers. This design, frequently used in school research, involves administering one treatment (TI) to an experimental group and another treatment (T2) to a comparison (control) group.

Non-equivalent control group designs usually involve intact experimental and control groups. For instance, if you taught high school English, you might select two classes (say, your fourth and sixth periods) to be involved in a study. You selected these two classes because both groups are somewhat equivalent in achievement levels or comparable in relation to the **variable** under study. (By the way, the word "non-equivalent" in the title of this design refers to the different or non-equivalent treatments both groups receive). Since non-equivalent control group designs involve intact classes, this design is associated with **ex post facto research** that involves group comparisons with intact classes (some consider this design **quasi-experimental**).

Reflection

What factor or factors would lead some researchers to describe this design as either quasi-experimental or ex post facto?

Non-equivalent control group designs can be used with two separate classes with or without the same teacher. You may even divide one class into two equivalent groups using the **matched pairs** technique, in which each member of one group has a direct counterpart in the other group. Let's say you have a fifth grade class comprised of 28 students and you want to divide them into two equivalent or comparable groups to assess the impact of a particular instructional strategy. To divide the class using matched pairs, you would follow these steps:

1. Administer a test to the entire class. If the content area of your study involves mathematics, for example, you would administer a mathematics test.

2. Rank the students who completed the test according to the grade achieved on the test. In other words, rank each member of the class from highest score to lowest score. For example, your results, in part, may appear as follows:

Mohammid B.	97
Fred D.	96
Juan S.	96
Fran Y.	93
Anita G.	91
Kim W.	88
Wendy L.	83

and so on

3. You then take the first *pair* (Mohammid B. and Fred D.) and randomly assign them to the experimental and control groups as follows, for example:

Experimental Group	Control Group
Fred D.	Mohammid B.

4. Continue the same procedure for the next pair (Juan and Fran) and do so with all 28 students.

Using matched pairs ensures that you now have two comparable groups, at least in terms of mathematics achievement. You are then ready to conduct your study using, for instance, a non-equivalent control group design.

Non-equivalent control group designs can only work when you begin the study with comparable groups. **Analysis of covariance (ANCOVA)** a statistical technique used in group comparison research when equivalence between the groups (usually only two in educational research) cannot be ascertained. To compute an analysis of covariance, you would use a computer program such as **STATPAK** (see Module 6 in Part Nine). Generally, the non-equivalent control group design is used when randomization is impossible, but groups are essentially comparable.

The next two designs are similar to the previous design except for the fact that randomization is possible. Randomization ensures equivalence between groups; i.e., whenever you randomize you can be certain that both groups are comparable. However, randomization is not easily used within classes because moving pupils from one classroom to another for research purposes may not be feasible or practical.

When could randomization be used? You may be able to randomly distribute students into classes before the start of the school year during reorganization.

Pretest/Posttest Control Group Design   EXPTL   RM → T1 → M
CONTRL   RM → T2 → M

The pretest/posttest control group design is a powerful design that incorporates randomization or **sampling**. The "R" indicates that the two groups have been formed by randomization procedures. As before, the "M" refers to the measurements taken prior to and after the introduction of the treatments (TI and T2).

Since randomization ensures equivalence between groups, the pretest/post test control group design allows you to draw conclusions about the effectiveness of the treatment. Statistically higher post test scores of the experimental group as compared to the control group would indicate that, for example, the special use of a new mathematics series with the experimental group contributed to the higher achievement scores.

A pretest is not necessary to establish a **baseline** so that a comparison can be made when the posttest is given. Pretest to post test gains are not made to ascertain the impact of a given treatment. Statistical work on posttest scores is all that has to be done once group equivalence is assured (see Part Nine).

As stated earlier, randomization ensures comparability or equivalence between groups. Therefore, if randomization is employed, why give a pretest? One might respond that a pretest can confirm equivalence. But such an assertion is really unnecessary because it is readily acknowledged that randomization assures equivalence. Sometimes, however, a pretest may yield some important information about content validity. Sometimes a pretest might be a reactive measure that might produce a change in the subject's behavior. For instance, a pretest that is given orally may be reactive in the sense that respondents or subjects may obtain clues about possible answers from voice inflections of the tester. If pretests appear to be reactive, then an alternate design such as the post test only control group design should be employed.

Pretest Only Control Group Design   RT1 → M
RT2 → M

This design should be used when the pretest may be a reactive measure; i.e., participants completing a test or a survey may receive clues from the pretest that may influence a positive score on the posttest. If a pretest is potentially reactive, don't use it. Since randomization is employed, there is no need to worry about equivalence between groups. This design allows you "to make defensible judgments about the value of a given treatment" (Popham, 1972, p. 149).

Interrupted Time Series Design   M1 → M2 → M3 T M4 → M5 → M6

This next design is somewhat different from the previous designs. The **interrupted time series design** is also commonly known as the **single-subject design**. In this design, one group is repeatedly pretested (usually with the same test), exposed to a treatment, and then repeatedly post tested at different times. In other words, in this design, a series of measurements is taken both before and after the introduction of the **treatment**. Measurements ("M") may be taken from existing archival data such as attendance records, standardized test scores, disciplinary records, and **school profiles**.

Interrupted time series designs usually involve *group* analyses with respect to a given **variable,** such as studying academic progress over time. When progress over time is assessed for *individuals,* another design is used. A **single-subject research design** allows a researcher to investigate one or just a few individuals with respect to a given variable (e.g., changes in behavior). Subjects are exposed to a treatment and then multiple measurements are taken over a period of time. The objective of this sort of research is to determine whether or not the treatment had any effect on the behavior of the subject(s).

Single-subject research design is a powerful method of studying the effectiveness of an intervention or treatment on a single subject or a small group. Measurements are repeatedly made until stability is established (a **baseline**), after which treatment is introduced and an appropriate number of measurements are made; the treatment phase is followed by a second baseline, which is followed by a second treatment phase.

Single-subject research design is popular for educational researchers because it is very useful to monitor and assess a particular treatment on individual students. This design is advantageous because results are easy to interpret, usually by visual inspection of the charted data points. Statistical analysis is also unnecessary.

A-B; A-B-A; or A-B-A-B research designs are *types* of single-subject designs. Before we discuss A-B, A-B-A, and A-B-A-B designs, two basic terms must be explained.

1. **Baseline** condition (Condition A)—refers to information collected on a specific *target behavior* before an intervention strategy is employed (see Figure 5.1). The purpose of establishing baseline data is to provide a description of the target behavior as it naturally occurs without treatment. The baseline serves as the basis of comparison for assessing the impact of a treatment. Taking a number of baseline measurements to establish a pattern of behavior is known as baseline stability. For instance, observing Sarah for a period of three days in a row for 45 minutes each time and noting the number of times she gets out of her seat without permission would establish baseline stability.

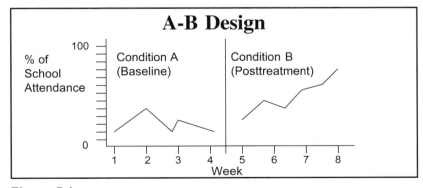

Figure 5.1.

2. **Treatment** (or **Intervention**) condition (Condition B)—during this phase, the treatment is introduced while **data collection** continues.

A word about *target behaviors:* Directly observing any subject in a school setting involves identifying a target behavior. The target behavior must be defined in such a way as to allow the observer to objectively and independently note and measure each behavior. Target behaviors must be observable and measurable. Independent observers must be able to see the behavior occurring and be able to quantify the behaviors by noting, for instance, the frequency and duration of each behavior. For example, observing Michael raising his hand in class, for any reason, is a target behavior because the observer can see the behavior occurring and is able to note the number of times Michael raises his hand in, say, a 45-minute period. An example of a nonobservable target behavior might be: Joshua will be cooperative during group work. The difficulty here, of course, is with the word "cooperative." What does "cooperative" mean? What does it mean to you? Can two independent observers agree that a particular student is being cooperative?

Reflection

Place a check next to the target behavior that can be observed and measured by two independent observers without defining the behavior prior to observation:

1. Johnny is acting out in class.

2. Natasha says "thank you" during the lesson.

3. Felicia is disruptive during art class.

4. Billy completes his class assignments.

5. Sally is behaving well.

6. Kisha raises her hand to ask or answer a question.

Numbers 2 and 6 are target behaviors that can easily be observed. The other choices require observers to define what they consider to be "acting out," "disruptive," "completes his assignments," and "is behaving well." Undertaking single-subject research design requires observers to clarify behaviors in advance.

A word about recording target behaviors: The most common way of recording data is by using frequency charts (checklists). These charts allow an observer to note the frequency of each target behavior. Interval recording is sometimes used to divide the observation period into equal intervals of smaller time periods (see Figure 5.2). Observers can then note whether the target behavior occurred (+) or had not occurred (-), during each interval. Note that the frequencies are not recorded, just the fact that the target behavior was noted during a specified period of time.

Frequency Recording Observation Form

Student's Name: _____

Environment: _____

Target Behavior: _____

Start Time: _____

Observer: _____

Date: _____

5-minute observation period: 30-second intervals

NAME		1	2	3	4	5
Maria						
Ronald						
Steve						

Key: + is marked for each occurrence of target behavior; – is marked if target behavior did not occur.

Figure 5.2.

A word about accuracy in recording behaviors: Here are some factors to consider that may potentially affect your **data collection** during **baseline** and **treatment** periods:

1. *reactivity*—The student observed realizes you are counting or noting the number of times, for example, she is talking to a neighbor. Reactivity can be minimized by not staring at the student as observations are made.

2. *observer drift*—This occurs when an observer daydreams or when an observer is unclear as to when a target behavior is occurring. As alluded to earlier, operationally defining (see **operational definitions**) the target behavior is the best method to minimize observer drift. For instance, how might you operationalize "getting out of one's seat"? Answer: when his buttocks are approximately 12 inches from his chair.

3. *recording procedures*—Make certain that charts for recording data are available at the time of the observation.

4. *location of observer*—The best place to observe is usually from the back of the room, as long as you have an unobstructed view of the class.

5. *observer expectations*—Biased observations or conclusions are minimized when target behaviors are clearly defined in advance.

6. *lack of practice*—That the observer should practice recording behaviors prior to actual study is sound advice.

7. **reliability**—**Interrater reliability** is achieved when there is a high percent of agreement between two or more observers.

Let's say two individuals are watching the number of times Jose leaves his seat without permission and the following data are collected by each observer:

Observer A-frequency = 5; Observer B-frequency = 10

Reliability could then be calculated by dividing 5\10 = 0.5 x 100 = 50%. You should strive for at least a 70% reliability factor.

A-B

The first type of single-subject design is known as A-B. Note Condition A (the baseline condition) and Condition B (the intervention condition). Don't forget, with single-subject research designs you are studying individuals, not groups of individuals.

The line in the center of Figure 5.1 indicates that the treatment has been introduced. You'll notice that the **baseline** was kept over a four-week period to establish stability before the introduction of the **treatment**. Measurements continue after the treatment is introduced to note any changes in attendance. From perusing the figure you may reasonably conclude that the treatment, indeed, had a positive effect on school attendance.

Can you draw a chart showing no change after the treatment is introduced? Can you think of a situation in which you might employ a single-subject research design? *Hint:* Think of a situation in which you want to monitor student behavior of some sort. Choose some target behavior; i.e., what exactly you are going to observe. Be very specific about target behaviors (e.g., number of times Howie gets out of his seat or the number of times Juan praises a fellow student in his cooperative group). Once a target behavior has been specified, start collecting **baseline** data during a specified period of time. Then introduce the **treatment** and keep collecting data. Record your data in chart or graph form.

One of the potential problems with an **A-B** design is how to determine that the change after the treatment was definitely due to the treatment and not due, perhaps, to some intervening **variable** or outside influence. That's why some researchers prefer a second type of single-subject design known as **A-B-A**.

A-B-A

This design is similar to the first design, except that you withdraw the **intervention** and then maintain **baseline** data. For example, as an educational leader you might want to introduce a program to increase attendance among students identified as at-risk of dropping out of high school. At a national convention you learn about a marvelous intervention strategy. You decide to implement this program (after, of course, becoming more familiarized with the program). How do you proceed? First, keep baseline data (Condition A) on each student's attendance records for a period of, say, four weeks to establish baseline stability. Then, introduce the treatment for a similar period of four weeks. You'll note, for example, that attendance rates dramatically increase. Before you conclude that the program is successful, what would you do? Right, withdraw the treatment and monitor student attendance rates by keeping additional baseline rates for four weeks. You might find a drop in attendance, but the attendance rates are better than they were prior to the introduction of the treatment.

An **A-B-A** design allows you to more confidently attribute the change in behavior to the treatment, as opposed to some extraneous factor or chance factor. Can you draw a chart or graph that illustrates the experiment described above?

A-B-A-B

The third type of single-subject research design is known as A-B-A-B. Again, this would be similar to the previous design, but would reintroduce the treatment. This design adds further credibility to your treatment. Can you explain why? Can you draw a graph illustrating this design? Can you think of a reason why an A-B-A-B design should not be used? *Hint:* Consider the ethics of removing a successful treatment.

A variation of the designs above is known as the Alternating Treatment Design (A-B-C-A-D-A) and is characterized by the introduction of three separate treatments (B, C, and D).

1. Starts off the same way as **A-B,** with B representing the use of positive reinforcement through verbal praise.

2. Then the first of two other treatments are introduced. The first treatment (B) is removed and a new treatment designated as C is introduced (e.g., positive reinforcement using only tokens, no praise) followed by A, which is a phase in which you record baseline data.

3. Then treatment C is withdrawn, and a new treatment (D) is introduced (e.g., positive reinforcement offered by sending daily letters home), followed by a phase in which you continue to record baseline data, A.

This design can be used when you want to assess the impact of various treatments before you select one as your primary choice.

Another major category of single-subject designs is known as Multiple-Baseline Designs. These designs are modifications of single-subject designs. With the use of multiple-baseline designs you can:

1. collect data on more than 1 subject, and/or

2. collect data on more than 1 behavior, and/or

3. collect data on more than 1 situation.

Multiple baselines are recorded because different subjects, behaviors, and situations are observed *Multiple-Baseline Across Subjects Design* involves utilizing one of the three single-subjects designs (A-B, A-B-A, or A-B-A-B) on two or more different subjects. For example, you may want to observe three of your students in terms of their frequency of violent behavior (i.e., your target behavior might be the number of times Steve, Maria, and Ronald hit someone in the classroom). Baseline data for Steve might be graphed as shown in Figure 5.3. Completing similar graphs for Maria and Ronald will allow for comparisons to be made regarding the frequencies of hitting, pretreatment, and post-treatment, for all three students.

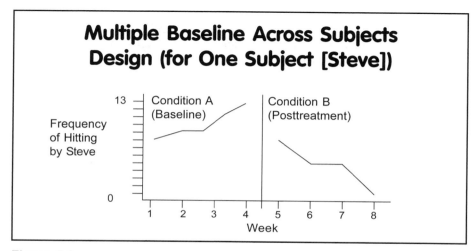

Figure 5.3.

What conclusion might you draw from Figure 5.3?

Multiple-Baseline across Behaviors Design involves utilizing one of the three single-subjects designs (A-B, A-B-A, or A-B-A-B) on one subject while observing two or more different behaviors. For example, you may chart the frequencies of hitting, yelling, and kicking for a given student or among three students. Comparisons, as before, can be easily made.

Multiple-Baselines Across Situations Design involves utilizing one of the three single-subjects designs (A-B, A-B-A, or A-B-A-B) in two or more different settings for one or more subjects. For example, you may chart the behavior of a given student or among three students in different settings (i.e., math class, cafeteria during lunch, and in the gymnasium). Comparisons, as before, can be easily made.

You are urged to consult Zirpoli and Melloy (1996) for an excellent overview of single-subject designs and other relevant information.

Table 5.1 contains a summary of the aforementioned research designs.

Table 5.1. Summary of Research Designs

Design and Symbol	
Unassessed Treatment	T →
Single Measurement	T → M
One-Group Pretest and Posttest	M → T → M
Static-Group Comparison	T → M
	→ M
Nonequivalent Control Group	M → T1 → M
	M → T2 → M
Pretest and Posttest Control Group	R M → T1 → M
	R M → T2 → M
Posttest-Only Control Group	R T1 → M
	R T2 → M
Interrupted Time Series	M1 → M2 → M3 T M4 → M5 → M6
Single Subject	__ A-B
	__ A-B-A
	__ A-B-A-B
	__ Multiple Baselines

Reflection

Pair and share with a colleague and describe each of these aforementioned designs, making certain to provide an example for each.

Getting Started: The Overall Research Plan

A **research design** is an overall plan for conducting educational research. An educational researcher begins by *clarifying the purposes* for undertaking a study and then *plans the logistics* or administrative items that are necessary to conduct a successful project. Selecting research *approaches* and *methods* are then considered. Planning and carefully considering an appropriate *design* are also essential elements in any research project.

In order to get started by choosing a sound research design, five steps should be followed:

1. clarify the purposes of your research;

2. attend to administrative and logistical aspects of your study;

3. decide on a quantitative and/or qualitative *approach;*

4. select a *method* and *type* of research; and

5. choose a *design* that is appropriate for the area of investigation.

Clarifying purposes

The first step you need to consider is the purpose for undertaking educational research. Four sets of questions should be initially addressed:

1. What is the purpose of my study or research project?

2. What do I want to accomplish? or What are my objectives?

3. Why is such a study important? Why do I want to spend time doing this?

4. How will information gleaned from my study help improve, for instance, the overall instructional program?

Here are some additional questions to ponder:

Why do I want to conduct an educational research study?

What are the primary concerns about my current instructional program?

What areas (instructional, curricular, administrative, social, etc.) need improvement?

How do I know that my instructional program is working to promote student achievement?

What is the impact of the new reading series on pupil achievement?

Are the new computers and multi-media technologies being effectively used?

Are parents adequately involved in instructional/curricular planning activities?

What are student attitudes toward the new extracurricular after-school program?

Are teachers adequately prepared to implement the new math series?

Does the school climate foster a sense of collegiality?

How might I better assist Sharon with her reading difficulties?

Are the needs of students, parents, and teachers met?

Are school goals and objectives continually evaluated?

How might multiple intelligences theory help my students achieve more?

How productive are the semi-annual parent/teacher conferences?

Is portfolio assessment meeting its intended objectives in grades K-3 or in my class?

What alternatives are there to traditional grading practices?

These are only some of the questions you might consider *before* undertaking any study or research project. Before you begin, you must clarify your purposes for conducting the study by focusing on what needs are to be addressed in your school, what you hope to accomplish, and why this project is so important.

Reflection

Think about and answer these questions:

1. Why do I want to undertake this educational research project? What do I want to investigate? What do I hope to learn?

   _____

   _____

   _____

2. What preliminary information should I gather to help me get started?

   _____

   _____

3. What question or questions should I ponder?

   _____

   _____

4. Who will be involved in this research project?

_____

_____

5. What administrative or logistical concerns should I attend to?

_____

_____

6. How will data be collected, analyzed, and reported?

_____

_____

7. What will I do with the results?

_____

_____

8. Will I incorporate quantitative and/or qualitative approaches?

_____

You are now ready to select an appropriate research design matched to your particular needs and concerns. Which designs make the most sense? Jot some notes below:

_____

_____

_____

Logistics

You have now identified the overarching purpose of your study including why and how the study will further improve your school/class/position and what goals and objectives you want to accomplish. You also know that data should be gathered from a variety of sources. You will try to utilize, when sensible, both qualitative *and* quantitative measures, including experimental and non-experimental types of research, including a variety of data gathering instruments (see Part Eight). Before we consider the heart or essence of **research design** (deciding which specific form of research to use), we need to consider some logistical matters first:

who will be involved in this study?;

who will collect data?;

how long will it take?; and

what will it cost in terms of time and resources (feasibility)?

Additional concerns include knowing how data are to be collected, analyzed, and reported, by whom, and what will be done with the results.

In summary, then, the first step in choosing a sound **research design** is to develop an overall plan for your study so that you are clear about your purposes, you understand the value of this undertaking, and you have attended to some logistics. Therefore, the following questions will serve as a guide in developing any research plan:

What research study will I undertake?

Why am I conducting this study?

How will this study help my school/class/position improve?

What are my goals and objectives?

Who will be involved in this study?

What other logistical concerns should I prepare for?

How will data be collected?

How will data be analyzed?

How will data be reported?

What will I do with the results?

Answers to these questions will enable you to start framing and preparing a plan. You need *not* answer all of the questions above definitively. Just begin thinking about them as you continue to plan the project.

The Plan

Now that you have clarified the purposes for conducting an educational research project and attended to various logistical concerns, a plan that specifies a **research design** must be articulated. Selection of a research design is really quite simple. The **design** used depends on the *question*(s) you ask and then selecting the appropriate research *methods* that can answer the questions you posed.

Preliminary steps in choosing a research design are:

1. specifying **research questions** and/or hypotheses;

2. selecting an appropriate **sample**; and

3. assigning individuals to **treatments.**

Specifying research questions and/or hypotheses will guide your study. Selecting an appropriate **sample** and assigning individuals or groups of individuals to various **treatments** are necessary.

What questions will guide your research?

Who will participate in your study?

How will they be selected?

Which group will be exposed to the treatment?

Who will you focus on for the case study?

Answering these questions is a prerequisite for selecting a suitable **research design.** Refer to Glossary for explanations of **sample, sampling, treatment, research questions,** and **hypotheses.**

Suggestions for Getting Started

Below are several key suggestions for helping you get started on an educational research project:

- Review and follow the 5 steps:

    1. clarify the purposes of your research;

    2. attend to administrative and logistical aspects of your study;

    3. decide on a quantitative and/or qualitative *approach;*

    4. select a *method* and *type* of research; and

    5. choose a *design* that is appropriate for the area of investigation.

- Think through the process before you begin. When asked to explain his high percentage of successful free throws from the line, basketball legend Michael Jordan said that before approaching the line he imagines himself holding the ball, aiming, and shooting. "I see the ball dropping into the hoop." We can learn from Jordan's approach by envisioning what our project will "look like down the road." Develop a vision of your project. Then, follow the next suggestion.

- Articulate your vision of educational research to a colleague. Talking about your plans to someone else will help clarify your project. New ideas will naturally arise or revising existing ones might be suggested.

- Collaborate with a colleague on a project. Often it is easier to begin any project by teaming with someone. The other person, if chosen correctly, will serve to spur you on towards success. Collaboration is also exciting and fun.

- Avoid those inevitable road blocks (stumbling blocks). Set backs will naturally occur. More often than not, these obstacles are beyond your control. As long as you keep your end goal in mind, you will be able to avoid nuisances that might serve to thwart your project.

Module 1 Review

In this Module you learned various research designs and to develop a research plan.

Self-Test Check

Exercises

1. INTERRUPTED TIME SERIES DESIGN
   Write in the space provided the letter or letters of the graph lines that support the conclusion that improvement was due to the treatment.

   _____ In this hypothetical research situation, we have measured pupil performance on equivalent problem-solving tests every 2 months during the year, and we have introduced a 3-week teaching unit (i.e., the treatment) on problem-solving problems during the middle of the year.

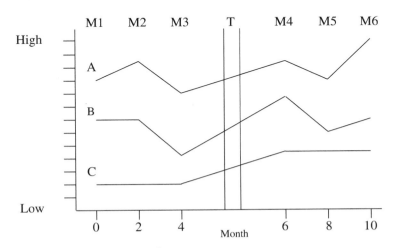

Answer: C. Only to group C can we attribute the increase to the treatment. Groups A and B reveal fluctuating pre- and posttreatment performance records, thus indicating that the same stimuli causing the pretreatment fluctuations could also have caused the posttreatment fluctuations.

---

2. IDENTIFYING TYPE OF DESIGN

Write the name of the design employed in this example in the space provided.

A school superintendent introduces a new music appreciation program throughout her school district that depends heavily upon tape recordings of classical masterworks. Although rather costly, the new program is considered a success by the superintendent and her staff at the end of the year.

DESIGN EMPLOYED:

_____

_____

Answer: Unassessed treatment (because no attempt is made to investigate the program)

3. IDENTIFYING TYPE OF DESIGN

Write the name of the design employed in this example.

A 10th-grade biology teacher institutes a new approach to the teaching of one-celled animal life based on a series of 7-minute single-concept films. Prior to starting the new unit, she develops a test covering the material and administers it to her class before and after the unit, noting with satisfaction a dramatic improvement by her pupils on the test.

DESIGN EMPLOYED:

_____

_____

Answer: one-group pretest and posttest

4. IDENTIFYING TYPE OF DESIGN

Write the name of the design employed in this example.

A researcher uses a table of random numbers to subdivide 15 junior high school classes into three groups of five classes each (30 pupils per class), as follows: Treatment A, Treatment B, and Control. The treatments are administered during the first 4 months of the school year, and at mid-semester a posttest is given to all of the 450 pupils involved.

DESIGN EMPLOYED:

_____

_____

Answer: posttest only

5. IDENTIFYING TYPE OF DESIGN

Write the name of the design employed in this example.

A school principal has received a federal grant to institute a new mathematics enrichment program. Using school records, he computes the average mathematics achievement score on a nationally standardized examination for his 5th-, 9th-, and 12th-grade pupils during each of the preceding 3 years. He plans to have the same tests administered for the 2 years following the institution of the new program. He wishes to compare the relative positions of the three classes during the 5-year period.

DESIGN EMPLOYED:

_____

_____

Answer: interrupted time series

6. SELECTING THE APPROPRIATE DESIGN

Select the design best suited to the following research problem and write its name in the space provided.

A school researcher hopes to test the merits of a new series of third-grade reading booklets. The booklets, commercially produced, are sold with a test that covers the skills ostensibly developed by learners during the 4-week period when the booklets are to be used. The researcher suspects that the pretest may structure the thinking of the pupils if it is administered to them prior to their exposure to the booklets. Twenty third-grade teachers have indicated a willingness to have their classes involved in the research as members of either the experimental or control groups.

BEST DESIGN:

_____

_____

Answer: posttest only (because of possibility for randomization and the potentially reactive nature of pretest)

7. SELECTING THE APPROPRIATE DESIGN

Select the design best suited to the following research problem and write its name.

A high school government teacher wishes to conduct a study in his class of the difference that weekly issues of current events newspapers will make in his pupils' scores on a current events test. He realizes that pupils will learn about current events outside school, so he is particularly interested in their pretest to posttest growth. He has a series of literature selections that he can give to students in the class who are not assigned to read the current events newspapers.

BEST DESIGN:

_____

_____

Answer: posttest only (because of possibility for randomization and the potentially reactive nature of pretest)

8. SELECTING THE APPROPRIATE DESIGN

Select the design best suited to the following research problem and write its name.

A school counselor wishes to test the influence on students' attitudes toward narcotics of a particular commercial film dealing obliquely with the use of narcotics. He devises a self-report questionnaire but is afraid if pupils complete the questionnaire prior to viewing the film, they will become sensitized to the narcotics issue. Random assignment of pupils is possible.

BEST DESIGN:

_____

_____

Answer: posttest only (because of the reactive nature of questionnaire)

9. SELECTING THE APPROPRIATE DESIGN

Select the design best suited to the following research problem and write its name in the space provided.

Faced with the necessity for evaluating a new set of general science kits, members of a small high school science department decide that they cannot randomly assign pupils among their first- semester general science classes because there would be conflicts. They have, however, administered science aptitude tests and have found that their four classes are remarkably similar. They hope to use the science kits with two complete classes, since two teachers have indicated unwillingness to use the kits with only a portion of their class.

BEST DESIGN:

_____

_____

Answer: nonequivalent control group design (with previously administered aptitude test at pretest)

10. SELECTING THE APPROPRIATE DESIGN

Select the design best suited to the following research problem and write its name.

Ms. Barbara Lewis, a school principal, wishes to assess the interest-building contribution of a school club program instituted 4 years ago. She decides to use daily attendance rates as an index of pupils' interest in school. She discovers that such data has been accumulated (in the school's archives) for every year since the club was inaugurated, as well as for the 10 years before it was initiated.

BEST DESIGN:

_____

_____

Answer: interrupted time series

11. Which statement is not true?
    a. Nonequivalent designs are used when randomization is not possible and groups are comparable.
    b. Posttest control group designs are used when randomization is possible.
    c. Interrupted time series designs are used when randomization is impossible or in a case in which two parallel treatments are not readily available.
    d. The purpose of matched pairs is to develop an accurate testing instrument.

    Answer: d

12. Divide into groups of three and consider that you are all principals who are evaluating some sort of program in your school. How could you use the following quantitative and qualitative approaches?
    a. observations
    b. surveys
    c. group comparison research
    d. ethnography

    Answers will vary

13. Identify the correct design:
    a. As a high school principal, I introduced a schoolwide restructuring program known as Housing. The high school was in desperate need to restructure because of high drop-out rates and low SAT scores. The ninth grade has completed its first year in the Housing program. The program appears successful, so I plan on including grade 10 next year.
    b. A supervisor of curriculum wanted to assess a new fourth-grade reading series used in two elementary schools in the district. Each school has three fourth-grade classes with comparable standardized reading test scores. She introduces the new reading series to one school in September, while the other school is monitored as they use the traditional reading series. Scores on the standardized reading test are compared at the end of May.
    c. An assistant principal wants to see the impact of a new in-school suspension program on the attendance record of selected students at-risk. She reviews attendance records for 3 years prior to the implementation of the in-school suspension program. She will compare these records to the attendance records for 3 years after the program starts.

    Answers: a) unassessed; b) nonequivalent control group design; c) time series

14. Write three realistic cases describing the use of any three adequate research designs. Cases should be drawn from either personal experience or an experience any supervisor or lead-teacher might encounter. Be specific, realistic, and practical.

    _____

    _____

    _____

    Answers will vary

15. MATCH

X		Y

____ A. unassessed treatment design

____ B. single measurement design

____ C. one-group pretest and posttest design

____ D. nonequivalent control group design

____ E. pretest and posttest control group design

____ F. posttest-only control group design

____ G. interrupted time series design

a. R T1 → M
    R T2 → M

b. M → T → M
    M → T1 → M

c. T →

d. M1 → M2 → M3 T
    M4 → M5 → M6

e. T → M

f. RM → T1 → M
    RM → T2 → M

g. M → T → M

Answers: A(c), B(e), C(g), D(b), E(f), F(a), G(d)

Study Questions

Consider these 20 questions as critical to a successful research project. You may not be ready to answer all of them in detail right now, but refer to them as you proceed.

1. What is my research problem or topic? (e.g., teacher expectations)

2. What variables will I examine? (e.g., teacher expectations and student participation)

3. What does the literature report about my topic and variables I've come up with given my preliminary review of the literature?

4. What will be my sample? (e.g., special education elementary school students)

5. What method or type of research seems most appropriate given my access to a particular sample?

    A. Descriptive research (via surveys, questionnaires, interviews, etc.)

    B. Correlational research (relationship between two or more variables)

    C. Experimental research (group comparison with randomization of individuals)

    D. Quasi-experimental research (group comparison with randomization of intact groups)

    E.   Ex post facto research (group comparison with groups already formed in respect to a particular independent variable e.g., pre-school attendance)

    F.   Historical research

    G.   Case study research

    H.   Ethnographic research

    I.   Mixed methodology (quantitative and qualitative approaches—be specific, which ones?)

6. How will I select my sample? (e.g., randomization, convenience, purposeful, other)

7. What ethical issues may come into play in my study?

8. What is a tentative title for my study given my answers to the questions above? (E.g., Impact of Teacher Expectations on Student Participation in an Elementary Special Education Classroom)

9. What are my research questions? (e.g., What impact do teacher expectations have on student participation?; What are students' perceived attitudes or feelings towards teacher expectations"; How might these attitudes or feelings affect their participation?; How might student participation be more effectively increased?)

10. What is my hypothesis (or hypotheses)? (e.g., High teacher expectations will significantly increase student participation)

11. Why is this study important?

12. What terms must I define (conceptually and operationally)?

13. How will I define these terms?

14. Have I conducted an extensive literature review?

15. What instruments must I develop to conduct my study? (e.g., questionnaires, teacher-made tests, interview protocols, etc.)

16. Have I attended to the validity and reliability of my instruments?

17. What threats may affect my study?

18. What are possible limitations of my research study?

19. How might I analyze my data (quantitatively, qualitatively, or both)?

20. How will I attend to all logistical concerns in carry out my study?

Activity

    1. Find a colleague and compare answers to the section above.

Part Six:

Thesis Overview—Chapter 3 of Thesis, Section 2: Research Design 2—Quantitative Approaches

Focus Questions

1. What are different types of quantitative approaches?

2. What are the advantages of using a quantitative approach to educational research?

3. What is the difference between a survey and a questionnaire?

4. How might you incorporate a quantitative approach in your project?

5. Can you think of a research project that would not call for a quantitative approach?

Module 1: Descriptive Research

Descriptive research is one of three methods of research that assumes a quantitative approach in studying a given educational issue or problem. Survey and observational reports are *types* of descriptive research. Descriptive research may use statistics or numbers (usually percentages) to describe data.

Although descriptive research is treated as a quantitative method, survey and observational reports can, in fact, be reported qualitatively if nonnumerical findings are reported. Some authorities in the field of educational research consider descriptive research as nonexperimental and can be either quantitative or qualitative. Yet, in educational research surveys and observations are usually reported quantitatively.

Let's say you distributed a questionnaire to teachers in your district and collected data about their attitudes towards bilingual education. To report your findings, you decide to note what percentages of teachers in various categories were favorably or unfavorably disposed to bilingual education. You report, in part for example, that 56% of elementary school teachers, as a group, are in favor of bilingual education as compared to 34% and 23% of middle school and high school teachers, respectively. This is an example of descriptive research because you describe findings of your study numerically.

Descriptive research may utilize simple mathematical notations such as percentages or more complicated statistical formulations (see Part Nine).

Two types of descriptive research can be employed by educational researchers: survey and observational.

Surveys

Survey can be defined as a general term for any **instrument** used to assess attitudes or views of respondents. Discussion of surveys in this section will highlight the most common type of survey used in educational research: **questionnaires.** Questionnaires are types of surveys that are distributed to a **sample** to ascertain attitudes about a particular issue or concern. Although questionnaires can, in fact, be assessed qualitatively, discussion of questionnaires has been included in this section because results are most often reported numerically.

Two other types of surveys, interviews and focus groups, whose results are reported verbally, will be discussed in the qualitative section.

Questionnaires are very useful tools to collect data about almost any given topic. Because they are relatively easy to construct and analyze, questionnaires are very popular in research projects. Questionnaires, especially anonymously collected, provide keen insights that might otherwise be overlooked or unrealized.

Questionnaires can be used to describe how, for instance, teachers in your school feel about the new literature-based reading program recently adopted. Questionnaires are one of the most common types of **data collection instruments** (or data sources) used in research projects.

Questionnaires, as a descriptive research methodology and as a data collection instrument, will be explained fully in Module 1 in Part Eight.

Reflection

Under what circumstances do you think you might utilize a questionnaire?

Observations

Survey and observational research can really be considered *both* quantitative and qualitative in approach. The determining factor that categorizes one or the other is the way the data are reported. I have included survey and observational research as quantitative approaches because in educational research projects they are often reported numerically. On the other hand, **ethnography,** as a qualitative form of observational research, uses verbal or non-numerical ways of reporting data.

Observational research, in this context, refers to studies that measure behavior of an individual or group of individuals by direct observation and report these observations in some numerical way.

Two common forms of observations are nonsystematic and systematic. When you, for instance, nonsystematically observe a classroom you may simply walk into a classroom unannounced and watch classroom interaction and may even begin taking notes on interactions observed. Nonsystematic observations are usually anecdotal and subjective. Systematic observation refers to a formal process of collecting data that is more scientific than nonsystematic observations in that data are collected with the aid of predetermined observation forms, audiovisual equipment, or some other observation instrument. Systematic observations are generally more accurate and desirable when conducting educational research.

An example of observational research conducted systematically in educational research projects is as follows:

You and a colleague observe three students in a classroom. These students have been identified as seriously disruptive. Both of you may simultaneously observe these students and record the number of instances of misbehavior within a predetermined period of time. Both observers must, of course, agree on what is considered "serious misbehavior." In advance of the observation they agree that serious misbehavior will be defined as any behavior that includes striking someone else in the class with one's body or any other object as well as verbal and nonverbal disruptions that include cursing, incessant calling out without permission, getting out of one's seat repeatedly, and so on.

During an observational research session both supervisors will record, for example, occurrences of misbehavior (i.e., target behavior) at various intervals or designated times using the Interval Recording Observation Form (see Figure 6.1)

Interval Recording Observation Form

Student's Name: _____

Environment: _____

Target Behavior: _____

Start Time: _____

Observer: _____

Date: _____

10-minute observation period: 30-second intervals

9:00		9:01		9:02		9:03		9:04		9:05		9:06		9:07		9:08		9:09	
1	2	3	4	5	6	7	8	9	10	11	12	13	14	15	16	17	18	19	20

Key: + is marked for each occurrence of target behavior; – is marked if target behavior did not occur.

Figure 6.1.

Although **validity** is maintained by predefining "serious misbehavior," **reliability** is determined through interrater reliability measures (or percentages of agreements between observers) (see **reliability** in Glossary).

Any numerical recording of data collected through direct observation is considered observational research. Several noteworthy works describe in detail various ways or methods of collecting data through observational research. Consult, for example, Acheson and Gall, 1997; Glickman, Gordon, and Ross-Gordon, 1998; Moore, 1995; and Willerman, McNeely, and Koffman, 1991. This latter work provides detailed explanations of how to use seating charts, verbal flow charts, nonverbal communication patterns, and anecdotal recordings using audio- and videotapes. I usually require my students to read portions of their excellent book.

Module 1 Review

In this Module you learned some basic information about descriptive research.

Self-Test Check

1. A study entitled "pupil attitude toward inclusion" would most likely be
   a. historical.
   b. descriptive.
   c. experimental.
   d. correlational.

2. You are an Assistant Principal in an elementary school and you want to raise student attendance rates in grade 5 by fostering school spirit. You initiate a program that fosters school spirit by involving students in school-wide projects, elections, and competitive academic contests. Which of the following methods of data collection would most accurately allow you to conclude that, indeed, school spirit affects higher rates of student attendance?
   a. descriptive data that includes pretest/posttest attendance rates
   b. attitudinal surveys distributed to students
   c. informal observations
   d. analysis of standardized test scores

Answers: 1) b; 2) b

Study Questions

1. How might you include descriptive research methods in your project?
2. Can you think of any study that in some way doesn't "describe" a phenomenon?
3. What kinds of surveys might you employ?
4. What are some different ways to observe an individual or situation?
5. What are the chief characteristics of descriptive research?

Activity

1. Locate a research article that incorporates this method and describe the kinds of surveys used.

Module 2: Correlation Research

Another possible *method* of research is known as correlational research (see **correlation** in the Glossary). Correlational research is used to explore the degree of relationship between **variables**, usually but not exclusively two. For example, as an educator you might be interested in correlating students' scores on math and science tests. You might **hypothesize** that the higher a student scores on math tests, the higher she is likely to score on science tests. A correlational analysis will indicate the degree to which these two variables relate to one another. The strength of the correlation (or relationship) between two variables may warrant that a specific instructional measure be taken on a grade level or by an individual teacher.

In the field of education causal relationships are infrequent. We cannot conclude, although we'd like to, that teacher use of praise, for instance, causes students to pay more attention which in turn raises achievement scores. We can say, however, that the two variables (teacher use of praise and student motivation) are related somehow. Correlational research studies the strength of that relationship. Once we conduct correlational analyses we are better able to understand a given phenomenon, event, or behavior. We might even be able to predict a future behavior or condition; e.g., that praise in the form positive reinforcement by Teacher X might influence a particular student to behave in a certain desirable manner. Moreover, correlational analyses might give us strong indications that one variable might, potentially, cause another. Caution is advised here since correlational analyses do not indicate cause and effect. For example, student absenteeism is highly correlated with student achievement. High incidents of absence, however, do not necessarily mean that under all circumstances students will perform poorly in a given academic area. Even though we might conclude that absenteeism is not recommended for school success, only by conducting an experimental study of some sort can we infer cause and effect. Again, correlational research cannot, by itself, indicate causality between variables. Therefore, any predictions made based on correlational research are tentative. Correlational research might be useful, for example, to study the following questions:

1. What is the relationship between leadership styles of principals and faculty morale?

2. What is the relationship between levels of stress among high school freshman (or any group for that matter) and achievement levels (in a given subject)?

3. What is the relationship between the availability of technologically oriented instructional materials in science and science achievement?

The most commonly used measure of correlation is r, the Pearson Product-Moment correlation coefficient (more about this statistic in Part Nine). The value of r may range from +1.00, which means a perfect positive correlation, to a -1.00, a perfect negative correlation. A zero r value means that there is no relationship between the variables.

Perfect correlations in education are rare, if they even exist. Hypothetically, however, when two variables are perfectly positively correlated we can say with certainty that as one value goes up (e.g., students' scores on math tests) so does the other value rise (e.g., students' scores on science tests).

Predictions, you see, are indeed possible when two variables are perfectly correlated. In reality, though, we in education are more likely to find somewhat strong or weak correlations, as in these examples:

1. amount of assigned homework and attitudes towards school

2. self-concept and motivation

3. parental involvement and student achievement

4. prior achievement in elementary school and achievement in middle school

5. early print experience and reading readiness

Two variables with an r value of +.91 is an example of a strong or high correlation. In contrast, a +31 value would indicate a weaker correlation. Two variables could also be negatively correlated as in the case of grade level and errors in simple reading comprehension activities. We could state that the higher the grade level the lower chance for errors on reading comprehension. That is, as one variable rises (e.g., grade level) the other drops (e.g., errors in reading comprehension).

Correlation coefficients (statistical way we measure the relationship between variables) of .00 indicate that the variables are not correlated at all as in the case of teacher hair color and student achievement.

Correlational studies may use research questions and/or hypotheses. Hypotheses are usually posed whenever statistical tests are required. Null hypotheses (see Module 3 in Part Three for a more complete discussion of hypotheses) are framed for correlational studies as in "No relationship exists between grade point average and student evaluations of teacher's work." Directional or non-directional hypotheses are used when the literature review indicates a specific substantial evidence in favor of one variable (independent) over the other (dependent) or when the review indicates that no one variable has more of a favorable effect on the dependent variable but that a difference between the variables is likely.

Reflection

Can you compose a directional and non-directional hypothesis for the null hypothesis previously stated? "No relationship exists between grade point average and student evaluation of a teacher's work."

Thus far, we've been discussing bivariate correlations; i.e., correlations between two variables or sets of scores. Some studies investigate relationships that call for multivariate correlations as in the relationships among self-concepts, student motivation, and student achievement, as in the following question: "What degree of relationship exists between self-concept and student motivation and student achievement?" The **multiple correlation coefficient** statistic R would be used in this case. The R statistic operates in a similar way to the simple correlation r. However, whereas r varies from -1.00 to +1.00, the R statistic varies from 0 to +1.00.

One type of multivariate correlation is known as a partial correlation. In this case the researcher looks for a relationship between two of the three variables by eliminating the effects of one of the variables. For instance, one might find a high correlation between math test scores of middle school students and computational abilities. Furthermore, both these variables (math test scores and computation) are highly correlated with I.Q. One may use "partial correlation" to discover the relationship between math test scores and computational abilities without considering I.Q. scores by removing the effects of I.Q. Similarly one could "partial out" the effects of math test scores to determine the relationship between I.Q.s and computational abilities.

Regression is an important concept related to correlation and represents a second type of multivariate correlation. Regression is used when researchers want to predict values of one variable from values of another variable. In regression analyses there is always one dependent variable (e.g., student achievement). In simple regression, we want to discover the degree to which we can predict one independent variable (e.g., teaching method) with another variable (i.e., dependent). In **multiple regression** there may be two or more independent variables.

Generally speaking, master's degree students rarely utilize multivariate correlations because they are simply too complicated. If this is a student's first thesis project, the objective, in my estimation, would be to keep things simple and manageable. For doctoral work, a strong working knowledge of the specifics and technicalities of multivariate analyses is needed. Other multivariate correlations such as **discriminant analysis**, **factor analysis**, and **path analysis** are also beyond the purview of readers of this volume.

As will be indicated in Part Nine, correlational analyses are relatively easy to compute with appropriate computer programs.

Module 2 Review

In this Module you learned some basics about correlation research.

Self-Test Check

1. "The correlation between the amount of time spent playing video games and scores on a science exam is .12." What does this mean?

    a. there is a strong relationship between the variables but no causal statements can be made

    b. there is practically no relationship between the 2 variables

    c. there is a strong negative relationship between the variables

    d. there is a cause and effect relationship between the 2 variables

    e. not enough information is given to assess this study

2. True or False: Causal conclusions are feasible with correlation research

3. True or False: Correlation research almost always uses hypotheses.

4. True or False: This statement is an acceptable form for a hypothesis in correlation research: No relationship exists between teacher use of praise and student achievement.

5. True or False: A correlation coefficient of +1.00 indicates a perfect positive correlation.

6. True or False: +1 and -1 are both perfect correlations.

7. True or False: Multiple correlation coefficients are symbolized by an R and indicate the strength of relationship between one variable and several others.

8. True or False: Correlation is a necessary but not a sufficient condition for determining causality.

9. True or False: The question "Do students like math when taught with computer technology" lends itself to correlational analyses.

10. True or False: The Pearson r can be used to calculate the degree of relationship between self-concepts and reading achievement.

Answers: 1) b; 2) f; 3) t; 4) t; 5) t; 6) t; 7) t; 8) t; 9) f; 10) t

Study Questions

1. In what way might correlation be useful in your research?

2. In what way might correlation be useful in your everyday practice as an educator?

3. What are the chief characteristics of correlation research?

Activity

1. Locate another research article that incorporates this method and describe its chief characteristics.

Module 3: Group Comparison Research

Group comparison research compares two or more groups according to some variable(s). Suppose as a middle school teacher you have two classes (e.g., periods 4 and 6) that were equivalent or comparable in terms of their math achievement. You volunteer to participate in a pilot program to want to determine whether or not the new district math program can significantly raise student math achievement. You randomly select one the two comparable classes to serve as the experimental group using the new teaching method (that we'll call Method A) while you continue to teach the other group (i.e., the control group) math the same traditional way you have for years (we'll call that Method B). You teach over a period of six months and then administer a post test that measures math achievement to determine which group scored significantly higher than the other, if in fact one group did. Such an experiment is a classic Group Comparison Study.

As previously explained group comparison research can be divided into three types: **experimental, quasi-experimental,** and **ex post facto research.** Regardless of which type of group comparison research you employ, the same basic structure applies: i.e., two or more groups are formed, a **treatment** is administered, post tests are given after a reasonable period of time, statistical comparisons are made, and conclusions are drawn.

The essential idea to keep in mind is that although the three types of group comparison approaches are similar, one factor distinguishes them; that is, how the groups are formed. The way in which the groups are formed determines statistical measures applied and the kinds of conclusions that you can draw from them. Keep this chart that distinguishes the three types of group comparison studies in mind:

Type of Study	Method of Forming Groups
Experimental	Individuals randomly assigned
Quasi-Experimental	Intact groups randomly assigned
Ex Post Facto	Groups already formed

Experimental research is a *type* of group comparison research that may not be suitable for many educational researchers (especially master's degree students) because of the requirement of **randomization.** Yet, some educators might indeed want to undertake experimental research when feasible because it is the strongest group comparison study due to the fact that when properly implemented causal conclusions may be drawn. I once conducted a study in which I had the opportunity to randomize when I was an assistant principal in New York City (see Glanz, 1994) strategies with fifth grade students by randomly assigning students to two groups: one group (experimental) received the **treatment** (also called the **independent variable**), that is, stress reduction instruction, while the other group (control) did not receive the treatment. The **independent variable** was stress reduction training and the **dependent variable** was levels of stress exhibited by students during various times of the school year. The fact that randomization was incorporated indicates the experimental nature of the study.

Reflection

Under what circumstances could you randomize individuals in order to conduct an experimental group comparison study?

How does **randomization** work? Although randomizing individuals or classes is not often very feasible in educational settings, opportunities may emerge in which randomization is possible and desirable. There are many ways of assigning subjects randomly to groups. Generally, here are some rules to keep in mind when you wish to randomize:

1. select the **population** you want to pull your **sample** from and make certain that all members of that population have an equal chance of being selected. For example, when I surveyed assistant principals in New York City (Glanz, 1994), I obtained a list of 3000 assistant principals. Then,

2. I assigned each subject (assistant principal) a number from 0000 to 2999. Then,

3. I consulted a table of random numbers (which can be found in almost any book on statistics) and arbitrarily selected a number. Then,

4. I looked at the last four digits of the numbers.

5. If that number was also assigned to a subject, that subject was selected for the sample; if not, I went to the next number. For example, notice this list of random numbers:

21880	78677
16899	90867
22500	12490
09823	73033
23460	89780
30494	23111
92412	80003
99780	00986

If you start with the top number and look at the last four digits (1880), that represents the assistant principal who was assigned #1880; in other words, the 1,880th assistant principal on the list. S/he is then chosen for my study. I then look at the last four digits of the next number (6899) and realize that it is a larger number than the list of names of assistant principals (maximum of 3000), so I skip that number and continue with the next number. The last four digits of the next number is 2500, so I select the 2,500th assistant principal on my list and s/he becomes the second AP in my study.

6. I continue this procedure until I have the desired **sample** (usually 10% of the population which, in this case, was 300 APs).

Other **sampling** techniques are described below:

Scenario: Let's say you want to randomly assign students to two groups. One group (the **experimental group**) will receive computer instruction to reinforce writing skills, while the other group will learn the same writing curriculum without computers. After a four-month period, you then compare the writing abilities of each group. Such comparisons enable you to assess the effect of the **independent variable** (computer assisted writing instruction) on the **dependent variable** (writing achievement). But how do you randomize individuals into each group?

Sampling (often synonymous with **randomization**) is a technique used to select participants for a study. Sampling involves a process by which members in the population have an equal chance of being selected into the experiment.

Types of sampling are:

A) *random sampling* involves each member of the population having an equal chance of being selected. The Table of Random Numbers, which can be found in any book on statistics as described above, can be used for studies involving many subjects. For smaller studies, simply shuffling cards with names of all the members of a population and then selecting a certain number of cards from the top of the deck (like pulling names out of a hat) could also be used as long as all members of the population have an equal chance of being selected.

B) *stratified sampling* involves identifying two or more subsets (e.g., gender, ethnicity, geographic location, etc.) in a population and taking a random sampling of each subset. Identifying subsets in advance of obtaining a sample reduces the possibility that an important group is left out of the sample.

Let's say you wanted a representative number of elementary, middle, and high school teachers for a survey you are conducting throughout a district on attitudes toward inclusion. You would identify the numbers of elementary, middle, and high school teachers and then take a random sampling from each category, thus ensuring representation from all three groups of teachers.

C) *systematic sampling* involves systematically selecting a fraction of the population (e.g., every tenth name on a list). Let's say you have 130 students in the population and wanted to randomly select a total of 40 of them into experimental and control groups. You would obtain a random list of all 130 students (not alphabetical or arranged according to some distinguishing characteristic such as gender, ethnicity, or achievement test scores) and then would arbitrarily select every third name until you have 20 students for each group.

D) *cluster sampling* is used by identifying a site (e.g., schools, a district, or classes) called a "cluster," and then taking a random sample from that cluster or site.

E) See Module 1 in Part Five for a description of **matched pairs** as a sampling technique.

Reflection

What is the connection and importance of obtaining a representative sample and the ability to generalize?

Parenthetically, qualitative sampling procedures may be quite different from techniques previously described. Obtaining a representative sample is less important in qualitative research studies because generalization is not a concern. Often, samples are chosen for qualitative studies based on convenience, individual preference, or happenstance. **Purposeful sampling,** for instance, is often used in ethnographic research in order to work with people who can provide essential information to the researcher. For instance, if you are conducting an ethnographic study about first year teachers and their ability to acclimate to the tensions of teaching for the first time, then you would want to purposely find individuals who recently began teaching. Purposeful sampling is not random, but can be used when for a specific purpose or objective.

Quasi-experimental research is a *type* of group comparison research in which groups, not individuals, are assigned to either experimental or control conditions. No **randomization** of individuals occurs in quasi-experimental studies. Quasi-experimental studies are the most commonly used in education because educators rarely have the opportunity to truly randomize subjects into groups. Educators usually deal with intact classes or groups of individuals. For example, let's say you wanted to compare Method A to Method B. As a high school teacher you might have two equivalent or comparable groups of 10th graders during periods 4 and 7. These are, of course, intact classes because you didn't randomly assign them to these classes; they are intact or preassigned. You can, however, randomly assign the *methods.* Period 4 may be assigned Method B and period 7 may be assigned Method A. In other words, quasi-experimental studies randomly assign intact groups to different *methods* rather than randomly assigning *individuals.*

The key idea to consider in quasi-experimental research is to ensure that both groups are equivalent or comparable. Usually, administering a pretest to both intact classes will determine whether or not the groups are equivalent in terms of the dependent variable.

Note that quasi-experimental research, as used in this volume, also refers to studies that do not use control groups. In Part Four we referred to single measurement, static, one-group pretest/post test, static group, interrupted time series, and single subject designs. These too are examples of quasi-experimental studies.

Ex post facto research (sometimes called causal comparative research because it attempts to define a cause and effect relationship between two variables) is one of the three types of group comparison research. Ex post facto studies involve intact classes which are assigned to either experimental or control conditions. No randomization occurs in these studies. In these studies groups are already formed because members of each group exhibit characteristics that the researcher has no control over (e.g., whether or not they had pre-school experience). Ex post facto, meaning, after the fact, indicates that the sample already exhibits certain uncontrollable characteristics in respect to a particular condition. For instance, let's say you wanted to examine reading readiness of kindergarten students. You might want to compare two groups: students who attended preschool with students who did not. You have no control over who had or didn't attend preschool. You simply identify a group of students who did attend preschool and another group who didn't. These two groups were not randomly formed but were assigned based on a precondition; in this case whether or not they attended preschool. You might ask, "Are students who attended preschool more reading ready than students who did not attend preschool?"

The major difference between ex post facto research and experimental studies is that in the former, neither groups nor individuals are randomized to form comparison groups. Comparisons are thus made with intact or pre-existing classes.

In conclusion, then, experimental research is used to identify cause and effect relationships; in other words, the effect that an independent variable (treatment) has on a dependent variable (outcome). Quasi-experimental research, in contrast is very similar to experimental research but that for a variety of reasons the researcher is not able to assign individuals randomly to treatment groups; rather, groups are randomly assigned to a particular treatment. In ex post facto research (also called causal-comparative because it explores possible causal relationships, although no cause and effect conclusions are usually drawn from such studies except under special circumstances (e.g., controlling for all confounding variables), as may be drawn from either experimental or even, to a lesser extent, quasi-experimental), the independent cannot be manipulated because participants already possess certain characteristics that the researcher has no control over (e.g., gender, car ownership, pre-school experiences, etc.).

Each of these types of group comparison studies has several factors that may threaten to interfere with the extent to which causal or any other conclusions may be drawn from them. Such threats to internal and external validity will be discussed in Part Nine. Also in Part Nine, I will discuss precisely how results from group comparison studies are analyzed.

Module 3 Review

In this Module you learned some basic ideas about group comparison research.

Self-Test Check

1. The purpose of giving a pretest to both the experimental and control groups is to
    a. ensure equivalence of post test results.
    b. define parameters of sampling techniques.

   c. ensure group comparability.

   d. develop reliability of assessments.

   e. all of these.

2. A "good" sample is one that is

   a. free of random errors.

   b. large.

   c. representative.

   d. small.

   e. systematic.

3. Sampling where every tenth name is picked from an alphabetical list of students would be an example of which type of sampling?

   a. cluster.

   b. stratified.

   c. random.

   d. systematic.

   e. none of these.

4. As an educator you will have to evaluate many programs in order to ascertain their effectiveness. Let's say you are experimenting with a new supervisory technique known as "clinical supervision." After five months of its implementation, you wish to evaluate its usefulness. You therefore prepare a number of evaluative tools in order to determine whether or not to continue its use,

   Clinical supervision in the example above is known as the

   a. dependent variable.

   b. extraneous variable.

   c. treatment.

   d. status dependent.

   e. coefficient.

5. Comparing self-concepts of mainstreamed and non-mainstreamed special education students is an example of

   a. ex post facto research.

   b. descriptive research.

   c. correlational research.

   d. all of these.

6. A researcher wishes to determine whether 6th graders taught language arts by Method A will score higher on a language arts test than will 6th graders taught by the Method B. The researcher identifies two classes and flips coin to determine which method will be used with each class. Thus, each group is randomly assigned to a method of instruction. This is an example of

    a. quasi-experimental research.

    b. ex post factor research.

    c. correlational research.

    d. ethnography.

7. True or False. A treatment is usually an independent variable.

8. True or False: Note that as a general rule, the larger the sample, the greater the likelihood for obtaining significant results.

9. True or False: It is improper to draw a causal inference from findings obtained from quasi-experimental and ex pos facto studies.

10. True or False: In quasi-experimental studies, existing intact classes are randomly assigned to the experimental or control group.

Answers: 1) c; 2) c; 3) d; 4) c; 5) a; 6) a; 7) t; 8) t; 9) t; 10) t

Study Questions

1. Can you think of a situation in which you might set up an experimental study, a quasi-experimental study or an ex post facto study?

2. Describe three ways to form an experimental and control group.

3. What are the chief characteristics of group comparison research?

Activity

1. Locate a research article that incorporates this method and describe its chief characteristics.

Part Seven:

Thesis Overview—Chapter 3 of Thesis, Section 3: Research Design 3—Qualitative Approaches

Focus Questions

1. What are different types of qualitative approaches?

2. What are the advantages of using a qualitative approach to research?

3. What is the difference between a case study and an ethnographic study?

4. How might you incorporate a qualitative approach in your project?

5. Can you think of an educational research project that would not call for a qualitative approach?

Module 1: Historical Research

Historical inquiry is one of three methods of qualitative research that attempts to understand past events by systematically examining primary and secondary sources. Although historical events or phenomena may be studied in their own right, they are often interpreted to better understand the past and be able to draw implications for present and future conditions. Historical research will not be extensively addressed in this text because master's degree students rarely, if ever, undertake historical inquiry as a separate research methodology. Sometimes, they may use historical inquiry to provide some background information for a case study or even as part of a literature review when appropriate and relevant. Due to its complicated (e.g., sources inaccessible) and arduous nature (e.g., time consuming), most of you will not undertake such inquiry. Doctoral students writing a dissertation are more likely to consider such research. My own dissertation focused on the history of public school supervision in the United States from 1875–1937.

Historical inquiry involves examining primary data sources that include first-hand accounts such as original documents, test scores, student records, interviews with participants, artifacts, autobiographies, etc. Access to such sources may be limited for the average master's degree student. Also, useful are secondary data sources; i.e., descriptions or accounts made by others not directly involved with the topic including biographies, newspaper articles, books, etc. Students often rely too heavily on secondary sources that may be useful to affirm a primary source but should rarely be used for substitution.

Historical research is most useful for educators when it attempts to explain the past and its interconnectedness to present conditions. History can be understood as an attempt to study the events and ideas of the past that have shaped human experience over time in order to inform current practice as well as to make more intelligent decisions for the future. Although historical inquiry would not usually be an educational researcher's first line of research, historical study does have particular relevance, especially when undertaking a needs **assessment** prior to initiating a new program. For example, a new principal would want to examine past records of levels of student achievement, records of dropout rates, or teacher attendance patterns. Data sources might include cumulative record cards, files, newspapers, original documents, and other archival information often found in **school profiles**. Interviewing individuals who can provide first-hand accounts of past events, for instance, is extremely beneficial. Triangulating data is critical in historical research.

Reflection

Why do you think triangulation is so critical in historical research?
How might you triangulate? Is triangulation any more important for historical inquiry than it is, for example, for quantitative research?

One of my former master's degree students was one of the few who chose historical inquiry for his project. He asserted that some of the problems and challenges his school encountered in 1990 stemmed from perceptions the community has historically had in terms of student body, ethnicity, and even physical facilities. He decided to explore the school over time to determine the extent to which situations of the past affected present circumstances in 1990. He posed very specific research questions including, among others, "how has the curriculum and instructional strategies changed?"; "how has the changing student body and ethnic makeup of the community affected curriculum and educational and non-educational resource allotments?"; and so on. Basically, he wanted to compare the school today with the school as it was ten, twenty, and thirty years ago. His data sources included individuals who worked in the school then and now, school records and documents including memoranda, curriculum guides, facilities reports, and demographic data culled from city and state records. Questionnaires and interviews were conducted as well. As he collected data he ensured their authenticity and realized that certain records may have been subjectively reported and that any information he gathered had to be contrasted with other pieces of data collected from a wide array of sources. He was also cognizant of "presentism" that cautions historians to avoid interpreting past events in light of present conditions and circumstances. For example, use of the "Negro" when referring to African American students or parents may not have been seen as derogatory in 1945 as compared to the term if used today.

Although historical inquiry as a complete project may be beyond the purview of most master's degree students, certain methods used by historians are very useful. Oral histories or testimonies, for instance, may be particularly useful for qualitative researchers. Oral histories involve open-ended interviews with a series of individuals involved in a particular issue.

Reflection

Can you think of an issue or situation in which an educator might want or need to undertake oral histories? Would you consider using oral testimonies (also simply called interviews) for your project? Explain.

Historical inquiry utilizes much the same steps as any other method of research. A problem is posed, research questions developed, research plan or design implemented, data collected and analyzed, and findings and conclusions presented. Although you are unlikely to conduct a full-blown historical study for your thesis project, you are more likely to utilize historical methods for writing case studies or providing background information in a literature review, as mentioned earlier.

Module 1 Review

In this Module you learned that historical inquiry is rarely used by master's degree students but some of the methods used are helpful to conduct research.

Study Questions and Activity

1. What else might you learn from historical researchers that would be helpful in carrying out your own study?

2. What problems do historical researchers encounter when they try to interpret historical data?

3. Examine several journals you subscribe to and locate any articles you find that are historical in nature or even incorporate some historical methods. How do the methods of historical inquiry differ from other methods of research?

4. What are the chief characteristics of historical research?

5. Conduct a historical study by examining the history of your current school. Collect primary (if possible) and secondary data and develop a historical picture of your school. What valuable information did you discover?

Module 2: Ethnographic Research

Ethnography is one of three methods of qualitative research and is perhaps the most common qualitative approach. Ethnography, a branch of anthropology, is a method of research in which individuals are observed in natural settings and are described in detail. In ethnographic research there is no attempt to generalize findings. An example of an ethnographic study would be to ask: What is a typical week in the life of five city-school superintendents? One would follow or shadow these superintendents and take extensive notes (called "thick descriptions" or "field notes"; see discussion in Module 2 of Part Eight) describing anecdotally the activities of these individuals. After a week, you would have accumulated a plethora of notes. You would read and reread your notes and perform a **content analysis** to determine any themes that emerge from your data (see **grounded theory**).

Note that it is possible to take detailed written descriptions of what was observed and, at the same time, make specific reflective or interpretative comments. As long as these subjective comments are kept separate from the descriptive data, use of the researcher's speculative comments is common in ethnographic research. In the brief, simple excerpt that follows, note that the researcher's subjective comments are identified and kept separate from the descriptive, more objective portion:

Field notes taken on October 27, 2004 at an after-school faculty conference at Lakewood Middle School

> *"I walked into the Lakewood Middle School main auditorium at 3:10 p.m. as the principal, Mr. Ernest Malcomb, was calling the meeting to order. Twenty-six people were sitting in seats scattered about the large auditorium. The principal requested that those individuals in the rear of the auditorium sit near the front. Three individuals moved from the rear to the middle of the auditorium. Seven individuals remained in the rear. The principal began to read the faculty notes. After two minutes had elapsed, he requested that Ms. Chapman report on the curriculum committee's findings and recommendations."*
>
> *Comments: The teachers in the rear of the auditorium seem defiant in their refusal to move their seats closer to the principal. As Mr. Malcomb read the faculty notes many teachers appeared bored.*

Field notes, then, are the researcher's written chronological account of what transpired during an observation session. Field notes consist of two parts:

1. an objective section that contains a detailed description of what has taken place and

2. a subjective part that contains the observer's reflections or speculations about what was observed.

Ethnographic research, then, clearly separates description from interpretation and judgment. Ethnographers are cognizant of their own biases and prejudices and how they may influence their observations. Although they may take measures to mitigate these influences, they readily acknowledge them and contextualize them within a framework of methodically and scientifically collecting data. They constantly scrutinize their findings and consider them along with the multitude of other pieces of data they collect. When biases are inevitable, ethnographers would encourage interrater reliability (see **reliability** in Glossary).

Reflection

Spend some time observing people in some social situation whether it be during a grade conference or standing outside waiting for the school bus. Take field notes to describe what you see and hear. Offer your comments and interpretations. How did you find the experience? What are some limitations of this method?

Some authorities in the field consider ethnography a form of descriptive research. Although ethnography does describe a particular situation, it does so usually without use of numbers, frequencies, or statistics. I have classified ethnography under qualitative research to indicate its non-mathematical orientation.

As an educational researcher employing ethnographic research, you would identify a topic, pose a research question or two, and collect data by documenting and explaining in great depth what you are observing. Data sources for an ethnographic researcher might include:

1. study of the social behavior of individuals (examples might include: shadowing an associate superintendent during the course of her day; observing the occurrences of misbehavior among three special education students; or observing teachers during a grade conference);

2. communication patterns among individuals or groups (examples might include: observing interactions between faculty and a principal at an after-school conference or observing students as they play in the school yard);

3. environmental conditions (examples might include: studying the impact of block scheduling on student movement in the hallways or observing the impact of early dismissal procedures on the number of incidents of reported accidents).

Several principles related to ethnography as well as for all qualitative research approaches should be reviewed:

-occurs in a natural setting

-attempts to explore the why, what, and, especially, how of an issue

-concentrates on fieldwork that may include observations, interviews, etc.

-focuses on a research problem and selection of a research site

-explores sites that are related to the problem, but not randomly selected

-stresses extensive use of field notes

-generates questions, collects data, and interprets data as a combined process

- generates theory from data (grounded theory)

-involves analyzing data as they are collected

Ethnographic studies, by their very nature, are usually long. Discussion of data collection methods useful in ethnographic research is presented in Part Ten. See discussion of observational techniques that can be used in ethnography in Module 2 in Part Eight. Refer to these classic works in ethnography: Wolcott, 1992; 1995; 1999.

Module 2 Review

In this Module you learned some characteristics of ethnographic research.

Self-Test Check

1. True or False: Ethnographic research is writing about people in their natural setting

2. True or False: Ethnographic research is well suited for those of us in education because it is based on human interaction in social settings.

3. True or False: Ethnographers have to be extra cautious for fear of their own biases and prejudices since they record what they see or experience.

4. True or False: Ethnographic research allows one to generalize.

5. True or False: One of the major benefits of ethnography is that it provides rich realistic descriptions of human behavior in natural settings such as classrooms.

6. True or False: Hypotheses are generally not used in ethnography.

7. True or False: Statistical analyses are common in ethnographic research.

Answers: 1) t; 2) t; 3) t; 4) f; 5) t; 6) t; 7) f

Study Questions and Activity

1. Examine the work of Diane Fossey, pioneering primatologist, whose research established the Karisoke Research Foundation in 1967 to study gorillas. Compare her research methods with the methods described in this module. Are there any differences or similarities? Can her research be considered qualitative?

2. Under what circumstance could you use statistics in ethnographic research?

3. What are the chief characteristics of ethnographic research?

Module 3: Case Study Research

This method of research is often used in qualitative approaches. Although case studies are actually ways of reporting ethnographic research, they are so common that I have included them as a separate category. Also note that some authorities have identified another method of research that they call phenomenological studies. In such studies the researcher attempts to study how one or more individuals experience a phenomenon. For instance, one may research how a high school student experiences a recent divorce between his mom and dad, and the impact this event has on his school work, or how a teacher candidate experiences the first year on the job as a certified teacher in a full-time position. Such phenomenological studies utilize case studies as the main method of reporting data. Therefore, I have not included phenomenological studies as a separate method of research.

Case studies involve in-depth investigations of an individual, group of individuals, a site, or a scene. Findings are stated verbally, not numerically. Case studies are reported by describing in detail observations made of individuals, groups, or school settings. Special education teachers, for instance, who use IEP's (Individual Educational Plans) are actually involved in some aspects of case study research. Case studies are written so that a better understanding of a situation is likely and so that educators may discuss possible implications for an individual, group, or school.

Case study research can also be conducted, as stated above, by examining a specific phenomenon such as a program, an event, a process, an institution, or a social group (Merriam, 1997). An example of how a case study approach was used in a research project can be found, for example, in Glanz (1995) in which a martial arts program for students at risk was implemented (see excerpt below).

Case studies differ subtly from ethnographic research in that case studies are written descriptively and objectively, while ethnographic accounts may contain interpretive material. Case studies are also more narrowly focused on a particular person, place, or scene. Case studies may also tend to create an idealized situation by merely using descriptive accounts. Case studies are often guided by a series of questions that the researcher tries to answer. The case study, in the end, provides an in-depth, descriptive account.

Incorporating a qualitative research methodology through the use of portraits (Donmoyer, 1993; Lawrence-Lightfoot, 1985) has gained favor in the educational community. Donmoyer and Kos (1993) have demonstrated the efficacy of this case study approach in examining the at-risk population. I would like to present, as an example, a brief, yet descriptive case study excerpt of one particular student who was in many ways representative of the students involved in the martial arts program mentioned above (Glanz, 1995). Data were gathered through the use of observations based on field notes, interviews, questionnaires, and video tape recordings. Information was gleaned from school personnel, especially the classroom teacher, the parent, the Sensei (martial arts teacher), and the student himself. Multiple observers, multiple data collection methods, and extensive "thick" descriptions were employed to attain as accurate a description as possible.

> *Ernest is a ten-year-old Mexican American fourth-grade student attending P.S. 563 in Elizabeth, New Jersey. Ernest was held-over once in grade 3 and is two years below grade level in reading and math. Ernest has had excellent attendance in*

school, but has been a severe discipline problem since the first grade. He has been suspended four (4) times within the last two years for the following incidents: striking another child across the face with his fist causing severe swelling and bleeding; throwing a chair at another student hitting the substitute teacher by accident; pulling the fire alarm during the school day; and threatening another child in his class with a knife.

Ernest has had an unstable family life in that he has not seen his father for nearly five years. His father is incarcerated for robbery and attempted murder and is serving a fifteen-year sentence. His mother, who has only reported to school once in the past three years, is a crack addict. Ernest lives with an "aunt" across the street from school. Ernest is an only child.

Ernest recently has been involved in a neighborhood gang of approximately fifteen other youth, mostly of junior high school age. Ernest is very intelligent and mature for his age. Although he is quite verbal, he does not participate in school. Teachers have reported the following comments appearing on report cards and cumulative record cards:

- *Ernest is an active youngster who needs constant supervision. (grade 2)*

- *Ernest is intelligent and can do work if he wants to. (grade 1)*

- *Ernest is very aggressive and hostile to his classmates. (grade 2)*

- *Ernest needs help in reading and math. He does not participate and is very playful in class. (grade 3)*

- *Ernest threatens others and shows no interest in school. (grade 4)*

- *Ernest has the potential, but clearly needs a more restrictive classroom environment.*

- *Ernest has been referred to the guidance counselor, assistant principal, and principal without any significant, long-standing change in behavior and attitude. Psychological tests indicate that he is of above average intelligence. Standardized tests as well as teacher-made tests indicate that Ernest is low achieving.*

When the guidance counselor tried to explore Ernest's thoughts and feelings the conversation typically went like this:

GC: *How are you doing Ernest?*

E: *(no response)*

GC: *Well?*

E: *Fine.*

GC: *Well, you know Ernest I have been receiving very disturbing reports about your behavior.*

E: (silence)

GC: *Do you like school?*

E: *Yeh.*

GC: *Well. if you like school, that's great, but*

E: *Do I have to be here? I wanna go.*

GC: *We know you are a very bright boy and want the best for you. Your teacher and Mr. XXXX really care about you.*

E: *(shrugs shoulders). I wanna go.*

GC: *Go where?*

E: *Out of here (storms out and runs through building for ten minutes before being apprehended by security and brought to the AP's office. At the AP's office, the same conversation repeats itself to no avail. Ernest is escorted back to class in time for lunch. He returns to class after lunch 30 minutes late. Excuse: playing basketball in the yard....]*

The case study continues to document attempts to assist Ernest. After participating in a martial arts class specifically designed to encourage greater self-discipline for students like Ernest, the following data were collected as part of the case study:

Ernest showed much enthusiasm about the Karate class in his discussions with the assistant principal (AP):

E: *Yeah, I'm really interested. When can I begin?*

AP: *You know, martial arts are very demanding and require discipline and lots of hard work.*

E: *I can do it.*

AP: *Why are you so interested in the martial arts?*

E: *I don't know, just am.*

AP: *You like the violence and fighting?*

E: *Yeah, I guess...You know Karate?*

AP: *Yep.*

E: *(nodding head in approval)*

AP: *You know the Sensei, teacher, is very strict and will not tolerate fooling around.*

E: *(no comment)*

AP: *You also should know that you can continue in the class as long as you continue to receive good reports from your teachers and me. And that you'll have to do homework and all that…Sensei will explain all that. Okay?*

E: *Okay.*

[Two weeks into the program]

Mr. Shurack, a state-certified teacher and first degree black belt instructor, was interviewed about Ernest's progress in the Karate class. The Sensei reported that Ernest had much difficulty adjusting to the rigors and demands of the class. Ernest grew impatient and had difficulty maintaining concentration. There seemed to be a dramatic change in his attitude and attention as a result of the number of visits to Ernest's classroom during the school day by the AP and Sensei where conversations were conducted about his progress. "It is due, I think," stated Sensei Shurack, "to the fact that Ernest received positive reinforcement and encouragement from his classroom teacher, the AP, the principal, and me that he was able to stick it out in class. The books and magazines (e.g., Karate Illustrated *and* Kung-fu *which were ordered through our school library) seemed to sustain Ernest's interest in those early weeks."*

As you can see from this excerpt, case studies provide descriptive and detailed information that is often missing from quantitative approaches.

Try writing a case study of your own school as an organization. The sample questions in Table 7.1 should serve as a guide. In the end, your case study will represent an attempt to describe your school as thoroughly as possible so that an outsider would be able to get a good sense of what your school is like.

Table 7.1.

Some Guiding Questions in Writing a Case Study of Your School

1. Describe the area in which your school is located. How is it reached by transportation? What is the social class that predominates in the area? Is the school in a residential or business area? Do many students come from the local community? Where else do students come from? Are students bused to the school? What is the ethnic makeup of the student body?

2. Is the school plant in good condition? How old is the building? How is it decorated, outside and inside? How do student treat the physical plant? Are the corridors well-lighted? What are the colors of the walls? Are they clean? Are bulletin boards displayed in the hallways? What do they contain? How many floors are there in the building? What special facilities or equipment exist?

3. What is the makeup (number, ethnicity, gender, etc.) of the faculty, staff, and administration? What are the responsibilities of administrators? teachers? What hierarchical relationships exist, if any? What is the relationship between teachers and administrators?

4. What services exist in the school? Are there nurses, doctors, and custodians in the school? Where is the cafeteria? What is the quality of the food services? Who is in charge? Are teachers and administrators on duty? Is there a library? What library resources exist? Are multimedia technologies present? Does each class have computers? What are the different kinds of software and hardware?

5. Does the school have a written statement of philosophy? Is there a student and/or teacher handbook? Are parents welcome and involved in the school? How do faculty and administration involve parents?

6. How much emphasis is placed on constructivist instructional strategies? What motivational strategies are employed? Describe the state of student discipline. What classroom management techniques and strategies are employed?

7. How are decisions made in the school? Who is involved in instructional decision making? Who is involved in administrative decision making? Does a learning community exist in the school? What is the relationship of the district office to the school?

These are only sample questions that might be framed. Many more questions about grouping practices, other instructional procedures, and logistical operations may be posed. Case studies provide an in-depth understanding of a particular situation. Remember, the educational researcher is likely to use a case study to describe a particular situation that can be then discussed or analyzed by others. Once a school, for instance, is described in detail using a case study, discussion of educational and/or instructional implications may occur.

Reflection

Can you think of a situation in which a case study
might be useful as you attempt to triangulate?

Readers interested in more detailed explanation of case studies, especially as they are used for advanced master's work and doctoral theses, please consult Merriam, 1997.

Module 3 Review

In this Module you learned some basics of case study research.

Self-Test Check

1. True or False: Ethnographic research is synonymous with case study research.

2. True or False: Case study research is qualitative by nature.

3. True or False: Case study researchers have to be extra cautious for fear of their own biases and prejudices since they record what they see or experience.

4. True or False: Case study research allows one to generalize.

5. True or False: One of the major benefits of case study research is the depth of analysis.

6. True or False: Hypotheses are generally not used in case studies.

7. True or False: Statistical analyses are common in case studies.

Answers: 1) f; 2) t; 3) t; 4) f; 5) t; 6) t; 7) f

Study Questions

1. How does one collect data for case study research?

2. What are the chief characteristics of case study research?

Activity

1. Locate a research article that incorporates this method and describe its chief characteristics.

Part Eight:

Thesis Overview—Chapter 3 of Thesis, Section 4: Research Design 4—Data Collection

Focus Questions

1. How many data collection techniques can you name?

2. Are some data collection techniques superior to others? Explain.

3. What does triangulation have to do with data collection?

4. How do you know when you have gathered enough data?

5. What is the difference between a survey and a questionnaire?

6. How might an educational researcher use multimedia to collect data?

Module 1: Writing Questionnaires

Questionnaires are one of the most common types of data collection **instruments** (or data sources) used in research projects. Their ease of use and uncomplicated methods of data analysis make questionnaires an invaluable means of collecting data for an educational researcher.

A questionnaire solicits respondents' attitudes toward a particular issue. Educators may distribute questionnaires to assess attitudes of students, parents, teachers, or supervisors about a variety of issues, such as instruction and school climate.

Sometimes, ready-made questionnaires that have been developed by companies are available for use. For example, the National Association of Secondary School Principals (NASSP, 1987) has developed several useful, ready-made questionnaires surveying school climate, teacher, student, and parent attitudes toward school. Also, you can call 1-800-228-0752 for the *School Effectiveness Questionnaire,* which can be hand-tabulated or computer-analyzed. In many cases, however, questionnaires may not be available to suit your unique needs. In such cases, you might have to construct your own questionnaire.

Two types of questionnaires are most common: **closed-ended** and open-ended questionaires. Open-ended questionnaires include questions that allow respondents to elaborate on a given question. A questionnaire, for instance, composed of questions to ascertain a teacher's attitude toward supervision may include the following open ended question: "Can you provide an example of a situation or experience in which you have benefited from supervision? Explain."

Note that while questionnaires are usually data collection instruments used in quantitative approaches, the responses to open-ended questions in questionnaires can be seen and interpreted as qualitative data. Very often comments generated from open-ended questions can prove very useful and even crucial in determining such things as the value of the program under study. (See Patton, 1990, p. 19, for a situation in which comments made in the open-ended portion of a questionnaire were the basis for a very important decision made by a school board, that would not have been made had only the closed-ended portion of the questionnaire been analyzed quantitatively.)

Closed-ended questionnaires, on the other hand, do not allow respondents to elaborate, but rather structure respondents' answers to predetermined choices. One of the most commonly used closed-ended questionnaires is known as the **Likert scale.** Many of us have taken a Likert scale questionnaire at one time or another. Right? You recall those choices it gives such as strongly agree, agree, disagree, and strongly disagree? A Likert scale is relatively easy to construct and easy to analyze.

Likert Scale Construction: Some Guiding Principles

1. Limit the number of items to as few as possible (ideally between 15 and 20 items). Long surveys are unlikely to be completed by respondents.

2. Avoid ambiguously worded statements. Construct items so that they may be interpreted in the same way by every respondent. Why is the following statement worded ambiguously?

   "How often do you observe your fifth grade teachers?"

   rarely   sometimes   often

Right. What is meant by "observe?" A casual look, an in-depth hour-long observation period, or some time in between? Moreover, what do the choices mean? How often is "sometimes"? Once a month, twice a month, or once a year?

Sometimes statements are just phrased ambiguously due to sentence structure problems. Have a colleague or potential respondent proofread your items for ambiguity.

3. Avoid leading questions; that is, don't suggest that one response will be more appropriate than another. For example, avoid using a question such as "Don't you agree that peer coaching is marvelous?"

4. Avoid sensitive questions to which respondents may not reply honestly. For example, don't ask: "Have you always acted so ethically?"

5. Statements should be concise, not overly lengthy.

6. Develop objectives before you write the items (see examples in sample questionnaire that follows).

7. Questionnaires should include statements that are conceptually related. If you are surveying attitudes of teachers toward bilingual education, then an example of a conceptually unrelated item would be: "I get along with my supervisor." This statement has little, if anything, to do with the major purpose of your questionnaire. One way to ensure that items are conceptually related is to match each item with your objectives. Does each item address one of the stated objectives?

8. Avoid response sets. Sometimes respondents will not really read the survey, but merely go down a column circling all the "strongly disagree" choices. To avoid response sets you must word half the items positively and half negatively. Placement of positively and negatively worded statements should be random. Don't intentionally place an item in the order you think is best. As long as about half of the items are positive statements and the other half are negative statements, and the items are randomly distributed, you will have avoided the response set problem.

Below is an example of two statements, one positively worded and the other in the negative:

Directions: Circle the response that best indicates the extent to which you agree or disagree with each statement below, where

SA = Strongly Agree

A = Agree

D = Disagree

SD = Strongly Disagree

1. Math is my favorite class.

2. Learning math is a waste of time.

If someone really enjoys math, she will circle SA for the first item and SD for the second. If the respondent circles SA for both items, you might have a response set. Too many response sets affect the **validity** and **reliability** of your questionnaire.

9. Preparation of cover letter: A cover letter should be brief and neat. The letter should explain the purpose of your study, emphasize its importance, give the respondent a good reason for completing the survey, and ensure the respondent's anonymity.

10. Field test your survey to ensure consensual **validity**.

The sample Likert-scale questionnaire below illustrates the objectives that were written prior to developing the items. Note that your objectives would not be shared with respondents.

SAMPLE QUESTIONNAIRE*

Team Teaching Class

Objectives:

1. Are students' physical needs met in the team teaching classroom?

_____

_____

_____

2. How is student achievement affected by team teaching?

_____

_____

_____

3. Does having two teachers increase your understanding of this topic?

_____

_____

_____

4. Are students finding their teachers more available for help?

_____

_____

_____

5. Are students comfortable participating in a team taught (larger) class?

_____

_____

_____

6. Does having two teachers help students to stay focused and attentive?

_____

_____

_____

*Developed by one of my graduate students, Jamie Horowitz.

Questionnaire:

Milburn High School
Mathematics Department

Place a check in the appropriate space below:

____male   ____female
____freshman   ____sophomore   ____junior   ____senior

This scale has been prepared so that you can indicate how you feel about the statements below. Please *circle* one of the letters on the left indicating how you feel about each statement (SA, strongly agree; A, agree; D, disagree; SD, strongly disagree).

SA   A   D   SD   1.   I understand explanations given by my teacher(s).

SA   A   D   SD   2.   I can see the board and overhead screen clearly.

SA   A   D   SD   3.   When something is unclear, I am not comfortable asking a question in class.

SA   A   D   SD   4.   Being in a class taught by two teachers helps me to be more attentive.

SA   A   D   SD   5.   I am not doing very well in this class.

SA   A   D   SD   6.   My teacher is available for extra help.

SA   A   D   SD   7.   I am not comfortable participating in this class by responding to teacher questions.

SA   A   D   SD   8.   I am confused by explanations given by my teacher(s).

SA   A   D   SD   9.   It's hard for me to see the board and overhead screen from where I'm seated.

SA   A   D   SD   10.   I am comfortable asking a question in class if I don't understand something.

SA   A   D   SD   11.   I find it harder to pay attention in class with two teachers.

SA   A   D   SD   12.   I am doing pretty well in this class.

SA   A   D   SD   13.   My teacher is not available when I need extra help outside the classroom.

SA   A   D   SD   14.   I am comfortable participating in class by responding to teacher questions.

Other types of scales:

1. Semantic Differential scale—a range of choices along a continuum of two contrasting concepts as in good/bad; fair/unfair, important/unimportant, etc. As in the following case:

Math Test

Fair ___ ___ ___ ___ ___ ___ Unfair

2. Checklists—Respondents are asked to check off items that relate specific requested information. As in the following simple cases:

Are you a teacher?

____ Yes

____ No

Check appropriate category:

____ Male

____ Female

For more information about questionnaire construction, consult the following excellent references: Fink (1998), Fink and Kosecoff (1985), Patten (1998), and Thomas (1999). On survey validity and reliability see Litwin (1995). For a comprehensive resource containing a collection of many easy-to-use assessment tools see Bum and Payment (2000).

Module 1 Review

In this Module you learned some basics of questionnaire construction.

Self-Test Check

1. An instrument which asks respondents to strongly agree, agree, disagree, or strongly disagree to a particular statement is called the
    a. Likert scale.
    b. **Chi Square** scale distribution.
    c. Null Hypothesis.
    d. Flander's Interaction Analysis.
    e. Eisner's Continuum.

2. Likert scales usually have half the items worded positively and half negatively in order to
    a. ensure validity.
    b. control for intervening variables.
    c. avoid response sets.
    d. calculate statistical regression.
    e. ensure a mathematical balance among the questions.

Answers: 1) a; 2) c

Study Questions

1. How might you use questionnaires in your study?

2. What's the difference between a survey and a questionnaire?

3. What steps should you take to ensure the development of a good questionnaire?

Activity

1. Locate three other questionnaires and describe their characteristics.

Module 2: Conducting Observations

A very common way to collect data in educational research settings is to observe and record information. In Part Six, Module 1 we discussed the difference between systematic and nonsystematic observation and explained that both forms of observation are valuable.

For qualitative research approaches, observation may take place in four ways:

1. *As a participant*—the researcher may conceal her or his role when gathering data. For example, a guidance counselor may want to study interactions among fellow guidance counselors at a conference. The researcher is able to observe firsthand social interactions among guidance counselors. Being actively engaged in the conference affords the researcher firsthand experience and data. Yet, the ethics of concealing one's purpose in interacting with others should be considered (see Module 4 in Part One).

2. *As an observer-participant*—the researcher's purpose is known by all participants. The researcher may record data as they occur. Yet, participants may be reluctant to share information if they know that what they will say or do will be recorded.

3. *As a participant-observer*—the researcher's observation role is secondary to the participant role. The researcher records data; however, the researcher may not attend to all data.

4. *As an observer*—the researcher observes without participating. Recording data can be accomplished without distractions, yet those being observed may feel uncomfortable with the researcher's sole role as observer.

Reflection

*Think how you might use these observational approaches
while conducting an ethnographic study.*

Keep in mind that observation can be obtrusive and thus compromise data collection.

Reflection

*How might observation intrude on data collection?
Provide a concrete example.*

Unobtrusive measures refer to **data collection** methods that are obtained without directly involving subjects or participants. An educational leader who determines, for example, staff morale by examining the quantity and pattern of staff attendance by collecting written reports and documents utilizes an *unobtrusive measure* in the sense that data can be obtained without conferring with the staff directly. Sometimes such an approach is not feasible. Remaining as unobtrusive as possible, especially when observing as number four above indicates, is essential. Always consider the impact your presence might have to contaminate data collection. Consider such a situation as a possible study limitation (see Module 1 in Part Twelve).

Regardless of the way you collect data through observation, several key questions should be kept in mind (thanks to my colleague Dr. Barry Friedman, a former principal in the New York City Public Schools and a professor at St. Joseph's College, for suggesting these questions):

1. What is the purpose of the observation?

2. Which individuals, events, settings, and circumstances are the focus of the investigation?

3. How are students, teachers, parents, and administrators behaving?

4. What activities are occurring?

5. How would you describe the social interaction?

6. How do people talk to each other?

7. What is the impact of my presence as an observer?

8. What instruments am I using to record data (e.g., pencil/paper, camera, video recorder, audio recorder, etc.)?

Two ways of collecting data through observation have been particularly useful for me. First, written descriptions are most often employed by educators when collecting data. For instance, when a leader observes a teacher, she may record information by taking field notes or "thick descriptions." Taking field notes is a convenient and simple way of recording observations. Although field notes are subject to observer bias and subjectivity, recording data anecdotally (without drawing conclusions or making value judgments) is highly recommended. Still, this method of recording data is incomplete in the sense that it is impossible to record all events during a given lesson, for instance. Observations are therefore necessarily limited and should rarely be used as a sole means of collecting data. This is why qualitative researchers, as we discussed, emphasize the importance of triangulating on the basis of various data collection methods.

A second way of collecting data through observation is preparing a checklist of some sort to facilitate observations. A checklist allows you to record instances of a particular behavior or practice. The checklist technique defines certain behaviors or events that can be checked off as they occur during a lesson, for example. Let's say that you are observing a teacher and want to keep a tally of the number of instances in which the teacher "gave directions," "praised," "criticized," "probed," and "asked questions" during a 15-minute segment of a lesson. Your checklist might look something like the one in Table 8.1. Checklists such as this one can assist systematic collection of data through observation.

Checklist Observation Technique					
Time	**Giving Directions**	**Praising**	**Criticizing**	**Probing**	**Questions**
Minute 1					
Minute 2					
Minute 3					
Minute 4					
Minute 5					
Minute 6					
Minute 7					
Minute 8					
Minute 9					
Minute 10					
Minute 11					
Minute 12					
Minute 13					
Minute 14					

Table 8.1.

Glickman, Gordon, and Ross-Gordon (1998) review several useful techniques for collecting data through observation. I suggest that you review the quantitative and qualitative techniques described by these authors. Also, consult Willerman, McNeely, and Koffman (1991) for a thorough discussion of observation instruments and Sullivan and Glanz (2005). In fact, some of the tables reproduced below come from this latter work.

Sample Observation Checklists or Forms

Consider each of these forms and ask yourself, "How might I use them for observational purposes?" Also ask, "How might I adapt them to suit my needs for when I conduct observations?"

Table 8.2. Teacher Verbal Behaviors

	Information Giving	Questioning	Teacher Answering Own Questions	Praising	Direction Giving	Reprimanding	Correcting
1							
2							
3							
4							
5							
6							
7							
8							
9							
10							
11							
12							
13							
14							
15							
16							

Time Ended:
Class:
Date:

Source: C. D. Glickman, S. P. Gordon, and J. Ross-Gordon, *SuperVision of Instructional Leadership: A Developmental Approach* (6th ed.), Copyright © 2004 by Allyn & Bacon. Reprinted/adapted by permission.

Reflection

Observe a colleague using the instrument above.
What conclusions can be drawn?

Table 8.3. Teacher Questions

Time began: _____

Question Category	Tally 5 min	Tally 10 min	Tally 15 min	Total	Percent	Comments
Evaluation						
Synthesis						
Analysis						
Application						
Comprehension						
Knowledge						

Total number of questions asked: _____
Time Ended: _____
Class:
Date:

Source: C. D. Glickman, S. P. Gordon, and J. Ross-Gordon, *SuperVision of Instructional Leadership: A Developmental Approach* (6th ed.), Copyright © 2004 by Allyn & Bacon. Reprinted/adapted by permission.

Reflection

Observe a colleague using the instrument above.
What conclusions can be drawn?

Table 8.4. Student On-Task and Off-Task Behavior

Time When Sweep Began

Student	9:00	9:05	9:10	9:15	9:20	9:25	9:30	9:35

Total:

Key:
A = at task
TK = talking (social conversation)
P = playing
O = out of seat
OT = off task

Source: C. D. Glickman, S. P. Gordon, and J. Ross-Gordon, *SuperVision of Instructional Leadership: A Developmental Approach* (6th ed.), Copyright © *2004* by Allyn & Bacon. Reprinted/adapted by permission.

Reflection

Memorize and practice using the Key. Select a few students and observe them using the instrument above. What conclusions can be drawn?

Table 8.5. Gardner's Model for Performance Indicators

Elements	Response			Observations
Logical/mathematical	Yes	No	N/A	
Bodily/kinesthetic	Yes	No	N/A	
Visual	Yes	No	N/A	
Musical	Yes	No	N/A	
Interpersonal	Yes	No	N/A	
Intrapersonal	Yes	No	N/A	
Linguistic	Yes	No	N/A	
Naturalistic	Yes	No	N/A	

Date:

Class:

Time:

Reflection

Observe a colleague teaching a lesson using the instrument above.
To what degree did the teacher utilize Gardner's intelligences?

Table 8.6. Hunter's Steps in Lesson Planning

Elements	Response			Comments
Anticipatory set	Yes	No	N/A	
Objective and purpose	Yes	No	N/A	
Input	Yes	No	N/A	
Modeling	Yes	No	N/A	
Checking for understanding	Yes	No	N/A	
Guided practice	Yes	No	N/A	
Independent practice	Yes	No	N/A	

Class:

Date:

Time:

Source: C. D. Glickman, S. P. Gordon, and J. Ross-Gordon, *SuperVision of Instructional Leadership: A Developmental Approach* (6th ed.), Copyright © 2004 by Allyn & Bacon. Reprinted/adapted by permission.

Reflection

Read a colleague's lesson plan using the instrument above.
To what degree did the teacher utilize Hunter's steps of lesson planing?

Table 8.7. Johnson and Johnson's Cooperative Learning

Elements	Response			Comments
Explanation of academic and social objectives	Yes	No	N/A	
Teaching of Social Skills	Yes	No	N/A	
Face-to-face-Interaction	Yes	No	N/A	
Position Interdependence	Yes	No	N/A	
Individual Accountability	Yes	No	N/A	
Group Processing	Yes	No	N/A	

Class:

Date:

Time:

Source: C. D. Glickman, S. P. Gordon, and J. Ross-Gordon, *SuperVision of Instructional Leadership: A Developmental Approach* (6th ed.), Copyright © 2004 by Allyn & Bacon. Reprinted/adapted by permission.

Reflection

Observe a colleague who uses cooperative learning using the instrument above.
To what degree did the teacher utilize Johnson and Johnson's elements?

Table 8.8. Teacher-Pupil Interaction

Time	Student: _____	Teacher: _____

Class:

Date:

Time:

Reflection

Observe a class of a colleague who complains that he cannot reach a particular student.
Chart the interactions between teacher and student as you observe for a class period.
Record observations. Can you draw any conclusions about their interaction?
What was learned, if anything?

Table 8.9. An Observation Chart

Nonverbal Technique	Frequency	Anecdotal Observations/ Student Responses
Proxemics 　Standing near student(s) 　Moving toward student(s) 　Touching student(s) 　Moving about room		
Kinesics a. Affirmation 　Eye contact 　Touching 　Smiling 　Nodding 　Open arm movements b. Disapproval 　Frowning 　Stern look 　Finger to lips 　Pointing 　Arms crossed 　Hands on hips		
Prosody 　Varies voice tone 　Varies pitch 　Varies rhythm		
Immediacy 　Responds with warmth [move over]		

Class:

Date:

Time:

Source: C. D. Glickman, S. P. Gordon, and J. Ross-Gordon, *Supervision of Instruction: A Developmental Approach* (6th ed.), Copyright © 2004 by Allyn & Bacon. Reprinted/adapted by permission.

Reflection

Observe a colleague teaching a lesson using the instrument above. How would you describe the teacher's use of non-verbal language? What insights were discovered, if any?

Table 8.10. Cultural Diversity

Teacher Indicator	Response Yes No N/A	Comments
Displays understanding of diverse cultures		
Displays personal regard for students of diverse cultures		
Uses instructional materials free of cultural bias		
Uses examples and materials that represent different cultures		
Promotes examination of concepts and issues from different cultural perspectives		
Intervenes to address acts of student intolerance		
Uses "teachable moments" to address cultural issues		
Reinforces student acts of respect for diverse cultures		

Class:

Date:

Time:

Source: C. D. Glickman, S. P. Gordon, and J. Ross-Gordon, *SuperVision of Instructional Leadership: A Developmental Approach* (6th ed.), Copyright © 2004 by Allyn & Bacon. Reprinted/adapted by permission.

Reflection

Observe a colleague teaching a lesson or unit on the topic of multicultural education or diversity using the instrument above. To what degree did the teacher address the indicators on the chart? What conclusions can you draw?

Table 8.11. English Language Learners

Accommodation/Modification	Response			What is the evidence?
	Yes	No	N/A	
Teacher talk is modified: slower speech, careful choice of words, idioms, expressions				
Teacher allows wait time and monitors teacher input vs. student output				
Definitions and language are embedded in content/context				
Real-world artifacts present that support comprehension				
Elicit and draw on students' backgrounds to build prior knowledge				
Teacher uses nonverbal cues to support comprehension				

Class:

Date:

Time:

Source: Sullivan and Glanz (2005).

Reflection

Observe a colleague teaching an ESL lesson using the instrument above.
To what degree did the teacher make accommodations as specified on the chart?
What conclusions can you draw?

Table 8.12. Guided Reading

Guided Reading Teacher Indicator	Yes / No / N/A	Comments / Examples
Management		
Was the transition from the mini-lesson to group work implemented in an orderly fashion?		
Were the other children on task while the teacher was in small-group instruction?		
Was the time allotted for the guided reading group appropriate?		
Instruction		
Was the text for guided reading introduced in a manner that provided support needed for students to read independently and successfully?		
Were the children interested in and did they grasp the concepts being taught?		
Was the text appropriate for the group as far as the level, content, and interest?		
Were support, challenges, and opportunities for problem solving evident from the teacher?		
Did the students read independently?		
What type of assessment took place?		
Did the teacher allow students to be responsible for what they already know?		
Did questions include the full range of Bloom's Taxonomy?		
Did the teacher help students strengthen their strategies?		

Class:

Date:

Time:

Source: This instrument was adapted from one that Suzanne Dimitri, a Brookly, N.Y., literacy coach, created. It is published with her permission. See Sullivan and Glanz, 2005.

Reflection

Observe a colleague teaching a lesson using the previous instrument.
To what degree did the teacher address the indicators?
What conclusions can you draw?

Reflection

In the preceding reflection activities you learned about and used the observation instruments.
Return to class to share your experiences. What worked and what didn't work?
What alterations, if any, would you make to the forms? Design an observation
instrument of your own now. Be certain to describe the precise context
in which it can be used. Share with colleagues.

Closing Comments

One final caveat before we close discussion in this module. Be wary of these potential biases in observation:

- *Halo Effect*—tendency to view participants positively or negatively. For instance, if you're observing Juan, a student who has a history of not conforming to classroom rules, you may tend to rely on his past experiences as you observe him in a new setting.

- *Leniency Effect*—tendency to give high observational ratings to all subjects regardless of real differences. Let's say you're observing Juan again and as you do so, you're your detached vantage point, you might not consider a behavior disruptive since his behavior is not directly related to you. A teacher, on the other hand, may see his behavior very differently.

- *Central Tendency*—reluctance to rate subjects either high or low and give average ratings—not unlike the previous effect.

- *Rater Indecisiveness*—inability to categorical judgments about subjects. Making recordings during observational periods takes skill and much practice.

- *Personal Bias*—tendency to rate subjects based on personal biases. Ask yourself, "do I have a personal bias that might interfere with my recordings?"

- *Contamination*—any conditions or circumstance that may impede or hinder the observation. Contamination may occur due to situational circumstances (e.g., fire drill, fight breakout in classroom, etc.) or due to observer (e.g., feeling ill).

- *Observer Omission*—inability for observer to record all relevant information. Although the nature of observation is selective, without practice the observer may not be able to record much of the relevant interactions in the setting. Developing a short-hand system or other method for recording data is essential.

Reflection

Did you encounter any of these biases?
Think of ways to avoid these potential biases in observation.

Module 2 Review

In this Module you learned some basics of observation.

1. Ways observations may occur

2. Key questions to keep in mind when observing

3. Ways of conducting observations

4. Sample observation forms

5. Avoiding biases in observation

Self-Test Check

1. For each of the five review items above, jot down as many ideas as you can recall.

2. Participant observation is frequently used in conducting
    a. correlational research
    b. ex post facto research
    c. ethnographic research
    d. quasi-experimental research

3. Which of the following is the best example of an "unobtrusive instrument?"
    a. supervisor walks into class for an on-the-spot observation
    b. supervisor peeks into window of classroom without letting the teacher see him/her
    c. supervisor determines staff morale by examining the quantity and pattern of staff attendance
    d. interviewing teachers
    e. anonymous questionnaire

4. True or False: Systematic observation refers to a formal process of collecting data that is more scientific than nonsystematic observations in that data are collected with the aid of predetermined observation forms, audiovisual equipment, or some other observation instrument.

Answers: 1) Refer to module; 2) c; 3) c; 4) t

Study Questions

1. What limitations of your study might result from conducting observations?

2. What cautions might you offer a beginning educational researcher you may want to utilize observation as a data collection technique?

3. Consider how you will use observational methods in your study?

4. Create an observation instrument of your own.

5. How will you attend to validity and reliability (see Module 6)?

Activity

1. Go to a sporting event, another social event, someone else's classroom, or simply look out your window (as long as you can see interactions among people). Practice taking field notes by recording what you see. Spend at least a half an hour doing so. Repeat this activity two or three times at the same location and compare/contrast observations.

Module 3: Conducting Interviews and Group Focuses

Seidman (1998) stated that interviewing is the most suitable **data collection** method if we are to understand the experiences of others and the meanings they make of them. Interviews enable the researcher to learn the complexities of the participants' experiences from his or her point of view. Following the advice of Mishler (1986), the best interviews are flexible and open-ended, allowing for natural conversation. The goal is to understand each participants' experiences and perceptions related to a given situation in a non-threatening way such that "meanings emerge, develop, and are shaped by and in turn shape the discourse."

Interviews are often audio-recorded and subsequently transcribed. Transcription, however, can be laborious and time consuming. Still, the time doing so will be well spent. Interviewing is a common and invaluable source of data for educational researchers.

Here are some guidelines to follow when using the interview technique for data collection:

1. Decide why you want to interview someone and what type of information you hope to glean from the interview.

2. Understand the difference between a structured interview and an informal one. A structured interview is one in which the interviewer has a high degree of control over the interview situation. A structured interview has an **interview protocol** which consists of a predetermined set of questions used by an interviewer. In contrast, an informal interview may occur without such a predetermined set of criteria or questions, but rather may be conducted informally, even casually, when speaking with someone. For those of you lacking interview experience, I recommend a structured format. As you develop confidence and skills, a more informal approach may be used.

3. Avoid the following: interrupting the participant; failing to pick up on a topic that the participant considered important; making inappropriate comments or jokes; asking irrelevant personal questions (e.g., "How many children do you have?" unless it comes up in the normal course of "small talk"); failing to check the tape recorder; asking leading questions such as "Don't you agree that principals should welcome teacher advice?"; asking multiple questions such as "Why was the supervisor union against shared decision making and what do you think about the superintendent who was against merit pay?"; and inferring something not said or meant by the participant.

4. Tips: Practice an actual interview with a friend, spouse, relative, or colleague; bring a tape recorder and extra blank tapes; organize your questions in advance; have fun; be a good listener; paraphrase the participant's main points; build rapport, especially at the beginning; probe when necessary; use a small inconspicuous tape recorder because a big one might make the participant self-conscious and consequently uncomfortable; ask questions when you do not understand what the participant meant; include open-ended questions such as "Take me through your day." or "Describe that meeting with the student."; and send out thank you cards/letters as soon as you complete interviews. Also, read Chapter

6 in Seidman (1998) for more detailed suggestions and information. See also Chirban, 1996.

Note the difference between the way qualitative and quantitative researchers would use interviews. The typical qualitative interview would be unstructured and open-ended. Using a protocol with a predetermined set of questions would generally be avoided. Qualitative interviewers want to encourage a relaxed atmosphere wherein ideas can be exchanged freely and easily. Qualitative interviews are really chats, rather than formal procedures. Also, a qualitative interviewer would not necessarily feign objectivity, but may, at times, interact with the participant in an open, lively dialogue.

Focus groups (Krueger, 2000; Vaughn, Schumn, & Sinagub, 1996) are groups of individuals selected by a researcher and consent voluntarily to share their views and opinions on specific topics related to a research project. As a type of survey, a focus group is not unlike a group interview.

For example, as an assistant principal in an elementary school, I asked my upper grade teachers to join me for a focused group session during lunchtime, during which I heard their opinions about the new textbook series adopted the previous year. Hearing their varied views provided an invaluable method of data collection that helped our textbook committee arrive at a decision about continuing or discontinuing the series.

Examine the sample Interview Protocol below. Notice the elements included (purpose, participants, circumstance, length of interview, introductory script, and actual questions). What do you think the purpose is for providing an introductory script? Be sure to consistently introduce the interview to each participant to avoid potential biases, extraneous statements, leading information, and so on. Make certain to achieve consensual **validity** for the questions you pose.

Interview Protocol for Teachers

Purpose: To find out teacher's views on the impact of sensory integration treatment on behaviors in adaptive developmental skills and academic achievement among preschool and elementary school aged students.

Participants to be Interviewed: Teachers of students with sensory integration issues.

Circumstance of Interview: Conference room in person.

Approximate length of interview: 15 minutes.

Hi, thank you for agreeing to participate in this study. The purpose of this interview is to hear your views on the impact of sensory integration dysfunction and treatment in your classroom. Be advised that participation in this interview indicates consent. You have the right to cease your involvement at any time. All names and other identifying factors will be kept confidential.

Thank you, your help is greatly appreciated.

1. What Sensory Integration issues, if any, have you noticed in your student(s) with Sensory Integration Dysfunction during classroom assignments? Describe.

2. What Sensory Integration issues, if any, have you noticed in your student(s) with Sensory Integration Dysfunction during lunch? Describe.

3. What modifications, if any, do you need to provide to accommodate students with sensory integration dysfunction in your classroom?

4. Have you found that Sensory Integration treatment has an impact on academic achievement? Explain.

5. Have you found that Sensory Integration treatment has an impact on daily living skills? Explain.

Whether you are conducting a group focus or one-on-one interview remain attentive and practice good listening skills:
Try this activity:

Turn to a neighbor. Each of you has one minute to share information about each other's professional and personal lives. Each of you talks for a minute. No one can take notes and no questions or discussion is allowed. At the end of two minutes, each of you should recount to each other or to the whole group what he or she has learned about the colleague. As you try to recount the information your colleague shared, you may be amazed to see how little you remember and how inaccurate some of your recollections are. This exercise awakens the need to develop listening skills.

The three types of techniques that follow promote effective listening and understanding (see Table 8.12)

- The first category, listening techniques, have a dual purpose: they encourage the speaker to continue and indicate that you are following carefully; they support your listening by inserting brief comments that relate to the content of the message.

- The second category, nonverbal clues, have similar effects: they clearly indicate to the speaker the listener's attention and free both the speaker and listener from physical distractions and barriers that hinder interactions.

- The third category, reflecting and clarifying techniques, are the most important in terms of verifying understanding and the most frequently omitted. Most miscommunication results from the speaker saying one thing and the listener hearing another. How often do children say? "You aren't listening to me!"

Table 8.12. Communication Techniques

Listening	Nonverbal Clues	Reflecting and Clarifying

"Uh-huh"
 "OK"
 "I'm following you"
 "For instance"
 "And?"
 "Mmm"
 "I understand"
 "This is great
   information for me"
 "Really?"
 "Then?"
 "So?"
 "Tell me more"
 "Go on"
 "I see"
 "Right"
	Affirmative nods and
	   Smiles
	 Open body language,
	   e.g., arms open
	 Appropriate distance
	   From speaker—not
	   too close or too far
	 Eye contact
	 Nondistracting
	   Environment
	 Face speaker and lean
	   Forward
	 Barrier-free space, e.g.,
	   Desk not used as
	   Blocker
		"You're angry because . . ."
		 "You feel . . . because . . ."
		 "You seem quite upset."
		 "So, you would like . . ."
		 "I understand that you
		   see the problem as . . ."
		 "I'm not sure, but I think
		   you mean . . ."
		 "I think you're saying . . ."

Source: Sullivan and Glanz, 2005

Adults are often not as open and hear from their own perspective without verifying. So many misunderstandings could be avoided through the use of these techniques. Now practice these three types of skills by pairing with a neighbor and have a conversation. Refer to the chart and see if you can appropriately use a particular communication technique.

Now, conduct a mock interview and intentionally use the listening, nonverbal clues, and reflecting and clarifying skills reviewed above.

Reflection

Think of ways to incorporate interviews and group focus interviews.

Module 3 Review

In this Module you learned some basics about interviewing and group focus, including: advantages as a data collection tool, some guidelines, and an example of a group focus interview.

Self-Test Check

1. The major purpose of using an interview protocol is to

    a. offer respondents a way to participate in the interview without having the interviewer present

    b. increase the chances that the respondent will respond honestly

    c. be able to conduct the interview in case the interviewer is not present

    d. provide the interviewer with a set of guidelines for conducting the interview

2. True or False: Interviews are generally considered qualitative in nature.

3. True or False: A Focus Group is a type of group interview.

Answers: 1) d; 2) t; 3) t

Study Questions

1. What are the advantages of using interviews as a data collection instrument?

2. What are its limitations?

3. How precisely may you be able to incorporate interviews or group focus interviews in your study?

4. What steps must you take to adequately prepare for an interview?

5. Do you think conducting a mock interview would help you conduct a real one? Explain.

Activity

1. Plan a mock interview with a classmate or friend. Role play the interview. Later describe what you would have done differently during an actual interview.

Module 4: Examining Test Data

Tests are perhaps the most common tools used to collect data by educational researchers. Two typical tests are commonly used in data collection:

1. **criterion-referenced tests** are one of two major types of **testing** instruments that measure minimum levels of student performance. Teacher-made tests are one example of a criterion-referenced test. The teacher usually establishes an objective (or criterion) and then measures the extent to which students meet the objective. Criterion-referenced tests are one of many possible data collection sources. (In contrast, see norm-referenced tests.)

2. **norm-referenced tests** (synonymous with **standardized tests**) are one of two major types of **testing** instruments that measure differences among individuals being tested. Each student's score is compared to the *norm* group, usually a nationally determined norm. A norm-referenced test, such as a standardized math test, can indicate how a given student, say 10-year-old Jerry, measures up against other ten-year-olds in the nation. For instance, if Jerry scores in the 65th **percentile**, this indicates that his score on the test was higher than 65% of ten-year-olds who took the test. Obviously, it also means that 35% scored higher than Jerry. Thus, norm-referenced tests compare students to other students on some pre-established norm or standard. Norm-referenced tests are usually used as important data collection sources.

Another data collection **instrument** (or data source) that is a kind of standardized or norm-referenced test is an **achievement test**. Achievement tests are commonly used measures or **assessment** tools in educational research. An achievement test assesses an individual's knowledge or proficiency in a given content area. The Stanford Achievement Test and the Iowa Test of Basic Skills are examples of standardized achievement tests.

An achievement test is one form of **data collection** that may be used by an educator, for instance, to arrive at a decision about levels of student achievement in a particular content area. Analysis of results of these achievement tests may yield valuable information in terms of needed remediation in specific content areas.

Achievement or standardized tests are, unfortunately, overused sometimes by supervisors and teachers who consider them the most important pieces of data when trying to arrive at a decision about levels of pupil achievement. Although an invaluable source of information, achievement tests should be considered as part of a **portfolio** of other assessment tools. No single assessment device should be used in making a decision about a program or practice. This book advocates a multidimensional, **triangular** approach to data collection.

Another data collection instrument that is a kind of standardized or norm-referenced test is an **aptitude test**. This test is designed to predict someone's ability to perform. The use of IQ tests is an example of an aptitude test. The SAT (Scholastic Aptitude Test) taken by precollegiate students is another example of an aptitude test.

Achievement tests are commonly used measures or **assessment** tools in educational research. An achievement test is a kind of **standardized test** in which an individual's knowledge or proficiency in a given content area is assessed. The Stanford Achievement Test and the Iowa Test of Basic Skills are examples of standardized achievement tests.

Aptitude test a kind of standardized test used as a data collection instrument (or data source) designed to predict someone's ability to perform. The use of IQ tests is an example of an aptitude test. The SAT test taken by precollegiate students is another example of an aptitude test.

Reflection

Think of ways to incorporate test data.

Module 4 Review

In this Module you learned some basics about test data, including types of tests commonly used in data collection.

Self-Test Check

1. Explain the difference between a criterion and norm referenced tests.

2. Explain the difference between an achievement and an aptitude test.

Answers: Refer back to module

Study Questions

1. What are the advantages and disadvantages of using test data?

2. What kinds of test data are available in your school or district?

Activity

1. Ask a principal to review summaries of test data, in confidence, in order to learn how such summaries are of value for collecting data.

Module 5: Other Means to Collect Data

School profile sheets may contain many of these aforementioned test scores. School profile sheets frequently analyze test scores over an extended period of time for various groups of students in different grades. As such, they are an invaluable source of information for an educational researcher.

Useful information may also be gleaned from tests that do not provide quantitative outcomes. Writing samples, for instance, are usually marked holistically and can be used as qualitative data. Although no longer as common as they used to be, oral examinations may be yet another kind of test used to collect data. Can you think of any others?

School Profile Data

School profile data sheets, generally available through the district office or state agencies, provide a wealth of important documentary information. These sheets provide reliable, clear data about a school's resources and students' needs in order to plan effectively for school improvement. These sheets provide achievement and background data over a period of years. Assessing student achievement over a four-year period, for example, is relatively easy. Data may include standardized reading and math scores by grade level over a four-year period; a statistical overview of a school's characteristics (percent utilization, capacity, staff-student ratio, repair orders, etc.); demographic backgrounds of faculty, staff, and students; teacher characteristics (e.g., certification or tenure status); student characteristics (including mobility, class size, attendance rates, etc.).

Data derived from such profile sheets are easily obtained and interpreted. Such information may prove invaluable for collecting data about a specific program, practice, or procedure.

Have you seen your school's profile sheet lately? Ask your principal to give you one to peruse and see how much information is readily available.

Multimedia

Too often researchers neglect this valuable source for collecting data. Use of multimedia (including audiotape recordings, videotapes, films, photographs, electronic mail surveys, among others) has many advantages over more traditional methods for collecting data. Don't overlook using any of these mediums when collecting data.

For example, taking pictures of students showing how they feel about their projects is a wonderful qualitative way of communicating information. Pictures *are* worth a thousand words. Pictures that show a group of eager, enthusiastic, and smiling kindergarten students holding their "Big Books" indicate the pride they must have felt in creating them. Using videotapes to film students' reading skills in September and videotaping them again in June will provide striking qualitative evidence of reading growth.

Although many researchers may indicate that use of videotape and photography may reflect a subjective bias, these forms of media, if incorporated properly and judiciously, can provide unique evidence. As long as you **triangulate,** that is, incorporate other valid and reliable data collection methods, multimedia use makes sense.

How might you use multimedia to collect data? What are its limitations?

Portfolios

Portfolios are **data collection instruments** (or data sources) that include a great deal of information about a particular individual or group of individuals. Portfolios may include a student's achievement test scores, book reports, homework assignments, art projects, in-class tests, oral presentations, self-assessments, artwork, etc. (see Wolf, LeMahiew, & Eresh, 1992). Portfolios are excellent ways of collecting data from a variety of perspectives. Portfolios may later be analyzed qualitatively to arrive at a decision about the achievement levels, for example, of a particular student in language arts. Portfolio use is very much in consonance with the concept of **triangulation**. What's the connection?

How might you use portfolios to collect data?

Records

School records, other than formal test data found in school profile sheets, are commonly referred to by educators. Educators, for example, may collect data by examining cumulative record cards (revealing information about students), teacher files (revealing professional data about teachers, such as record of service), anecdotal records, and diaries/journals/logs.

How might you use records to collect data?

Reflection

What other means are at your disposal to collect data?

Module 5 Review

In this Module you learned some alternative ways to collect data including: school profile sheets, multimedia, portfolios, and records.

Activity

1. Examine several journal articles to discover three other ways data are collected.

Module 6: Validity and Reliability of Instruments

Aside from the word "statistics," the words "validity" and "reliability" *frighten* neophyte researchers. Fear not, but proceed slowly. Discussion of validity and reliability is included in this module even though the terms are relevant for quantitative and qualitative data analyses (Parts Nine and Ten) because they are initially most crucial when collecting data.

What is Validity?

Validity refers to the extent to which a test, survey, or some other **instrument** measures what it is intended to measure. If you were asked to complete a pretest on your knowledge of some aspects of research and the pretest was comprised of mathematical questions only, then the test would *not* be valid as it did not measure your knowledge of research, but rather your ability to compute and solve mathematical problems.

What are some Types of Validity?

There are four (4) general types of validity: *concurrent, construct, content,* and *predictive.* Descriptions of each type of validity are not necessary since for research projects you will unlikely ever need to use any of these four types of validity.

Perhaps the only exception would be use of *content* validity, to some extent. In the previous example, a **content analysis** of the curriculum or knowledge base of educational research would be undertaken and then the test items on the pretest would be compared to the *content* base to ascertain that the questions on the pretest reflect the content.

Have you ever taken a test in which you said, "we never covered this stuff?!" If you were to administer, for example, a test to a group of 12th graders based on Chapter 12 in their social studies textbook, you would check for *content* validity after writing the test to see whether or not answers to each question can be found in the chapter. If each question is, in fact, derived from the content of Chapter 12, then your test may be said to have *content* validity. By the way, determining content validity for standardized tests involves more sophisticated procedures.

Two other types of validity, although not thought of highly by many experts in the field, are useful for research purposes: *consensual* and *face* validity.

Consensual validity would be ascertained by asking people who will not be administered the test or survey (e.g., a colleague or a student in another class) whether or not the questions selected for inclusion are appropriate given the purpose of the assessment.

Face validity would be ascertained by asking participants or subjects to share their views about how valid a test or survey appears. Ever take an examination that was fair because it accurately reflected the content of the course? Such an exam might have high face validity. The converse could, of course, also be true if the content of the course didn't match the questions asked on the exam.

Reflection

Under what circumstances might you use content,
consensual, and face validity? Be specific.

What are Two Forms of Validity?

Internal validity refers to the extent to which the independent variable (i.e., treatment) is the true cause of the change in the dependent variable (i.e., outcome). Can you state with a degree of certainty, for instance, that the Teaching Method A (the independent variable) produced an observed effect on Student Achievement in Reading (the dependent variable)? Perhaps other extraneous or **confounding variables or factors** had greater effects than Teaching Method A. If some other variable was responsible for the effect, then one can say that the study has low internal validity. Conversely, if few if any extraneous variables affected the outcome, then the study might have high internal validity.

Confounding factors can cause erroneous conclusions to be drawn from a study. In group comparison studies, for example, changes in the **dependent variable** may not be caused by the **treatment** under study, but may, in fact, be influenced by some other intended or unforeseen factors. Two such confounding factors are the Hawthorne and John Henry effects.

The Hawthorne Effect occurs when members in the **experimental group** know they are receiving "special" **treatment** and, thus, will improve no matter what treatment they are receiving. Members of such experimental groups consider themselves special or privileged. The original Hawthorne studies were conducted by Elton Mayo and his associates in the late 1920s and early 1930s at the Hawthorne Plant of Western Electric near Chicago.

The John Henry Effect, the opposite of the Hawthorne Effect, occurs when subjects in the **control group** know they are, in a sense, competing with some other group (experimental) and, consequently, expend extra effort to perform better than the **experimental group.**

Both the Hawthorne and John Henry effects may cause erroneous conclusions to be drawn from your study and are, thus, called confounding factors. Obviously, every effort to make each group "feel" special would avert problems with the Hawthorne Effect, for example. In **group comparison** research (e.g., assessing the effect of computer-assisted instruction on computational skills between two groups) both groups should be exposed to some special **treatment** (computers, in this case) without letting the participants know what you are measuring. For example, the control group may use computers to enhance writing skills, while using traditional methods to learn computational skills. The experimental group is exposed to computers to enhance their mathematical computational skill development. Participants in this study do not know what you are measuring and, thus, the Hawthorne Effect is minimized.

A number of other extraneous variables might affect the results of a study. These variables are known as "threats to internal validity." They are:

- *History* refers to effects on data when collected at differing times. History can negatively affect data collection when, for instance, data are collected at the beginning of the academic year when respondents may not have had enough time to assess the impact of a particular program or practice. If you collected data on the impact of computer assisted instruction on reading achievement at the beginning of the year, you might find not see any impact because not enough time has elapsed to indicate an impact.

Too much time can also affect results. The more time that passes, other factors may influence the dependent variable. Once I was conducting a study using a special teaching method. A major snowstorm hit New York City and we lost many days of school. The weather pattern repeated itself for over six weeks resulting in many lost days. Impact of the treatment on the dependent variable was seriously compromised.

Reflection

Think of some reasons why this may be so.

- *Mortality* (or attrition) refers to a situation in which respondents or subjects of a study drop out for one reason or another (e.g., illness, moved) – also called "subject attrition." A poor rate of return of a questionnaire is an example of mortality. Fewer returns of the questionnaire reduces the number of participants in your study, and, thus, becomes a threat to internal validity.

- *Maturation* refers to students who do well due to natural maturation (physical or mental) and not necessarily due to the **treatment**. Therefore, if the treatments extend too long of a time, participants may have improved in respect to the dependent variable not due to the treatment but due to the natural maturation process. In other words, they would have improved regardless of the treatment.

- *Reactivity* refers to the likelihood that a pretest administered will affect post test results. Respondents to a **questionnaire,** for example, may figure out what "you are looking for" and respond accordingly on the post test.

- *Instrumentation*—refers to problems associated with the instruments used in data collection. Using two different tests to assess math knowledge, for instance, will not enable you to draw sound conclusions regarding the impact of the treatment on the dependent variable. If instrumentation is flawed in any way, a serious threat to validity occurs.

- *Statistical Regression* occurs when subjects are selected because of their low or high scores. The tendency of subjects who score extremely low on a pretest, for instance, to score closer to the mean on a posttest, regardless of the impact of the treatment is called statistical regression. In other words, students who score very low are likely to score higher on a posttest regardless of the treatment.

All of the cases above are a threat to validity because they have the potential to distort conclusions you can reasonably make.

Reflection

Think of ways to avoid these threats to internal validity

External validity a second form of **validity** that is synonymous with **generalizability**; i.e., the degree to which results can be generalized to other populations. Educational research studies, especially of a qualitative nature, are rarely generalizable and, therefore, have weak external validity. This lack of external validity does *not*, in any way, diminish the significance of research.

What is Reliability?

Reliability the degree to which an instrument yields consistent results under repeated administrations. When you hear the term "reliability" you should immediately think of "consistency."

Usually, if you want to know whether a particular **instrument** was reliable you would consult the test maker's manual. Reliability, whether reported by a manual or computed on one's own, is reported in terms of a **correlation coefficient.** The closer the coefficient of correlation, which is expressed in hundredths, comes to + 1.00, the higher the reliability factor. Thus, for instance, a reliability coefficient of .80 would indicate that the **instrument** (e.g., a test) is reliable. Remember that no test is ever 100% reliable.

What are Two Forms of Reliability?

In qualitative approaches to research, two forms of reliability are common:

A) *external reliability* refers to the degree to which your study can be replicated by others. In other words, if someone followed your procedures and methods, they would likely report similar findings. Yet, the nature of qualitative research is so personal that external reliability is difficult to attain.

In a study I completed (Glanz, 1998), I wanted to ascertain the kinds of images of principals that were depicted in film and television. After previewing dozens of sitcoms and movies, I identified, through **content analysis,** three categories of images. External reliability was confirmed, in this case, by having independent researchers view the same episodes to confirm my categories.

B) *internal reliability* is synonymous with *interrater reliability* (see below).

What are Some Common Reliability Tests?

A) the *test-retest method,* in which the same test is repeated over a period of time. Two test administrations are required. **Correlations** are taken between the two sets of test results. The resultant **correlation coefficient** is the index of reliability. Note that **correlations** can be inflated if the time interval between tests is short. Why do you think this is so?

B) the *parallel (or equivalent) forms method,* similar to the previous method, in which you retest the same group with an equivalent form of the test. This method requires two administrations (Form A of the test administered, for instance in September, and then Form B administered to the same group in March). The two sets of scores are correlated as they were in the test-retest method.

C) the *split-half method,* in which the test is split into two parts (or halves), such as odd-numbered items and even-numbered items. The test is administered to the same group. Two sets of scores are obtained for each person: a score based on the odd-numbered items and a score based on the even-numbered items. These two sets of scores are correlated to obtain a reliability coefficient. Note that the longer the test, the more reliable the test will be. Why do you think this is so?

Note that a split-half reliability quotient may be calculated by conducting a Pearson r (see Module 6 in Part Nine and the statistical software described) between the odd-numbered and even-numbered items. Whatever r value you come up with, double it (e.g., r=.67; 2 X .67 = 1.34). Then, add 1 to the r value (i.e., 1 + .67 = 1.67). Then, take the doubled r value (i.e., 1.34) and divide it by the value in which you added a 1 (i.e., 1.34 and 1.67). Therefore, 1.34/1.67 = .80. The .80 value is the split-half reliability coefficient. Whether or not you consider the .80 reliable or not depends on the purpose of your study. It's a subjective decision you make as a researcher. For the most part, any r value above .50 can be considered reliable.

You may also refer to Crowl's 1986 book titled *Fundamentals of research: A practical guide for educators and special educators,* published by Horizons, Inc., in which easy-to-follow, step-by-step procedures for calculating Pearson r's and split-halfs are provided in his appendixes.

D) *KR-21* (Kuder-Richardson Formula), used to measure the consistency of an **instrument** in which all items have the same characteristic or degree of difficulty. Tests that include diverse items or varied levels of difficulty should be subjected to split-half reliability assessments. KR-21 may be calculated by referring to Crowl's work cited above.

E) *Interrater reliability* (also known as *internal reliability),* used in **qualitative research** and **single subject research designs,** involves comparing ratings or rankings given by independent observers. The more similar the rankings, the higher the reliability. Interrater reliability, therefore, refers to the percentage of agreement among independent observers.

Teachers use this form of reliability in grading standardized writing tests. Three teachers rate a given essay separately and an average score is then computed. In this way, no single rating is given preference.

Reliability is enhanced by use of multiple data sources.

Reflection

Why do you think this is so? Moreover, if reliability of qualitative studies is enhanced through the use of multiple observers, why do you think this is so?

What is the Relationship between Reliability and Validity?

A valid test is always reliable, but a reliable test is not always valid. If a test is not reliable it cannot be valid. But, if a test is not valid, it may or may not be reliable.

Reflection

Based on what you've learned thus far, explain why the preceding is so. Share thoughts with a colleague and then with your professor.

Module 6 Review

In this Module you learned some of the nuts and bolts of validity and reliability.

Self-Test Check

1. True or False: A threat to internal validity can occur whenever an extraneous event occurs that affects the dependent variable.

2. True or False: The following description might be considered a threat to internal validity: Let's say you wanted to assess a particular workshop on teacher morale in your district. If at the same time of this study or in the recent past a budget crisis loomed that froze teacher wages, results from your study might be influenced by this budgetary situation and not be caused by the series of workshops offered.

3. Can you think of a situation in which you conduct a quantitative study that has low external validity?

4. This can cause erroneous conclusions to be drawn from a study
    a. confounding factors
    b. contextual validity
    c. inter-rater reliability
    d. statistical significance
    e. sample exclusion

5. This refers to the degree to which your study can be replicated by others
    a. internal reliability
    b. external reliability
    c. internal validity
    d. external validity
    e. none of these

Answers: 1) t; 2) t; 3) For instance, when numbers of participants are low; 4) a; 5) b

Activity

1. Examine several journal articles to discover how internal and external vaidlity/reliability are reported.

Part Nine:

Thesis Overview—Chapter 3 of Thesis, Section 5: Research Design 5—Quantitative Data Analysis

Focus Questions

1　Why do you think that calculating statistics in the 21st century is so easy?

2.　Why is data analysis so important?

3.　What is the simplest way to quantitatively analyze data gathered from a questionnaire?

4.　What would you want to know that would allay your apprehensions about statistics?

Module 1: Statistical Analyses

Sadistic statistics?! Not really. With the advent of computer technology, use of statistical analysis has become relatively easy. No longer do you have to take out the abacus, calculator, or compute by longhand complicated formulae. Computers can conduct statistical analyses faster than you can say "hey, that's significant." Computers are readily available at campus computer lab centers and appropriate software packages are menu-driven for easy use.

The only slightly difficult thing to do is to be able to select the correct statistical calculation to match the type of research conducted. Programs exist today to help you do even that. So, as we discuss some statistics, don't fret since the computer can do it all.

Please note, therefore, that longhand calculations will not, for the most part, be described in this chapter. No educator would spend the time doing that kind of calculation. Learning how to analyze statistics on a computer is essential and will be part of your training in an educational research course or workshop.

Two common types of statistics are:

1. **descriptive statistics** and

2. **inferential statistics.**

Descriptive statistics is one category or type of statistics that is used to describe and summarize data. Two of the most common ways to describe data statistically are by determining the mean and the **standard deviation.**

Mean is synonymous with average score. Mean indicates how a typical person scored on your test or survey. Mean is computed very simply by adding the numbers and dividing by the total number of numbers used. What would be the mean of these numbers: 23, 45, 12,45, 23? Right, 29.6. Simply add the five numbers (23 + 45 + 12 + 45 + 23) and divide by five (since there are five total numbers).

Standard Deviation (symbolized *S.D.*) indicates how much scores vary from each other.

For example, consider the means of these two sets of scores:

        Group X = 5 scores   Group y = 5 scores
        50 50 50 50 50   100 50 45 35 20
        250\5 = 50   250\5 = 50

Note that although both groups have the same mean, the scores in group X seem much more homogeneous than the scores in group Y. How do we describe the differences in the variation of the scores in both groups? Right, using standard deviation will indicate how much scores in this group vary. Standard deviation is easily calculated by using a calculator or computer.

Both mean and standard deviation are accurate **descriptive statistics** since they provide a good picture of a given distribution of scores. Means, of course, tell us the average score. Why do you think it may be important to know the mean of a given group of scores?…Knowing the standard deviation tells us how dispersed scores are in a given group. If you find a high *S.D.*, you might want to explore further reasons why scores in this group varied so much from one another. This knowledge may encourage us to examine our treatment and/or design of the study. Also, *S.D.* helps us draw conclusions about the population from what we know about the **sample.** How mean and standard deviation can be used is described later in the chapter.

Percentages, as will be explained later, can also be considered descriptive statistics in research projects.

Thus, descriptive statistics describe and summarize data numerically. For purposes of educational research, the following are the most useful and common **descriptive statistics:**

(A) **Mean** (symbolized *X* or *M*)—a measure of central tendency indicating the arithmetic average;

(B) **Standard deviation** (symbolized *S.D.*)—a measure of dispersion indicating the amount scores vary from each other;

(C) **Percentage** (symbolized %)—a measure denoting "percentage" of individuals who gave a particular response or achieved a particular score;

(D) **Correlation coefficient** (symbolized *r*)—a measure of relationship indicating the degree to which two or more **variables** are related to each other.

In contrast to descriptive statistics, **inferential statistics** tell us how much confidence we can have in generalizing from a **sample** to a **population.** Although educational research projects generally do not involve studies that seek generalization, certain useful and common inferential statistics are:

Tests of significance (see level of significance in the Glossary) include:

(A) **t-Tests**—determine significance of difference between means of two groups;

(B) **sign tests**—determine significance of difference between means of one group;

(C) **Mann-Whitney U-Tests**—determine whether two small groups differ significantly (works similar to a t-Test); and

(D) **Chi square analyses**—(often symbolized by X^2, the 22nd letter of the Greek alphabet) determine the relationship between two or more **nominal variables** (see **scales of measurement** below and in the Glossary).

Scales of measurement are important to determine what types of statistical analyses are appropriate.

Four (4) scales of measurement are:

Nominal (categorical) is the lowest scale of measurement. Nominal categories are not quantifiable; i.e., non-numerical, such as gender, ethnicity, and religious affiliation. An easy way to remember nominal variables is to know that nominal = naming. That is, a nominal variable just names things. For instance, gender (male or female), names of states (e.g., Texas or California), socioeconomic status (upper, middle, lower), and political party affiliations (Republican, Democratic, etc.) are nominal. Nominal variables have no order (from high to low), one category is not better than another; they are non-numerical. **Chi square** analyses are conducted with nominal data.

Ordinal (order) is a scale that puts subjects in order from high to low, but does not indicate how much higher or lower one subject is in relation to another. An example of an ordinal variable is: ranking height from tallest to shortest (e.g., Mary #1; Sue #2; Fran #3; Bill #4); or ranking three brands of cereal by consumer preference. Note that **Likert scales** are really ordinal, but in education they are treated statistically as **interval.**

Interval is a scale of measurement that tells us how much subjects differ from one another. For example, **raw scores** are interval scales. Subject 1 (S1) with a raw score of 100 (out of 100) has 50 points more than subject 2 (S2) with a score of 50. Although we can say that SI scored 50 points higher than S2, we can't say that S1 is twice as smart as S2 because interval scales have no absolute zero point (as do **ratio** scales). Differences between categories in interval data are considered real differences in that the difference between a raw score of 4 and a raw score of 2 is the same difference between raw scores of 6 and 8.

Ratio is the highest and most precise scale or level of measurement. The ratio scale is the same as the interval scale, except that it has an absolute zero point. Weight, for example, is based on a ratio scale. Someone who weighs 140 lbs. is twice as heavy as someone who weighs 70 lbs.

Here's a mnemonic to help you recall the 4 **scales of measurement:** No One Is Ready (**N** = nominal; **O** = ordinal; **I** = interval; **R** = ratio).

Note that **parametric statistics** are statistical techniques, more common than **nonparametric statistics**, used to analyze data for interval or ratio data or when nominal or when data are normally distributed. In education, we generally deal with data that are normally distributed (i.e., the proverbial bell curve) such as test and attitudinal scores. **Nonparametric statistics** are statistical techniques used to analyze data for nominal or ordinal data or when data are not normally distributed.

The remainder of this module will be devoted to more fully explaining some of these descriptive and inferential statistics. An explanation of many other statistical analyses will not be undertaken because they are not usually utilized in research projects by masters students. Note that many statistical operations can today be easily computed using a computer with a popular and easy-to-use statistical package.

Application of Mean, Standard Deviation, and Percentage

In this section, results of a survey distributed to teachers about their attitudes toward supervision will be analyzed. Results that follow are fictionalized. The purpose of the analysis that follows will be to demonstrate how you, as a researcher, can easily apply some basic descriptive statistics to analyze survey research. Other forms of descriptive statistic such as correlational analyses can be easily carried out by using one of the many computer programs.

Other than **standardized tests,** the most common **data collection** technique used by researchers is the questionnaire. Let's illustrate how to apply three very common descriptive statistics: **mean, standard deviation,** and percentages. Let's apply them to a survey disseminated to teachers in Public School XY. The **Likert scale questionnaire** was designed to determine teachers' attitudes toward supervision.

The survey was disseminated to a group of 34 teachers. In order to analyze the data, you must develop an answer sheet of sorts that indicates favorable responses. Since the questionnaire is designed to assess attitudes toward supervision, which choices on the Likert scale questionnaire indicate favorable attitudes toward supervision?

Let's say you develop a 20-item questionnaire that includes, for example, the following two items, among others:

1. Your supervisor provides helpful feedback after a formal observation, and

2. Your supervisor offers little, if any, support in student disciplinary matters.

Since you've developed a Likert scale, the choices listed are Strongly Disagree (SD), Disagree (D), Agree (A), and Strongly Agree (SA). Choices are stated as follows:

SD D A SA 1. Your supervisor provides helpful feedback after a formal observation.

SD D A SA 2. Your supervisor offers little, if any, support in student disciplinary matters.

What response for each question indicates a favorable attitude toward supervision? Well, for the first question the most favorable response would be *SA* and least favorable response would be *SD*. Since four choices are provided (*SD, D, A, SA*), you would award 4 points to the most favorable response (*SA*), 3 points to the next favorable response (*A*), 2 points to *D*, and 1 point to *SD*, the least favorable response.

How might you code the second question?…Right, the most favorable response this time is *SD* which receives a 4, *D* receives a 3, and so on. Notice that the value awarded for each response varies depending on the question. You determine favorable responses based on what would be considered to be generally accepted among educators.

If your questionnaire has 10 items, what would be the highest possible favorable score?…Right, 40 (10 items, each receiving a 4 for the most favorable response equals 40). And what would be the lowest possible score, indicating the least favorable attitudes toward supervision?…Right, 10 (10 items, each receiving a 1 for the least favorable response equals 10).

Mini-exercise: What would be the highest and lowest scores for a questionnaire that has 20 items?

Here's an example of how a researcher coded the following questions indicating favorable attitudes toward supervision (note that the higher the score, the more favorable respondents' attitudes are toward supervision):

1. Supervision facilitates instructional improvement.

    SA   A   D   SD

    4   3   2   1

2. Supervision is a waste of time.

    SA   A   D   SD

    1   2   3   4

Now, if 32 individuals completed the questionnaire, you would have a total score for each of them as follows, for example:

$$S1 = 40$$
$$S2 = 34$$
$$S3 = 10$$
$$S4 = 18$$
$$S5 = 26$$
$$S6 = 30$$
$$S7 = 14$$
$$S8 = 20$$
$$S9 = 10$$
$$S10 = 30$$

and so on

Obviously, subject 4 (S4) has a more unfavorable attitude toward supervision than subject 1 (S1). Who has the least favorable attitude toward supervision?

Now, how would we apply the three basic descriptive statistics to analyze these data? The results below, for two questions, is one common and easy way to indicate results.

Teachers' Attitudes Toward Supervision: Survey Results

1. *Your supervisor provides helpful feedback after a formal observation.*

   N = 32

   21.9% Strongly Disagree (Raw score = 7)

   75.0% Disagree (Raw score = 24)

   3.0% Agree (Raw score = 1)

   0.00% Strongly Agree (Raw score = 0)

   Mean = 1.81

   Standard Deviation = .47

   Conclusion: An overwhelming percentage of respondents maintain that the supervisor doesn't provide helpful feedback after an observation.

2. *Your supervisor offers little, if any; support in student disciplinary matters.*

   N = 32

   0.00% Strongly Disagree (Raw score = 0)

   15.6% Disagree (Raw score = 5)

   62.5% Agree (Raw score = 20)

   21.9% Strongly Agree (Raw score = 7)

   Mean = 1.94

   Standard Deviation = .62

   Conclusion: An overwhelming percentage of respondents maintain that the supervisor offers little, if any, support in student disciplinary matters.

Notice in the example above that we first note that N = 32. This indicates that 32 individuals responded to the first question. Therefore, *N* signifies the *number* of respondents. Raw scores indicate the number of respondents who filled in a given choice (e.g., 7 individuals responded "Strongly Disagree" to the first question).

Percentages are calculated by dividing the raw score (e.g., 7 in the first question above) into *N* (therefore, 7/32 = 21.9%). Calculate the other percentages on your own now....

Many researchers only rely on percentages for analyzing data. However, use of means and standard deviations are also commonly employed. Means and standard deviations are calculated easily using a calculator or by using a computer program such as **STATPAK**, as follows:

You would enter the STATPAK's main menu and select calculations for Mean and Standard Deviation. You will then be asked to enter a number for the first entry. Note that you will have 32 entries because 32 individuals responded to the first question. To calculate the mean and standard deviation, you need to look back at your key to determine how many points are awarded for a given choice. In the first question above, we awarded 4 points for a "Strongly Disagree" response because that would be considered the most favorable response to the first question. We also need to note the raw score for each response.

Since a "Strongly Disagree" response gets 4 points and 7 individuals respond "Strongly Disagree," we would enter the number "4" seven times into the STATPAK program. Why? Because seven individuals are awarded 4 points each for the "Strongly Disagree" choice.

The next choice, "Disagree," is awarded 3 points. How many individuals responded "Disagree"?…Right, 24. Enter 3, twenty-four times. The next category is "Agree." How many respondents chose "Agree"?…Right, only 1. Therefore, enter the number 2 (indicating 2 points) only once. Since no one responded "Strongly Disagree," no entry is made for the next choice.

Follow directions on the STATPAK menu and in a few seconds you will see the following page:

Standard Deviation for Samples and Populations

STATISTIC	VALUE
No. of Scores (N)	32
Mean	3.19
Standard Deviation	0.47

Compute the mean and standard deviation for the second question above using a calculator or the STATPAK program (or any similar program, for that matter).

Sometimes, a Likert Scale may incorporate other choices such as *Very much, Somewhat,* or *Not at all.* Also, results are often stated simply using percentages rather than means and standard deviations. Examine the analysis of results derived from a questionnaire (below) which indicates results based on student attitudes toward school:

1. *Indicate the degree to which your classes were informative and educational.*

   N=27

   61.0% Very Much

   28.0% Somewhat

   11.0% Not at all

2. *Indicate the degree to which you enjoy your academic studies.*

   N=34

   70.0% Very Much

   20.0% Somewhat

   10.0% Not at all

3. *Counseling has met my expectations*

     N= 35

     11.0% Very much

     61.0% Somewhat

     28.0% Not at all

Can you, for extra credit (just a joke), figure out how many people responded for each choice above?! It's really quite simple. Multiply each percentage by N (the total number of respondents). For example, for question number one: multiply .61 by 27 = 16.47, rounded off to 16 people. That means that 16 people responded "very much" to the first question. Then, multiply .28 by 27 = 7.56 = 8; and .11 by 27 = 2.97 = 3. Thus, 16 + 8 + 3 = a total of 27 people who responded to the first question.

Whenever you want to determine a raw score, you multiply the percentage by the number (in this case, the number of total respondents). Therefore, for example, if I told you that Jeremy received an 70% on his math test and that there were 20 questions, what would be his raw score (i.e., number of correct responses)? That's right, multiply .70 by 20 = 14 correct responses. Now, figure out the number of people who responded for each choice in questions two and three above (answers can be found after exercise 2 below).

The examples illustrated above analyze results for one group. Sometimes, however, you might want to compare attitudes of two different groups, such African American parents' attitudes toward the school versus attitudes of Hispanic American parents. To analyze results from two groups, you would follow the same procedures for each group as you did before. You would now have, however, two sets of scores, one for each parent group. Although you could analyze each group using percentages, means, and/or standard deviations as explained above, you might consider another approach, such as the use of **correlational analysis** or **t-Test** analysis on both groups.

A correlational analysis would indicate the degree of relationship between both sets of group scores. You might conclude, for example, that there is a significant relationship between the way African American parents feel about the school and the way Hispanic American parents feel. To ascertain whether there is a significant statistical difference, however, between the two groups, a t-Test analysis should be undertaken, as will be explained in the next module.

Tables, Graphs, and Charts

Whether you employ quantitative and/or qualitative analyses, using tables and graphs, whenever possible, to summarize your findings will not only better facilitate data interpretation (see Part Ten), but will serve as a way to display data after analysis, and serve as an easy, convenient, and visual way for reporting your data to others. "A picture (i.e., table or graph) is worth a thousand words." Use your imagination to devise tables and/or figures to summarize your findings. A sample of a table, a graph, and a chart are included to demonstrate how data can be displayed visually.

Table 9.1 illustrates how data can be presented in a table. This table indicates that two groups were comparable at the start of the project. How do we know this? The means and a t-Test (t = .19) did not indicate a significant difference. Yet, after the administration of the posttest, presumably months later, a significant difference between both groups was apparent (t = 8.69). Therefore, the original hypothesis ("failing sixth grade math students who participate in the after-school tutorial programs will have higher math scores than failing math students who do not participate in the after-school math tutorial programs") was supported. Please note that further discussion of the t-Test occurs in the next module.

See Figure 9.1 for a sample graph. Graph your data whenever possible.

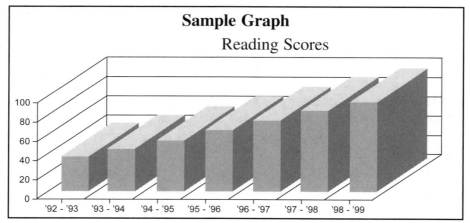

Figure 9-1. Bradley School reading scores. Percent of students reading on grade level in the fourth grade from 1993 to 1999.

Exercises

1. You've analyzed the result of an AIDS questionnaire distributed to 70 high school freshmen as follows:

   A. AIDS can reduce the body's ability to fight disease.

SA	A	D	SD
53	14	3	0
75.7%	20%	4.3%	0%

   $\overline{X} = 3.71$
   $S.D. = .54$

   B. AIDS attacks the immune system in the body.

SA	A	D	SD
50	18	2	0
71.4%	25.7%	2.9%	0%

   $\overline{X} = 3.69$
   $S.D. = .53$

C.   A person can be infected with the AIDS virus (HIV) but not have the disease AIDS.

SA	A	D	SD
41	20	7	2
58.6%	28.6%	10.0%	2.9%

$\overline{X} = 3.43$
$S.D. = .79$

Describe how you would compute the percentages, means, and standard deviations. Based on this excerpted data, describe what the survey indicates. What do the means and standard deviations tell us?

_____

_____

_____

Check answers in sections above

2.   Develop a 5-item questionnaire, a coded answer sheet, and provide some dummy data. Compute means, standard deviations, and percentages for each item.

_____

_____

_____

Answers will vary. Answers for questions two and three in the previous section are, respectively: 24, 7, and 3 people; and 4, 21, and 10 people.

3. Examine the table below and draw four comparisons between the Cooperative Learning experimental group and the Whole Class control group. This table is culled from a study of a group of secondary school teachers in Israel conducted by Sharan and Shachar, 1988 (reprinted with permission, Springer-Verlag, Inc.)

	Effects of Complex Cooperative Learning in a History Course by SES			
	Groups			
	Experimental Cooperative Learning		**Control Whole Class**	
Test	**High SES**	**Low SES**	**High SES**	**Low SES**
(Pretest)				
M	20.99	14.81	21.73	12.31
S.D.	9.20	7.20	10.53	7.05
(Posttest)				
M	62.60	50.17	42.78	27.03
S.D.	10.85	14.44	14.40	13.73
Mean Gain:	41.61	35.36	21.05	14.92

_____

_____

_____

Answer: Any of the following comparisons can be made: (1) In the pretests the lower-SES students scored significantly lower than the higher-SES students; (2) The lower-SES students taught by cooperative learning achieved over two times higher than those of the lower-SES students taught by whole class instruction; (3) Lower-SES students taught with cooperative learning scored higher than High-SES students taught with whole class instruction; (4) High-SES students scored higher than High-SES students with whole class instruction.

Module 1 Review

In this Module you learned some of the fundamentals of statistics for educational research. Students tend to shy away from statistical procedures, especially inferential ones. The truth of the matter is that quite often students don't use them because as master's degree students who work as educators in school settings they are unable to conduct group comparison studies and so they opt for either descriptive statistics or something more qualitative. That is fine as long as you don't avoid inferential statistics simply because you think it's too hard. Your professor will demonstrate that computing statistics is quite easy via the use of computer software (see Module 6).

Self-Test Check

1. True or False: Correlation coefficients are statistical measures that indicate the degree of relationship between two variables.

2. True or False: Inferential statistics use significance tests.

3. This statistic (often symbolized by X^2) is a statistical technique for assessing the relationship between two or more nominal variables
   a. descriptive
   b. Mann-Whitney
   c. chi square
   d. t-Test

4. This category or type of statistics that tells us how much confidence we can have in generalizing from a sample to a population.
   a. descriptive statistics
   b. Halo Effect
   c. inferential statistics
   d. t-tests
   e. significance tests

5. Check yourself by defining these terms: t-Tests, S.D., scales of measurement, parametric statistics.

   Answers: 1) t; 2) t; 3) c; 4) c; 5) Refer to module

Study Questions and Activity

1. How might you use statistics to analyze data?

2. What else do you need to know in order to feel more comfortable using statistics?

3. Although you might not be able to utilize inferential statistical procedures, brainstorm a situation wherein you might. Establish "dummy" (made-up) data and compute various statistical procedures, including a t-Test. Share results with a colleague. Was it difficult? Explain why or why not.

Module 2: The t-Test

A t-Test is a popular and common statistical technique that determines the degree of significance between the **means** of two groups. In other words, the purpose of a t-Test is to determine whether the difference between two means is statistically significant (see **statistical significance**). Parenthetically for those of you who are trivia buffs, the t-Test, one of the best and most common statistical procedures used by masters degree students conducting quantitative analyses, was developed by British statistician William Gosset in 1908.

There are two types of t-Tests:

a. Independent t-Tests – Used when comparing scores between two independent or unrelated samples, or when the number of scores of both groups are different.

b. Non-Independent t-Tests (also called paired samples) – Used with scores derived from matched pairs or with one-group repeated measures. With this test, the number of scores of both groups must be equal.

Let's say you've divided your class into two equivalent groups using the **matched pairs** technique previously described in Module 1 of Part Five. Or, let's say you are a middle or high school teacher who wants to compare two equivalent classes (say, periods 4 and 6) in terms of science achievement. Both groups or classes would be exposed to a **treatment** and then a posttest would be administered. The results of the posttest are indicated in Figure 9.2 for two classes of five students each. Note that a t-Test would not ordinarily be used for groups less than 15 participants. I've used five students in each class to merely simplify the explanation of the t-Test. For groups less than 15, a **Mann-Whitney U-Test** should be conducted (see discussion in Module 4).

Posttest Results for t-Test Computation	
CLASS I	**CLASS II**
S1 = 85	S1 = 73
S2 = 82	S2 = 76
S3 = 78	S3 = 80
S4 = 75	S4 = 70
S5 = 72	S5 = 65

Figure 9.2.

The numbers in Figure 9.2 represent raw scores or interval data (see **scales of measurement**) based on posttest results. A score of 85, for instance, in Class I indicates a student's raw score on a science achievement test.

A cursory perusal of the data in Figure 9.2 may lead one to conclude that the students in the first class scored higher posttest scores than students in the second class. In other words, students in the first class have higher achievement in science than the other students. However, can we conclude that this difference is statistically significant? No, we can't.

To determine statistical significance requires that some sort of statistical operation be conducted. In this case, a t-Test would be the appropriate choice.

Computation of a t-Test can be performed using a calculator with a square root function or, more simply, using **STATPAK**, a computer-based statistical program that was introduced earlier in this chapter. It seems to me that no supervisor, teacher, or other practitioner would choose to expend the effort to compute any statistical calculations other than by using a computer-based program. Therefore, an explanation of any "long-hand" statistical computations will not be undertaken in this text.

To determine whether or not the post test scores of these classes are significantly different from one another, one would simply input the raw scores in a computer-based program, such as STATPAK, by pressing a couple of keys. STATPAK is very user-friendly and all you need to do is follow the menu-driven instructions on the screen. (Your professor will certainly demonstrate the ease of computer-based programs and you will have the opportunity to practice t-Test calculations on your own.)

While some programs actually indicate whether or not the t-Test result is significant (e.g., SPSS), STATPAK does not. To determine significance, you must consult a t-Test Table that is, by the way, very easy to interpret.

After inputting the information in Figure 9.2 (using a t-Test for non-independent means), you will find that the t value equals 2.49 (ignore the minus sign). The **degrees of freedom** *(df)* equal 4. Now, all you have to do is consult a t-Test Table that can be readily found in almost any statistics book. I have, however, included an abbreviated t-Test set of values in Table 9.1 for your use in this chapter. You would go down the left column *(df)* to the number 4 and look across at the values noted. Since your t-Value was 2.49, you would look for the value that is less than 3.00. In other words, to be significant, your t-Value must be higher than the values noted on the table. In this case, a t-Value of 2.49 is higher than the value under the .05 column (2.48), but lower than the value under the .01 column (5.02). Therefore, there is a **statistically**

Table 9.1.

Abbreviated Table of t-Values

Number of Subjects (df)	.05	.01
4	2.48	5.02
5	2.35	4.54
6	2.13	3.75
7	2.02	3.37
8	1.94	3.14
9	1.90	3.00
10	1.86	2.90
11	1.83	2.82
12	1.81	2.76
13	1.80	2.72
14	1.78	2.68
15	1.77	2.65
16	1.76	2.62
17	1.75	2.60
18	1.75	2.58
19	1.74	2.57
20	1.73	2.55
22	1.73	2.53
24	1.72	2.51
26	1.71	2.49
28	1.71	2.48
30	1.70	2.47
40	1.68	2.42
100	1.65	2.35

Note: t-values for directional hypotheses are presented.

significant difference between the posttest results of these two classes at the .05 level. One may, therefore, conclude that the differences between the two classes may be attributed to the **treatment** and not to a chance error factor (see **level of significance**).

In other words, there is a significant difference in achievement between the two groups. If these were posttest scores on attitudes toward science, and not achievement scores, then you could conclude that one group had more favorable attitudes toward science than the other group.

The level of significance is indicated in the following statement:

$$t = 2.49, p < .05$$

This statement indicates the obtained t-Value (2.49) and the probability (p) that differences between the two groups were due to chance error factors is less than 5%. In other words, you can conclude with 95% certainty that the differences between the two groups were true differences that resulted from the treatment.

Complete the following exercise that helps reinforce some of the ideas expressed above.

Exercise

1. Compare t-test results for the following cases:

	I				II		
Class 1		**Class 2**		**Class 1**		**Class 2**	
S1	83	S1	83	S1	10	S1	9
S2	83	S2	83	S2	8	S2	8
S3	80	S3	80	S3	7	S3	10
S4	99	S4	87	S4	7	S4	6
S5	98	S5	77	S5	5	S5	6
S6	76	S6	75	S6	4	S6	3
S7	63	S7	88				
S8	97	S8	75				
S9	79	S9	88				
S10	100	S10	75				
S11	40	S11	84				
S12	83	S12	79				
S13	75	S13	83				
S14	76	S14	84				
S15	77	S15	76				

III				IV		
Class 1		**Class 2**		**Class 1**		**Class 2**
S1	90	S1	73	S1	85	S1	73
S2	87	S2	76	S2	82	S2	76
S3	85	S3	80	S3	78	S3	80
S4	80	S4	70	S4	75	S4	70
S5	78	S5	65	S5	72	S5	65

Answers: I, $t = 0.20$; II. $t = 0.00$; III, $t = 5.50$; IV, $t = -3.00$.
Consult a t-test table to determine whether or not
differences are significant.

Module 2 Review

In this Module you learned the basics for employing the very common and really easy to use statistic known as the t-Test.

Self-Test Check

1. A test of significance used to determine whether there is significant difference between two means at a selected probability level is known as

   a. ANOVA.

   b. self-report research.

   c. chi square.

   d. t-Test.

   e. analysis of covariance.

   Answer is of course the _____.

Study Question

1. Under what circumstances do you think you could use a t-Test for data analysis?

Activity

1. Examine several journal articles to discover how t-Tests are used.

Module 3: The Sign Test

One of the common statistical techniques or procedures used in research to determine whether the post test scores are different from the pretest scores in **one-group pretest-posttest designs** is known as the Sign Test. Although we cautioned against using one-group pretest/posttest designs because of the inability to control for extraneous factors or **variables** that might have influenced results on the post test, this **design** is still popular in research and can be utilized if analyzed properly.

Let's say you are working with a teacher who wants to encourage her pupils to read more books and write more book reports {this example is culled from Willerman, McNeely, & Koffman, 1991). The method the teacher has traditionally used is the "Stars on the Chart" method. You remember that chart, don't you? A chart is displayed on a wall in the classroom with an alphabetical listing of all the names of the students. Stars are placed next to names to indicate the number of books read. You notice Ms. Smith's use of these charts and you surmise that many students are simply turned off to reading because the competition inherent in this "Stars on the Wall" approach is too much to bear for some students. You recommend another approach that you recently read about in *Instructor* magazine. You clip out the article for Ms. Smith and encourage her to try the new method.

Ms. Smith is intrigued by this new method of writing and publishing class newspapers that includes book reports written by the students. Newspapers are to be published weekly and disseminated throughout the school and community. Ms. Smith decides to try this approach. She wonders if this new method for encouraging book reports will significantly increase the number of books read by her students.

She states her **hypothesis** in null form: "There will be no difference in the number of books read by students whose book reports are rewarded by charting them with stars on the classroom bulletin board and students whose book reports are printed in a classroom newspaper."

Note that there are not two separate groups in this case. One group at a time will be treated with a method for encouraging students to read more books. She now collects her data in the following way:

1. For one month she counts the number of books read by students in her class. This is considered the pretest.

2. During the second month she begins to publish book reports in the classroom newspaper and disseminates them throughout the school. She records the number of books read by students. This is considered the posttest.

3. She charts results by comparing pretest scores (number of books read using the star method) with posttest scores (number of books read using the newspaper technique). A plus sign (+) (see Figure 9.3) indicates an increase from pretest to post test; a minus sign (-) indicates a decrease from pretest to post test; and a zero (0) indicates no change in scores.

Sign Test Computations			
Student	**Pretest Score**	**Posttest Score**	**Sign**
Mary	6	4	-
Zakia	4	5	+
Juan	6	7	+
Michael	5	6	+
Rochelle	6	4	-
Natasha	3	4	+
Jacob	3	4	+
Jessie	4	6	+
Kevin	6	5	-
Carlos	5	5	0
Mansa	6	7	+
Cynthia	5	6	+
Huan	7	8	+
Linda	5	6	+
Tim	4	7	+
Karim	5	5	0
Rolanda	4	5	+
Joseph	6	7	+

Figure 9.3.

Then, she follows these next steps to carry out the **sign test** to determine if there is a significant difference between pretest and post test scores:

1. As you note in the chart, Ms. Smith has 18 students who are identified as $N = 18$ (number of students equals 18). She counts the number of scores that were *not* the same, which happens to be 16 (18 - 2). Therefore, N now becomes 16 ($N = 16$).

2. She counts the number of pluses and minuses and assigns the smaller number the X value. Therefore, there are 13 pluses and 3 minuses; $X = 3$.

3. Now that you have $N = 16$ and $X = 3$, you refer to the "Sign Table" that can be found in a statistics book. I have, however, included an abbreviated Sign Test set of values in Table 9.2 on page 240 for your use in this chapter. Find where on the table the X value and the N value intersect. You'll note that the table shows a probability value of .011.

Table 9.2.

	X values						
N	**0**	**1**	**2**	**3**	**4**	**5**	**6**
5	.031	.188	.500	.812	9.69		
6	.016	.109	.344	.656	.891	.984	
7	.008	.062	.227	.500	.773	.938	.992
8	.004	.035	.145	.363	.637	.855	.965
9	.002	.020	.090	.254	.500	.746	.910
10	.001	.011	.055	.172	.377	.623	.828
11		.006	.033	.113	.274	.500	.726
12		.003	.019	.073	.194	.387	.613
13		.002	.011	.046	.133	.291	.500
14		.001	.006	.029	.090	.212	.395
15			.004	.018	.59	.151	.304
16			.002	.011	.038	.105	.227
17			.001	.006	.025	.072	.166
18				.004	.015	.048	.119
19				.002	.010	.031	.084
20				.001	.006	.021	.058

Table title: Abbreviated Table for the Sign Test

How do we interpret this value? We learned earlier that in education the generally accepted level of significance is .05; i.e., only a 5 percent chance error factor. For the **sign test,** the minimum **level of significance** is .10, which means a less stringent level of significance is used. To find a significant difference between the two sets of scores, the number found on Table 9.2 must be lower than .10. Since .011 *is* lower than .10, we can therefore reject the null hypothesis that no difference would be found between the pretest and post test scores. We may conclude, then, that the use of classroom newspapers to encourage students to read more books was a more effective approach than using the star method.

As a general rule, one-group pretest/posttest designs use the **sign test.** The weakness of this design, of course, is that there is no **control group.** However, the sign test does provide the educator with **empirical** data to help make a good educational decision.

Complete the following exercise that helps reinforce some of the ideas expressed above.

Module 3 Review

In this Module you learned the basics of the Sign Test, commonly used by educators.

Self-Test Check

1. Without looking back at this brief module, describe a Sign Test to someone who never heard the term. Can you? Check back of course if you must.

Activity and Study Questions

1. Think of scenario in which you could use a Sign Test to analyze data. Share ideas with a colleague. The Sign Test is really easy to use and should not be avoided when appropriate.

2. Can you think of another situation, other than the one described in this module, in which a Sign Test could be used?

Module 4: The Mann-Whitney U-Test

A second type of statistical test commonly used in research is known as the Mann-Whitney U-Test. The Mann-Whitney U-Test can be used to analyze results for small groups of students (under 15 per group) when two groups are formed by:

1. dividing one class into two groups using the **matched pairs** technique described earlier; or

2. comparing two separate classes that are comparable (e.g., two sections of a math class in high school).

The **Mann-Whitney U-Test** is used for small groups and operates not unlike a **t-Test.** The t-Test is preferable for groups larger than 15 students per group.

Let's examine how a Mann-Whitney U-Test might work (this example is also culled from Willerman, McNeely, & Koffman, 1991).

Let's say you'd like to assist a teacher to assess the effect of computer-assisted instruction on mathematical computation skills among third graders. You'd suggest that the teacher follow these steps:

1. Administer a pretest and with the results divide the class into two groups using **matched pairs.**

2. One group would be allowed to use computers to assist them in computational work (the **experimental group**), while the other group would learn computation the traditional way without use of computer-assisted instruction (the **control group**). (A null **hypothesis** could be framed that there will be no difference between the two groups). Of course, to avoid the Hawthorne Effect (see **confounding factors**) you might want the latter group to have equal access to computers, but not to assist them in mathematical computations. You might allow them to use computer-assisted instruction to enhance vocabulary development.

3. At the end of a given period of time (for instance, two months), a posttest is administered to both groups and scores are ranked. See Figure 9.4, on page 243.

The table in Figure 9.4 indicates that the first group consists of 9 students (N = 9) and the second group consists of 12 students (N = 12).

Control and Experimental Group Test Scores and Rank Order for a Mann-Whitney U-Test

Control			Experimental		
Student	**Score**	**Rank**	**Student**	**Score**	**Rank**
Fran	87	11.5	Al	98	20
Bob	72	4	Paul	93	15
Tania	65	2	Margie	76	6.5
Jerry	54	1	Stacey	88	13
Ralph	67	3	Allison	96	18
Renaldo	73	5	Melissa	90	14
Ro	78	8.5	Candida	87	11.5
Vivian	82	10	Mark	76	6.5
Sharon	95	17	Cary	94	16
			Helen	99	21
			James	97	19
			Noreen	78	8.5

Figure 9.4.

Scores are on the post tests are ranked as follows:

Considering both groups together, the *lowest* score achieved regardless of group would receive a 1. The second lowest score receives a 2, and so on. Jerry, with a score of 54, has the lowest score of either group and therefore is awarded a rank of 1. Tania has the second lowest score and thus is awarded the rank of 2.

In the event of a tie, as occurs with Margie and Mark, you would compute their ranks as follows:

Since one subject would have received a rank of 6 and the other a 7 if their scores had not been the same, you add 6 plus 7 and divide by 2 (the number of subjects involved). Therefore, 6 + 7= 13; 13 + 2 = 6.5. Both Margie and Mark are awarded a rank of 6.5. If three scores were to be tied, then you would add them together and divide by three to attain the rank score for each subject.

Try to complete the table by ranking the other scores and check your answers with Figure 9.6. Now the Mann-Whitney U-Test can be calculated as follows:

Step 1. Once scores have been ranked, multiply the number of subjects in the control group by the number of subjects in the experimental group. Thus, 9 x 12 = 108.

Step 2. Calculate the U1 and U2 with the following formula:

$$U1 = N1\ N2 + \frac{N1\ (N1 + 1)}{2} - R1$$

$$U2 = N1\ N2 + \frac{N2\ (N2 + 1)}{2} - R1$$

Key:
N1 = number of subjects in control group
N2 = number of subjects in experimental group
R1 = sum of ranks for control group
R2 = sum of ranks for experimental group

Try the calculations on your own using a calculator. Now that you have attained U1 and U2 values, you are ready to check the "Table of U-Values."

U1 should equal 91 and U2 should equal 17.

You should consult a U-Value Table, which can be found in many statistics books. I have, however, included an abbreviated U-Value Table in Table 9.3 for your use in this chapter. Select the smaller U-value to estimate the level of significance. If the value of the table is *larger* than the lower U-value, then the groups are statistically significant.

Look where 9 and 12 intersect on the table. You'll notice two points identified on the chart. The 26 is the lower limit and the 82 is the upper limit. Now, you notice that our U1, which was 91, falls above the upper limit on the table, whereas the U2, which was 17, falls below the lower limit. Since we are looking at the lower

Table 9.3.

Abbreviated U-Table for the Mann-Whitney U-Test

	1	2	3	4	5	6	7	8	9	10	11	12	13
1													
2								$\frac{0}{16}$	$\frac{0}{18}$	$\frac{0}{20}$	$\frac{0}{22}$	$\frac{1}{23}$	$\frac{1}{25}$
3					$\frac{0}{15}$	$\frac{1}{17}$	$\frac{1}{20}$	$\frac{2}{22}$	$\frac{2}{25}$	$\frac{3}{27}$	$\frac{3}{30}$	$\frac{4}{32}$	$\frac{4}{35}$
4				$\frac{0}{16}$	$\frac{1}{19}$	$\frac{2}{22}$	$\frac{3}{25}$	$\frac{4}{28}$	$\frac{4}{32}$	$\frac{5}{35}$	$\frac{6}{38}$	$\frac{7}{41}$	$\frac{8}{44}$
5			$\frac{0}{15}$	$\frac{1}{19}$	$\frac{2}{23}$	$\frac{3}{27}$	$\frac{5}{30}$	$\frac{6}{34}$	$\frac{7}{38}$	$\frac{8}{42}$	$\frac{9}{46}$	$\frac{11}{49}$	$\frac{12}{53}$
6			$\frac{1}{17}$	$\frac{2}{22}$	$\frac{3}{27}$	$\frac{5}{31}$	$\frac{6}{36}$	$\frac{8}{40}$	$\frac{10}{64}$	$\frac{11}{49}$	$\frac{13}{53}$	$\frac{14}{58}$	$\frac{16}{62}$
7			$\frac{1}{20}$	$\frac{3}{25}$	$\frac{5}{30}$	$\frac{6}{36}$	$\frac{8}{41}$	$\frac{10}{46}$	$\frac{12}{50}$	$\frac{14}{56}$	$\frac{16}{61}$	$\frac{18}{66}$	$\frac{20}{71}$
8		$\frac{0}{16}$	$\frac{2}{22}$	$\frac{4}{28}$	$\frac{6}{34}$	$\frac{8}{40}$	$\frac{10}{46}$	$\frac{12}{51}$	$\frac{15}{57}$	$\frac{17}{62}$	$\frac{19}{69}$	$\frac{22}{74}$	$\frac{24}{80}$
9		$\frac{0}{18}$	$\frac{2}{25}$	$\frac{4}{32}$	$\frac{7}{38}$	$\frac{10}{44}$	$\frac{12}{51}$	$\frac{15}{57}$	$\frac{17}{64}$	$\frac{20}{70}$	$\frac{23}{76}$	$\frac{26}{82}$	$\frac{28}{89}$
10		$\frac{0}{20}$	$\frac{3}{27}$	$\frac{5}{35}$	$\frac{8}{42}$	$\frac{11}{49}$	$\frac{14}{56}$	$\frac{17}{63}$	$\frac{20}{70}$	$\frac{23}{77}$	$\frac{26}{84}$	$\frac{29}{91}$	$\frac{32}{97}$

U-value (U2 in this case) and since the values on the table (26 and 82) are larger than U2, we conclude that there is a significant difference between the posttest scores of both groups. We, therefore, reject the null hypothesis and conclude that computer-assisted instruction had a significant effect on pupil achievement in mathematical computational skills.

Module 4 Review

In this Module you learned the basics of employing the Mann-Whitney U Test, another easy to use statistic . . . right?

Self-Test Check

1. When would you employ a Mann-Whitney U-Test?
    a. in collaborative planning
    b. assessing posttest results in a quasi-experimental study
    c. assessing posttest results in a single measurement design
    d. when randomization is impossible

Answer: 1) b

Activity and Study Questions

1. Think of scenario in which you could use a Mann-Whitney U-Test to analyze data. Share ideas with a colleague. The Mann-Whitney U-Test is really easy to use and should not be avoided when appropriate.

2. Can you think of another situation, other than the one described in this module, in which a Mann-Whitney U-Test could be used?

Module 5: The Chi Square Test and Other Statistics

A third common statistic, the **chi square** (pronounced kiy-square and represented by X^2) is used for nominal data (see **scales of measurement**). Nominal data refer to categories such as gender (male, female), ethnicity, socioeconomic status, etc. Any study that uses nominal data is analyzed using the chi square statistic.

Let's say you are a principal of a high school and want to know if there's a relationship between gender and teacher morale in the school. You would use the X^2 to determine, for instance, whether low morale is more closely associated with femaleness or maleness.

We will *not* outline the steps for calculating a chi square but will only mention that such calculations can easily be conducted using statistical programs such as **STATPAK**. More important is to know when to use each statistic. A summary of relevant and friendly statistics will conclude this section.

Aside from the use of means, standard deviations, sign tests, t-Tests, and Mann-Whitney U-Tests, which have previously been explained, only four other statistics may likely be used by researchers: the Spearman Rho, Pearson r Correlation Coefficient, **ANOVA**, and **ANCOVA**.

The Spearman Rho (also known as Rank Correlation) shows the degree of relationship between two sets of scores collected from the same group (and is usually measured by an ordinal scale). According to Willerman, McNeely, and Koffman (1991), "the Spearman Rho correlation is useful to teachers who do research because it can be used with groups that have small numbers of subjects and with data that are in either interval or ordinal form" (p. 139).

The Pearson Product Moment Correlation Coefficient (better known as simply the Pearson r, after Karl Pearson, a British statistician) is a common statistic used to correlate two variables. In other words, the Pearson r would be used to determine the degree of relationship between two variables, such as science test scores with math test scores.

Suppose you wanted to correlate (i.e., examine the relationship) between two **variables** such as teachers' attitudes toward supervision and years of teaching experience. You might have **hypothesized** that teachers with more years of experience have less favorable views toward supervision. Yet, a correlational study or analysis of these two variables might indicate no significant relationship or correlation. If that were so, you might find a .15 **correlation coefficient**.

Correlation coefficients are expressed from +1.00, which indicates a perfect correlation between two **variables,** to -1.00, which indicates a perfect negative correlation between two variables. A 1.00 coefficient indicates that as one variable increases, the other increases proportionally. The most common statistic used to calculate correlation is the Pearson Product Moment Correlation Coefficient (usually abbreviated as *r*; i.e., coefficients of correlation are expressed by the mathematical symbol *r*). Another statistic, used with ranked data, is the rank order correlation coefficient (called *rho*), but can be computed through computer analysis.

Correlation is NOT causation. A relationship between two variables does not necessarily mean that a cause and effect relationship exists. Research may indicate a strong correlation (i.e., relationship) between teacher use of positive reinforcement and positive pupil behavior in the classroom. Praise, for instance, may be a potent force to mitigate misbehavior, however, one cannot conclude that praising a student will *cause* a positive change in behavior. Any experienced teacher will testify to the fact that effective use of praise doesn't always yield positive student behavior. For some students, praise is ineffective. Yet, correlational studies do indicate a strong relationship that may warrant teachers to learn how to effectively and judiciously use praise and other forms of positive reinforcement.

Correlational analyses usually involve one group and two variables (e.g., fourth grade students' math scores correlated with science achievement scores).

NOTE: Pearson's Product Moment Coefficient is most often used as a precise statistic, but generally used with continuous variables. With ordinal or ranked data use the Spearman Rank Order Coefficient (p). The Phi Correlation Coefficient is a form of the Pearson's Product Moment Coefficient that is used with dichotomous variable (e.g., male/female, pass/fail, etc.)

Regression analyses are use for making prediction based on finding unknown values from known values (e.g., predicting high school GPA from known middle school GPAs).

Multiple regression analyses is similar but it attempts to predict an unknown value from two or more known variable (e.g., predicting high school GPA from known middle school GPA and standardize test scores).

The **Analysis of variance** (**ANOVA,** sometimes called the F test) is a statistical technique for determining whether or not significant differences can be found among the means of *three* or more groups. To compute an analysis of variance, you would use a computer program such as **STATPAK.**

Suppose you want to determine possible differences in social studies achievement among three separate groups of eighth graders taught by three different teachers using different methods of instruction. An analysis of variance (ANOVA) statistical test would be applied to determine whether or not a statistically significant difference in social studies achievement exists among the three different groups of students. This statistic operates not unlike the **t-Test.** The ANOVA computes statistical differences for three or more groups, while the t-Test, as you recall, only works with two groups. Although not frequently used in research, the ANOVA can be effectively used under certain circumstances.

Another statistic not commonly employed by researchers, yet nevertheless valuable, is an **Analysis of covariance** (**ANCOVA**). The ANCOVA is a statistical technique used in **group comparison** research when equivalence between the groups (usually only two in educational research) cannot be ascertained.

Let's say you are comparing the achievement levels of two groups of seventh graders, one of which is treated with computer-assisted instruction. In **group comparison** research, post test scores of both groups are compared to determine which group had higher achievement scores. (We don't measure growth between pretests and post tests, as was explained previously). Yet, without assuring that both groups were initially comparable or equivalent (i.e., had somewhat equivalent achievement levels to begin with), you cannot draw any conclusions from posttest scores.

Why can't comparisons be made? Comparisons cannot be made because one group may have started with higher achievement levels than the other group. How, then, can anyone conclude that the **treatment** (i.e., computer-assisted instruction) had any effect on achievement? How do you know that, for instance, high achievement levels can be attributed to the treatment as opposed to the fact that the **experimental group** had higher achievement scores initially? Thus, such comparisons cannot be made.

The analysis of covariance statistic can be used when you cannot ascertain group equivalence at the outset of a study. ANCOVA would be conducted with posttest results of both groups. This statistical procedure takes the pretest scores and adjusts them statistically so that they can be treated identically.

You don't have to understand how this works mathematically or statistically. All you need to understand is that the analysis of covariance statistic can be used when noncomparable (nonequivalent) groups are being studied.

The statistics mentioned above can be easily computed using STATPAK or any other computer program. Inputting data and following menu-driven instructions is all you have to do. Your professor or workshop leader will likely demonstrate the ease of using such computations.

The following references are very useful in more fully explaining these statistics as well as providing easy-to-follow instructions for computations: Crowl, 1996, 1986; Fitz-Gibbon and Morris, 1987; Urdan (2001); Willerman, McNeely, and Koffman, 1991. Note that the Crowl, 1986 work is especially useful, in that easy-to-follow step-by-step calculations are provided in his appendixes.

Activity   Quantitative Data Analysis Worksheet

1. What is the purpose of analyzing the data I collected? (Use additional paper to record your responses if necessary.) _____

   _____

2. Will I use both quantitative and qualitative analyses? _____

   _____

3. Which computer program will I use to analyze my data? _____

4. Who will be responsible for analyzing and presenting the data? _____

5. What tables and/or figures might I develop to summarize my data? _____

   _____

6. Statistical and Non-statistical Analyses:

QUANTITATIVE

____ Descriptive statistics
____ mean   ____ standard deviation   ____ percentage   ____ correlation coefficient

____ Inferential statistics
____ t-tests   ____ sign tests   ____ Mann-Whitney U-tests   ____ chi square
____ Spearman Rho   ____ Pearson r   ____ ANOVA   ____ ANCOVA   ____ other

Module 5 Review

In this Module you learned some of the basics of other statistics that can be easily computed using a software package as is described in Module 6.

Self-Test Check

1. Can you name and define each of the statistical procedures covered above?

Activity and Study Questions

1. Think of scenario in which you could use a statistic to analyze data. Share ideas with a colleague. These statistics are really easy to use and should not be avoided when appropriate.

2. Can you think of another situation, other than the one described in this module, in which these statistics could be used?

Module 6: Using SPSS or STATPAK

In the "old days," we used an abacus for statistical computations. In my day, we used a calculator and had to grapple with very long and complicated mathematical equations. Crowl (1986) provided a very useful way to avoid calculations using these mathematical equations. He gave his readers easy steps to follow that avoided equations, but still needed a calculator. Today, we have computers to assist us. Computer technology has really made data analysis much easier and quicker. Still, knowing what statistic should be used in a given situation is imperative. Knowledge about data analysis and interpretation are key. For my students' research projects, I find that computerized statistical packages are most desirable. For advanced students of research (usually those completing their doctoral dissertations), Statistical Packages for the Social Sciences or now called Statistical Product and Service Solutions (more commonly known as SPSS) is the most frequently used program. SPSS can be used for master's degree work though. Below you'll find a somewhat easy to use step-by-step guide to some basics:

Using SPSS: A Step by Step Condensed Approach

1. Click on SPSS Icon

2. "What would you like to do?" window pops up. Click on "Type in data."

3. SPSS Data Editor window pops up. You are now ready to type in data (a data set, if you please) Click on the "Variable View" on the bottom

4. In the 1st box under "Name" type in "GroupX" (no space between the word and the "X"); Click on box 2 in the same column and type in "GroupY"

5. Now, click on the "data View" box on the bottom

6. You'll notice "groupx" and "groupy" are named. Type in these post test raw scores for each of two groups:

    Group X= 10, 8, 7, 7, 5, 4

    Group Y= 9, 8, 10, 6, 6, 3

7. Now that you have finished inputting the test scores for each group

8. To save the data set, click the word "File" in the menu bar on top and click on "Save As" and name it "testscores1.sav"

9. Let's analyze this data set using descriptive statistics. Click on "Analyze" in the menu bar on top. A drop-down menu will appear and select the "Descriptive Statistics" command, and click on "Descriptives" – the Descriptives dialog box opens.

10. Click on "groupx" and click on arrow box; Do the same for "groupy" – you notice that they moved to the variables box

11. Now click on the "Options" box; The "Mean" and "Std. Deviation" boxes are already checked off. Click "Continue", then "OK"

12.   The Descriptive Statistics results box appears:

Descriptive Statistics

	N	Minimum	Maximum	Mean	Std. Deviation
GROUP X	6	4.00	10.00	6.8333	2.13698
GROUP Y	6	3.00	10.00	7.0000	2.52982
Valid N (listwise)	6				

By the way, do you know how I copied the Descriptive Statistics box? I clicked on the Edit function on the menu bar and click on copy; then, I opened my Word file and pasted it by hitting CTRL V.

13.   Now, let's compute a correlational analysis on this data set. Go to File on menu bar and click on "Open," then "data" and scroll to file name "testscores1"

14.   Click on "Analyze" in the menu bar on top. A drop-down menu will appear and select the "Correlate" command, and click on "Bivariate"—the Bivariate Correlation box appears.

15.   Click on "groupx" and click on arrow box; Do the same for "groupy"—you notice that they moved to the variables box

16.   Now click on the "Options" box; Click "Continue", then "OK"

17.   The Correlations results box appears:

Correlations

		GROUP X	GROUP Y
GROUP X	Pearson Correlation	1	.777
	Sig. (2-tailed)	.	.069
	N	6	6
GROUP Y	Pearson Correlation	.777	1
	Sig. (2-tailed)	.069	.
	N	6	6

18. .777 really equals .78, which is a fairly strong correlation and is significant at the .05 level (if you consulted a correlation table you would confirm this significance).

19. Now, let's use this same data set to compute a t-Test. Go to File and open data set, saved under "testscores1"

20. Click on "Analyze" in the menu bar on top. A drop-down menu will appear and select the "Compare Means" command, and click on "Paired-Samples t-Test" - the "Paired-Samples t-Test" box appears.

21. Click on "groupx" and then on "groupy" so that they both appear in bottom box as Variable 1 and Variable 2 respectively.

22. Now click on the "Options" box; Click "Continue", then "OK"

23. The t-Tests results box appears:

Paired Samples Test

		Paired Differences					t	df	Sig. (2-tailed)
		Mean	Std. Deviation	Std. Error Mean	95% Confidence Interval of the Difference				
					Lower	Upper			
Pair 1	GROUP X - GROUP Y	-.1667	1.60208	.65405	-1.8479	1.5146	-.255	5	.809

24. The significance box reads .809, which means it is not significant because its value is more than the minimal .05 significance level.

Essentially, you now understand how to use SPSS. I'd advise you purchase the superb work on SPSS: Corston and Colman, 2003.

You can input the same data for use in STATPAK, which is a really easy to follow (menu-driven) statistical program to achieve the same results for the data set above. Read below.

Still, SPSS, in my opinion, may be too complicated and advanced for most statistical analyses that students enrolled in research courses would need. Still, I highly recommend the best resource on the market currently available for learning SPSS, the aforementioned Corston and Colman, 2003 work!

A number of companies offer other user-friendly statistical packages. The professional educator, knowledgeable about applying research, should become familiar with a statistical computer program. I find that STATPAK, an acronym for "Statistical Package," is one such user-friendly package, but, in truth, any similar program will do. STATPAK is available for use with Macintosh and IBM-compatible computers. STATPAK can be obtained from Frisbie (1992) and Gay (1996).

Installation procedures are supplied as well as directions on how to use STATPAK. STATPAK is completely menu-driven, is very, very easy to use, and best of all, it's free. STATPAK can be downloaded from my website at http://www.wagner.edu/faculty/users/jglanz/web/

You can compute the following operations, among others, using STATPAK: **mean, standard deviation, correlation coefficients, t- Tests, ANOVAS,** and **Chi Squares.** I'm certain that as part of a course on educational research you will have opportunities to use some of these computer software programs.

Other comparable statistical packages include, among others:

GB-STAT automatic statistical graphs. Contact Dynamic Microsystems, (301) 384-2754.

PRO STAT. Poly Software International, (801) 485-0466.

MYSTAT for Windows (ISBN 1-56527-166-1).

Module 6 Review

In this Module you learned the importance of using computer software to analyze data.

Part Ten:

Thesis Overview—Chapter 3 of Thesis, Section 6: Research Design 6—Qualitative Data Analysis

Focus Questions

1. Why aren't statistics necessary to analyze qualitative data?

2. How do you think results from open-ended questionnaires can be best analyzed?

3. How do you think you might analyze data collected in notation form?

4. What are the chief ways qualitative data analysis differs from quantitative analyses?

5. Have you noticed how journal articles incorporate qualitative data analysis? Explain.

Module 1: Analytic Procedures

Analyses of qualitative data differ from analyses of quantitative data. Data analysis, as was explained, is the process of bringing structure and meaning to the mass of data collected. Remember, qualitative research, relying on extensive field notes, yields a bulk of data that is not easily analyzed. Analyzing such data, especially for practicing educators, can be time consuming and arduous, albeit, at times, fascinating and creative. Data analysis of quantitative data is not always straightforward, logical, and statistical. Similarly, data analysis for qualitative studies is often complex and not readily convertible into standard measurable units. In fact, research in general involves decisions by the researcher: omitting cases from the sample, recoding categories, dealing with missing or incomplete data, and choosing appropriate techniques to analyze the data. As researchers we have to explain and justify choices or decisions we make.

In addition, while quantitative analyses are conducted at the end of a study, qualitative analyses are ongoing; that is, they may occur as data are being collected. Moreover, qualitative analyses tend to be somewhat eclectic in that there is no one "right way" or pre-established criteria to follow. Data analysis "requires that the researcher be comfortable with developing categories and making comparisons and contrasts" (Creswell, 1994, p. 153). Creswell delineates several guiding principles, however, when undertaking qualitative data analysis:

1. *Simultaneity*—In contrast with quantitative data analyses, qualitative data may be analyzed simultaneously with data collection. As you interview various people, for instance, certain phrases or themes may be readily apparent. Making note of these phrases or themes, as you continue data collection, will aid thematic development in subsequent interviews. A summary chart at the end of this chapter can be used to record such data.

2. *Decontextualization or reduction*—These terms refer to the qualitative researcher taking the voluminous data collected and reducing them to patterns, categories, or themes. Reduction is often accomplished by a procedure known as coding. Coding involves attaching meaning to a particular scene, document, or event. For example, in viewing different types of leaders in films, one may categorize the different leaders by their style by first coding each leader with a given leadership style. **Content analysis** is a process that makes decontextualization or reduction possible.

Content analysis is a method of data analysis in which you analyze the content in a given document according to prescribed categories or criteria while following explicit rules of coding. When conducting content analysis of any document, categories should emerge naturally based on your analysis rather than using the analysis to verify preexisting categories. As you peruse the data in a document, you would identify key words to create research categories. Krippendorf (1980) reports that content analysis allows for making inferences from the data context using the procedure above.

Let's say you wanted to investigate whether principals were favorably depicted in popular culture (e.g., television and film). You would first obtain several television shows and movies for viewing. You would then identify several categories that would guide your viewing. These categories would depend on the purposes of your research. Let's say you were interested in understanding the different ways principals were depicted in these forms of popular culture. You could identify the following three categories: (a) favorable scenes about principals; (b) unfavorable or unflattering scenes; and (c) neutral scenes. As you watch these shows and movies, you would describe each scene thoroughly and might even transcribe dialogues. You would then classify each scene into one of the aforementioned categories. Frequencies of scenes in each of the three categories are tabulated, and on the basis of content analysis, you would arrive at a conclusion about the way principals are depicted in the television shows and films you watched.

Content analysis, then, is a method of analyzing data through a process of categorization.

Reflection

How might you use content analysis to analyze data?

Grounded theory—This refers to the comparison of collected data to extant theory or literature in search of a pattern or theme. Themes emerge as a consequence of collecting data. One should not develop a theme and then look for data to confirm one's expectations (Strauss & Corbin, 1990). Generally, grounded theory works when you start with a general question or problem (e.g., student misbehavior in a school). You interview parents, administrators, teachers, staff, and of course students themselves. You gather a lot of data. You review your data and a theme or theory emerges as a possible explanation for the problem. A theory is developed and then tested through empirical research.

Analytic Procedures

Drawing from the work of Marshall and Rossman (1999) analytic procedures for qualitative studies essentially fall into three categories:

1. *Organizing the Data*—Accumulate your data collection types (e.g., observations, interviews, documents, and audiovisual materials) and read and reread all the data. Make notes of anything that strikes you as significant or unusual. You should also make a list of all the main topics you have covered and may begin to cluster together similar topics. Major topics and sub-topics may emerge. This stage familiarizes you with all the data you have collected. Computer analysis may be helpful at this initial stage.

2. *Generating Categories, Themes, and Patterns*—This phase of data analysis can be cumbersome, yet interesting. Often simple scanning the data several times will result in some emerging pattern or theme. Feel free to make educated guesses or hunches at this stage.

    Developing coding categories occurs at this stage. Our discussion of decontextualization or reduction above comes into play at this phase. Coding systems enable you to see themes emerge from the data. You can choose from a "family of codes" (Anderson, Herr, & Nihlen,

259

1994; Bogdan & Biklen, 1997). I will introduce some of these codes. Further discussion of these codes can be found in the previous citation.

    a.   *Perspectives held by participants*—includes codes of ideas or perspectives held by individuals (e.g., liberal or conservative views).

    b.   *Activity codes*—includes codes that demonstrate a regularly occurring behavior (e.g., smoking, cutting class, or attending faculty meetings).

    c.   *Event codes*—includes codes that occur infrequently or only once (e.g., a teacher's strike or a teacher's dismissal).

    d.   *Strategy codes*—includes codes that refer to methods and techniques that people use to accomplish various things (e.g., behavior management strategies or various instructional strategies).

Working data into codes is an especially laborious process that, to be honest, educational researchers are not likely to attempt with as much rigor as someone undertaking a doctoral research project. For more detailed information, consult Wiersma (1999).

3.   *Testing Emergent Hypotheses*—As categories or themes begin to emerge you will want to initiate the process of framing some sort of hypothesis in order to determine whether or not the theme or category is consistent with the data. What kinds of questions can you pose to verify that the theme you selected is indeed inclusive of most, if not all, of your data?

As themes emerge and are verified, separating each one onto index cards, in folders, or into a data base is a matter left to the discretion of the researcher. Themes, at this point, can be compared to extant theory. Let's say bureaucratic themes have emerged in your study of the way district office supervisors relate to school personnel. That is, a consistent pattern emerges in a particular district in which district office supervisors, by and large, do not relate to teachers in professional, collaborative ways, but are rather officious, aloof, and bureaucratic. You might review literature to determine whether this observation or theme that has emerged from your data is representative of the way, for instance, most district office personnel relate to school faculty. In other words, does the literature support your findings? This inductive process of collecting data, developing a theme, and comparing the theme to extant literature is known as grounded theory. That is, your findings are "grounded" in real and verifiable data you have collected. You did not develop some theme and then look for data to support it. I should add that, at times, referring to literature as you collect data in an attempt to discover a theme is also an accepted practice in qualitative research.

An application: Imagine that you have collected data on the attitudes of parents and teachers toward inclusion. The qualitative data collection types include observations, interviews, documents (minutes of teacher/parent council meetings), and audiovisual materials (photographs and videotapes of students in inclusive settings).

Reflection

How might you incorporate the data analytic procedures described above?

There are many different and personalized ways to analyze qualitative data. The first step you might take is to separate the written data into three groups: observation data, interview data, and document data. A fourth group would include the visual data from the photographs and video-tapes. You would then read and view all the data. As you do so for each group, you would make both mental and written notes highlighting interesting and possibly significant pieces of information or even obvious emerging patterns. This might include underlining key words, phrases, or sentences in text or even color coding different pieces of data. Any logical and workable method can be applied. Whether you use index cards, folders, or a laptop is a matter of personal preference.

Analytic procedures can also be applied during, and not only after, data collection. The purpose of this initial stage in data analysis is to take all the data that have been collected and to organize and separate them into workable units.

Remember: The goal of analysis is to discover patterns, ideas, explanations, and understandings.

Once you are familiar with the data and have taken preliminary notes that identify key words, phrases, or events that seem relevant, you are now ready to generate categories or themes that might emerge from the data. For each group, you would select appropriate codes that highlight appropriate information and better organize the data. Use of codes and subcodes would be in order. For example, from the interview data a major code might be "Friendships" and sub-codes might include "with other included students" or "with paraprofessionals." The idea is that a particular interview reveals that included students have developed friendships with other students and paraprofessionals in the inclusive classroom. Each interview might have many different codes and sub-codes. If a qualitative researcher has interviewed five individuals, then several pages of coded data might be taken. This procedure would be followed for each data group. How do you think coding might work for videotaped data?

Reflection

*Observe any social situation in which there is much activity. Spend 30 minutes
doing so and take field notes. Practice analyzing your data with a colleague
using coding. Share with colleagues. Describe the experience. What did you learn?
What might you do differently next time?*

Once categories or themes emerge such as "teachers' resistance to inclusion" (note that several different, even competing themes may emerge, such as teachers against inclusion, but parents for inclusion), the researcher might review the themes and compare them to extant literature or theory in order to uncover a general theoretical framework that would explain the data. This process is known as grounded theory.

A brief word about the credibility of qualitative data analysis is in order. **Triangulation** enhances the credibility of qualitative data analysis. The use of varied data collection instruments and the comparison of emerging themes in one data collection instrument to other instruments contribute to the credibility of the analysis. If the pattern, for example, emerges consistently in the videotaped data as well as in interviews, observations, and documents, then the trustworthiness of the analytic procedures is apparent. As alluded to earlier and explained in the Glossary, **reliability** and **validity** of qualitative data also contribute to its credibility.

Reflection

How do you think reliability and validity of qualitative data is achieved?
Here's a bonus question: How does the concept of grounded theory contribute to internal validity?

When analyzing qualitative data, I recommend charting data collection techniques with key findings as follows:

Data collection technique	Key findings
Questionnaire	58% of parents dislike idea of inclusion.
Interview	Teacher X: "I don't think inclusion will work."
School Profile	Test scores indicate...
Multimedia	Videotapes demonstrate...

Computer Applications

Qualitative analyses are enhanced by state-of-the-art computer applications. Software programs are available to sift through qualitative data (e.g., "thick descriptions" from field notes) to locate specified words and phrases, creating indexes, attaching codes to various parts of the text, developing categories, and so on. The possibilities of computerized data analysis for qualitative research are currently being considered.

General and useful programs include word processors, database managers, spreadsheets, and text retrievers. Word processors are designed for production and revision of text and thus useful for taking, writing, and editing field notes. Most of you are likely quite familiar with the advantages of a word processor. How might a word processor help in data analysis of qualitative material? At what phase or phases of data analysis would a word processor come in handy?

Reflection

How might the CTRL Find function assist in data analysis?

A data base program can input text data according to a structured format. Let's say you wanted to use a data base program to keep track of interview data. You could set up a data base that records and keeps records of each interview subdivided into important pieces of information including name of interviewee, date of transcription, time of interview, and other information. Retrieval of various files aids in data analysis.

A spreadsheet program, although established for accounting purposes, can be used to create tables. A spreadsheet allows you to record information in each vertical column and in each horizontal row. Keeping track of your research project will be easier using a spreadsheet. Think of two specific ways a spreadsheet may help analyze data.

A text retriever is a sophisticated text search program that allows you to locate all instances of words, phrases, and combinations of phrases in one or more files. How might a text retriever assist in data analysis?

The following web sites provide specific software programs available (for purchase) for qualitative data analysis. Ask your professor if the college subscribes to any of them:

1. http://www.atlasti.de

2. http://www.qualisresearch.com

3. http://qsr-software.com

These sites will allow you to download free demo versions to determine which suits your needs the best.

Module 1 Review

In this Module you learned about three major ideas related qualitative data analysis:

1. Guiding principles for undertaking qualitative data analyses (i.e., simultaneity, decontextualization, and grounded theory)

2. Three categories for employing analytic procedures related to qualitative research (i.e., organizing the data, generating categories, themes and patterns, and testing emergent hypotheses).

3. Qualitative analyses through the use of computer software.

Self-Test Check

1. Explain the difference among simultaneity, decontextualization, and grounded theory.

2. Explain how content analysis is related to decontextualization.

Answers: refer back to module

Activity and Study Questions

The following activity worksheet allows you to easily analyze your data. This worksheet is meant to allow you to brainstorm different ideas. Answer each question. Changes in your plan can always be made at a later date. This worksheet also serves as a review of the ideas discussed in this module.

Exercise

1. *What is the purpose of analyzing the data I collected? (Use additional paper to record your response if necessary.)* _____

   _____

2. *Will I use both quantitative and qualitative analyses?* _____

   _____

3. *Which computer program will I use to analyze my data?* _____

4. *Who will be responsible for analyzing and presenting the data?* _____

5. *What tables and/or figures might I develop to summarize my data?* _____

   _____

Part Eleven:

Thesis Overview—Chapter 3 of Thesis, Section 7: Research Design 7—Results

Focus Questions

1. Should you include your interpretations of your study results in this section of the thesis?

2. What exactly is included under the "Results" section?

3. How do you know what results to report?

4. What format should you use to report your findings?

Module 1: Presenting Results

The final sub-section of Chapter 3 of your thesis will contain the results of your study. You've collected data thus far and have gone through them to determine how to best answer your research questions and/or hypotheses. For instance, if you hypothesized that "Students exposed to Teaching Method A would score significantly higher than students exposed to Teaching Method B," then your results would be stated perhaps in statistical form with an accompanying table. For qualitative studies, you'd probably have to provide representative data as your results. In other words, you couldn't possibly include all data collected from, for instance, interviews. Rather, you'd generate some themes of the interviews and then select quotations from respondents or informants whose statements best represent the theme.

One of the most important ideas to keep in mind when you write this section of your thesis is to simply state the results as you found them. No interpretation or discussion (e.g., opinions) should be stated. Save these discussions for Chapter 4 of the thesis under the sub-section "Conclusions or Discussion."

Also, always state your results in narrative form and include tables as a visual aid whenever possible.

Below you will find three sample "Results" sections:

Sample 1

Results

When comparing the Computer Software/Hardware Skills and Access section of the questionnaires from March 2000 and October 2000 the following results were found (See Table 1):

- Daily access to computers increased from 75% to 88%

- Regarding knowledge of using Windows 95 or 98, in March 2000 a total of 75% did not feel they knew how to use it. In October 2000, that total number dropped to 34%.

- In March 2000, 25% of the teachers felt strongly that they could not use Microsoft Word, but in October 2000, none of the teachers who responded strongly felt they could not use Microsoft Word.

- 50% of the teachers in March 2000 agreed that they knew how to use Microsoft Word, in October 2000 that number increased to 71%.

- In March 2000, 95% of the teachers felt that they did not know how to use Microsoft PowerPoint. 55% of the teachers in October 2000 still felt they did not know how to use Microsoft PowerPoint.

- 20% of the teachers felt they knew what the internet was and how to search on it, but in October 2000 that number increased to 53%.

Table 1

Computer Software/Hardware Skills and Access	March 2000				October 2000			
	Strongly Disagree	Disagree	Agree	Strongly Agree	Strongly Disagree	Disagree	Agree	Strongly Agree
I have daily access to a computer.	5%	20%	20%	55%	0%	6%	12%	76%
I know how to use Windows 95 or 98.	15%	60%	20%	5%	5%	29%	47%	18%
I know how to use Microsoft Word.	25%	25%	35%	15%	0%	29%	47%	24%
I know how to use Microsoft PowerPoint.	90%	5%	5%	0%	20%	35%	35%	6%
I know what the internet is and how to search on it.	45%	35%	15%	5%	5%	41%	35%	18%

In the Computers in Personal Work section of the March 2000 and October 2000 questionnaires, the following results were found (See Table 2):

- In March 2000, 25% of the teachers strongly agreed that they were afraid to use computers for personal use. In October 2000, none of the teachers who responded felt the same way. Furthermore, the total of teachers who agreed that they were afraid to use computers for personal use decreased in October 2000 to 29% from the 65% in March 2000.

- 10% of the teachers in March 2000 felt strongly that they were not afraid to use computers for personal use, this number increased to 20% in October 2000.

- When asking teachers if they used computers often in personal work, 25% of the teachers agreed that they did in March 2000. There was an increase to 47% in October 2000.

Table 2

Computers in Personal Work	March 2000				October 2000			
	Strongly Disagree	Disagree	Agree	Strongly Agree	Strongly Disagree	Disagree	Agree	Strongly Agree
I am afraid to use computers for personal use.	10%	25%	40%	25%	20%	47%	29%	0%
I use computers often for personal work.	30%	45%	20%	5%	20%	29%	29%	18%

When comparing the results from the Computers in Professional Work section of the March 2000 and October 2000 questionnaires, the following results were found (See Table 3):

- The total number of teachers who agree that computers can help enhance the learning of their students in March 2000 was 85%. This number increased to 94% in October 2000.

- In March 2000, 5% of the teachers responded that they often use computers with their students, this number increased to 24% in October 2000.

- 50% of the teachers agreed that they used computers often when preparing materials for their classes. In October 2000, there was an increase of 32% to a total of 82%.

- In October 2000, 59%of the teachers responded that they knew many ways computers can be integrated into their content area. This was an increase from the 15% who responded in the same way in March 2000.

- In March 2000, 5% of the teachers agreed that they used many different content area software packages. In October 2000, this number increased to 12%.

- 95% of the teachers in March 2000, felt they did not know what to look for when purchasing software for their classes. This number decreased to 83% in October 2000.

- In March 2000, 20% of the teachers who responded agreed that computers were "toys" for students, not tools for good teaching. This response decreased to 12% in October 2000.

Table 3

Computers in Professional Work	March 2000				October 2000			
	Strongly Disagree	Disagree	Agree	Strongly Agree	Strongly Disagree	Disagree	Agree	Strongly Agree
I believe computers can help enhance the learning of my students.	0%	15%	70%	15%	0%	6%	65%	29%
I often use computers with my students.	85%	10%	5%	0%	50%	18%	12%	12%
I often use computers when preparing materials for my classes.	30%	20%	35%	15%	0%	18%	41%	41%
I know many ways that computers can be integrated into my content area.	20%	65%	10%	5%	10%	29%	41%	18%
I have used many different content area software packages (ex: Might Math, Inspiration).	85%	10%	5%	0%	65%	12%	12%	0%
I know what to look for when purchasing software for my classes.	85%	10%	5%	0%	65%	18%	6%	0%
I believe computers are "toys" for students, not a tool for good teaching.	15%	65%	20%	0%	25%	59%	12%	0%

The following results from the interviews were found:

- All of the teachers interviewed were motivated or inspired to use computers at some level

- With regard to the teachers' feelings if the training was successful:
  - 50% of those interviewed felt the training was effective if the teachers had prior knowledge of computers.

- In response to being questioned if incorporation of technology in the classroom has increased since training:
  - Two of the teachers tried to incorporate technology, but had problems.
  - Two of the teachers felt they needed more training before using technology in classroom.
  - One of the teachers increased his incorporation of technology in the classroom.
  - One of the teachers has no interest in using technology at all in her classroom.

- When asking teachers about their use of computers in general, the following responses were given:
  - One teacher felt her knowledge of computers was strengthened, but she did not increase her use of computers.
  - Five of the teachers felt their use of computers has increased.

Sample 2

Sample Write-Up of Quantitative and Qualitative Methods and Results

Methods (Excerpted with permission from Sullivan & Glanz, 2002.)

Both qualitative and quantitative methods were used in this study. Quantitative assessment included the creation and validation of a survey assessing the knowledge and implementation of the Teacher Performance Review (TPR). The survey consisted of two parts. Part I asked for some basic demographic information. Part II was directed at personal knowledge of the performance review agreement (see Appendix). Content validity was established by distributing the survey to educators and administrators for review and comments. Quantitative analysis utilized descriptive statistics to report the findings.

We used a stratified sample of seven schools representing elementary, middle, and high schools within the New York City public school was used. This sample included two elementary schools, three intermediate schools, and two high schools from the New

York City boroughs of Brooklyn and Staten Island, serving a total of 10,108 students. A total of 696 staff members from these seven schools received the surveys in their school mailboxes. Attached to each survey was a stamped envelope with a return address. We received responses from 158 faculty members (23%).

In order to address the process of implementation of the professional development initiative, qualitative data was collected by conducting interviews with staff from the seven schools. Two formats were used: a) focus group interviews of teachers and administrators; and b) individual interviews of teachers, administrators and union representatives. Dialogues and interviews focused on the following:

- Documentation of professional development policies.
- Analysis of what worked, what didn't work, and why.
- Staff development practices.
- Support services.

The following questions were used to begin the discussions, with follow-up questions as needed:

1. *What do you know about the Teacher Performance Review and its implementation in your school?*

2. *What do you feel impeded the implementation of the Teacher Performance Review Initiative?*

3. *What do you feel facilitated the implementation of this item of the contract agreement?*

4. *How could the TPR have been implemented more effectively? What suggestions would you have for future teacher development initiatives?*

5. *What professional practices do you consider effective in your building?*

6. *What professional practices haven't worked, and why?*

7. *What impact has the TPR had on the professional development of teachers?*

8. *What is its value versus traditional teacher evaluation?*

9. *What specific alternatives have teachers selected?*

10. *What criteria have principals used to assess the effectiveness of these alternative approaches?*

The research team synthesized the data in written narratives. A modified form of grounded theory was implemented in order to reveal patterns and to analyze the data. Clear, consistent patterns emerged from the constant comparison of the results of the survey and the interviews. The comparative analysis of these results lead to the findings, conclusions, and implications (Strauss & Corbin, 1990).

Results

I. Analysis of Responses to the survey

A total of 158 people responded to the survey. Part I of the questionnaire referred to the background characteristics of the respondents. The overwhelming majority of respondents were teachers (85%). The remaining 15% of the sample included UFT representatives, assistant principals, counselors, deans, and project coordinators.

The majority of respondents indicated that they had tenure status (78%). However, approximately 50% of those surveyed reported that they had 2 years or less of teaching experience, while 50% reported having more than 3 years of experience teaching. Approximately 17% of the respondents reported having more than 6 years of teaching experience.

Table 1 represents the frequencies and percentages of responses to Part II of the survey regarding personal knowledge of the performance review agreement.

Table 1: Personal Knowledge of the Teacher Performance Review

Question	Yes	No	Missing	Total N
1. I have read the Performance Review Resource Handbook that explains the Teacher Performance Review Initiative.	27 17%	127 80.4%	3 1.8%	154
2. My principal or assistant principal discussed the Performance Review Resource Handbook or the Initiative guidelines with the staff.	37 23.4	119 75.3%	2 1.3%	156
3. The UFT representative discussed the handbook or guidelines with the staff.	34 21.5%	120 76%	4 2.5%	154
4. I attended a borough wide conference to acquaint staff with the new Teacher Performance Review model	4 2.5%	154 97.5%	4 2.5%	154
5.* I attended district workshops to acquaint staff with the new Teacher Performance Review model.	10 6.3%	147 93%	1 .6%	157

Table 1: Personal Knowledge of the Teacher Performance Review (*Continued*)

6. Teachers and administrators in my school have received on site training on performance review procedures.	24 15.2	116 73.4	18 11.3%	140
7. Parents in my school received a brochure describing the new citywide Characteristics of Good Teaching and new Teacher Performance Review procedures.	9 5.7	114 72.2	35 22.1%	123
8. The faculty voted on the adoption of the guidelines as a school-based option during the first three years of the union contract	20 12.5%	113 71.5%	25 16%	133
9. I have the opportunity to select either component A or B	47 29.7%	52 32.9%	59 37.4%	99
10. I selected Component A (annual performance options) for my performance review in the Spring of 1999	14 8.9	62 39.1	82 52%	76
11. I selected Component B (the traditional classroom observation) for my performance review in the Spring of 1999	48 30.4	35 22.2	75 47.4%	83

*Only 10 respondents of the 158 reported attending workshops. Of this group of 10 who attended workshops, 4 reported attending 1 workshop, 4 reported attending 2 or more workshops, and the remaining 2 respondents did not answer.

Table 1 above clearly demonstrates that most teachers did not get information about the Teacher Performance Review option. Of those who were informed about the option, less than 9 percent selected the annual performance option for their performance review and only 3 teachers (1.8%) provided information concerning the activities that they selected as part of that option.

<u>Analysis of additional survey questions requiring information about the Teacher Performance Review Option:</u>

Of the 20 respondents who indicated that faculty had adopted the guidelines as a school based option (see question #8 above), no one indicated the performance option that the school utilized. When asked to indicate activities utilized in the implementation of the performance option (see checklist on P. 2 of questionnaire in Appendix): one person indicated classroom visits, one indicated portfolios and one indicated "other." There were no other responses to this question.

II. Analysis of Surveys: Qualitative

Respondents were asked to provide additional comments on the Teacher Performance Review Initiative. Of those who provided comments, the majority (70%) of respondents indicated a lack of information regarding the Teacher Performance Review (TPR). Several teachers indicated that they were not given forms to record a choice for the initiatives. Comments from teachers included the following:

"What is the Teacher Performance Review?"

"Parts of this initiative may be in place in my school, but initiatives were not presented as such in any training or communications within the school."

"As a new teacher, I should have been observed more often… This is the first time I am hearing of the Teacher Performance Review model."

"I don't think anyone does it here."

Several respondents who were aware of the initiative mentioned that implementation of the TPR was impeded because they had received little or no training, as evident in the following remarks:

"…At the time it was introduced at my school little information was provided…"

"…It (TPR) has not been widely publicized at our school site."

Some teachers' responses indicated that they had felt pressure by school administration to select component B (observation). The following response indicates evidence of strong encouragement on the part of supervisors to select the observation over component B:

"…at the time it was introduced in my school little information was provided and my direct supervisor encouraged the use of component B."

273

Both teachers and supervisors thought that traditional observations were less time consuming as supported by the following comments:

"I found it less time consuming to just be observed."

"No one wanted to be bothered...it's too involved."

Two respondents reported being afraid that selecting component A would be viewed as hostile by their supervisors. They therefore selected component B in order to avoid future harassment.

"Although myself and some other colleagues wanted to select A, we decided to stick with B...We felt that if we chose A (TPR), it would be viewed as hostile by our supervisors and they would harass us in the future..."

One of the factors that impeded selection of Option A was the fact that teachers did not feel invested in a new performance review option. Some teachers indicated that the Teacher Performance Review option (A) was not a better choice than being observed (option B). In fact, 20% of the respondents indicated that being observed by a supervisor was preferable to option B. These teachers did not believe that option A was better in any way than traditional observation. Some teachers indicated that the descriptions of the Teacher Performance Review options were unclear and they were therefore better off with the traditional observation.

"I think it's easier to be observed."

"Option A (TPR) was considered to be vague and could be interpreted by ourselves and supervisors in different ways... which could lead to conflict."

Clearly both teachers and administrators did not feel that the new TPR would be more beneficial than the traditional observation.

III. Analysis of Interviews

Representatives from four New York City schools were interviewed regarding the implementation of the Teacher Performance Review. In each of the four schools the principal, union leader and at least one teacher were interviewed. A total of 10 people were interviewed. In one of these schools an "alternative assessment" model has been implemented, where teachers select a project to complete instead of being observed. However, school personnel have not developed criteria to assess the effectiveness of selected projects. Participants who were interviewed from the remaining three schools indicated that traditional observations were the mode of assessment.

A. *Findings regarding Knowledge and Implementation of the Teacher Performance Review option:*

Principals from two schools needed to be reminded about the details of the Teacher Performance Review. Except for one school, where school personnel described the implementation of the alternative assessment model as successful, the Performance Review option was not being implemented and was not viewed as having any impact on the professional development of teachers.

One of the researchers held a small focus group with principals about the Teacher Performance Review. Her findings are summarized below.

She met with a small group of principals to ascertain what they knew about the guidelines for and implementation of the teacher Performance Review. The group was composed of three active principals and one principal who had retired the previous year (1998). Two of the principals were from Brooklyn, one from Manhattan, and the fourth from Staten Island. All are middle school principals; one runs a sixth through twelfth grade school.

All but one Brooklyn principal seemed familiar with the Guidelines publication. "It looks familiar." "I think I received it a couple of years ago." One didn't remember it at all. Only one principal had been involved in any professional development related to the Guidelines. She mentioned that a couple of principals in her district were officially implementing the program. She had attended one workshop (LIFE) that an arm of the Council of Supervisors and Administrators (CSA) had offered in her district. Her next comment was that some teachers in her school were involved in that type of professional development without being officially involved: "They're doing it without realizing that they are." She had not pursued the official program herself.

When asked how the program had been implemented, only one principal spoke clearly about a process. She said, "The UFT representative could present it to the staff in the fall and that individual teachers could request to participate." Although it had not been officially presented in her school, one of the authors was involved in providing peer coaching workshops for a mini-school in her building. The researcher mentioned that the superintendent in her district had commented that it hadn't taken hold in the district because, during the first three years of implementation, the union contract stipulated that it had to be voted as a School-Based Option (the previously mentioned official staff vote with 75% of the faculty voting for the proposal). The principal responded, "So many initiatives are presented and demands made that the superintendents can't keep track of them." None of the principals was aware of any other staff development opportunities related to the initiative.

B. *Views on the Impediments to the implementation of the Teacher Performance Review Option:*

The overwhelming response on impediments to implementation was a lack of sufficient training. In the words of one principal whom we interviewed:

> "There isn't sufficient training so that supervisors (can) feel comfortable approving requests… Training was not well organized or meaningful. People don't remember, it's not something you do once and not repeat. You need to revisit it regularly…"

Both teachers and administrators viewed Option A (TPR) as vague in terms of how to set up professional goals. Teachers and administrators in the New York City schools are products of a bureaucratic culture that, until recently, prescribed what teaching and leading were. The researchers have seen many instances of bewildered staff members who have difficulty reflecting and creating without defined parameters, thereby resulting in a fear of changes that provide choices. A teacher and dean of students explained his feelings in the following conversation:

> "…(it is) difficult to determine how to approach goals… (it is) difficult to know what goals are important and what type of professional development (is needed) to address goals… No one is saying how to do this."

Part of the problem with instituting the TPR option is the outlook of both teachers and administrators that Option B (observation) is the preferred option as it allows administrators to see the classroom. Several principals who were interviewed believed that teacher observation was critical:

> " The traditional observation is a lot more concrete and immediate in assessing performance."

> "The observation shows me the teacher's instructional ability. I think observations are critical."

It is clear from these responses that many administrators don't look at performance review as a means to further teacher development. Instead it is seen as solely an evaluative experience; a tool for an administrator to use to gauge the performance of his or her staff. Therefore observations are clearly a necessary part of the TPR. From the perspective of teachers, the impediment to a novel type of performance review was shown to be the investment of time and energy into something new whose value as a means of teacher growth as opposed to its use as an evaluation tool has not been clearly demonstrated. Teachers clearly preferred a performance review that was a known phenomenon and easy to implement:

"No one wanted to be bothered. It's too involved." (teacher)

"People wanted to do the observation and get the process over with. The other is too involved." (teacher)

The view that teachers as a group don't like or want change is evident in the following remarks made by a principal:

"Teachers as a group are routinized in what they've done. They are frightened of change." (principal)

Finally, both teachers and principals view competition with other reforms (such as assessments and curricular changes) as impediments to the implementation of the TPR.

Sample 3

Results

The following tables present the tests results from this study. Table 1 provides an overview of the study procedure. The first lesson and initial multiple choice test was on October 4th. The student scored 90% on this test. Two weeks later the student took the same test to test for delayed retention. He scored the same score of 90%. The second lesson and initial short answer test was given on October 6th. The student received a score of 85%. Two weeks later on October 21st the student retook the test and scored 80%. The third lesson was given on October 11th, with the student anticipating an immediate test following the lesson. However, the researcher informed the student that he was lucky – and today there would be no test on what he just finished learning about! A mixed format delayed retention test on lesson #3 was given two weeks later on October 25th; the student scored 75% on this post test. The final fourth lesson was given on October 13th. This time the student was told that he would not be tested initially on the day's lesson. No immediate post-test was administered. Two weeks later on October 27th a mixed format test on lesson #4 was given to the student, and marked with a score of 65%.

Table 1: Study timeline with test scores

OCTOBER - 2004

Sun.	*Monday*	*Tues.*	*Wednesday*	*Thurs.*	*Fri.*	*Sat.*
Week #1	**Oct. 4** Lesson # 1 American Revolution Followed by Initial Multiple choice test on lesson #1 =90%		**Oct. 6** Lesson #2 Civil War Followed by Initial Short Answer test on lesson # 2 =85%			
Week #2	**Oct. 11** Lesson #3 World War 1 **NO** test given on lesson # 3		**Oct. 13** Lesson # 4 **World War 2** **NO** test anticipated and given on lesson # 4			
Week #3	**Oct. 18** Delayed Retention Multiple Choice test on lesson #1 =90%		**Oct. 21** Delayed Retention Short Answer test on lesson # 2 =80%			
Week #4	**Oct. 25** Delayed Retention mixed format on lesson # 3 =75%		**Oct. 27** Delayed Retention mixed format test on lesson #4 +65%			

Tables 2–3 compare the initial-immediate tests scores with the same test given two weeks later to assess delayed retention and long-term memory.

Table 2: Comparison of initial (immediate) test results with delayed retention post tests scores:

Test Format	*Initial Test Score*	*Post Test Score*
1. 10 question Multiple Choice quiz	**90%**	**90%** *
2. 10 question Short Answer quiz	**85%**	**80%** *
3. Mixed format (five m.c. / five s.a.)	No test given	**75%**
4. Mixed format 2 (five m.c. / five s.a.)	No test anticipated or given	**65%**

* Delayed Retention is measured by a test score of 80% or higher

Table 3

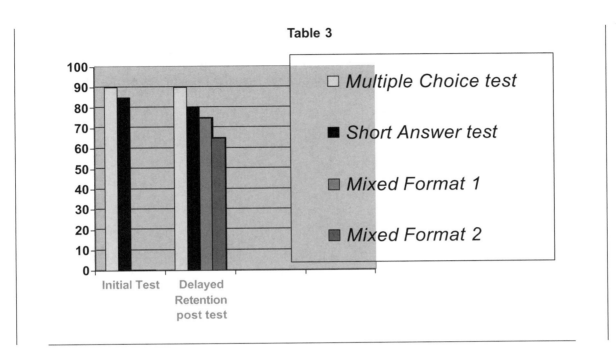

Reflection

What conclusions can you draw about reporting results from analyzing the examples above? Describe how quantitative results reporting differs from qualitative approaches.

Module 1 Review

In this Module you learned the basics in reporting the results of your study as samples were provided.

Keep in mind these guidelines:

1. State results and do not offer interpretations or present conclusions.

2. Present all results including quantitative and qualitative portions.

3. Report all relevant findings (i.e., those that directly answer your research questions and/or hypotheses).

4. Use concise narrative and tables, charts, or figures.

5. Readers should be able to clearly ascertain your findings from this section of your thesis.

Activity

1. Conduct a quick survey of at least 20 people on some topic of interest to you and them. Report your findings by constructing a table to visually present your findings

Part Twelve:

Thesis Overview—Chapter 4 of Thesis—Implications for Practice/Research

Focus Questions

1. Why is specifying study limitations so necessary?

2. You've collected all your data. How do you plan on interpreting them in order to draw accurate and fair conclusions?

3. What is included in the "Discussion" section of your thesis?

4. How will you determine what implications you will draw from your study?

5. What kinds of implications are likely?

Module 1: Specifying Limitations

This section is part of Chapter 4 of your thesis. The section informs readers of the limitations of your findings. Every study has limitations. No study is flawless. Specifying limitations acknowledges them and helps readers to place your findings within proper context. Too many theses and even published articles in academic journals do not attribute or acknowledge critical limitations of the particular study. Limitations of a study may or may not affect the strength or usefulness of your study. It is indeed possible to have significant limitations that caution readers that further research may be necessary to support the findings of a particular study. Specifying limitations is an ethical matter that you should take seriously. Please note that just because your study may have serious limitations doesn't denigrate your efforts. It merely underscores your professional responsibility as an educational researcher.

Often in published articles limitations may be included with the conclusions or discussion section. In theses work, I require my students to specify study limitations as a separate section and I have them list them in outline form rather than in a narrative (just my preference). Each limitation should be stated precisely with a brief explanation as to why it's a limitation, if it's not obvious, and the consequences of the particular limitation. For instance, you might state that the relatively small number of participants in your study is an important limitation so that readers are cautioned not to generalize your findings to other samples or to the population as a whole.

I've included two sample limitations below to give you some ideas as you write your own section:

Sample 1

The limitations of this study were as follows:

- Sample size—The number of teachers used for this study was limited to those who participated in the professional development program, which was twenty teachers. Results, therefore, cannot be generalized to all teachers.

- Validity of Questionnaires—Internal validity of the questionnaire may have been threatened due to 50% response rate. Furthermore, reactivity to the questionnaire/interviews also may have threatened internal validity based on an assumption of what respondents may have thought the researchers were expecting.

- Time Factor—Internal validity may have further been compromised due to the fact that there was a four-month gap between the training completion and the interviews portion of the study. Other factors may have influenced participants that may not be attributed to the study treatment.

Sample 2

Limitations of the Study

1. The sample of this study was limited to one 5th grade student. An in depth case study on the affects of various testing procedures was conducted with this student. Therefore, results of this study could not be generalized to all 5th grade students, and certainly not to all students.

2. Researcher is a tutor of this fifth grade student, which may cause bias. The researcher has known this student for some time, and the bias lies in the researcher already having some knowledge of the student's capabilities. This limitation was overcome through inter-rater reliability measures.

3. The researcher does not have knowledge or availability of all known testing forms, and not all testing forms were administered to the student.

4. The research is limited to a certain amount of time, which may affect the learning process and accurate assessment of long-term learning.

5. The results of the various test forms on the student may not be a representation of the true influence of these tests on the student. Internal reliability was not ensured, due to the fact that the researcher was unable to control many, if not all factors affecting test results. In addition while attempts to ensure that all tests were designed fairly, the researcher was unable to verify that the tests and lessons were equally fair for this particular student, despite attempts to attain validity and reliability measures.

Reflection

What conclusions can you draw from these limitations?
What other possible limitations might develop in your study?

283

Module 1 Review

In this Module you learned the importance of specifying study limitations.

Self-Test Check

1. What should be your first reaction when you hear a radio commentator report that a recently published article indicates that a particular drug may reduce the risks for cancer?

   a. disbelief the study

   b. accept it as accurate

   c. it's a PR push by a pharmaceutical company

   d. consider study limitations

   Answer: 1) d

Study Questions

1. What should a limitations section include?

2. Why are there differences in the way the limitations are presented by different authors?

Activity

1. Examine several journal articles to discover how "limitations" are presented.

Module 2: Interpreting Data

Having collected and analyzed your data, you are ready to reach certain conclusions so that you can more intelligently discuss your findings (see Module 3). The graphs and figures you've accumulated merely present the data in visual form, but do not indicate how this data is to be used or interpreted. The fact that you have found, for example, statistically significant findings regarding a particular **treatment** does *not* necessarily mean that a change in educational programming is inevitable. There is a distinction between **statistical significance** and educational significance. A .05 statistical difference may not necessarily warrant implementation of a new textbook series, because other factors may need to be considered before investing money and expending additional efforts.

Reflection

*What other factors may possibly influence your decision
to adopt or discard the new textbook series?*

Maybe data collected qualitatively indicate that teachers find the teacher's editions complicated and not very useful. Perhaps parents complain that the textbook doesn't represent the cultural diversity of the community. Perhaps the cost of the textbook series is prohibitive. Despite statistically significant findings that the **experimental group** who used the new textbook series increased reading comprehension levels, adoption of the series may be precluded by other factors. Obviously, then, the decision to adopt or not adopt the textbook series depends on a variety of factors. Interpretation of data must be viewed as a decision-making process that includes these many possible factors.

How, then, does one decide whether to adopt or discard the new textbook series? In other words, how can we best interpret our data to make informed decisions about the instructional program in our school? Ultimately, interpreting data must be based on those decisions that are likely to help achieve your goals and objectives. What do you eventually hope to accomplish? Will this program, product, or procedure move you closer to your goals? What evidence exists that this program, product, or procedure is effective? Is this evidence overwhelming or are there conflicting findings? (One of my mentors once quipped: "If in doubt, do without!"). Reflecting on these and similar questions will assist in appropriately interpreting data from your study.

If you are using this study to in some way influence your practice as an educator then I have found that establishing a steering committee that is in charge of interpreting data is quite helpful. The steering committee is provided with relevant data summaries that they can peruse and discuss. After a period of time, the committee makes recommendations for your consideration. Note that in **collaborative** or **schoolwide** educational **research** projects, the steering committees would actually decide on the efficacy of a given program or practice.

Another strategy for interpreting data is using prespecified standards. You would chart expected results for each **data collection** instrument employed and note the extent to which the standard was met. Conclusions are then drawn. Final decisions are then made based on the conclusions drawn. For an excellent guide to interpreting data, see Chapter 5 in Herman and Winters, 1992. Table 12.1 has been adapted from the aforementioned work.

Table 12.1.

Using Prespecified Standards to Interpret Data

Instrument	Standard	Percentage Meeting	Conclusion
Science Aptitude Test	*50% above 50th percentile*	*61% above 50th percentile*	*Above goal; success*
Problem-solving science question	*At least 50% scoring "acceptable" or above*	*37% last year; 52% scored acceptable, but only 20% for girls*	*Met goal overall but examine achievement for girls*
Portfolios	*Average rating: 4 out of 6*	*20% were rated 4 out of 6 or higher*	*Problem here; let's examine*
Parent survey	*At least 80% registered satisfaction with new program*	*90% approval rate*	*Met goal; success*

You'll notice that Table 12.1 displays data and compares results with prespecified standards for an elementary school science program. The table demonstrates various instruments, standards established, percentages met, and appropriate conclusions that can be drawn. Your perusal of the table will allow you to interpret results fairly easily. Multiple indicators should always guide your decision making.

A cautionary, albeit parenthetical, note should be made about the interpretation of test scores. Test scores are still the most frequently used data source in many schools. Misinterpretations of test scores are too common. Although test score interpretation goes beyond the purview of this text, pointing out a few general cautions that apply to the interpretation of any test score is in order (for more detailed information consult, e.g., Gronlund & Linn, 1990):

A test score should be interpreted in terms of the specific test from which it was derived. In other words, look beyond the test title to evaluate a pupil's performance in terms of what the test actually measures. For example, one type of **achievement test** may measure a pupil's ability to compute mathematical problems, yet another achievement test may measure problem-solving ability. To use, for instance, the former test and thus conclude that the pupil needs remedial assistance in mathematics may be an inaccurate generalization. The evidence more accurately indicates that the pupil may need help in computational skills, but that her/his ability to problem-solve may be, in fact, satisfactory.

A test score should be interpreted in light of all the pupil's relevant characteristics. In other words, consider such factors as motivational levels, physical health, and any disabilities that may impair performance. Test performance may be affected by these and other factors.

A test score should be interpreted according to the type of decision to be made. Attempting to predict, for example, a pupil's success in college from a **criterion-referenced test** is not justified when **norm-referenced tests** more accurately provide such information. Remember to match the test score to the type of decision that needs to be made.

A test score should not be interpreted as a specific value. A grade equivalent score of, say, 5.3, doesn't indicate that a pupil is exactly one month ahead in reading of a pupil who scores 5.2. These scores, as well as other types of scores, should be considered as merely small differences and not significant in and of themselves. To make a decision about a pupil's performance based on a specific value will lead to erroneous conclusions.

A test score should be considered along with other supplementary evidence. Making a decision about a pupil's academic performance should involve a variety of data sources. Relying solely on test score information is shortsighted and will lead to erroneous conclusions. **Triangulation** of data sources is essential for judicious data interpretation.

Using prespecified standards to interpret data may fit nicely with quantitative data, but how do we interpret qualitative data? As with data analysis, interpretation of qualitative research is different than for the quantitative approach. While generalizations can usually be drawn from quantitative research (although as you recall not all quantitative approaches in educational research lend themselves to generalization), no generalizations may be made for qualitative findings due, in large measure, to the small samples that are used. Conclusions that are drawn from qualitative studies are tentative and speculative and must be viewed within a unique context. In other words, findings from an ethnographic study might be applicable to the particular school under study, but may not be applied to all similar schools.

Since triangulation is so important, findings from both quantitative and qualitative studies should be carefully examined. Overall results from quantitative studies might yield numerical or statistical evidence to support the use, for example, of a particular textbook series, but qualitative findings that present detailed insights into "how" these books are being used on a daily basis might add some important information as well. It is not a matter of deciding that one approach yields more reliable findings than another. Rather, the cumulative effect of both approaches or methodologies provide the best insight into whether or not a district or a school should expend thousands of dollars to adopt the textbook series. Sometimes quantitative and qualitative findings support similar conclusions and sometimes different ones. Ultimately, you, as educational researcher, will have to decide what the weight of evidence suggests. The important point is that employing a **mixed methodology** (both quantitative and qualitative approaches), when feasible, is the best way to conduct research.

Another strategy for data interpretation is to allow a colleague or two to peruse your results and to have them draw likely conclusions. Do their assessments match yours? Are there major or minor differences? How will these assessments influence your interpretation of data?

Module 2 Review

In this Module you learned some strategies for data interpretation that include:

1. Consider statistical significance versus educational significance.

2. Use prespecified data tables.

3. Have a colleague or two review your findings and draw conclusions.

Module 3: Drawing Conclusions/Discussion

This section is part of Chapter 4 of your thesis. The section informs readers of the conclusions you've drawn from the study that were directly related to the research questions or hypotheses. This is the section where you can "discuss" your findings, share your interpretations, compare conclusions to others studies in the literature, raise questions, etc. A satisfactory job here can be accomplished in as few as five or six paragraphs or as long as several pages. I've included sample sections below to give you some ideas as you write your own section. Note that the samples are drawn from actual theses. With theses work, I require my students to actually reproduce the research questions or hypotheses and answer them directly, and then to discuss each one or all of them as a whole:

Sample 1

Discussion

Literature and research has demonstrated that tests impact long term memory and retention of knowledge. Previous studies have shown that the very act of students engagement in test taking, and or anticipating a test led to improved and longer lasting retention of the subject. (Haynie, 1990, 1991, 1994). Earlier research has also concluded that multiple choice tests were more effective than short answer tests in the promotion of long term memory (Haynie, 1994).

The purpose of this research was to examine the impact of various testing measures on the impact of long term memory in a fifth grade student. As predicted, any form of testing was found to be more effective in the long term than no testing. In addition the test format of multiple choice was found to measure higher than other test forms in both initial tests and delayed retention test scores.

The findings in this case-study on a fifth grade student confirmed previous literature and research. The research questions addressed in this study can now be answered and discussed.

1. *What influence does initial testing of information have on long term retention of knowledge of history facts in fifth grade students?*

   A: Based on this study results, initial testing of information has influenced long term retention, based on higher test scores in a fifth grade student. This was evidenced by the student learning four history lessons, and initially tested on two of them. The material that was initially tested on, received higher scores on the delayed retention post test administered two weeks later.

   However, it should be noted that the delayed retention test was the same test given initially, and test scores may have been influenced by the student having taken the same test originally.

<u>2.</u> *<u>What impact does the anticipation of an upcoming test on the information being learned have on retention learning of history facts in fifth grade students?</u>*

A: According to study results, the anticipation of a test has impacted the student to actually perform better on the delayed retention test compared to the delayed retention test given when a test was not anticipated. The conclusion here is that, in general, students do likely study more earnestly when they expect a test than if they do not, but maximum benefit in retention is gained only by having students anticipate and then actually take a test.

<u>3.</u> *<u>How does the long term effectiveness of initial testing with multiple-choice tests compare with initial testing by short-answer tests?</u>*

A: Based on the study executed on this particular fifth grade student, multiple choice tests were shown to be more effective than short answer tests in promoting long term memory and recall of information. While both tests received scores above 80%, which measure retention of knowledge, the student performed better on both sets of the multiple choice tests.

It should be noted that the higher test score for multiple-choice was seen on both the initial and post test score. This may indicate that the student was more familiar with the content on the multiple-choice test in the first place. Furthermore, the student performed better on the initial multiple-choice which may have led to a higher grade on the post test as well.

While on the surface, the previous research and the research questions addressed have been confirmed and explained, some aspects of the results may not accurately describe the actual findings.

During the study itself, the researcher observed how the basic content of the information on the tests were not identical or similar to the student. The content on the multiple-choice test appeared to more familiar to the student, which may have affected his higher test scores, and do not definitely show that he remembers more through multiple choice tests.

The above conclusions mainly confirm and resolve the original research questions, yet further research in various settings is needed to further develop and verify these results for a broader setting.

Sample 2
(*Thanks to my student Sima Mikhli*)

Research Questions

- How does sensory integration treatment impact the behaviors of preschool and elementary school aged students in their adaptive development skills?
- How does sensory integration treatment impact the behaviors of preschool and elementary school aged students in academic achievement?

Possible Explanations for Differences in Findings of Previous Research Compared to Present Study

Many studies which involved children who have sensory integration dysfunction have shown no impact of sensory integration treatment on behaviors in learning, yet have shown significant improvements in behaviors on sensory motor function (Din & Lodato, 2001; Shuman, 1996). A possible explanation of the discrepancy between the findings of those studies and the present study is that the previous studies involved children with multiple disabilities or maladaptive behaviors in addition to sensory disorders while the present study involved students who have only sensory integration dysfunction. Another possible explanation for the discrepancy is that the participants in the previous studies were high-school students as opposed to the children in the present study who were of a younger age range. This may be due to the fact that the earlier the intervention the more effective the treatment will be.

Conclusions

Sensory integration treatment is individualized occupational therapy sessions which are developed specifically to remediate sensory integration dysfunction in children. Treatment involves active participation and self direction of the child with the therapist. Activities are tailored to the specific needs and interests of the child (Mailloux & Parham, 2001).

The occupational therapist will design a program based on the child's particular needs. The therapist will guide the child through activities that challenge the child's ability to respond successfully to sensory stimuli in an organized way. For example, a child may have difficulty jumping, climbing, pedaling tricycles, and getting dressed. However, these problems can not be "fixed" by teaching the child specifically how to jump, climb, pedal and put on a jacket, when the underlying problem is sensory dysfunction. The child does not need jumping lessons but opportunities to integrate all sensations.

During these therapy sessions, a child actively takes in movement and touch information in a playful, meaningful, and natural ways that help the brain modulate these fundamental neural messages. The child responds favorably to sensory integration treatment, because his nervous system is pliable and changeable (Kranowitz, 1998).

This study confirms that sensory integration treatment impacts behaviors in adaptive developmental skills and academic achievement among pre-school and elementary school aged students. Most teachers, parents, and occupational therapists found that sensory integration treatment improved their student's or children's cognitive abilities as well as their adaptive developmental skills. However, occupational therapists reported conflicting views on the impact of sensory integration treatment on academic achievement. 75% of therapists stated sensory integration treatment has a strong impact on children's academic achievement. On the contrary, 25% of therapists responded that other factors may impact the child's academic achievement. The child may be receiving other treatments like behavior modification, counseling, or experiencing an environmental change, that are impacting their academic performance besides the sensory integration treatment.

According to Dr Ayres (1969 as cited in Kranowitz, 1998, p. 46) "Sensations that make a child happy tend to be integrating." When the child is actively involved in therapy, the child becomes more organized, has fun and feels happy.

Reflection

What conclusions might you draw from the information above?

Module 3 Review

In this Module you reviewed two samples of a "Drawing Conclusions or Discussion" section.

Module 4: Implications for Practice

This section is part of Chapter 4 of your thesis. The section informs readers of some of the important implications of your study. The section answers the question, "So what?" As a result of undertaking your study, discuss the implications of your research for practice related to teaching or your specific area of specialty (e.g., counseling, administration, etc.). A satisfactory job here can be accomplished in as few as three or four paragraphs or as long as nine or ten. I've included two very brief sample sections below to give you some ideas as you write your own section.

Sample 1

Implications for Practice

Three main implications for teaching practice emerged from this study.
On the basis of this study it is recommended that:

a. When useful for evaluation purposes, classroom testing should continue to be employed due to its positive impact on retention learning.

b. Students should know in advance that they will be tested because of the affect this information may have on their learning and study habits.

c. Multiple-choice tests should be utilized as a tool to reinforce, review and retain knowledge.

The researcher of this study intends to continue to notify students of all upcoming tests so as to reinforce positive learning and study habits. Multiple-choice tests will be used most frequently as an aid for delayed retention learning.

Sample 2

Implications for Practice

Parents should create a sensory oriented environment in addition to the sensory integration treatment their child is receiving. This stimulating environment will help ensure successful results in treatment for their child.

Teachers can play a significant role in their students' sensory development. They should be encouraged to implement sensory techniques or activities recommended by the occupational therapists in their classrooms.

Occupational therapists should collaborate and communicate with the student's parents and teachers about their concerns of the individuals with sensory disorders.

Module 4 Review

In this Module you reviewed two brief samples of an "Implications for Practice" section.

Module 5: Implications for Further Research

This section is part of Chapter 4 of your thesis. The section offers readers of your thesis suggestions for further research. In fact, I inform students undertaking the thesis project during the first semester as they are generating ideas for a possible topic to consult the "Implications for Further Research" section of another thesis for possible ideas. If written well, this section provides ideas for further investigation. Perhaps the current researcher was unable to undertake a certain avenue of research that now in hindsight s/he would have. S/he now offers advice for future researchers. Suggestions offered here can vary. The section is relatively brief. A satisfactory job here can be accomplished in as few as three paragraphs or as long as seven or eight. I've included two sample sections below to give you some ideas as you write your own section.

Sample 1

Implications for Further Research

The positive results of this research study should not be considered definitive. This study should be viewed as a step towards more knowledge about the application of testing in the teaching and learning process.

The value of tests in the promotion of retention learning has been demonstrated here and research questions about anticipation of tests have been addressed. However, there remain many more potential questions about testing and long term retention of knowledge.

Therefore, studies similar in design that use different materials and are conducted with diverse populations will be needed to achieve more definite answers to these research questions.

This research was conducted on a single fifth grade student. In order to further develop these results a larger sample should be employed. A similar study should assess long term retention over longer periods of time. A larger sample would help confirm the results and may draw conclusions of a larger framework, which can then be incorporated into the classroom and curriculum. Internal and content validity need to be ensured as much as possible to guarantee accurate outcomes.

Sample 2
(Thanks to my student Sima Mikhli)

Implications for Further Research

Three parents in this study indicated difficulty determining the impact of treatment on their child's behaviors in the adaptive developmental skills and academic achievement because their child has been receiving therapy for a short span of time. Therefore, further research should include longitudinal studies that implement sensory integration treatments and their impacts on children's behaviors.

In the present study children with sensory integration dysfunction were not directly observed. Information was obtained via surveys to parents, teachers, and occupational therapists. Additional detailed information may have been derived by directly observing the individuals with sensory integration dysfunction. Thus, further studies should include children with sensory integration dysfunction as participants, so they can directly observe individuals with sensory integration dysfunction and obtain more information.

Module 5 Review

In this Module you reviewed two samples of an "Implications for Further Research" section.

Part Thirteen:
Putting It All Together

Focus Questions

1. What kinds of information would you need to assist you in writing your thesis?

2. What is APA and why is it important for thesis writing?

3. Why is writing an "abstract" so important in order to help you "put it all together?"

4. Would you welcome some advice and suggestions for writing and completing your thesis? (If so, see Module 4)

5. What criteria are important in terms of evaluating or assessing the quality of a thesis?

6. What would you need to know in order to become a better consumer of research?

Module 1: Writing the Thesis

This module in the final part of *Fundamentals of Educational Research* is comprised of several invaluable web sites that you are encouraged to visit and explore. Each web site has important information to assist you in writing and completing a successful thesis project.

I   www.apastyle.org

This web site is a must visit because it supplies you with research tools to write and complete your thesis.

II   http://www.bartleby.com/141/

This wonderful web site provides you with additional research tools including an encyclopedia, dictionary, thesaurus, and probably the best little book on writing titled *The Elements of Style.* Refer to Strunk and White's masterpiece often.

III   www.m-w.com

This most useful web site provides you with the Merriam-Webster dictionary and thesaurus. Whenever I need the right word or need to check a spelling I click on this site.

IV   Writing help

Simply conduct a google search by typing in "writing tips" and you'll have more than enough advice!

V   Plagiarism

Simply conduct a google search by typing in "plagiarism" and you'll have more than enough advice on this critical subject! Note that plagiarism seems to be on the rise or at least reported cases on the rise. I would highly suggest that you consult your own university or colleges' policies on academic integrity. Inadvertent or unintentional plagiarism may get you into trouble. Understanding what is and what is not plagiarism is important.

VI   "Thesis Writing" on the Web

For a thesis site with some very useful information, type in "thesis writing" at www.google.com and explore at your leisure varied web pages.

Module 1 Review

In this Module you were given six ideas for helping write a thesis, or any paper for that matter:

1. APA

2. The Elements of Style

3. Dictionary, thesaurus, etc.

4. Writing suggestions

5. Plagiarism

6. Thesis writing tips

Module 2: Incorporating APA

The *Publication Manual of the American Psychological Association* (APA) (2001) is the accepted manual of style for writing reports in the social sciences. I recommend that my students adhere to this manual of style for several reasons:

(1) APA is relatively easy to learn and use;

(2) APA is widely used and known; and

(3) APA enhances the professional appearance of reports.

Although you may have to refer to the *Publication Manual* for details about specific guidelines for documenting sources, here are twelve (12) basic rules and sample references that should, at least, get you started:

(1) APA uses no footnotes.

(2) All references are placed in the main body of the text as follows: Jones (2000) stated that...

To find the Jones reference you would consult the list of *references* placed at the end of the report that lists alphabetically, by author's last name, all works referred to in the report. In this example, you merely paraphrase what Jones stated, rather than quoting directly from the source. Since paraphrasing is used, no mention of page numbers is necessary.

If you quote an author in the text of your report without mentioning her/his name, you might reference the work as follows: It is maintained that cooperative learning is an effective means of...(Johnson & Johnson, 1990). Note the use of the ampersand (&). The ampersand is always used, instead of *and*, when referenced with parentheses (for more explanation see below). To find the reference in which "cooperative learning" is explained, consult the list of *references* placed at the end of the report. Note that since paraphrasing is again employed, no mention of page numbers is necessary.

A direct quote within the text is referenced as follows: Moreover, Tanner and Tanner (1987) were correct when they stated that "the development of public education and the field of supervision are so completely intertwined that they defy separation, even for purposes of analysis" (p. 4).

Note that a page number is cited because a direct quote is used. Page is abbreviated as "*p.*" Notice the placement of the period after the closed parenthesis. Also, notice that *and* is used in "Tanner and Tanner" because you mention the names of the authors within the text, instead of just in parentheses.

Offset a lengthy quote as follows:

Spears (1953) stated:

> *Thirty or forty years ago, when supervision was first settling down in the organizational scheme of things as a service to the classroom teacher, a supervisor was a supervisor. Today, when supervision is attaching itself to almost anything that has*

to do with furthering learning, a supervisor masquerades under a miscellaneous array of titles. Supervision today often travels incognito. (p. 84)

Note the page number placement at the end of the quote with parentheses, but without a period afterwards.

(3) In general, APA recommends use of past tense when reporting research findings: Smith (2001) reported, not reports.

(4) Use of "and" or "&". In reference list at the end of the report, always use "&". In text, the "&" is used within any parentheses, but when noting authors within text, without use of parentheses, the "and" is used. For example, in text you write Welfel and Ingersoll (2001) reported that...

(5) Document a book in references as follows:

Glanz, J. (1991). *Bureaucracy and professionalism: The evolution of public school supervision.* Madison, NJ: Fairleigh Dickinson University Press.

Note several unique aspects of APA when referencing a book:

(A) Title of book is italicized (or underlined), including period.

(B) Always use initials for first and middle names.

(C) Only first letter of first word in title is capitalized as well as first letter in any word appearing after a colon. Always capitalize first letter of proper nouns wherever one appears in title.

(D) Year is placed in parentheses followed by a period.

(E) Usually two spaces placed after:

(a) name before year

(b) year before title

(c) title before place of publication

(F) When only state or country for place of publication is referenced, type complete spelling as in "New Jersey." However, when more specific information about place of publication is presented, reference as follows: "Cranford, NJ". Note that abbreviation for state is used with no periods as might usually be found in "N.J."

(6) Document an article in references as follows:

Glanz, J. (1994). Dilemmas of assistant principals in their supervisory role: Reflections of an assistant principal. *Journal of School Leadership, 4,* 577–593.

Note several unique aspects of APA when referencing an article:

(A) Title of journal name is italicized (or underlined), including period, volume number, and comma following volume number.

(B) As with a book, always use initials for first and middle names.

(C) Only first letter of first word in title of article is capitalized as well as first letter in any word appearing after a colon. Always capitalize first letter of proper nouns.

(D) As with a book, year is placed in parentheses followed by a period.

(E) Usually two spaces placed after:

    (a) name before year

    (b) year before title

    (c) title before name of journal.

(F) Volume number is referenced by simply placing the number after name of journal preceded by a comma. Sometimes, an issue number is referenced as follows: "76(3)", which refers to volume number 76, issue number 3. An issue number is only referenced for journals that begin new pagination with each issue. For example, the *NASSP Bulletin,* a prominent journal in the field, begins each issue with page 1. Therefore, referencing any article published in this journal would include an issue number:

Glanz, J. (1994). Where did the assistant principalship begin? Where is it headed? *NASSPBulletin, 78*(564), 35–41.

Notice that only the volume number is italicized along with journal name, but not issue number, which is always placed in parentheses.

(G) Page numbers follow without designations of "p." or "pp.". Don't abbreviate numbers, such as "14–7", but rather state as "14–17". Note comma before page numbers to separate from volume number.

(7) Document a chapter or article in an edited volume as follows:

Garman, N. B. (1996). Is clinical supervision a viable model for use in the public schools? No. In J. Glanz & R. F. Neville (Eds.), *Educational supervision: Perspectives, issues, and controversies* (pp. 143–178). Norwood, MA: Christopher-Gordon Publishers.

Note several unique aspects of APA when referencing a chapter or article in an edited volume:

(A) Title of book is italicized (or underlined), including period.

(B) Always use initials for first and middle names.

(C) Only first letter of first word in title is capitalized as well as first letter in any word appearing after a colon. Always capitalize first letter of proper nouns.

(D) Year is placed in parentheses followed by a period.

(E) Usually two spaces placed after:

    (a) name before year

    (b) year before title of chapter or article

    (c) title before place of publication

(F) When only state or country for place of publication is referenced, type complete spelling as in "New Jersey". However, when more specific information about place of publication is presented, reference as follows: "Cranford, NJ". Note that abbreviation for state is used with no periods as in "N .J .".

(G) Names of editors (first initials, then last names). Editors' names separated by an ampersand. When only two editors', no comma between names. For three or more editors, comma is placed before ampersand.

(H) Page numbers of chapter or article appear in parentheses as noted.

(8) Document a magazine article as follows:

> Henry, W. A. (1990, April, 9). Beyond the melting pot. *Time, 135,* 28–31.

Note several unique aspects of APA when referencing a magazine article:

(A) Title of journal name is italicized (or underlined), including period, volume number, and comma following volume number.

(B) As with a book, always use initials for first and middle names.

(C) Only first letter of first word in title of magazine article is capitalized as well as first letter in any word appearing after a colon. Always capitalize first letter of proper nouns.

(D) As with a book, year is placed in parentheses followed by a period. However, include month and day magazine was published along with year of publication, as noted above.

(E) Usually two spaces placed after:

    (a) name before year

    (b) year before title

    (c) title before name of magazine.

(F) Volume number is referenced by simply placing the number after name of journal preceded by a comma.

(G) Page numbers follow without designations of "p." or "pp.".

(9) Document a newspaper article as follows:

> Schwartz, J. (1993, September 30). Obesity affects economic, social status. *The Washington Post,* pp. A1, A4.

(A) Same documentation is used as with a magazine article except abbreviation "pp." for pages is used. "A1, A4" indicates that article appears on discontinuous pages.

(10) Document an edited book as follows:

Glanz, J., & Neville, R. F. (Eds.). (1996). *Educational supervision: perspectives, issues, and controversies.* Norwood, MA: Christopher-Gordon Publishers.

(A) Same documentation is used as with a regular book except abbreviation "Eds." is used to note the "editors".

(11) Document an electronic source as follows:

Glanz, J. (1997). Supervision news. [Online] Available: Http:// www.kean.edu/~jglanz/

(12) Document a citation as follows:

In text: (Rodriguez, 2000 as cited in Mullen, 2001). In other words, you consulted Mullen's work to obtain Rodriguez's quotation. You did not locate Rodriguez's work directly.

To obtain more information on electronic sources for APA citations, consult: *Publication Manual of the American Psychological Association*, 5th ed., 2001 (ISBN: 1557987912). Also, check out www.apastyle.org

Sample Portion of a Paper in APA Style

The study of history is a struggle to understand the "unending dialogue between the present and the past" (Carr & Smith, 1961, p. 8). As such, the notion of temporality is relevant to understanding the flow of historical events. People and events cannot be explained only in terms of the present, but must be understood in terms of a past and a future as well. The past, present, and future, according to Cassirer, form an "undifferentiated unity and an indiscriminate whole" (Cassirer, 1953, p. 219). Kummel and Barnes (1966) explained this notion of temporality as a historical process "in which the past never assumes a final shape nor the future ever shuts its doors. Their essential interdependence also means, however, that there can be no progress without a retreat into the past in search of a deeper foundation" (p. 50).

The experience of reflective consciousness through historical inquiry implies an awareness of the past and its interconnectedness to present conditions and future possibilities. History, then, can be understood as an attempt to study the events and ideas of the past that have shaped human experience over time in order to inform current practice as well as to make more intelligent decisions for the future (Marsak, 1970).

History is more than simply recording all past experiences and events. Historians are interested in those aspects of the past that have historical significance. Since what may be historically significant to one may be irrelevant to another, the reconstruction of the past must be undertaken from different perspectives by different people. Moreover, significance is granted only when a sufficient amount of time has lapsed in order to ensure that contemporary demands alone do not dictate what is considered historically important (see e.g., Davis, 1992). Seen in this way, history is the retelling and interpretation of significant events of the past (Kliebard, 1995; Stephens, 1974).

The value of history is its concreteness, its placing of events, people, and theories within context (see e.g., Goodson, 1985; Kliebard, 1987). History supplies the context with which to view current proposals. More fundamentally, understanding how the field has come to take the shape it has is a compelling reason to undertake historical inquiry of supervision. History can also explore antecedents of current innovations or theories. Thus, having a supervision history will deepen and strengthen identity as a field of scholarship and provide a collective consciousness (Garrett, 1994).

References

Carr, E. H., & Smith, J. (1961). *What is history?* New York: Alfred A. Knopf Publisher.

Cassirer, E. (1953). *An essay on man: An introduction to a philosophy of human culture.* New York: Doubleday & Co.

Davis Jr., O. L. (1992). Memory, our educational practice, and history. *The Educational Forum, 56,* 375–379.

Garrett, A. W (1994). Curriculum history's connections to the present: Necessary lessons for informed practice and theory. *Journal of Curriculum and Supervision, 9,* 390–395.

Goodson, F. (1985). History, context, and qualitative methods in the study of the curriculum. In R. G. Burgess (Ed.), *Strategies of educational research: Qualitative methods* (pp. 121–152). London: Falmer Press.

Kliebard, H. M. (1987). *The struggle for the American curriculum: 1893-1958.* New York: Rutledge & Kegan Paul.

Kliebard, H. M. (1995). Why history of education? *The Journal of Educational Research, 88,* 194–199.

Kummel, F., & Barnes, M. N. (1966). Time as succession and the problem of duration. In J. T. Fraser (Ed.), *The voices of time* (pp. 31–55). New York: George Braziller.

Marsak, L. M. (1970). *The nature of historical inquiry.* New York: Holt, Rinehart, and Winston.

Stephens, L. D. (1974). *Probing the past: A guide to the study and teaching of history.* Boston: Allyn & Bacon.

Note two additional items:

    (1) In text, when two or more references are noted within one set of parentheses, alphabetize according to author's last name. For example, as noted above: (see e.g., Goodson, 1985; Kliebard, 1987). Note: "e.g." is the abbreviation for "for example."

(2) In references list, if one author has two or more works cited, the earlier one is referenced first, as in:

> Kliebard, H. M. (1987). *The struggle for the American curriculum: 1893–1958.* New York: Routledge & Kegan Paul.
>
> Kliebard, H. M. (1995). Why history of education? *The Journal of Educational Research, 88,* 194–199.

A Final Word

You will notice that the form and format for APA is a bit awkward, with its use of capitalization, no mentioning of author's first name, etc. You should consult the APA manual in order to accurately apply other rules for documentation. My purpose is only to introduce the style briefly and to indicate its importance. Investment in the *Publication Manual* is suggested. Knowledge of APA will serve you well in other courses and in writing any reports during your professional career. Happy referencing.

Reference

American Psychological Association. (2001). *Publication manual of the American Psychological Association* (5th ed.). Washington, DC: Author.

Module 2 Review

In this Module you learned some basics for using APA. The best way to learn APA is to actually apply it as you write your paper. This module is not meant to be read, but rather referred to as needed. Again, purchasing the Publication Manual of the APA is highly recommended as is visiting www.apastyle.org.

Self-Test Check

1. Below you'll find three references with errors present. Can you locate them?

   Reference #1:

   > Acheson, K. A. & Gall, M. D. (1997). *Techniques in the clinical supervision teachers.* New York: Longman.

   Reference #2:

   > Alfonso, R. J., & Firth, G. R. (1990). Supervision: Needed Research. *Journal Curriculum and Supervision, 5,* 181–188.

   Reference #3:

   > Benedetti, T. (1997). Tips from the classroom. *TESOL Journal, 7*(1), pp. 41–47.

Answers:

1. Comma needed after K.A.; 2. The "R" in word "Research" should be lower-cased.; 3. no need for "pp."

Study Questions

1   Why is it useful to learn and know the APA style?

2.   How might you use APA in writing other than for a thesis?

Module 3: Writing the Abstract

What is an **abstract** and why is it important? An abstract is a summary of your study that contains a brief version of the statement of the problem, a description of the research methodology, the results of the study, and conclusions and/or implications. The abstract is written as the last part of the thesis and contains about 100–150 words. All information appearing in the abstract should appear in the body of the paper or article. Many research journal articles contain an abstract. An abstract is important because it provides the reader with a quick idea of what the study is about. A well written abstract will attract the readers attention and will encourage her/him to read the complete article. I am certain that you appreciated well written abstracts when you were in the midst of reviewing the literature. You certainly couldn't read every article you came across. The abstract gave you just enough information needed to make a decision of the worth of a particular article.

Here is a checklist to determine whether or not you have included all the necessary elements of an abstract:

_____1. Purpose of study noted

_____2. Reference to research questions/hypotheses made

_____3. Research methodology explained

_____4. Results highlighted

_____5. Conclusions/implications briefly mentioned

_____6. Written in one paragraph

_____7. Contains 100–150 words

_____8. Written clearly and precisely

Below you will find four abstracts. Each one has a different problem. Identify each problem and compare your responses to the suggested answers that follow:

Abstract #1:

This group-comparison study examined the effects of cooperative learning (group instruction) and traditional learning (whole class instruction) on mathematics achievement among 3rd grade bilingual students (N = 12) in a self-contained classroom. Equivalent groups were formed using matched pairs based on a pre-test. The control group (n = 6) was taught mathematics using whole class instructional methods, while the experimental group (n = 6) was exposed to cooperative learning strategies. After a 4-week treatment period, a post-test was administered to both groups. A t-test for non-independent means was utilized to determine whether or not there was a significant statistical difference between the mean scores of both groups. To increase sample size, a repeated measures assessment was utilized and mean post-test scores were similarly analyzed.

Abstract #2:

This study assessed the impact of teaching about the Holocaust through literature on a class of sixth-grade Language Arts students. The study was based upon the premise that teaching about the Holocaust is assumed to be important. The study took place at Stevens School in Holmesdale. Support for this assumption is based upon a variety of reasons, including the fact that The State of New Jersey has a requirement that the Holocaust and genocide be taught in some manner in all schools from kindergarten through grade twelve. Upper elementary-grade students need to be taught about the Holocaust by utilizing age-appropriate materials and techniques. This project is important because students must be able to understand not only facts that pertain to the Holocaust itself, but also specific lessons that need to be extrapolated from the topic. More precisely, these lessons include the importance of defending what is morally right, even if one must stand alone, the roles of bystanders, perpetrators, victims, and rescuers, and that understanding and practicing tolerance must be a vital part of one's life.

Abstract #3:

The purpose of this study was to determine whether various testing procedures affect the long term memory and retention of knowledge of history facts in school-age children. A fifth grade male student participated in the case-study assessment and comparison of various testing methods. This study compared two types of teacher made tests (multiple-choice and short-answer) with a no test (control) condition to determine their relative effectiveness as aids to retention learning. The investigation involved instruction via four teacher lessons followed by initial testing of learning, and delayed testing to assess information that was retained two weeks after the initial instruction and testing occurred. After a six week study period, data were analyzed and the results indicated that multiple-choice test formats had a greater impact on long term retention of history facts than short-answer tests. However, any form of testing was superior to no testing. Test anticipation also contributed to higher test results. The study ends with suggestions to continue employing anticipated tests due to its positive effect on retention learning.

Abstract #4:

Research provides conflicting evidence as to whether or not sugar impacts children's behavior. A number of previous sugar-behavior studies concluded that sugar causes adverse behaviors in children. Other studies, however, refuted these claims. The present study intended to assess possible impacts of sugar on various behaviors in children. Parents and several health professionals from the New York area were surveyed regarding their children's/clients' behaviors after consumption of sugared foods. Data from survey responses were analyzed qualitatively. Approximately one third of the children described in parental questionnaires were reported to show behavior changes after sugar consumption, with irritability and overactivity being the most common reported behavioral reactions. Health professionals believed that sugar exacerbates adverse behaviors in children. Parents, pediatricians, and teachers are recommended to encourage children to eschew sugar consumption. Future research should include longitudinal studies that follow groups of children on diets differing in sugar content. Also, research should include schoolteachers as participants in studies involving children's sugar consumption.

Suggested answers:

Abstract #1:

Results and conclusions/implications missing; otherwise first part is fine.

Abstract #2:

Unclear about what the study actually accomplished. It's more of a rationale or explanation as to why the study is important more than it is an abstract.

Abstract #3:

In the last sentence, use "affect," not "effect."

Abstract #4:

Pretty good one; Can you make a suggestion?

Below you will find three abstracts that are satisfactory and that can be used as models for your own:

Abstract #1:

This qualitative study sought to integrate Gardner's Theory of Multiple Intelligences into science classes for the Deaf and Hard of Hearing. A series of science lessons and workstations using Multiple Intelligence Theory was developed in conjunction with the science curriculum approved by the Board of Education. The lessons were conducted in a multi-age, multi-level class with students whose hearing impairments ranged from moderate to profound. Gardner's Theory of Multiple Intelligences proved useful in many aspects of the students' educational development. Multiple observers noted that all students, regardless of their age, ability, or degree of hearing loss participated in the lessons and took part in the workstations with heightened interest and enthusiasm. Observation instruments were used to record data and case studies were written. Improvements in both signed and verbal communication skills, self-esteem, student motivation, and quality of work were observed and recorded qualitatively. Evidence was presented in case study form. Suggestions for Integrating Gardner's theory into other curricula were made.

Abstract #2:

Research indicates that the educational objectives of mathematics instruction have shifted away from computational proficiencies and textbook applications of isolated math skills. Emphasis is now placed upon open ended problem solving skills requiring students to think critically and make valid connections between relevant mathematics and everyday applications. Neurological research is rapidly gaining momentum as it dovetails with new technology, continually revealing information about how the brain learns. These discoveries may provide insights that enable teachers to create more productive teaching/learning situations. Strategies more compatible with the brain's natural tendencies could enhance retention of learning. A quantitative study of two groups of eighth grade math students was conducted to measure the effects of regular logic based instruction with brain compatible strategies. A pretest was given to establish comparability between experimental and control groups. After a 3 1/2-month instructional period, a post-test was administered to assess measurable differences in problem solving ability. Post-test results were subjected to a t-Test analysis but no statistically significant results were found.

Abstract #3

Research provides inconsistent findings on sensory integration treatment and its impact on learning and adaptive development of children with learning disabilities. Previous studies have shown that sensory integration techniques impact a child's academic achievement. Other studies have shown minimal or no evidence regarding the impact of sensory integration treatment. The present study intended to assess possible impacts of sensory integration treatment on behaviors in adaptive developmental skills and academic achievement among preschool and elementary school aged students. Parents of children with sensory integration dysfunction, teachers, and several health professionals were surveyed via questionnaires and interviews. Data from survey responses were analyzed qualitatively. Detailed descriptions based on data collected indicated that positive behavioral changes in adaptive developmental skills and academic achievement after receiving sensory integration treatment were noted. Future research should include longitudinal studies that implement sensory integration treatments and their impacts on children's behaviors.

Module 3 Review

In this Module you learned the basics for writing an abstract. A good abstract includes these elements: a brief version of the statement of the problem, a description of the research methodology, the results of the study, and conclusions and/or implications.

Self-Test Check

1. Write an abstract with data made up. Don't refer back to module yet. This will be good practice. After you've written an abstract, check back at beginning of the module to determine whether or not you included each abstract component appropriately.

Study Questions

1. Locate five abstracts from five journal articles and assess their quality in terms of the criteria outlined in this module.

2. Plan your own abstract. Even though you may not have completed your study, sketch out a tentative, even hypothetical abstract. After you have written one, use the checklist in the module to ensure you've covered all aspects of a well written abstract. How does yours compare?

Module 4: Advice and Suggestions

As you "put it all together" in this final part of this book, below are some suggestions for success I culled from the experiences of my former and current students. I hope they are of assistance to you. Note that some of the following suggestions are relevant before beginning your thesis while others relate to the latter stages. Earlier in the book in Module 3 in Part One I recommended that you skip to read this module as well. So, here's some more advice and suggestions:

- Relax. All students confronting the challenges of completing a thesis project experience stress pangs. They are short-lived. Speak to former students and even ask your professor for sample thesis projects as samples. Think, "Others before me have succeeded." (For you pessimists, keep in mind that in all my years of teaching few, if any, graduate students ever failed to complete a thesis. Certainly the quality of student projects has varied, but I found that graduate students, largely are earnest, caring, intelligent, and diligent. You can and will succeed.).

- Read the textbook or chapters assigned. Many students feel they can "go it alone." Such an attitude usually gets them in trouble. So, read all assigned readings.

- Develop a study team. Find like-minded students to join to complete, for example, literature reviews and survey development together. Brainstorming ideas and just working with others in a similar situation will serve to allay your apprehensions.

- Team up with a partner to complete a project. Some professors allow two students to team up to complete a single project. If your professor allows this option, be aware of the advantages and disadvantages of such an undertaking:

  Advantages: 1) two heads are better than one; 2) you can work problems through together; 3) when one person is unavailable, the other can pick up the slack; 4) workloads can be divided equally.

  Disadvantages: 1) you are dependent on the promptness and earnestness of someone else; 2) if one person cannot complete her/his phase of the project, you will either have to pick up the slack or just sit it out and wait; 3) you will get one grade from the professor.

- Develop a timeline for completing the project. Certain phases of the project will take longer than others. Also, know that there may be a lot of "waiting around" time especially during data collection. Don't get complacent. Remain vigilant and aware that when the data arrive you must get ready for data analysis and interpretation.

- Rely on your professor for assistance. Most professors remind students that they can submit sections for her/his review prior to the end of the semester. You'd be surprised to know that most students never take up this generous offer. If you do so, you will more successfully complete the project.

- Follow the 5 easy steps, previously explained in various Parts of this book, that include: Identify a Topic; Write the Literature Review; Develop a Research Plan; Carry Out the Plan; and Write up the Results. Each step is reviewed below:

Step 1: Identify a topic

- Don't rush when selecting a topic
- Choose a topic that is of *interest* to you, is *researchable*, and is *feasible* to carry out.
- Be ready to tolerate initial uncertainty
- Brainstorm a list of things that you wonder about:
- Your classroom
- Your school
- Your profession
- An educational issue
- Discuss your choices with a colleague or two
- Select one broad topic, then try to narrow down your area – develop researchable questions
- Skim the text
- Go to the library or scan the web – Locate articles, books, and journals that interest you – look for studies on the general topic. Locate dictionaries (e.g., *Dictionary of Education* or *Dictionary of Multicultural Education*), encyclopedias (e.g., *Encyclopedia of Education* or *International Encyclopedia of Education, Encyclopedia of Educational Research*), handbooks (e.g., *Handbook of Educational Psychology, Handbook of Research on Curriculum*, or *Handbook of Research on School Supervision, Handbook of Reading Research*, or *Handbook of Research on Teaching*)
- Discuss your ideas again with a colleague or two
- Meet with professor
- Voila! You now have a topic

Step 2: Write a Literature Review

- Your literature review does not have to be exhaustive. You don't have to locate every study completed on your topic. The purpose of a literature review is to find out and acknowledge what work has been done on the topic. Your literature review, then, merely has to represent accurately what the experts have to say about it.

- Include pro *and* con perspectives. Present a balanced fair review. For instance, if you are reviewing the use of phonics, you should include the work of those who support and oppose its use. You should also review the literature on whole language instruction to place the subject in proper perspective.

314

- Scan the web using key websites. Review educational databases (e.g., ERIC) to obtain leads. Copy articles that seem relevant and then read each article. For each article, keep an index card that includes: title, author, other publication information necessary to write a reference, summarize article including purpose, methodology, findings, implications, and conclusions. Simply use your own words and be concise. Number the card and the article. That way you can refer to the article later. If you decide to include quotations on the card, make sure you include accurate quote and correct page numbers. Label cards my topic e.g., Pros of Cooperative Learning, Cons, Research Studies at the High School Level, etc.

- Divide your literature review as you would any story: a beginning, middle, and end. The beginning includes a one or two paragraph introduction that states the purpose of the literature review and what will be included. The middle may include several subsections. Use the various topics you noted on the cards above to guide development of the middle subsection. The end is just a concluding statement summarizing what you found.

Step 3: Develop a Research Plan

- A Research Plan is developed after you have identified and topic and have conducted a literature review. The Plan outlines what you intend to do in terms of conducting some research on the topic chosen.

- Know what is included in a Research Plan: Statement of the Problem, Research Questions and/or Hypothesis, Sample, Instrumentation, and Procedure.

Step 4: Carry Out the Plan

- At this stage, you are prepared to conduct your study (carry out the Procedure as stated above.

- Implement your plan by carefully methodically and consistently. Collect data and properly file them for later analysis.

- Analyze your data. See Parts Nine and Ten.

- Interpret your results. See Module 2 of Part Twelve.

Step 5: Write Up the Results

TITLE PAGE

ACKNOWLEDGEMENTS

ABSTRACT

LIST OF TABLES

LIST OF FIGURES

CONTENTS

CHAPTER 1: INTRODUCTION

    Background

    Importance of the Study

    Statement of the Problem

    Hypothesis and/or Research Question(s)

    Definition of Terms

CHAPTER 2: REVIEW OF LITERATURE/RELATED RESEARCH

CHAPTER 3: RESEARCH DESIGN/METHODOLOGY

    Sample

    Instrumentation

    Procedure

    Analysis of Data

    Results

CHAPTER 4: IMPLICATIONS FOR PRACTICE AND RESEARCH

    Limitations of the Study

    Discussion/Conclusions

    Implications for Practice

    Implications for Further Research

REFERENCES

APPENDIXES

Here are some guidelines compiled from several of my former students:

Suggestions... Recommendations.... from former students

- Welcome to the research course, if you've gotten this far then you know you are almost through with the program... now it's time for some different type of work... research!

- While this project may sound very difficult and confusing... We hope you can be comforted by the fact that many students before you successfully completed the thesis.

- I particularly wasn't so fond of research, but when you get down to doing the actual work on a topic you are INTERESTED in, it's really not that bad and even gets interesting!

- But, you need to choose a topic that you really want to know more about and one that you will and can stick with for a while...

- When choosing a topic, do not try to be too creative or original. Think about your daily environment (work, home, school, neighborhood) and come up with a study that will be easy and meaningful for you to carry out!

- I found communication via email extremely helpful. Your professor should be available to help and guide you, so be thankful and take the opportunity to email questions, drafts etc...

- OH! When you decide on a topic and are in the midst of planning your study, take the time to go through your ideas with a friend, teacher, etc... to help you clarify and make the most of your study! It's worth the extra thoughts to choose a study design that will be worthwhile...

- Most of my literature I received from ERIC online, others from books on my topic, or copies from journals at the library.

- To find additional articles for your literature review, scan the reference section of a journal article you have for titles that seem pertinent to your topic. Try to get a hold of those articles. Each article should lead you to many more.

(Continued next page)

- To find additional articles for your literature review, scan the reference section of a journal article you have for titles that seem pertinent to your topic. Try to get a hold of those articles. Each article should lead you to many more.

- Ask your librarian if your library has an inter-library loan service (ILL). This service allows a library to request journal articles and books from other libraries that are outside the library's system. This process takes time—it can take a few weeks to receive an article—but you will obtain articles you could not get by doing your own searches. Many articles that I wanted for my literature review were in journals which most libraries do not have. The only way I was able to get these articles was through the ILL service of my library.

- For those of you who will compose a questionnaire for your study, have at least one person who will not participate in your study complete the entire questionnaire before you distribute it to the participants in your study. Someone who actually goes through the questionnaire will be able to point out which questions or directions he/she finds confusing or unclear.

- To sum up, take it easy, do what you need to do when you are supposed to do it… and you'll be just fine!

Module 4 Review

In this Module you learned about some suggestions that will help to successfully complete your thesis.

Module 5: Evaluating the Thesis

I always believed that students should be made aware in advance as to the criteria used to evaluate their work. The rubric on the next page is one I have found useful in my attempt to both guide and evaluate student thesis work. The rubric is basic and generic so the instructor may have additional criteria but you have at least some sense of basic expectations.

THESIS RUBRIC

Place score below

Components	1	2	3	SCORE= 1, 2, or 3	
	Unacceptable	Acceptable	Target		
Topic	Insignificant and unrelated to area of specialization	Significant and related to area of specialization	Significant, related to area of specialization, and made a unique contribution to the field		
Content	Insufficient; lack of information; superficial understanding of research	Acceptable; information provided; researched	Substantial; detailed information; thorough and well researched		
Format	Guidelines not followed; disorganized and sloppily arranged	Guidelines followed; organized and arranged in a logical, presentable order	Guidelines followed precisely; Well organized and arranged logically; aesthetically presented		
APA (citations)	APA not adhered to (3 or more errors)	APA generally adhered to (1 or 2 errors)	APA meticulously adhered to (no errors)		
Control	Poor "technical control"; incomplete sentences, spelling errors, incorrect punctuation, improper use of grammar, poor paragraph development, etc.	Correct "technical control"; few, if any, incomplete sentences, few, if any, spelling errors, correct punctuation, proper use of grammar, correct paragraph development, etc.	Excellent "technical control"; complete sentences, no spelling errors, correct punctuation, proper use of grammar, excellent paragraph development, etc.		

Qualitative comments: (on reverse side)　　　　　　　　**OVERALL SCORE-** _____

Evaluation Criteria for Report

Some prefer the criteria list below to a rubric. Students need to be informed in advance how their projects will be evaluated. Below is a list of criteria students have found useful (note that each instructor will have her/his own criteria):

The research project will be graded based on the following criteria (serious deficiency in anyone of these criteria can affect your grade):

(1) *Content:* Does your paper reflect a knowledge and understanding of the content/topic/ problem? Is the problem stated clearly and precisely? Is the author aware of critical issues that relate to the problem?

Comments:_____

_____

_____

(2) *Citations:* Are appropriate and sufficient authorities cited? Does the research include at least 12 articles and 3 books (15 references)? Are the references timely (within the last 5 years)?

Comments:_____

_____

_____

(3) *Coherence:* Is the paper well organized so that ideas "hang together"? Are ideas developed clearly? Are all sections of the research project included?

Comments:_____

_____

_____

(4) *Clarity:* Is the paper clear and easy to read? Is it aesthetically pleasing?

Comments:_____

_____

_____

(5) *Control:* Does the writing reflect good "technical control," i.e., complete sentences, spelling, correct punctuation, grammar, paragraph development, etc.?

Comments:_____

_____

_____

Module 5 Review

In this Module you learned the criteria that may be used to evaluate your thesis project and/or research paper.

Study Questions

1. How do the rubric criteria help you frame your project?

2. What other evaluative information would be of assistance? (Inform your professor)

3. What else do you need in order to complete your thesis project successfully? (share ideas with a colleague and/or professor)

Module 6: Becoming an Intelligent Consumer of Research

"Study demonstrates that 1800 men and women who are apple-shaped with thin legs are more susceptible to heart ailments."

This vitamin "will not prevent cancer, stroke, or Alzheimer's but research has shown that it can lesson your risk for getting these diseases."

"4th grade standardized math scores have shown a rise of 20% over 4th grade scores last year. Students are clearly doing better in math."

"Brand X of cars has increased in quality and is on top of cars in three categories."

We are bombarded by the media on an almost daily basis with many studies purporting new insights, if not panaceas. As an educational researcher, you now have the skills to become a more intelligent consumer of research. One of the most fundamental premises underlying research is that every study has some sort of limitation or limitations.

Reflection

What limitations come to mind as you reread each of the research-based statements at the start of this module?

We began this book with outlining the importance of reflection. Maintaining a research mindset and disposition that values scientific inquiry enables you to reflect on important educational matters that affect your work and that promote student learning and better schools. Reflective practice creates a systemwide mindset for school improvement—a professional problem-solving ethos. It instills a commitment to continuous improvement. Reflecting on research data enhances decision making. It provides a greater feeling of competence to solve problems and make sound instructional decisions. In other words, educational research provides for an intelligent way for making decisions. Moreover, reflecting on research creates a more positive school climate in which teaching and learning are foremost concerns.

Educators who undertake educational research should accept without criticism theories, innovations, and programs at face value. With a research-oriented mindset, you are able to make more intelligent decisions about the quality of educational research and its usefulness for educators. As you examine the research literature (i.e., studies) consider these, among other, factors for evaluating the quality of research in education.

1. Was the study peer reviewed?

2. Does the study have a representative sample?

3. Is there an adequate sample size?

4. Are instruments valid and reliable?

5. Has the study been replicated?

6. Does it make sense from a practical point of view?

7. What are its limitations?

Module 6 Review

In this Module you learned that becoming an intelligent consumer of research requires knowledge of research methodology but, perhaps as important, you need to maintain a research-oriented mindset.

Self-Test Check

1. For each of the studies or situations below, explain any possible limitations or cautions you might point out. What does the study reliably tells us, if anything?

    a) A 4-year study conducted by university researchers with grades 3, 6, 9, and 12, that included 1300 students, concludes that Teaching Method A is the best method for teaching reading in Mansfield School District.

    b) At a school board meeting, the superintendent unveils a new reading series that he says has been heralded nation-wide for raising student reading scores. He wants the district to adopt the series.

    c) As a classroom teacher, you read about a new approach to teaching phonics. You decide to try it out with your class.

    d) As a guidance counselor with twenty years of experience, you know what works best for middle school students in terms of allaying their apprehensions and anxieties. You read an article in a research journal that discusses a longitudinal study that indicates that a special counseling method has proven statistically significant as being effective. You are intrigued about the findings of this study. You decide to try it out.

    e) At a faculty meeting, the principal informs teachers that the district has adopted a new approach to teaching writing and that "research indicates a high level of success using this approach." He states that all language arts teachers will receive training in this new approach and that all teachers are expected to adopt it as the main approach for teaching writing in the upcoming school year.

Study Questions

1. How might the information you learned in this book help you to become a better consumer of research?

2. How might the information you learned in this book help you to become a better educator?

3. If you were asked by your principal to speak to beginning teachers about the importance of educational research, what would you tell them?

4. What lessons have you learned about educational research in general?

Activity

1. Collect 10 different news items reported on TV, radio, or newspaper. Describe the accuaracy of each study, noting possible limitations or cautions about readily accepting the report.

References

Acheson, K. A., & Gall, M. D. (1997). *Techniques in the clinical supervision of teachers.* New York: Longman.

Anderson, G. L., Herr, K., & Nihlen, A. S. (1994). *Studying your own school: An educator's guide to qualitative practitioner research.* Thousand Oaks, CA: Corwin Press.

Bates, J. D. (2000). *Writing with precision: How to write so that you cannot be misunderstood* (4th ed.). Washington, D.C.: Acropolis Books.

Beck, L. G. (1994). *Reclaiming educational administration as a caring profession.* New York: Teachers College Press.

Best, J., & Kahn, J. (1998). *Research in education* (8th ed.). Needham Heights, MA: Allyn & Bacon.

Bogdan, R. C., & Biklen, S. K. (1997). *Qualitative research for education: An introduction to theory and methods* (3rd ed.). Boston: Allyn & Bacon.

Bum, B., & Payment, M. (2000). *Assessments A to Z: Collection of 50 questionnaires, instruments, and inventories.* Port Chester, NY: National Professional Resources.

Calhoun, E. F. (1993). Action research: Three approaches. *Educational Leadership, 51,* 62–65.

Calhoun, E. F. (1994). *How to use action research in the self-renewing school.* Alexandria, VA: Association for Supervision and Curriculum Development.

Calhoun, E., & Allen, L. (1996). *The action research network: Action research on action research.* In B. Joyce & E. Calhoun (Eds.), *Learning experiences in school renewal.* Eugene, OR: Clearinghouse on Educational Management.

Charles, C. M. (1997). *Introduction to educational research.* New York: Addison-Wesley Longman.

Chirban, J. T. (1996). *Interviewing in depth.* Thousand Oaks, CA: Sage Publications.

Corston, R., & Colman, A. (2003). *A crash course in SPSS for Windows.* Malden, MA: Blackwell Publishing.

Creswell, J. W: (1994). *Research design: Qualitative and quantitative approaches.* Thousand Oaks, CA: Sage Publications.

Crowl, T.K. (1986). *Fundamentals of research: A practical guide for educators and special educators.* Columbus, OH: Publishing Horizons, Inc.

Crowl, T.K. (1996). *Fundamentals of educational research: A practical guide for educators and special educators* (2nd ed.). Boston, MA: McGraw Hill.

Crowl, T. K., Kaminsky, S., & Podell, D. M. (1997). *Educational psychology.* Madison, WI: Brown & Benchmark.

Denzin, N. K., & Lincoln, Y. S. (Eds.). (2000). *Handbook of qualitative research* (2ⁿᵈ ed.). Thousand Oaks, CA: Corwin Press.

Donmoyer, R. (1993). The purpose of portraits: Rethinking the form and function of research on students at risk. In R. Donmoyer & R. Kos (Eds.), *Students at risk: Portraits, policies, programs, and practices* (pp. 37–48). New York: State University of New York Press.

Donmoyer, R., & Kos, R. (1993). *Students at risk: Portraits, policies, programs, and practices.* New York: State University of New York Press. *Equity and Choice.* (1993), 10(1).

Farkas, R.D. (2003). Effects of traditional versus learning-style instructional methods on middle school students. *The Journal of Educational Research, 97*(1), 42–51.

Fink, A. (1995). *The survey kit.* Thousand Oaks, CA: Sage Publications.

Fink, A., & Kosecoff, J. (1998). *How to conduct surveys: A step-by-step guide* (2ⁿᵈ ed.). Thousand Oaks, CA: Sage Publications.

Fitz-Gibbon, C. T., & Morris, L. L. (1987). *How to analyze data.* Newbury Park, CA: Sage Publications.

Gay, L. R. (1996). *Educational research: Competencies for analysis and application* (5th ed.). Englewood Cliffs, NJ: Prentice Hall.

Glanz, J. (1994). Redefining the roles and responsibilities of assistant principals. *The Clearing House, 67*(5), 283–288.

Glanz, J. (1995). A school/curricular intervention martial arts program for students at risk. *The Journal of At-Risk Issues, 2*(1), 18–25.

Glanz, J. (1998). Images of principals in film and television: From Mr. Wameke to Mr. Rivelle to Mr. Woodman. *The Journal of Educational Leadership and Administration, 10,* 7–24.

Glanz, J. (2000). *Relax for success: A practical guide for educators to relieve stress.* Norwood, MA: Christopher-Gordon Publishers.

Glickman, C. D. (1998). *Renewing America's schools: A guide for school-based action.* San Francisco: Jossey-Bass Publishers.

Glickman, C. D., Gordon, S. P., & Ross-Gordon, J. M. (2004). *Supervision of instruction: A developmental approach* (6th ed.). Boston: Allyn & Bacon.

Gronlund, N. E., & Linn, R. L. (1990). *Measurement and evaluation in teaching* (6th ed.). New York: Macmillan.

Hunter, M. (1967). *Reinforcement theory for teachers.* El Segundo, CA: TIP Publications.

Krippendorf, K. (1980). *Content analysis: An introduction to its methodology.* Beverly Hills, CA: Sage Publications.

Krueger, R. A. (2000). *Focus groups: A practical guide for applied research* (3ʳᵈ ed.). Thousand Oaks, CA: Sage Publications.

Lawrence-Lightfoot, S. (1985). *The good high school.* New York: Basic Books.

Litwin, M. S. (1995). *How to measure survey reliability and validity.* Thousand Oaks, CA: Sage Publications.

Marshall, C., & Rossman, G. B. (1999). *Designing qualitative research* (3rd ed.). Newbury Park, CA: Sage Publications.

McGuire, M., Stilborne, L., McAdams, M., & Hyatt, L. (2000). *The Internet handbook for writers, researchers, and journalists.* New York: The Guilford Press.

McMillan, J. H., & Schumacher, S. (2000). *Research in education: A conceptual introduction* (5th ed.). Glenview, IL: Scott, Foresman.

Mishler, E. G. (1986). *Research interviewing: Context and process.* Cambridge, MA: Harvard University Press.

McMillan, J. H., & Schumacher, S. (2000). *Research in education: A conceptual introduction* (5th ed.). Glenview, IL: Scott, Foresman.

McNiff, J. (1995). *Action research: Principles and practice.* London: Routledge.

Merriam, S. B. (1997). *Qualitative research and case study applications in education.* San Francisco: Jossey-Bass Publishers.

Moore, K. D. (1995). *Classroom teaching skills.* New York: McGraw-Hill.

NASSP. (1987). *Comprehensive assessment of school environments.* Reston, VA: National Association of Secondary School Principals.

Oja, S., & Smulyan, L. (1989). *Collaborative action research: A developmental approach.* London: The Falmer Press.

Osterman, K. F., & Kottkamp, R: B. (2001). *Reflective practice for educators: Improving schooling through professional development.* Newbury Park, CA: Corwin Press.

Patton, M. Q. (1990). *Qualitative research methods* (2nd ed.). Beverly Hills, CA: Sage Publications.

Patten, M.L. (1998). *Questionnaire research: A practical guide.* Los Angeles, CA: Pyrczak Publishing.

Popham, W. J. (1972). Simplified designs for school research. In R L. Baker & R. E. Schutz (Eds.), *Instructional product research* (pp. 137–160). New York: American Book.

Publication Manual of the American Psychological Association. (2001). Washington, DC: American Psychological Association.

Sagor, R. (1992). *How to conduct collaborative action research.* Alexandria, VA: Association for Supervision and Curriculum Development.

Schon, D. A. (1983). *The reflective practitioner: How professionals think in action.* New York: Basic.

Schon, D. A (1984). Leadership as reflection-in-action. In T. J. Sergiovanni & J. E. Corbally (Eds.), *Leadership and organizational culture: New perspectives on administrative theory and practice* (pp. 36–63). Urbana: University of Illinois Press.

Schon, D. A. (1987). *Educating the reflective practitioner: Toward a new design for thinking and learning in the professional.* San Francisco: Jossey-Bass Publishers.

Scieczka, J. (1996). *The true story of the 3 little pigs.* New York: Viking Press.

Seidman, I. E. (1998). *Interviewing as qualitative research: A guide for researchers in education and the social sciences* (2nd ed.). New York: Teachers College Press.

Starratt, R. J. (1995). *Leaders with vision: The quest for school renewal.* Thousand Oaks, CA: Corwin Press.

Strauss, A., & Corbin, J. (1990). *Grounded theory: Basics of qualitative research.* Newbury Park, CA: Sage Publications.

Stringer, E. T. (1999). *Action research: A handbook for practitioners.* Thousand Oaks, CA: Sage Publications.

Strunk, W., Jr., & White, E. B. (2000). *The elements of style* (4th ed.). New York: Macmillan.

Sullivan, S., & Glanz, J. (2000; 2005). *Supervision that improves teaching: Strategies and techniques.* Thousand Oaks, CA: Corwin Press.

Sullivan, S., & Glanz, J. (2002). Good intentions, questionable results: Implications for the professional development of teachers. *Education and Urban Society, 32,* 451–476.

Thomas, S.J. (1999). *Designing surveys that work! A step-by-step guide.* Bloomington, IN: Phi Delta Kappa.

Urdan, T.C. (2001). *Statistics in plain English.* Mahwah, NJ: Lawrence Erlbaum Publishers.

Vaughn, S., Schumm, J. S., & Sinagub, J. M. (1996). *Focus group interviews in education and psychology.* Thousand Oaks, CA: Sage Publications.

Webber, I. E. (1976). *It looks like this: A point-of-view book.* San Francisco: International Society for General Semantics.

Whitaker, K. S. (1995). Principal burnout: Implications for professional development. *Journal of Personnel Evaluation in Education. 9,* 287–296.

Wiersma, W. (1999). *Research methods in education: An introduction* (7th ed.). Boston: Allyn & Bacon.

Willerman, M., McNeely, S. L., & Koffman, E. C. (1991). *Teachers helping teachers: Peer observation and assistance.* New York: Praeger.

Wolcott, H. (1992). *Writing up qualitative research.* Newbury Park, CA: Sage.

Wolcott, H. (1995). *The art of fieldwork.* Walnut Creek, CA: AltaMira.

Wolcott, H. (1999). *Ethnography: A way of seeing.* Walnut Creek, CA: AltaMira.

Wolf, R M., LeMahiew, P. G., & Eresh, J. (1992). Good measure: Assessment as a tool for educational reform. *Educational Leadership, 49*(8), 8–13.

Zirpoli, T. J., & Melloy, K. J. (1996). *Behavior management: Application for teachers and parents* (2nd ed.). New York: Macmillan.

Glossary

A-B; A-B-A; or A-B-A-B research designs are types of single-subject designs. See **Single-Subject Research Designs.**

Abstract is a brief summary of the study that contains a brief version of the statement of the problem, a description of the research methodology, the results of the study, and conclusions and/or implications. The abstract is written as the last part of the thesis and contains about 100–150 words. All information appearing in the abstract should appear in the body of the paper or article. See Module 3 in Part Thirteen for more details.

Accurate disclosure is an ethical principle related to conducting research that assures that participants in research are informed accurately about the general topic under investigation as well as any unusual procedures that may be used in the study. See Module 4 in Part One for more details.

Achievement tests are commonly used measures or **assessment** tools in educational research. An achievement test is a kind of **standardized test** in which an individual's knowledge or proficiency in a given content area is assessed. The Stanford Achievement Test and the Iowa Test of Basic Skills are examples of standardized achievement tests.

Analysis of covariance (ANCOVA) is a statistical technique used in group comparison research when equivalence between the groups cannot be ascertained. To compute an analysis of covariance, you would use a computer program such as STATPAK or SPSS. See Module 6 in Part Nine for more details.

Analysis of variance (ANOVA, sometimes called the F test) is a statistical technique for determining whether or not significant differences can be found among the means of *three* or more groups. To compute an analysis of variance, you would use a computer program such as STATPAK or SPSS. See Module 6 in Part Nine for more details.

Aptitude test is a kind of standardized test used as a data collection instrument (or data source) designed to predict someone's ability to perform. The use of IQ tests is an example of an aptitude test. The SAT test taken by precollegiate students is another example of an aptitude test.

Assessment is a process of interpreting information to aid decision making. Assessments include all information an educator collects to help make an informed, thoughtful decision. Thus, assessment is a general term for interpreting data collected. As an educator, for example, you may collect data (by various **measurements,** e.g., **interviews,** observations, **portfolios,** and **surveys,** among others) about teachers in your school. Assessment occurs when you interpret the meaning of these data. Your interpretation of the data may lead you to conclude that a particular teacher is having trouble dealing with disruptive students. Your assessment leads you to believe, in other words, that this teacher needs classroom management training.

Since the terms assessment, measurement, and evaluation are often used synonymously, an attempt to clarify differences may be in order. Measurement refers to the process of gathering information and is often expressed numerically. In the case above, for instance, the number of times this teacher refers students to the dean or vice-principal is one form of measurement. Ordinarily, scores on tests are considered measurements. However, a measurement really refers to any way of collecting data, including **questionnaires, aptitude tests,** and other surveys.

Assessment is a broader term that includes measurements, but also includes interpreting measurements in order to make some sort of decision. Concluding that a student is reading on the 6th grade level or that a teacher is suffering from burnout are derived though assessment; i.e., interpreting various measurements.

Evaluation, in contrast, refers to the process of making a decision based on the assessment process. For example, referring a burnt out teacher to counseling might be a decision made as a result of interpreting the data collected. Placing a student in a remedial class is an evaluative measure taken after having interpreted or assessed various measurements or data collected.

Every competent educational leader is continually taking measurements, assessing them and, then, taking a course of action by making some decision or evaluation.

Beneficence is an ethical principle related to conducting research that ensures all participants that no harm will befall them. See Module 4 in Part One for more details.

Baseline is a graphic record of measurements taken prior to introducing an **intervention** or **treatment** in **single-subject** research designs such as a time-series design. See Part Five.

Case study research is one of three methods of qualitative research. Case studies involve in-depth investigations of an individual or group of individuals. Findings are stated verbally, not numerically. Case studies are reported by describing in detail observations made of individuals, groups, or school settings. See Module 3 in Part Seven.

Causal-comparative – see **ex post facto**

Chi square (often symbolized by X^2) is a statistical technique for assessing the relationship between two or more **nominal variables.** "Chi" is pronounced "kiy (long i sound)." To compute chi square, you would use a computer program such as STATPAK or SPSS. See Module 6 in Part Nine.

Closed-ended questions are questions on a **questionnaire** that limit possible responses by providing specific choices or options (e.g., yes, no, uncertain) to a respondent. **Likert scales** are examples of **close-ended** questionnaires.

Collaborative action research (and schoolwide action research) are forms of action research in which parents, teachers, and principals might be involved in an ongoing program of **assessment**

and improvement. Each group member shares in the planning, implementation, and analysis of the research.

Conceptual definitions are one of two ways to define terms in a research study. A conceptual definition is a typical dictionary-type definition of a term or concept. Sources for conceptual definitions usually are authorities in the field. The following is an example of a conceptual definition:

> Cooperative Learning "involves positive interdependence among students, face to face interaction, individual accountability for mastery of material and the development of personal and small group skills." (Johnson & Johnson, [year, page]).

See **operational definitions** for a second way of defining terms.

Confounding variables or factors can cause erroneous conclusions to be drawn from a study. In group comparison studies, for example, changes in the **dependent variable** may not be caused by the **treatment** under study, but may, in fact, be influenced by some other intended or unforeseen factors. Two such confounding factors are the Hawthorne and John Henry Effects.

The Hawthorne Effect occurs when members in the **experimental group** know they are receiving "special" **treatment** and, thus, will improve no matter what treatment they are receiving. Members of such experimental groups consider themselves special or privileged. The original Hawthorne studies were conducted by Elton Mayo and his associates in the late 1920s and early 1930s at the Hawthorne Plant of Western Electric near Chicago.

The John Henry Effect, the opposite of the Hawthorne Effect, occurs when subjects in the **control group** know they are, in a sense, competing with some other group (experimental) and, consequently, expend extra effort to perform better than the **experimental group.**

Both the Hawthorne and John Henry Effects may cause erroneous conclusions to be drawn from your study and are, thus, called confounding factors. Obviously, every effort to make each group "feel" special would avert problems with the Hawthorne Effect, for example. In **group comparison** research (e.g., assessing the effect of computer-assisted instruction on computational skills between two groups) both groups should be exposed to some special **treatment** (computers, in this case) without letting the participants know what you are measuring. For example, the control group may use computers to enhance writing skills, while using traditional methods to learn computational skills. The experimental group is exposed to computers to enhance their mathematical computational skill development. Participants in this study do not know what you are measuring and, thus, the Hawthorne Effect is minimized.

Discussion of other confounding factors are included in the "limitations" section of your report (see Module 1 in Part Twelve). Although your study may be limited by several factors (see **internal validity**), confounding factors only refer to those factors or situations which may cause erroneous conclusions to be drawn.

Content analysis is a method of data analysis in which you analyze the content in a given document according to prescribed categories or criteria while following explicit rules of coding.

Control group (sometimes called comparison group) is the term used in **group comparison** studies to identify the group, sometimes assigned randomly, that remains untreated or receives a **treatment** other than the one received by the **experimental group.** Data collected from individuals in a control group are compared with data collected from members of an **experimental group.** These groups serve as comparisons or controls for subjects who are receiving special treatments.

Convenience sampling refers to obtaining a sample from whoever happens to be available (see **sampling**).

Converted scores refer to **raw scores** that are converted into **grade equivalents, percentiles, stanines,** or other forms. Raw scores that are converted are more easily understood, compared, and interpreted.

Correlation (synonymous with the word "relationship") is a statistical technique for evaluating the degree to which two **variables** relate to one another.

 Correlational analyses are most easily computed using STATPAK or any similar program (see Module 6 in Part Nine).

Correlation coefficient (or coefficient of correlation) is a statistic (r) that indicates the degree of relationship between two or more **variables,** as explained above.

Correlational research is one of three methods of research that assume a quantitative approach (see Figure 2.1 in Part Two) in studying a given educational issue or problem.

Criterion-referenced tests are one of two major types of **testing** instruments that measure minimum levels of student performance. Teacher-made tests are one example of a criterion-referenced test. (In contrast, see **norm-referenced tests**).

Data collection is the process of collecting information to answer one's **research questions** and/or confirm or reject an **hypothesis.** One of the major steps of the **scientific method,** data collection should be comprehensive and multiple (as described in Part Eight).

Degrees of freedom (usually abbreviated as "*df*") is a term used in statistical inference to connote the "degree of freedom" a researcher has in selecting a given **sample** for one's study. Degrees of freedom is one of the more difficult statistical terms to fully understand. All you have to know is that *df* always = N - 1; i.e., the number of subjects in your sample minus one subject.

 Let's say I asked you to choose any 5 numbers you would like, as long as the **mean** was 10. You would have, theoretically, 4 "degrees of freedom" to choose any four numbers you wish. Try this: choose any number. Okay, say you chose 5. Now, choose another number and say you chose 9. Now choose a third number, 7, and still another number, say, 10. Stop. You have selected 4 numbers (5, 9, 7, 10). You have had complete "freedom" to choose any four numbers you wished. The mean of these four numbers, however, is…well, you figure it out…Right, add them and divide by 4 to get a mean of 7.75. But, wait, I said the mean must be 10. So in selecting a fifth number, you have no "freedom." You must select the number 19. Right? Add, 5, 9 ,7, 10, and 19 and divide by 5 to get a mean of 10. Therefore, *df* always equals N - 1; in this case, 5 - 1.

 This concept of degrees of freedom (*df)* will come into play when you interpret **statistical significance,** as you have seen in Part Nine.

Dependent variable (see **variable**) is the term used for the "outcome" variable in **group comparison research.** In such research, the experimenter manipulates one variable (the **independent variable**) and measures its effect on a second variable. That second variable is known as the dependent variable; i.e., the variable that *depends* on the other variable (the independent one). In order to easily remember which variable is dependent, know that the dependent variable is synonymous with the word "outcome."

Consider this **research question**: How is math achievement affected by computer-assisted instruction? What is the desired outcome in this research question? Of course, it's math achievement. Math achievement is the dependent variable.

Descriptive research is one of three methods of research that assumes a quantitative approach in studying a given educational issue or problem. **Survey** and observational reports are *types* of descriptive research. Descriptive research may use statistics or numbers (usually percentages) to describe data.

Descriptive statistics is one category or type of statistics (the other is **inferential statistics**) that is used in **descriptive research** to describe and summarize data.

Two of the most common ways to describe data statistically are **mean** and **standard deviation.**

Design See **research design.**

Discriminant analysis is an advanced statistical procedure, usually beyond the needs of thesis students, in which differences in participants' scores on several variables are examined to determine if differences separate participants into their respective groups.

Effect size is a statistic that is used when one synthesizes findings from many studies to determine the practical significance of the results. It demonstrates how well the experimental group did compared to the control group. Effect sizes of 0.33 or larger generally are considered to have practical significance.

Empirical research refers to methods of systematic investigation based on observations. In other words, any study you conduct that involves investigation by observation is considered empirical research. Observing Juan, who's been in special education classes, react when he's placed in an inclusive classroom for the first time, for instance, is an example of empirical research.

ERIC (Educational Resources Information Center) database consists of two files: the Resources in Education (RIE) file of document citations and the Current Index to Journals in Education (CIJE) file of journal article citations from over 750 professional journals. In addition, ERIC now contains over 850 ERIC Digest records that feature the full text of the original document. ERIC is an information system sponsored by the U.S. Department of Education that generates the U.S. national bibliographic database covering the literature of education. NOTE THAT ERIC IS LIKELY TO CHANGE AS EXPLAINED IN MODULE 5 OF PART ONE. SIMPLY GO TO THE WEB SITE TO DISCOVER ANY CHANGES IN THE SYSTEM. ESSENTIALLY, THOUGH ERIC WILL FUNCTION THE SAME, EVEN THOUGH ICONS, ADDRESSES, MAY CHANGE.

Ethics refers to principles and guidelines that guide educational researchers to fair, equitable, and just standards when planning, conducting, and reporting research studies.

Ethnography (or **ethnographic research**) is one of three methods of **qualitative research** discussed in this book. It is used to observe individuals or groups of individuals in natural settings. Detailed analyses and descriptions are made of th subjects under study. In ethnography, more detail of fewer subjects is superior than less detail with many more subjects. The ethnographic researcher takes many notes describing what was observed. Further information can be found in Module 2 of Part Seven.

Evaluation is an ongoing decision-making process about the quality of a program, product, or procedure. Evaluation takes place only after measurements have been taken and **assessment** (interpretive) procedures completed. Once data are collected and interpreted, an educator can now make a better decision or judgment. Evaluations may occur informally or formally.

Evaluation research is the most common use of action research. Evaluation research is *not* a separate research method, as is ethnographic or correlational research. Rather, as defined here, evaluation research is a common use of action research that may incorporate quantitative and/or qualitative approaches.

Experimental group is a group, assigned randomly in **experimental research,** that receives a special treatment. Data are then collected to determine the effect that this treatment has on the experimental group. The experimental group is contrasted with data collected from a **control group.**

Experimental research is one of the three types of **group comparison** research that utilizes quantitative approaches. Experimental studies assign individuals to either experimental or control conditions. **Randomization** occurs in experimental studies. See discussions of experimental research designs in Part Five.

Ex post facto research (sometimes called causal comparative research because it attempts to define a cause and effect relationship between two variables) is one of the three types of group comparison research that utilizes quantitative approaches. Ex post facto studies involve intact classes which are assigned to either experimental or control conditions. No randomization occurs in these studies. In these studies groups are already formed because members of each group exhibit characteristics that the researcher has no control over (e.g., whether or not they had preschool experience). See discussions of ex post facto **research designs** in Part Five.

Briefly, ex post facto research studies involve groups already formed, such as intact classes (e.g., classes in periods 2 and 4 in a high school). In other words, the study is carried out after the fact (ex post facto); i.e., after classes or groups have been formed. You as the researcher have no control over the fact that these students are part of periods 2 and 4. That is a fact or condition beyond your control. Studies that use intact or ex post facto groups are called ex post facto research. A study involving self-concepts of mainstreamed and non-mainstreamed students is an example of ex post facto research because mainstreamed and non-mainstreamed groups already exist with varying degrees of self-concept. You are merely using these preexisting or intact classes as part of your study to compare self concepts.

Therefore, the major difference between ex post facto research and experimental studies is that in the former, neither groups nor individuals are randomized to form comparison groups. Comparisons are thus made with intact or pre-existing classes.

External validity is a form of **validity** that is synonymous with **generalizability**; i.e., the degree to which results can be generalized to other populations. Qualitative and action research studies are rarely generalizable and, therefore, have weak external validity. This lack of external validity does *not*, in any way, diminish the significance of qualitative research.

For further explanation, see **validity.**

Factor Analysis is an advanced statistical procedure, usually beyond the needs of thesis students, in which many variables are correlated with one another. Then, groups of variables, called factors, are identified to determine if they correlate with one another.

Focus groups are groups of individuals who are selected by a researcher and consent voluntarily to share their views and opinions on specific topics related to a research project. As a type of **survey**, a focus group is not unlike a group interview. See Module 3 in Part Eight for more details.

Generalizability is the degree to which findings derived from one context or under one set of conditions may be assumed to apply to other settings or conditions. Qualitative research studies do not generally yield findings that are generalizable.

Studies, for example, with large numbers of subjects or participants are more likely generalizable than research studies that involve a small group of individuals. Again, the lack of generalizability does not diminish the impact of qualitative research as a viable tool. See more under **sample.**

Grade equivalents are converted scores that report how well or poorly a student has done on a **standardized test. Raw scores** on standardized tests are converted into grade equivalents by indicating grade levels and months. A grade equivalent of 5.3 in reading, for example, indicates that a student is reading at a fifth grade level in the eighth month. Grade equivalents are usually reported in **school profiles.** Although more revealing than **raw scores,** grade equivalents are not as accurate as **stanines** or **percentiles.**

Grounded theory is a theory developed by qualitative researchers (usually ethnographers) as they gather data in a naturalistic setting. In grounded theory, the researcher does not develop a set theory or premise and then go about searching for evidence to confirm or reject the theory. Rather, data are gathered and theories or ideas emerge from the process. Tentative conclusions from these data may be drawn, but they are continuously examined in light of new data that emerges.

Group comparison research is one of three methods of quantitative research that can be used by educational researchers. In these studies, the researcher administers different **treatments** to groups and then compares the groups on a **dependent variable.** Groups are formed by random assignment of intact groups.

Hawthorne Effect (see **Confounding factors**)

Historical research is one of three methods of **qualitative research** that uses written documents of the past (primary and secondary sources) and oral testimonies to provide insight into phenomena or events.

Honesty is an ethical principle related to conducting research that ensures that you, as researcher, will remain truthful in all aspects of conducting your research (e.g., data collection, data analysis, and data reporting). See Module 4 in Part One for more details.

Hypothesis (**hypotheses**) is a researcher's educated or informed guess about the relationship between two or more **variables.** A hypothesis is a statement of prediction, an anticipated outcome. Hypotheses are utilized only in quantitative studies.

There are three major types of hypotheses: *directional non-directional,* and *null.*

Directional hypotheses indicate some direction between the variables under study, as in the following example: Teachers supervised by clinical supervision will have more favorable attitudes towards their supervisors than teachers supervised by traditional forms of supervision. Note that this hypothesis indicates that one group will demonstrate more favorable attitudes, thus, indicating that a particular variable will influence or *direct* the other. Can you construct your own directional hypothesis?

Non-directional hypotheses, in contrast, indicate, as in the previous example, that there will be a difference between teachers who are observed, but do not specify a direction between the two variables. "There will be a difference between self concept levels between mainstreamed and non-mainstreamed students" is an example of a non-directional hypothesis. Construct a non-directional hypothesis of your own.

Null hypotheses indicate that no relationship or difference between the two groups or variables is likely. "There will be no difference in self concept levels between mainstreamed and non-mainstreamed students" is an example of a null hypothesis. As was indicated in Module 1 of Part Nine, null hypotheses are usually employed when statistical analyses are calculated.

In traditional educational research, hypotheses are generated only after an extensive review of the literature on a given topic. I advise my students to always frame their hypotheses in the null form, especially when some statistical work will be done. See Module 3 in Part Three for more details.

Independent variable (see **variable**) refers to the variable manipulated by the experimenter in group comparison research to determine its effect or influence on another variable (i.e., the dependent variable).

Let's say you're interested in researching the following question: How is teacher satisfaction (morale) influenced by leadership style of the principal? Leadership style is the independent variable that is manipulated by the researcher to determine its impact on the dependent variable *(outcome,* remember?), in this case *teacher morale.* The independent variable is considered *manipulated* because the researcher could have chosen any variable in order to study its effect on teacher morale. Also, it's manipulated in the sense that various leadership styles may be studied in a given context or situation. For example, democratic leaders may influence morale differently than autocratic styles, under various circumstances.

An easy way to remember which variable is dependent and which is independent is: Dependent variables always signify outcomes, whereas independent variables can be manipulated.

Consider this research question: How is math achievement affected by computer-assisted instruction? What is the desired outcome in this research question? Think....Of course, it's math achievement. Math achievement is the dependent variable. The other variable, therefore, has to be independent. It's independent because you could have selected any variable to study its influence on math achievement. It's also independent because you can *independently* assign one group to computer-assisted instruction, while another group is exposed to some other **treatment.**

Inferential statistics are one category or type of statistics (the other is **descriptive statistics**) that tells us how much confidence we can have in generalizing from a **sample** to a **population.** Qualitative research is not concerned with inferential statistics (see definition of **Generalizability**).

Institutional Review Board (IRB) is a group of individuals that review and monitor research involving human subjects. It is important to consult your college or university to determine the process, if any, that is needed to seek permission to conduct a research study. One college I am familiar with requires students to submit a 2–4 page proposal containing the following information:

    a. Brief introduction stating the background information, justification for the study, and hypothesis or research question(s)

    b. A section describing the study design and explicit description(s) of protocol(s)

    c. A section describing recruitment of subjects and a specific desciption of sample

    d. A section of how confidentiality willbe protected (including the location of stored data if anmes are attached to the data)

    e. Provide informed consent forms (e.g., for study with minor children) and any surveys with directions for respondents (i.e., each survey must contain clear and complete intruction on the top)

Instrument is any device used to collect data such as a test, **questionnaire,** portfolio, etc.

Internal validity is a form of **validity** that assesses the degree to which data you collect are unbiased and undistorted. The following two measures, for instance, increase internal validity:

    A) longer periods of **data collection.**

    B) more subjects (e.g., more respondents to a survey).

While these aforementioned factors increase internal validity, the following factors are threats to internal validity:

    A) mortality refers to a situation in which respondents or subjects of a study drop out for one reason or another. A poor rate of return of a questionnaire is an example of the concept of mortality. Fewer returns of the questionnaire reduces the number of participants in your study, and, thus, becomes a threat to internal validity.

    B) maturation refers to students who do well due to natural maturation (physical or mental) and not necessarily due to the **treatment.**

C) history refers to a situation unrelated to the study that may influence a change in behavior or achievement levels. Let's say you wanted to assess a particular workshop on teacher morale in your district. If at the same time of this study or in the recent past a budget crisis loomed that froze teacher wages, results from your study might be influenced by this budgetary situation and not be caused by the series of workshops offered.

D) reactivity refers to the likelihood that a pretest administered will affect post test results. Respondents to a **questionnaire**, for example, may figure out what "you are looking for" and respond accordingly on the post test.

Intervention (See **treatment** because the two terms are synonymous)

Interview is one method of collecting data based on surveying the views of an individual or group of individuals. Although face-to-face interviews are the most common type, phone interviews are frequently employed in qualitative research projects. See Module 3 in Part Eight for further discussion on interviews.

Interview protocol is a predetermined set of questions used by an interviewer to conduct an interview.

  If you were to interview your superintendent, you might want to prepare a set of interview questions in advance of the actual interview. These questions are known as the interview protocol. An interview protocol, especially for an inexperienced interviewer, will lessen anxiety and structure the interview positively. Sometimes the protocol may be shared with the interviewee to allow her/him to see the range of questions that may be asked.

John Henry Effect (see **Confounding factors**)

Level of significance is a term used in quantitative studies to refer to the probability that the difference between the **variables** studied occurred by chance and not due to your **treatment**. In most educational studies, the desired level of significance is 5% (.05). For some research studies (e.g., action research) the level is less stringent (10% or .10) (see, for example, the **sign test** in Module 3 of Part Nine). In other words, there's only a 5% or 10% chance that differences between the **experimental** and **control groups** could have occurred by pure chance without any **treatment**.

  Levels of significance are represented by the "*p*" level or "alpha" level. You are likely to see a level of significance reported as follows: $p < .05$, meaning that the probability that differences between both groups were due to chance factors are less than 5 chances in 100 or 5%. Further explanation of levels of significance are discussed in Part Nine.

Likert scale is a type of **questionnaire**, developed by Rensis Likert, that utilizes the following categories of possible responses: strongly disagree, disagree, agree, and strongly agree. For a complete discussion on designing and interpreting Likert scales see Part Eight.

Mann-Whitney U-test is a statistical technique used to determine whether or not two *small* groups differ significantly from one another. This test is often used for **static-group comparison** designs. This test operates like a t-test and was discussed in Module 4 of Part Nine.

Matched pairs is a technique for equating groups on one or more **variables**, resulting in each member of one group having a direct counterpart in another group. Matched pairing is used to form equivalent or comparable groups when **randomization** is not possible. A teacher, for instance, may divide her intact class into two comparable groups for purposes of conducting a **group comparison** study. Matched pairs is a very useful technique used by masters degree researchers. See Part Five for more details.

Mean is the arithmetic average of a group of scores. The mean is calculated by the sum of the scores divided by the number of scores. (See discussion above—**descriptive statistics**, as well as applications of mean in Par Nine).

Meta-analyses are quantitative reviews of previous studies that uses some rather new and advanced statistical procedures (beyond the scope by the way of most masters thesis students) to systematically combine results from many previous studies on a particular topic in order to come up with some sort of conclusion of evidence. These reviews are useful to consult for literature reviews or simply to develop a possible topic of study for a thesis project.

Methodology (see **Research Design**) – Note that "Methodology" is a term generally used in qualitative studies whereas "Research Design" is a term used in quantitative studies.

Mixed methodology combines both quantitative and qualitative approaches to research. Using such a methodology encourages triangulation.

This book has emphasized the importance of two basic approaches to research: quantitative and qualitative. Both approaches have different purposes, each having strengths and weaknesses. Current thinking in the field of educational research suggests that neither approach is superior to the other, although earlier views held that the quantitative approach, with its emphasis on traditions of positivism, was far more "scientific" than qualitative approaches. The predominance of this social science perspective has only recently undergone criticism in light of the emergence of qualitative, including ethnographic and biographical, analyses. Still, the quantitative research approach is appropriate in some situations, while qualitative research approaches are more suitable in other situations. Sometimes, both approaches can be applied in a given research project. Utilization of one particular approach depends on what is being researched, the aim of the project, and the researcher's preference, rather than the inherent superiority of one approach over another.

Quantitative and qualitative approaches have arisen from different research needs. The quantitative research approach seeks to establish facts through the utilization of the scientific method. In quantitative research, the researcher is considered to be "an outsider to the research" (Carr & Kemmis, 1986, p. 16) or an objective observer. Results from quantitative analyses are presented numerically, often using some statistical procedures. The research goal of this approach is discovery of some generalized truth (see **generalization** in the Glossary).

In contrast, qualitative research emphasizes the researcher's subjective viewpoint as integral to disciplined inquiry. Qualitative inquiry provides in-depth analysis into a given problem that might not otherwise be gleaned from statistical results derived from quantitative studies. Results, in qualitative studies, are verbally expressed in great detail. Qualitative approaches enable in-depth analyses into social, interpersonal, and cultural contexts of education more fully than do quantitative studies. For many educators, qualitative research provides richer and wider-ranging descriptions than quantitative methods.

Thus, rather than conceptualizing quantitative and qualitative approaches as diametrically opposed to research, both approaches should be seen as part of one naturalistic (qualitative)-positivistic (quantitative) continuum. Mixed methodology encourages both approaches where appropriate and feasible. See Module 1 in Part Two for more details.

Multiple correlation coefficient is an advanced statistic (R) used to determine the degree of relationship among three or more variables.

Multiple regression is an advanced statistical procedure for predicting values of one variable on the basis of values from two or more variables.

Multivariate Analysis of Variance (MANOVA) is a statistical technique used to determine the extent to which two or more groups differ in respect to a combination of several different dependent variables.

Non-equivalent control group design a **research design** used in **ex post facto** studies involving at least two groups. Both groups are pretested, while one group receives a **treatment.** Both groups are then post tested. Individuals are not randomly assigned to groups.

Nonparametric statistics are statistical techniques used to analyze data for nominal or ordinal data or when data are not normally distributed. In education, we generally deal with data that are normally distributed such as test and attitudinal scores.

Norm-referenced tests (synonymous with **standardized tests**) are one of two major types of **testing** instruments that measure differences among individuals being tested. Norm-referenced tests are usually used as important **data collection** sources.

One-group pretest-posttest design is a **research design,** sometimes called preexperimental research design, involving one group that is pretested, exposed to a treatment and post tested. This design is considered weak because no comparison group is utilized. Yet, one-group pretest-posttest designs are commonly employed by practitioners because often only one group is available and it's relatively easy to administer and analyze.

Although such a design is not usually one's first choice, one-group pretest-posttest designs can be used effectively by employing the sign test for analysis, as was demonstrated and explained in Module 3 of Part Nine.

Operational definitions are one of two ways to define terms in a research study. Operational definitions involve observable, measurable, and quantifiable descriptions of key terms in a research study. Science achievement, for example, can be operationally defined as follows: a passing score of 70% on a teacher-made science test. A supervisor-made questionnaire could also be defined operationally by stating the nature of the survey (e.g., **Likert**), the design (e.g., designed by researcher, as opposed to using some commercially developed **instrument**), and how the questionnaire will be measured (e.g., a favorable attitudinal score would be 25 and above). Operational definitions do not merely define the terms conceptually (see **conceptual** definitions), but rather describe them and state how they will be measured.

Parametric statistics are statistical techniques, more common than **nonparametric statistics**, used to analyze data for interval or ratio data or when nominal or when data are normally distributed. In education, we generally deal with data that are normally distributed such as test and attitudinal scores.

Path Analysis is an advanced statistical procedure, usually beyond the needs of thesis students, to determine the extent to which there is a causal relationship among variables from correlational data.

Percentile indicates the percentage of individuals who scored above or fell below a given score. For instance, if a third grader scored at the 76th percentile, her score exceeded 76% of the third graders who took that same test (see **norm-referenced tests**). Percentiles are **converted scores.**

Raw scores are frequently converted into percentiles so that comparisons can be made among individual test or questionnaire scores. A raw score of 32 does not indicate how well or poorly a certain individual performed on a test. The score merely indicates the number of correct responses. Once the raw score is converted into percentiles (e.g., 89%), one might then ascertain how this particular individual performed in relation to the other test-takers. In this case, we may conclude that the individual scored higher than 89% of the test-takers.

Percentages, in contrast, denote the "percentage" of individuals who gave a particular response or achieved a particular score. Percentages are often used to describe and analyze data.

Participants, often derogatorily called subjects (we don't want to "subject" anyone to do anything they don't want to do), are vital to most research studies. The **sample** we select "participate" with us in the study. They voluntarily join in educational research. See discussion of "ethical principles" in Part One, Module 4).

Periodical is a term that applies to journals, magazines, and other educational documents.

Population refers to the large or total group from which a **sample** is derived. For example, all male college students, all principals in New Jersey, or all graduates under age 25 are considered populations. As a researcher, I want to draw a **sample** from a given population. Members of a sample are called **subjects** (Ss) or participants.

Portfolio is a **data collection instrument** (or data source) that includes a great deal of information about a particular individual or group of individuals. Portfolios may include a student's achievement test scores, book reports, homework assignments, art projects, in-class tests, oral presentations, self-assessments, art work, etc. Portfolios are excellent ways of collecting data from a variety of perspectives.

Posttest-only control group design is a **research design** used in **experimental research** involving at least two randomly formed groups in which one group receives a **treatment** and then both groups are post tested for comparison. (See discussion of this design in Part Five).

Pretest-posttest control group design is a **research design** used in **experimental research** involving at least two randomly formed groups in which one group receives a **treatment** and then both groups are pretested and post tested. (See discussion of this design in Part Five).

Purposeful (or purposive) sampling is used as a sampling procedure in qualitative research (usually ethnography) in which participants are identified because they have certain attributes needed for the study.

Qualitative research approaches examine questions that can best be answered by *verbally* describing how participants in a study perceive and interpret various aspects of their environment. Participant observational methods, for instance, are an important tradition in qualititative research. See discussion of various forms of observation in Module 2 of Part Eight, Data Collection.

Quantitative research approaches examine questions that can best be answered by collecting and statistically analyzing *numerical* data.

Quasi-experimental research is one of the three types of **group comparison** research that utilizes quantitative approaches. Quasi-experimental studies assign groups, not individuals, to either experimental or control conditions. No **randomization** occurs in quasi-experimental studies. See discussions of quasi-experimental **research designs** in Part Five.

Quasi-experimental studies are the most commonly used in education because teachers and supervisors rarely have the opportunity to truly randomize subjects into groups. Intact classes or groups are most common. For example, let's say you wanted to compare Method A to Method B. As a high school teacher you might have two equivalent or comparable groups of 10th graders during periods 4 and 7. These are, of course, intact classes because you didn't randomly assign them to these classes. You can, however, randomly assign the *methods*. Period 4 may be assigned Method B and period 7 may be assigned Method A. In other words, quasi-experimental studies randomly assign intact groups to different *methods* rather than randomly assigning *individuals*.

Note that quasi-experimental research, as used in this volume, also refers to studies that do not use control groups. Part Five referred to single measurement, static, one-group pretest/post test, static group, interrupted time series, and single subject designs as examples of quasi-experimental studies.

Questionnaire is a type of **survey** that is distributed to a **sample** to ascertain attitudes about a particular issue or concern. A questionnaire, then, is a type of survey; the two terms are not necessarily synonymous. Module 1 in Part Eight discussed questionnaire construction. (Also, see **Likert scales**).

Randomization (or **sampling**) See **sampling**.

Raw score (or number) is a numeral that indicates a score obtained on a test or a **questionnaire** before the score is converted into a **percentile, grade equivalent, stanine,** or some other analogous form. A raw score of 56, for example, indicates the number of correct responses attained by an individual on a test or a questionnaire. Raw scores are considered **interval** data (see **scales of measurement**). Although raw scores are a preferable way of obtaining quantitative data (since data analysis is much easier using raw scores as opposed to using percentiles, grade equivalents, or stanines, sometimes you might want to convert raw scores in some way in order to make them more easily understood and comparable (see **converted scores**).

Reliability is the degree to which an instrument yields consistent results under repeated administrations. When you hear the term "reliability" you should immediately think of "consistency."

Usually, if you want to know whether a particular **instrument** was reliable you would consult the test maker's manual. Reliability, whether reported by a manual or computed on one's own, is reported in terms of a **correlation coefficient.** The closer the coefficient of correlation, which is expressed in hundredths, comes to + 1.00, the higher the reliability factor. Thus, for instance, a reliability coefficient of .80 would indicate that the **instrument** (e.g., a test) is reliable. Remember that no test is ever 100% reliable.

In qualitative approaches to research, two kinds of reliability are common:

A) *external reliability* refers to the degree to which your study can be replicated by others. In other words, if someone followed your procedures and methods, they would likely report similar findings. Yet, the nature of qualitative research is so personal that external reliability is difficult to attain.

In a study I recently completed, I wanted to ascertain the kinds of images of principals that were depicted in film and television. After previewing dozens of sitcoms and movies, I identified, through **content analysis,** three categories of images. External reliability was confirmed, in this case, by having independent researchers view the same episodes to confirm my categories.

B) *internal reliability* synonymous with *interrater reliability* (see below).

Common reliability tests include:

A) the *test-retest method,* in which the same test is repeated over a period of time. Two test administrations are required. **Correlations** are taken between the two sets of test results. The resultant **correlation coefficient** is the index of reliability. Note that **correlations** can be inflated if the time interval between tests is short. Why do you think this is so?

B) the *parallel (or equivalent) forms method,* similar to the previous method, in which you retest the same group with an equivalent form of the test. This method requires two administrations (Form A of the test administered, for instance in September, and then Form B administered to the same group in March). The two sets of scores are correlated as they were in the test-retest method.

C) the *split-half method,* in which the test is split into two parts (or halves), such as odd-numbered items and even-numbered items. The test is administered to the same group. Two sets of scores are obtained for each person: a score based on the odd-numbered items and a score based on the even-numbered items. These two sets of scores are correlated to obtain a reliability coefficient. Note that the longer the test, the more reliable the test will be. Why do you think this is so?

Note that a split-half reliability quotient may be calculated by referring to Crowl's 1986 book titled *Fundamentals of research: A practical guide for educators and special educators,* published by Horizons, Inc., in which easy-to-follow, step-by-step procedures are provided in his appendixes. If out of print, email me for copies.

D) *KR-21* (Kuder-Richardson Formula), used to measure the consistency of an **instrument** in which all items have the same characteristic or degree of difficulty. Tests that include diverse items or varied levels of difficulty should be subjected to split-half reliability assessments. KR-21 may be calculated by referring to Crowl's work cited above.

E) *Interrater reliability* (also known as *internal reliability)*, used in **qualitative research** and **single subject research designs,** involves comparing ratings or rankings given by independent observers. The more similar the rankings, the higher the reliability. Interrater reliability, therefore, refers to the percentage of agreement among independent observers. Teachers use this form of reliability in grading standardized writing tests. Three teachers rate a given essay separately and an average score is then computed. In this way, no single rating is given preference.

Reliability is enhanced by use of multiple data sources (triangulation). Why do you think this is so? Reliability of qualitative studies is enhanced through the use of multiple observers. Why do you think this is so?

Are reliability and validity related? A valid test is always reliable, but a reliable test is not necessarily valid. Can you explain why?

See Module 6 in Part Eight for more details.

Research design or Methodology was discussed in 3 ways:

(1) As an overall plan—The research design, explained in Part Five, is the overall plan for conducting systematic inquiry.

(2) As a quantitative plan—See Part Five

(3) As a qualitative plan—See Part Five

Research questions are the questions posed by educational researchers as they undertake qualitative studies, although may be used in quantitative research as well. Research questions guide the research and are answered as a result of conducting the study. See Module 2 in Part Three for more details.

Response set the tendency to respond in a particular way to the content of a questionnaire. See Module 1 in Part Eight for a detailed explanation.

Reviewing the Literature refers to the process of locating, reading, and evaluating research dealing with a particular topic. See Module 2 in Part Four for more details.

Running head is a shortened version of the title of a thesis project that appears at the top of each page. Running heads are often found in published journal articles as well. The running head for "Effects of the use of phonetic reading strategies within a literacy based program on the word recognition scores of 1st grade boys and girls in an urban elementary school" could be: "Literacy based program and word recognition." Using one or two words would be used for a running head in journal articles, but for theses projects two to six words are common.

Sample refers to the group of subjects or participants chosen from a larger group, known as the population. On sample selection, see **sampling.** A sample, technically, can consist of only one person as in case study research, although with such a small sample nothing can be related to the

population. Several rules of thumb apply: 1) The larger the sample, the higher possibility for generalization and statistical significance (if the sampling procedure is sound; e.g., random, stratified, cluster, and systematic); 2) For a large population (e.g., all teachers in a district) a sample of 10% is generally acceptable for generalization; 3) For correlation research a minimum sample of 30 is needed; and 4) For a group comparison study a minimum of 15 per group is necessary in order to generalize from sample to population and to offer anything substantive related to statistical significance. **Purposeful sampling** or **convenience sampling** rarely, if ever, can lead to generalization.

Sampling (often synonymous with **randomization**) is a technique used to select participants for a study. Sampling involves a process by which members in the population have an equal chance of being selected. Note that as a general rule, the larger the **sample,** the greater the likelihood for obtaining significant results.

Types of sampling are:

A) *random sampling* involves each member of the population having an equal chance of being selected. The Table of Random Numbers, which can be found in any book on statistics, can be used for studies involving many subjects. For smaller studies, simply shuffling cards with names of all the members of a population and then selecting a certain number of cards from the top of the deck (like pulling names out of a hat) could also be used as long as all members of the population have an equal chance of being selected.

B) *stratified sampling* involves identifying two or more subsets (e.g., gender, ethnicity, geographic location, etc.) in a population and taking a random sampling of each subset. Identifying subsets in advance of obtaining a sample reduces the possibility that an important group is left out of the sample.

Let's say you wanted a representative number of elementary, middle, and high school teachers for a survey you are conducting throughout a district on attitudes toward supervision. You would identify the numbers of elementary, middle, and high school teachers and then take a random sampling from each category, thus ensuring representation from all three groups of teachers.

C) *systematic sampling* involves systematically selecting a fraction of the population (e.g., every tenth name on a list).

D) *cluster sampling* used by identifying a site (e.g., schools, a district, or classes) and then taking a random sample from that cluster or site.

Qualitative sampling procedures may be quite different from techniques previously described. Obtaining a representative sample is less important in **qualitative research** studies because generalization is not a concern. Often, samples are chosen for qualitative studies based on convenience (some call this **convenience sampling**), individual preference, or happenstance. **Purposeful sampling**, for instance, is often used in ethnographic research in order to work with people who can provide essential information to the researcher. For instance, if you are conducting an ethnographic study about first year teachers and their ability to acclimate to the tensions of teaching for the first time, then you would want to *purposely* find individuals who recently began teaching. Purposeful sampling is not random, but used when for a specific purpose or objective.

Scales of measurement are important in order to determine what types of statistical analyses are appropriate.

Four (4) scales of measurement are:

nominal (categorical) is the lowest scale of measurement. Nominal categories are not quantifiable; i.e., non-numerical, such as gender, ethnicity, and religious affiliation. An easy way to remember nominal variables is to know that nominal = naming. That is, a nominal variable just names things. For instance, gender (male or female), names of states (e.g., Texas or California), socioeconomic status (upper, middle, lower), and political party affiliations (Republican, Democratic, etc.) are nominal. Nominal variables have no order (from high to low), one category is not better than another; they are non-numerical. **Chi square** analyses are conducted with nominal data.

ordinal (order) is a scale that puts subjects in order from high to low, but does not indicate how much higher or lower one subject is in relation to another. An example of an ordinal variable is: ranking height from tallest to shortest (e.g., Mary #1; Sue #2; Fran #3; Bill #4); or ranking three brands of cereal by consumer preference. Note that **Likert scales** are really ordinal, but in education they are treated statistically as **interval.**

interval is a scale of measurement that tells us how much subjects differ from one another. For example, **raw scores** are interval scales. Subject 1 (S1) with a raw score of 100 (out of 100) has 50 points more than subject 2 (S2) with a score of 50. Although we can say that SI scored 50 points higher than S2, we can't say that S1 is twice as smart as S2 because interval scales have no absolute zero point (as do **ratio** scales). Differences between categories in interval data are considered real differences in that the difference between a raw score of 4 and a raw score of 2 is the same difference between raw scores of 6 and 8.

ratio is the highest and most precise scale or level of measurement. The ratio scale is the same as the interval scale, except for the fact that it has an absolute zero point. Weight, for example, is based on a ratio scale. Someone who weighs 140 lbs. is twice as heavy as someone who weighs 70 lbs.

Here's a mnemonic to help you recall the 4 **scales of measurement**: No One Is Ready (N = nominal; O = ordinal; I = interval; R = ratio).

Summary:

N = Shaquille O'Neal is tall, and I am short

O = Shaquille O'Neal is taller than I

I = Shaquille O'Neal is 7' tall and I am 5' tall

R = Shaquille O'Neal is 7\5ths as tall as I am

School profile is a document that summarizes quantitative data about a given school. Usually published annually by the district office or board of education, a school profile includes demographic data and detailed summaries of student achievement levels. A school profile summarizes important data from a variety of **instruments** and, as such, is an invaluable means of **data collection**. Obtain a recent profile of your school to see the kinds of useful data provided.

Scientific method is a four-step approach to disciplined inquiry. The scientific method is most usually applied to quantitative studies. As an educator who wishes to examine the impact of a new literature series on reading comprehension achievement of two equivalent groups of students, you would apply the scientific method as follows:

   (1) define the problem to be investigated;

   (2) state the **hypothesis**;

   (3) collect and analyze the data; and

   (4) confirm or reject the hypothesis.

Let's analyze each step in the **scientific method.**

   (1) *define the problem* Let's say you wanted to determine the impact of invented spelling on kindergartners' ability to spell. The first step would be to express the problem as specifically as possible. Problems need to be expressed behaviorally. Problems that are not defined precisely cannot be investigated scientifically. To ask "Is invented spelling good for kindergarten students?" is imprecise because of our inability to measure "good." Defining the problem more accurately one might ask: "What is the impact of invented spelling on kindergartners' ability to spell?"

   (2) *state the hypothesis* In the case above, one might hypothesize as follows: "Kindergarten students taught spelling by invented spelling will score significantly higher on a spelling test than students taught by another method." When some statistical work will be done, hypotheses should be framed in the null form. Can you restate the directional hypothesis above in null form?…Right, "there will be no difference in spelling achievement between kindergarten students taught by invented spelling and students taught by another method."

   (3) *collect and analyze data* We collect data to test our hypothesis. How might we collect data to determine the impact of invented spelling on kindergartners' ability to spell? Yes, we might administer some sort of spelling test. This test would be our primary means of collecting data. We might also, of course, collect data by noting the amount of words spelled correctly during class work.

      After collecting the data, we analyze the data, statistically, to confirm or reject our hypothesis. (See Part Nine).

   (4) *accept or reject the hypothesis* At this point in the scientific method, analysis of collected data will provide evidence to either reject or accept the hypothesis. If the evidence supports the hypothesis, then the hypothesis is accepted. If the evidence is contrary to the hypothesis, then the hypothesis is rejected. Students often think that a rejected hypothesis

means a less worthy study. Such a conclusion could not be farther from the truth. As long as you have applied the steps of the scientific method properly, your study is valid regardless of findings contrary to existing literature in the field.

Search engine develops a large database of web pages by using software called spiders or webcrawlers to search the Internet for information; e.g., altavista.com, google.com, hotbot.com, etc. Try typing in "homeschooling" on each of these sites and compare what you find.

Sign test is a simple statistical technique or test to determine if the posttest scores are different from the pretest scores in **one-group pretest-posttest designs.** See Module 3 in Part Nine for a complete explanation of the **sign test.**

Single-subject design (a type of **time series design**) is a **research design** used in **quasi-experimental research** that can involve only one individual and sometimes up to four or five individuals. **Single-subject designs** allow a researcher to investigate one or just a few individuals with respect to a given **variable** (e.g., changes in behavior). Subjects are exposed to a **treatment** and then multiple measurements are taken over a period of time. The objective of this sort of research is to determine if the treatment had any effect on the behavior of the subject(s).

This design is frequently used in special education. Applicability for action researchers is significant as well. See Part Five for more details.

SPSS is an abbreviation for Statistical Product and Service Solutions (formerly and popularly known as Statistical Package for the Social Sciences) is the oldest, most advanced and most popular computer programs available for statistical analysis. There are many books that aim to teach you how to use SPSS, but, in my view, the best one is: Corston, R., & Colman, A. (2003). *A crash course in SPSS for Windows.* Malden, MA: Blackwell Publishing. See Module 6 of Part Nine for more details.

Standard deviation is a **descriptive statistic** that measures the variability of a group of scores. The higher the value of the standard deviation, the wider the spread of scores. (See applications of standard deviation in Module 1 of Part Nine.)

Standardized tests See **norm-referenced tests** because the two terms are synonymous. It should be noted that some authorities don't equate norm-referenced tests with standardized tests since some **criterion-referenced** tests may also be standardized.

Stanines are converted scores that are frequently reported in **school profiles.** Stanines convert individual scores into bands of scores. Stanines are divided into nine bands; hence, the term is derived from *standard nine.* In other words, the range of scores is divided into nine bands. A student scoring in the first stanine scores the lowest, while a band of nine represents the highest score. The average or **mean** score is found in the fifth band. Although test results are usually reported in more easily understood ways (e.g., **grade equivalents** or **percentiles**), a basic understanding of stanines may come in handy to show the relative position within which all scores are distributed.

Static-group comparison design a **research design** is used in **quasi-experimental research** involving two groups in which only one group, the experimental group, receives a **treatment.** Although a posttest is administered to each group (experimental and control), no pretest is administered. Individuals are not randomly assigned to groups. See Part Five.

Statistical significance is a term used in **quantitative research** to refer to results when the probability of their occurrence by chance is less than .05 in educational research in general, and less than .10 in action research projects. Significant findings do *not* mean that your study is necessarily important or meaningful (see distinction between statistical significance and educational significance in Module 2 of Part Twelve). Significant findings mean that the probability that your research findings would have occurred by chance, without the **treatment,** is low (**see level of significance**).

Let's say you were conducting a study by comparing two groups (e.g., period 4 and period 7 classes) as regards their achievement levels in science. You set up a **non-equivalent control group design** and after a period of 4 months you post test both groups on science achievement. You employ a statistical technique (e.g., the t- Test) to determine whether or not one group (class) scored *significantly* higher than the other group. Let's say the t-Test analysis indicates the following finding: $p < .01$ (for an explanation on how to arrive at this statistically significant finding, see Module 2 of Part Nine). This means that the probability (p) that the difference in achievement levels occurred by mere chance is less than 1% (less than one chance in a hundred), which is a statistically significant finding.

How do you know that this finding is statistically significant? Recall, as noted above, that in order to assert a statistically significant finding you must achieve a p (probability factor) of less than .05 in educational research in general, and less than .10 in action research projects. Since $p < .01$, your findings are statistically significant.

A caveat: many people think that arriving at a statistically significant finding is, by itself, sufficient to incorporate a particular practice or program, for example. This may not be necessarily true.

STATPAK, an acronym for "Statistical Package," is a user-friendly program to compute simple statistics. It's easier to use than SPSS. It's a free, public domain software. To download go to my web page at http://www.wagner.edu/faculty/users/jglanz/web/html/statpak.html

Survey is a general term for any **instrument** used to assess attitudes or views of respondents. **Questionnaires, interviews,** and **focus groups** are types of surveys. Surveys are, perhaps, the most common methods for **data collection** used in master's degree research.

t-Test is a popular and common statistical technique that determines the degree of significance between the means of two groups. In other words, the purpose of a t-Test is to determine whether the difference between two means is statistically significant. See Module 2 of Part Nine for a complete explanation and application.

Teacher-made tests testing or **assessment** procedures are created by educational researchers for purposes of measuring growth in a particular content area. Three types of teacher-made tests are common: **norm-referenced, criterion-referenced,** or **performance-based.** In master's degree research projects, teacher-made tests are quite commonly used.

Testing refers to any form of measurement that yields clear, consistent, meaningful data about a person's knowledge, aptitudes, intelligence, or other traits. **Standardized** and **norm-referenced tests** are examples.

Theory is a statement of interrelated sets of assumptions and propositions which help us to explain our world. Theories are like mental road maps, guiding the way we perceive the world. Master's degree research contributes very little, if at all, to theory development. Still, one may conduct a research project to assess a particular theory.

Time series design (See **single-subject design** because the two terms are related.)

Treatment (synonymous with **intervention** and **independent variable**) is any specific instructional practice, program, or procedure that is implemented by a researcher in order to investigate its effect on the behavior or achievement of an individual or a group.

Examples of treatments or interventions are behavioral management strategies, various textbook series, different methods of teaching, use of instructional technology as well as a host of other instructional methods, and many other programs, procedures, and practices. As an educator, you'll need to evaluate such treatments in order to decide whether they should be retained, modified, or discarded.

Triangulation refers to multiple research approaches, data sources, **data collection** procedures, and analytic procedures. Triangulation strengthens the credibility of data collection and analysis as well as findings. Educational researchers should appreciate that the inclusion of both qualitative and quantitative methods is desirable. Triangulation can also be used within each approach to research, especially in qualitative studies. Qualitative researchers emphasize the importance of triangulating on the basis of data sources, data collection methods, researcher perspectives, and theoretical frameworks. To the extent to which you can *triangulate,* you will make more effective decisions. For further explanation see the Preface.

Unobtrusive measures refer to **data collection** methods that are obtained without directly involving subjects or participants. An educational leader who determines, for example, staff morale by examining the quantity and pattern of staff attendance by collecting written reports and documents utilizes an *unobtrusive measure* in the sense that data can be obtained without conferring with the staff directly.

Validity refers to the extent to which a test, survey, or some other **instrument** measures what it is intended to measure.

If asked to assess your knowledge of some aspects of research, you were administered a pretest comprised of mathematical questions only, then the test would *not* be valid as it did not measure your knowledge of research, but rather your ability to compute and solve mathematical problems.

Have you ever taken a test in which you said, "we never covered this stuff?!" If you were to administer, for example, a test to a group of 12th graders based on Chapter 12 in their social studies textbook, you would check for *content* validity after writing the test to see whether or not answers to each question can be found in the chapter. If each question is, in fact, derived from the content of Chapter 12, then your test may be said to have *content* validity.

Two other types of validity, although not thought of highly by many experts in the field, are useful for master's degree research purposes: *consensual* and *face* validity.

Consensual validity would be ascertained by asking people who will not be administered the test or survey (e.g., a colleague or a student in another class) whether the questions selected for inclusion are appropriate given the purpose of the assessment.

Face validity would be ascertained by asking participants or subjects to share their views about how valid a test or survey appears. Ever take an examination that was fair because it accurately reflected the content of the course? Such an exam might have high face validity. The converse could, of course, also be true if the content of the course didn't match the questions asked on the exam.

Know that, like **reliability,** the coefficient of validity is determined. The validity coefficient is likewise expressed in hundredths and the closer the coefficient comes to + 1.00, the more valid the instrument is considered. See explanation of **internal validity** and **external validity** above.

Variable is any factor having two or more values or distinguishably different properties or characteristics. Two examples of variables are:

Sex or *gender*—two distinct properties are maleness and femaleness,

Mathematics achievement—multiple properties are represented by different student test scores.

There are two (2) main types of variables: dependent and independent:

A **dependent variable** is one that represents a desired instructional *outcome,* such as student achievement or high school attendance.

An **independent variable** is one whose relationship to the dependent variable is being investigated (i.e., the **treatment**). In a study that attempts to correlate gender and science achievement, gender is the independent variable and reading achievement is the desired outcome or dependent variable.

Some independent variables cannot be manipulated by the researcher to determine their effect on a particular dependent variable. For example, if you were to investigate the years of experience of a group of teachers on morale levels, the independent variable in this case (the number of years of experience) cannot be manipulated because you have no control over a teacher's experience. In other words, years of experience is a characteristic of a particular teacher that you, as researcher, cannot manipulate or control, You can't say, for instance, "for purposes of my study subject 1 (S1) will be assigned ten years of experience." In this case, the independent variable is non-manipulable.

Examples of manipulable variables are: type of textbook series, exposure to computer-assisted instruction, or a particular method of teaching (e.g., cooperative learning). Can you name one example of a non-manipulable variable and one example of a manipulable variable?

Three other types of variables are:

1. Continuous variables – indicate numerical distinctions along a continuum. The following are examples of such variables along with an example:

    a. Height – Jose is 69" tall whereas Joseph is 65" tall.

    b. Academic achievement – Jose answered 58 out of the 100 questions correctly whereas Joseph earned a raw score of 51.

2. Discrete (categorical) variables – indicate categorical distinctions. In other words, individuals may be classified into one of several categories. The following are examples of such variables along with an example:

    a. Ethnicity – Jose is Hispanic American, Josephine is African American, and Henry is Asian American.

    b. Type of instructional method – Jose is taught via the use of computer-assisted instruction (a discrete variable) whereas Josephine is taught via the use of a textbook (another discrete variable).

3. Dichotomous variables – discrete variables that have only two possible categories The following are examples of such variables along with an example:

    a. Gender – Jose is male whereas Josephine is female.

    b. Language spoken – Jose speaks English whereas Josephine speaks non-English. Notice of course that a dichotomous variable may be converted into a discrete variable if defined differently.

Test Bank

Directions: These 200 test items may be used, in part or in total, as a pretest or posttest. Instructors may use some of these questions for constructing their own tests as well as develop their own. Readers (students) should use these questions as a means of assessing how well they have mastered the contents of this book and as a study guide. Certainly, test items are only one measure of mastery; ultimately, the ability to translate the ideas and concepts underlying these questions in order to write a thesis is the true test of mastery. The questions below are not in any particular order in terms of book contents. Types of questions are randomly distributed throughout the Test Bank. Also, I've intentionally mixed "true or false" items with "multiple choice" questions and other types of questions. Answers to items are found at the end.

1. Which of the following is an example of empirical research?
   a. A study of the impact of a literature-based reading series on the attitudes of 5th graders towards reading
   b. A review of the literature on cooperative learning
   c. A historical overview of home-schooling
   d. All of these are examples of empirical research

2. Which is an example of an ethnographic study?
   a. Images of principals in the media
   b. Relationship between math and science scores among 11th graders
   c. A day in the life of a local school superintendent
   d. Programmed textbook instruction versus computer-assisted instruction

3. True or False. Stating one's class rank (i.e., freshman, sophomore, etc.) is considered a nominal variable

4. True or False: Ranking once preference for desserts is considered an ordinal scale of measurement.

5. True or False: Birth order is considered ordinal data.

6. True or False: Number of traffic tickets is considered a ratio scale of measurement.

7. True or False: The Likert scale is an example of an interval scale.

8. True or False: Ratio scales are seldom used in educational research.

9. True or False: A population is drawn from a sample.

10. True or False: "What is the effect of single parent homes on student achievement" is an ex post facto study.

11. True or False: "Parents attitudes towards inclusion" is an example of a descriptive study.

12. True or False: "The relationship between amount of homework and student achievement in science" is an example of a quantitative study.

13. True or False: Correlation coefficients are statistical measures that indicate the degree of relationship between two variables.

14. True or False: The larger the standard deviation, the more variability there is in a group of scores.

15. True or False: Two groups may have different means but the same standard deviation.

16. True or False: Inferential statistics use significance tests.

17. True or False: "Students taught with Method A exhibited significantly higher post test scores than students exposed to Method B." This can be reported as follows: t (32) = 2.76, p<.05. The *p* stands for the "probability of being incorrect" where as the 32 is called the degrees of freedom which is equal to the number of subjects in both groups minus 2. In other words, chances are less than 5 in 100 that one would not find that Method A works better than Method B.

18. True or False: This hypothesis is acceptable. Students taught by Method B will be better spellers.

19. True or False: The null hypothesis is generally used for statistical purposes.

20. True or False: If the literature indicates that Method A is better than Method B, the researcher should formulate a hypothesis to conform with the findings of the literature review.

21. True or False: Terms defined operationally are described in how they are measured.

22. True or False: In correlational studies it is not possible to conclude that there is a definite causal relationship.

23. True or False: A sample of convenience is used when random sampling is impossible and the researcher is forced to use whatever subjects are available.

24. True or False: In matched pairs sampling subjects are ranked according their pre-test scores.

25. True or False: A valid test must be reliable.

26. True or False: A reliable test may or may not be valid.

27. True or False: If a test is not reliable it's not valid.

28. True or False: Quantitative researchers assume an objective reality, study human behavior in natural or contrived settings, and use statistical methods to analyze data.

29. True or False: Qualitative researchers study humans in natural settings, discover concepts after data have been collected, and sometimes become personally involved in the study.

30. Which is not a good suggestion for writing a literature review?

    a. use frequent headings and subheadings to help reader follow topics more easily

    b. describe weaknesses and strengths of methods used in various research studies

    c. express yourself clearly and precisely

    d. include every research study on a given topic that you can find

31. True or False: "All seeing is essentially perspective and so is all knowing" can be addressed by triangulating.

32. Which is not a good running head for this title: "Impact of Cooperative Learning Strategies in Elementary Classrooms on Student Motivation to attend School"?

    a. Cooperative Learning

    b. Elementary Classrooms

    c. Cooperative Learning in Elementary Schools

    d. Cooperative Learning and Student Motivation

33. Mr. Solomon is a supervisor in an elementary school. Mr. Jones, a 6th grade teacher, complains that one student, Billy, is disruptive and recalcitrant. Mr. Solomon tells the teacher to record Billy's behavior in anecdotal form for two weeks before scheduling a conference with the guidance counselor. During the first week, Mr. Jones discovers that Billy acts out 26 times. During the second week, he acts out 22 times. During the third week, Mr. Jones meets with the guidance counselor to work out Billy's problems. The counselor sets up a special reward system for Billy. During the fourth week, Billy acts out 18 times. During the fifth week, the disturbances decrease to only 5 times. Mr. Jones and the counselor conclude that the technique used with Billy is successful. What research design was employed?

    a. pretest-posttest control group design

    b. control group only design

    c. interrupted time series design

    d. single measurement design

    e. non-equivalent control group design

34. Mrs. James teaches computers at P.S. 999. She has a new programmed instruction textbook which she wishes to use with her classes. She decides to test the effectiveness of the new

textbook. She chooses two classes that rank similar in ability on a pretest in computer literacy. She gives her programmed text to group A but with group B she continues her normal instruction. At the end of the semester, she gives a test on computer knowledge and discovers that the class using the new text outperformed the other group (B). She concludes that the new text should be incorporated in all the classes. What research design did Mrs. James use?

    a. non-equivalent design

    b. interrupted time series design

    c. pretest-posttest design

    d. pretest-posttest control group design

    e. control group only design

35. Consider 50 4th grade students, assign 25 randomly to one class and 25 randomly to the other class. Both groups are measured beforehand. Two different treatments are presented, then a follow-up measurement is given. Which type of design is this?

    a. pretest-posttest control group design

    b. pretest-posttest only design

    c. one-shot case study

    d. non-equivalent control group design

    e. one-group pretest-posttest design

36. A quasi-experimental design involving one group which is repeatedly pretested, exposed to an experimental treatment, and repeatedly post tested is known as a

    a. pretest/post test design

    b. post test only design

    c. time-series design.

    d. revolving series design

    e. none of these

37. Classify the following study:

RESEARCH HYPOTHESIS: Achievement in Spanish is affected by class size

PROCEDURE: At the beginning of the school year the students in Highpoint High School are randomly assigned to one of two types of Spanish classes: a class with 20 students or less and a class of 40 or more. The two groups are compared at the end of the year on Spanish achievement.

    a. historical

    b. descriptive

    c. correlational

    d. experimental

38. Janice Barnett, Supervisor of Curriculum, wanted to evaluate a new reading series that her district was considering. She decided to study 5th graders in a particular school. She selected one class of 5th grade students who were introduced to the new reading series. Another comparable 5th grade class would use the "old" reading series. At the end of the year, Ms. Barnett tested all students in reading comprehension. What type of study is this?

    a. pretest-posttest control group

    b. non-equivalent

    c. case study

    d. historical

39. To determine if a particular textbook is appropriate for a 5th grade class, your analysis would entail which type of research?

    a. content analysis

    b. ethnography

    c. case study

    d. naturalism

    e. simulation

40. The major purpose of using an interview protocol is to

    a. offer respondents a way to participate in the interview without having the interviewer present.

    b. increase the chances that the respondent will respond honestly.

    c. be able to conduct the interview in case the interviewer is not present.

    d. provide the interviewer with a set of guidelines for conducting the interview.

41. You are a principal in an intermediate school with a population of 750 students. As indicated by recent district-wide tests, student reading achievement has increased. You are interested in discovering how well the students in your school perform in reading compared to students in other schools throughout the country. Which of the following instruments of measurement would you use?

    a. a classroom achievement test

    b. observation

    c. examination of school records

    d. a questionnaire

    e. a standardized test

42. Below you will find "References" section that a student prepared. Critique the references according to APA style. Note any errors and offer suggestions for improvement:

References

Miller, D. (2002). *Reading With Meaning: Teaching Comprehension in the Primary Grades.* Portland, ME: Stenhouse

Taberski, S. (2000). *On Solid Ground.* Portsmouth, NH: Heinemann

Gillet, J. W., & Temple, C. (2000). *Understanding Reading Problems.*

Claprice, Albert. (1996). *The Quotable Einstein.* Princeton, NJ: Princeton University Press.

43. See the "Literature Review" introduction below written for a study entitled, "Impact of Explicit Comprehension Strategy Instruction on Second-grade Students." Critique the introduction.

Literature Review

Introduction

Educators and the public are in frenzy over how to boost reading comprehension scores. In some school systems, children fill out comprehension skill sheets, again and again. In others they struggle diligently through thick workbooks in an effort to improve reading scores. Neither approach teaches students to use strategies that will, in fact, help them understand texts better. Worse, neither approach develops the love of reading, which invites the student into a lifetime of reading.

Reading encompasses both decoding and the making of meaning. The first entry on the word read in Webster's New World Dictionary (1991) defines reading as, "getting the meaning of something written by using the eyes to interpret its characters."

44. For the same study, critique these sections of a study:

Importance of Study

Much of the research underlying the No Child Left Behind Act comes from the work of the National Reading Panel (NRP). The NRP report, "Teaching Children to Read: An Evidence-Based Assessment of the Scientific Research Literature on Reading and Its Implications for Reading Instruction" (2000), summarized and synthesized research on reading over the last thirty years. The NRP findings highlighted important areas of instructional need. One particular area of need stated in the NRP review is in the area of comprehension instruction. The NRP concluded that explicit instruction in cognitive strategies is absolutely necessary to improve students' reading comprehension. Both struggling and accomplished readers need to build a repertoire of comprehension strategies that they can call on when attacking new text.

Palinscar and Brown (1984) determined that improvement occurs when teachers demonstrate, explain, model, and guide interaction with students as they move through the text. In fact, the NRP determined, "Readers who are not explicitly taught these procedures are unlikely to learn, develop, or use them spontaneously" (p 44). Therefore, students' comprehension strategies can improve, but only with explicit instruction, modeling, and scaffolding.

Unfortunately, many students have not been receiving the comprehension instruction they need. Studies by Durkin (1979), Duffy, Lanier, and Roehler (1980) and Pressley (1998) have shown that only a small percentage of instructional time is devoted to teaching reading comprehension. The studies showed that teachers spent little time teaching and demonstrating the skills, strategies, and processes that students could use to help them comprehend information in the text.

This study will try to determine if teacher modeling reading comprehension strategies will increase second grade students' use of comprehension strategies. It will focus on teacher modeling the comprehension strategies and how well the students use these strategies while reading a text. Hopefully, by carefully analyzing this data I will be able to conclude if modeling reading comprehension strategies will increase students' use of comprehension strategies while reading independently.

Research Questions
1) Will using reading comprehension strategies improve students' understanding of text?

2) Will modeling the eight strategies most commonly associated with proficient readers as they read unfamiliar text increase students' use of each comprehension strategy?

45. For the same study, critique this abstract:

Research confirms that one of the biggest problems facing schoolteachers today is that many students come into their classrooms without the knowledge, skills, or dispositions to read and comprehend materials that they are expected to understand. This creates major challenges in the area of reading education including understanding how children learn to comprehend the text they are reading, how to design and deliver instruction that promotes comprehension, how to assess comprehension, and how to prevent poor comprehension outcomes. This study will address the issue of promoting proficient reading, while focusing on the development of reading comprehension and the capacity to acquire knowledge through reading. The purpose of this research study is designed to help teachers meet these challenges that they face each day.

46. When a group of subjects sense that they are part of an experiment and react in a special way it is known as the

    a. John Henry effect

    b. Norton's Law

    c. Halo effect

    d. Hawthorne effect

    e. Pearson r

47. This is an ethical principle related to conducting research that assures that participants in research are informed accurately about the general topic under investigation as well as any unusual procedures that may be used in the study.

    a. accurate disclosure

    b. fair-mindedness

    c. ethics

    d. beneficence

48. This statistic (often symbolized by X^2) is a statistical technique for assessing the relationship between two or more nominal variables

    a. descriptive

    b. Mann-Whitney

    c. chi square

    d. ANOVA

    e. t-Test

49. This can cause erroneous conclusions to be drawn from a study

    a. confounding factors

    b. contextual validity

    c. inter-rater reliability

    d. statistical significance

    e. sample exclusion

50. This occurs when subjects in the control group know they are, in a sense, competing with some other group (experimental) and, consequently, expend extra effort to perform better than the experimental group.

    a. Hawthorne Effect

    b. John Henry Effect

    c. Western Electric Effect

    d. John James Effect

    e. all of the above

51. ERIC is comprised of CIJE and

    a. LIE

    b. RIE

    c. Ed Index

    d. ERIC Descriptors

    e. Dissertation Abstracts

52. This category or type of statistics that tells us how much confidence we can have in generalizing from a sample to a population.
    a. descriptive statistics
    b. Halo Effect
    c. inferential statistics
    d. t-tests
    e. significance tests

53. Statistical techniques used to analyze data for nominal or ordinal data or when data are not normally distributed are
    a. nonparametric statistics
    b. parametric statistics
    c. significance statistics
    d. error factors
    e. path analyses

54. This refers to the degree to which your study can be replicated by others
    a. internal reliability
    b. external reliability
    c. internal validity
    d. external validity
    e. none of these

55. This type of validity would be ascertained by asking participants or subjects to share their views about how valid a test or survey appears
    a. consensual
    b. content
    c. predictive
    d. face
    e. none of the above

56. Which is not a component in a research proposal?
    a. Conclusions/Discussion
    b. Statement of Problem
    c. Methodology or Research Design
    d. Definition of Terms

57. Participant observation is frequently used in conducting

    a. correlational research

    b. ex post facto research

    c. ethnographic research

    d. quasi-experimental research

58. A research hypothesis should be stated in the form of a

    a. value judgment

    b. hypothetical construct

    c. research question

    d. predictive statement

59. In order to establish whether or not there is a causal relationship among variables, it is necessary to carry out

    a. a correlational study

    b. an experimental study

    c. a descriptive study

    d. an ex post facto or causal comparative study

60. It is desirable to administer pretests if the design of a study is

    a. ex post facto

    b. experimental

    c. correlational

    d. quasi-experimental

61. In cluster sampling the unit of sampling is

    a. the individual subject

    b. the population

    c. a naturally occurring group of individuals

    d. the proportion of subjects

62. The basic purpose of reviewing the literature is to

    a. find out if the study you are planning to carry out has already been done

    b. provide a documented rationale for your hypothesis

    c. convince the reader of your study that you are thoroughly familiar with your topic and that you are an expert on your topic

    d. uncover all studies whose findings may contradict your prediction

63. True or False: Qualitative research generally has low generalizibility.

64. True or False: Defining a term by how we measure it is conceptual.

65. True or False: Triangulation is preferred under most circumstances.

66. True or False: Interviews are generally considered qualitative in nature.

67. True or False: The unassessed treatment design is superior to the static group comparison design.

68. True or False: "Attitudes of Parents towards Inclusion" can be considered a descriptive study.

69. Critique the "excerpts of a Research Design" below:

    Statement of the Problem

    The study was conducted to determine whether or not the professional development program offered in the Spring 2005 on the use of computers and related technology in the classroom increased the participants' understanding and use of computers and related technology.

    Research Questions

    The research questions are "How did the teachers who participated in the professional development program increase their understanding and use of computers and related technology, if at all, from the training?" and "How have the teachers increased their incorporation of computers and related technology in their instruction?"

    Sample

    The sample for this study was a group of 20 teachers from Howard High School. There were 7 male and 13 female teachers of various ages and ethnic backgrounds. The teachers were all high school teachers from grades 9–12, and they teach a variety of academic subjects. Nine of the teachers participating in this study were untenured.

    The teachers in this study all volunteered to participate in the professional development program that we are evaluating. Each teacher received an hourly wage for their time spent in the training sessions, and were paid an additional hour each week in order to practice the skills learned.

70. Critique this reference list (according to APA):

    REFERENCES

    Abrahms, S. (1998, August 16). Bringing teachers into the computer age. <u>Boston Globe,</u> E5.

    Adams, S. (1997). <u>Learning together: Cooperative learning in action.</u> Albany, NY: SUNY Press.

    Bartles, L. (2000, September). Gathering statistics. Retrieved March 15, 2006 from http://www.electronic-school.com/2000/09/0900f5.html.

    Beattie, R. M. (2000, September). The truth about tech support. Retrieved March 15, 2006 from http://www.electronic-school.com/2000/09/0900f3.html.

Bouie, E. (1998, September). Spotlight on...technology integration: Creating an information rich environment. T.H.E. Journal, 26(2), 78–79.

Bracey, B. (1996, March). Kick-start technology for teachers. The Education Digest, 61(7), 42–45.

71. Critique this questionnaire:

Howard High School
Technology Professional Development Program

Congratulations! You have been selected to participate in Howard High School's new technology professional development program. This program has been developed to give teachers opportunities to learn how to use computers and related technology. There will be a focus on how to integrate these technologies into your instruction.

In order to prepare a professional development program that is challenging, useful, and effective, we must gather information on what your needs are in the area of instructional technology. Please answer the questions below and return to Jane Smith by **March 29.**

Thank you for your help and for volunteering to be a part of this new program. We look forward to working with you. If you have any questions, please call Sam Davis at extension 351.

Sincerely,

The Technology Team

Read each statement below and check off how much you agree or disagree with it.

	Strongly Disagree	Disagree	Agree	Strongly Agree
Computer Software/Hardware Skills and Access				
I have daily access to a computer.				
I know how to use Windows 95 or 98.				
I know how to use Microsoft Word.				
I know how to use Microsoft PowerPoint.				
I know what the internet is and how to search on it.				
Computers in Personal Work				
I am afraid to use computers for personal use.				
I use computers often for personal work.				
Computers in Professional Work				
I believe computers can help enhance the learning of my students.				
I often use computers with my students.				
I often use computers when preparing materials for my classes.				
I know many ways that computers can be integrated in my content area.				
I have used many different content area software packages (examples: Mighty Math, Inspiration)				
I know what to look for when purchasing software for my classes.				
I believe computers are "toys" for students, not a tool for good teaching.				

In addition, please list any special needs or interests you would like to investigate during our sessions together. (example: *I'd like to learn how to use a scanner.*)

72. A researcher wished to test the effectiveness of a new reading program as compared to an older one. If the difference between the two programs was statistically significant at the $p < .05$ level, this means that
    a. the new program made meaningful changes in the student's reading skills.
    b. the results are probably due to the researcher's program and not a chance occurrence.
    c. the probability of being incorrect is 95 chances out of 100.
    d. the new program should be introduced to all grades.
    e. the statistical analysis used was the correct one and the program has educational significance.

73. True or False: Using prespecified data tables helps to interpret data.

74. In qualitative data analysis the goal is to
    a. discover patterns among the data.
    b. uncover errors in data interpretation.
    c. compare findings to quantitative studies.
    d. all of the above.

75. The degree to which a test consistently measures whatever it measures is
    a. reliability.
    b. validity.
    c. coefficient.
    d. statistical analysis.
    e. none of these.

76. To determine if a particular textbook is appropriate for a 10th grade class, your analysis would entail which type of research?
    a. content analysis
    b. ethnography
    c. case study
    d. grounded theory
    e. ex post facto

77. Which of the following is the best example of an "unobtrusive instrument"?
    a. supervisor walks into class for an on-the-spot observation
    b. supervisor peeks into window of classroom without letting the teacher see him/her
    c. supervisor determines staff morale by examining the quantity and pattern of staff attendance

    d. interviewing teachers

    e. anonymous questionnaire

78. Which correlation is stronger: .85 or - .55?

79. True or False. External validity, referring to generalizibility, in quantitative studies is similar to that in qualitative studies.

80. True or False. Grounded theory is a theory deductively arrived through quantitative analyses.

81. Which of the following questions lends itself best to survey research?

    a. What does a guidance counselor do all day?

    b. Is Method A more effective than Method B?

    c. How do special educations students feel about inclusion?

    d. Who built the school and when?

82. Explain as concisely as possible this statement: "randomization ensures equivalence."

83. Provide an example of an operational definition.

84. Distinguish between a sample and a population.

85. Name 1 form of validity and 1 form of reliability.

86. Name 1 difference between an experimental study and a quasi-experimental study.

87. Why do we prefer to use the word "impact" instead of "effect," generally, in non-experimental research studies?

88. How might you triangulate if you wanted to study the impact of something on something else?

89. Name one way to avoid response sets.

90. Examine the research study excerpt below that applauds Wagner College for being one of two top institutions that adequately prepare students for teaching. The data was collected by a nonprofit organization in NYC in the spring of 1998. The NYC Board of Education sent surveys to all teachers listed on the personnel list with 4 or fewer years of experience. A total of 2,956 usable surveys were returned. The survey asked new teachers to rate their preparedness and their personal views about teaching. Recruits were asked to assess how well prepared they felt when they entered teaching. Read the excerpts below and answer the question that follows:

> The programs with significantly higher mean ratings were Program 3, Bank Street College, and Program 98, Wagner College, a small college on Staten Island. Bank Street College graduates, who are primarily elementary teachers, rated their preparation higher than the average teacher education graduate on 30 items and significantly so on 6 items ($p<.05$), especially those dealing with understanding children and developing curriculum, two hallmarks of Bank Street training. Wagner College graduates rated their preparation

higher than the average on 39 of 40 items and significantly so on 21 items (p-.05). Among these were preparation to use technology, an area in which teacher education graduates and nongraduates alike generally felt under prepared. On the 5 items evaluating preparedness to use technology, Wagner College graduates' rating ranged from 3.14 to 3.52 whereas other program graduates' ratings ranged from 2.18 to 2.83.

On the other hand, graduates of two programs- both campuses of the City University of New York-rated some aspects of their preparation lower than the average teacher education graduate.

Wagner College, a small college located on Staten Island, does not have Bank Street's national reputation, but its graduates had the most positive preparation perceptions of all teacher education program graduates in our sample. Wagner prepares about 110 elementary and secondary teachers each year, a cohort of 70 graduates who take a three-semester program. Most graduates take teaching jobs in New York City.

Wagner emphasizes a strong liberal arts education plus intensive preparation for teaching. Elementary education students take a dual major in a discipline and in education. Secondary candidates major in the discipline they want to teach and minor in education or stay on for a 5th year of education coursework. In addition to their disciplinary major, students complete coursework in English, mathematics, science, and social studies (for elementary education majors); a year of language other than English; a computer science course; and professional coursework-three courses in foundations of education and five courses in methods and content of education, including two courses in math and science methods for elementary teachers and three courses in clinical practice, including student teaching. A series of course-linked practicum experiences combined with two rotations of student teaching result in about 24 weeks of supervised clinical work, of which at least on placement must be urban. In recent years, Wagner has decreased the number of schools involved in student teaching placements to build partnerships with the schools. In some cases, Wagner's methods courses are taught at the schools and offer professional development for school faculty as the college moves toward a professional development school model.

In addition to strong school relationships, Wagner College and Bank Street share an emphasis on extensive, carefully supervised clinical work (24 or more weeks of student teaching in settings selected to ensure modeling of desired teaching strategies) tightly linked to coursework that places significant attention on the development of content-based pedagogy.

Question: Name one possible flaw with this study.

91. Which of the following questions lends itself best to qualitative research?

    a. Which learning strategy is better than another (A or B)?

    b. Does invented spelling increase students' spelling achievement?

    c. How did teachers teach in the 1890s?

    d. Is it unethical to conduct research without asking permission of students?

92. True or False: Ethnography may have an experimental treatment.

93. True or False: A primary document used in historical research is a first-hand account of an incident.

94. Which of the following parts of a thesis goes last?
    a. definition of terms
    b. research questions
    c. description of instruments
    d. importance of study

95. The use of a times series design in single-subject research overcomes the problem of
    a. having no control group.
    b. obtaining a baseline measure of behavior.
    c. having to obtain several measures to the same behavior at different points in time defining variables in quantitative terms.

96. True or False. Bilingualism is considered a preexisting condition in ex post facto research that cannot easily be manipulated and therefore causality of ex post factor studies is not as feasible as it is under pure experimental studies.

97. What is a confounding variable?

98. Correlation is to relationship as dependent variable is to outcome as reliability is to
    a. validity.
    b. inter-rater.
    c. independent variable.
    d. consistency.

99. True or False: One may never be able to generalize from a convenience sample even though the sample consists of 150 people.

100. True or False: A valid test is always reliable, but a reliable test is not necessarily valid.

101. What is the mean of 1, 4, 4, 5, 5, 5, 5, 6, 7, 8?

102. True or False: An F statistic (F Test) measures the significance of the difference between three or more means.

103. True or False: Inferential statistics and descriptive statistics are synonymous.

104. True or False: APA sometimes uses footnotes.

105. True or False: Theses can be written in future tense.

106. True or False: History is one example of internal validity in that when treatments extend over too long a period, factors other than the treatment might exert influence and thus put research conclusions into question.

107. Internal validity is to accuracy of results as external validity is to
    a. threats to validity
    b. causality realities
    c. triangulation
    d. generalizibility

108. True or False: The correlation between amount of time for study and student achievement in science is .49 which indicates a moderate correlation.

109. True or False: p<.01 is a more significant finding than p<.001.

110. A statistical procedure that aims to determine the significance between two variables is called the _____.

111. A brief summary of what appears in an article or in a thesis is called the _____.

112. True or False: Education usually deals more with basic research than applied research.

113. Which of the following is an empirical statement?
    a. "I found the student's rather obnoxious."
    b. "I know Marian has increased the number of completed homework assignments because I've been monitoring her progress for months."
    c. "I just know Scott will improve."
    d. "I always had confidence in Daniel because he tries so hard in my class."

114. Deductive reasoning is exemplified by which of the following first steps?
    a. the researcher begins to observe Steven on Tuesday morning
    b. the researcher states a hypothesis
    c. the researcher gathers data
    d. the researcher searches for patterns of behavior

115. Research involving the examination of the same variables with different people and in different ways is called
    a. experimentation
    b. expectation theory
    c. grounded theory
    d. replication

116. Which of the following best describes the mixed methodology approach to research?
    a. statistical reports of significance exclusively used
    b. particularistic findings
    c. quatitative and quantitative approaches
    d. descriptive, narrow, and well defined

117. Which is an example of a categorical variable?

    a. ethnicity

    b. age

    c. anxiety level

    d. dropout rate

118. True or False: Ex post facto research utilizes a discrete or categorical variable.

119. _____ is a kind of qualitative, inductive approach to research that generates and develops a theory from data collected.

120. Under what circumstance(s) would you not use a mixed methodological approach?

121. True or False: Theses follow the exact same format as articles published in peer reviewed journals.

122. True or False: There is no need to visit the library to conduct research when you have the Internet.

123. True or False: The following question is an example of descriptive research: "Does Teaching Method A produce an change in Student Achievement?"

124. Which question reflects a qualitative approach?

    a. Can Reading Technique A produce a change in student achievement?

    b. Does socioeconomic level predict success in high school?

    c. How does the social context of a classroom influence students' enjoyment of school?

    d. What is the relationship between reading test scores and science test scores?

125. In which part of your thesis would you address the answer to this question?: What appropriate actions did the researcher take to control potential biases?

    a. Introduction

    b. Method

    c. Results

    d. Discussion

126. True or False: In published research articles sometimes the implications for future research are explained in the "Discussion" section.

127. What should be your first reaction when you hear a radio commentator report that a recently published article indicates that a particular drug may reduce the risks for cancer.

    a. disbelief the study

    b. accept it as accurate

    c. it's a PR push by a pharmaceutical company

    d. consider study limitations

128. Potential participants of a study must give you the researcher _____ before they can participate in the study.

129. True or False: It is never reasonable to mislead or withhold information from research participants.

130. Which organization is research oriented?

    a. AERA

    b. AFT

    c. BBX

    d. ASCD

131. True or False: This citation is correctly referenced according to APA: Meade, R.P., & Smith, L. (2004). *Reading instruction in schools.* New York: Allyn and Bacon.

132. The scale of measurement that uses rank-order but also provides equal intervals is known as a(n) _____ scale.

133. True or False: A reliable test is always valid.

134. Which question is not appropriate on a questionnaire?

    a. Do you like math?

    b. Don't you agree that math is fun?

    c. How do you study?

    d. What do you like most about school?

135. True or False: A Focus Group is a type of group interview.

136. True or False: The best sample is one that represents the population.

137. This kind of sampling is used when the researcher tries to locate certain individuals who have special characteristics that the researcher might be interested in _____.

138. What is a major flaw of the pretest posttest design?

    a. is has just one pretest

    b. is has just one posttest

    c. you can't control for other variables that might have impacted the results

    d. only one group is used

139. Which threat to internal validity occurs when pretest and posttests are administered at a rather lengthy interval?

    a. history

    b. maturation

    c. externalization

    d. instrumentation

140. True or False: ANCOVA is a statistic that equates groups that differ on the initial pretest.

141. True or False: An A-B-A design includes the reintroduction of the treatment.

142. The _____ _____ design focuses on two or more different behaviors in the same person, on the same behavior exhibited by two or more people, or the same behavior exhibited by one person but in different situations.

143. _____ occurs in research when a historian examines the past using biases of the present.

144. Which is phrased properly?

    a.   None of us is perfect.

    b.   None of us are perfect.

145. _____ _____ uses probability to make inferences and draw statistical conclusions about populations based on sample data.

146. True or False: p<.03 is statistically significant.

147. One of the first steps in conducting a preliminary review of the literature might be to

    a.   conduct an ERIC search

    b.   scan through some textbooks in previous courses

    c.   read someone else's thesis

    d.   read the *Encyclopedia of Educational Research*

148. Which of the following is the best example of a suitable topic?

    a.   Methods for teaching mathematics

    b.   Mathematics performance of English Language Learners in elementary school

    c.   5th graders exposed to computer assisted instruction in mathematics will score higher on the State's standardized test than students taught using the textbook approach

    d.   Is bilingual education a good approach?

149. Topic: cooperative learning and science achievement. Which is best research question?

    a.   is cooperative learning related to science achievement?

    b.   is science achievement measurable?

    c.   is cooperative learning a viable teaching strategy and can it promote science achievement?

    d.   all of these are satisfactory

150. Name three reasons for conducting research as an educator.

151. Explain what the following quotation by Goethe (1749–1832), means to you about completing your thesis project? What specific suggestions can you make to assist one to complete the project?

> Lose this day loitering- t'will be the same story tomorrow and the next more dilatory. Then indecision brings its own delays, and days are lost lamenting over lost days. Are you in earnest? What you dream to do or think you can do, only begin it. Then the mind grows heated. Begin it, and work will be completed.

152. Consider each of these studies and determine what decision you can make about them: "Peer Acceptance of Students with Disabilities in Inclusive Settings"; "Students' and Teachers' Views of the Impact of Inclusion on the Non-Disabled Students"; "Extrinsic and Intrinsic Motivational Strategies for Promoting Interest in Mathematics Among Students with Learning Disabilities.":

    a. they are clearly experimental in nature
    b. they are correlational
    c. they are essentially descriptive
    d. they all likely will incorporate a time-series design

153. True or False: A -1.00 correlation is considered a perfect correlation.

154. Independent variable is to treatment as standard deviation is to

    a. reliability
    b. consistency
    c. mean
    d. variability

155. True or False: It is possible for two groups to have different means but the same standard deviation.

156. Provide an example of a non-directional hypothesis.

157. True or False: Only data collected by means of an experimental study can permit you to determine causality.

158. True or False: Although experimental studies are preferable because they yield useful research information, they are generally difficult to carry out in educational settings.

159. True or False: Do not initiate a study with receiving permission to do so.

160. True or False: Larger sample sizes are always better than smaller sample sizes in order to make inferences from sample to population.

161. Provide an instance when you would want a stratified random sample.

162. True or False: Although most desirable, samples of convenience in education are acceptable as long as you note possible limitations.

163. Explain how matched pairing works for sampling.

164. Provide an example of a way to minimize the John Henry Effect.

165. True or False: A split-half reliability test has the advantage over the test-retest and parallel forms methods in that there is no need to get the same group of people together twice for the purpose of administering the tests.

166. Explain the difference between consensual and face validity.

167. True or False: Data measured with an interval scale permits one of the most powerful, if not most powerful, statistical techniques available.

168. True or False: Scales of measurement that do not yield numerical scores are called ordinal data.

169. The process of locating, reading, and evaluating research articles is known as _____.

170. True or False: A convenience sample is a group of participants selected because of availability.

171. True or False: In the Test-Retest Reliability method for ascertaining reliability of an instrument participants are administered the instrument twice at different intervals using one version of the instrument.

172. Translate this research question into a directional hypothesis: "What effects will providing knowledge of results have on the spelling performance of fourth-grade students?"

173. Explain the difference between applied and basic research.

174. True or False: Quantitative researchers disregard description as a goal of their scientific experiments.

175. Explain the difference between a survey and a questionnaire.

176. True or False: A questionnaire typically begins with a question.

177. True or False: Effects sizes of lower than .33 are significant.

178. Explain the difference between parametric and nonparametric statistics.

179. Which of the following is the best example of a secondary source?
    a. a teacher's roll book of a one-room school house during 1889
    b   the acceptance speech delivered by a newly elected president of the PTA
    c. a textbook on education during the middle ages
    d. a handwritten letter by Benjamin Franklin

180. A study entitled "pupil attitude toward mainstreaming" would most likely be

    a. historical

    b. descriptive

    c. experimental

    d. correlational

181. Which of the following is an empirical statement?

    a. "I found the Mr. Smith rather obnoxious."

    b. "I know George has increased the number of reading projects because I've been monitoring his progress for months."

    c. "I just know Sam will fail."

    d. "I always had confidence in Joshua because he tries so hard in my class."

182. Why do we prefer to use the word "impact" instead of "effect," generally, in non-experimental research studies?

183. Action research differs most from typical professional practice in its

    a. concern for fostering students' learning

    b. concern for discovering generalizable knowledge

    c. promotion of practitioners' professional development

    d. systematic collection of data as a guide to improving practice

184. True or False: Under most circumstances, hypotheses are only used for quantitative studies (even though they can be used when appropriate in qualitative studies).

185. True or False: Using a standardized test ensures reliability, under normal circumstances.

186. True or False: It is better to say "Johnson (2005) designed the study" than "The study was designed by Johnson (2005)."

187. True or False: Systematic observation refers to a formal process of collecting data that is more scientific than nonsystematic observations in that data are collected with the aid of predetermined observation forms, audiovisual equipment, or some other observation instrument.

188. True or False: Regression is used when researchers want to predict values of one variable from values of another variable.

189. Describe some differences between a case study and ethnography.

190. Describe the Halo Effect.

191. Critique the following title for a study: "IMPACT OF MOTIVATIONAL STRATEGIES ON ATTITUDES TOWARDS READING AMONG SPECIAL EDUCATION STUDENTS."

192. Critique the following table of contents for a research proposal:

STATEMENT OF THE PROBLEM **3**

RESEARCH QUESTION **3**

DEFINITION OF TERMS **3**

IMPORTANCE OF THE STUDY **5**

LIMITATIONS OF THE STUDY **7**

    REVIEW OF LITERATURE **8**

        INTRODUCTION **8**

        RATIONALE **8**

        CREATING AN ENVIRONMENT THAT BUILDS MOTIVATION **12**

        SUMMARY 16

    RESEARCH DESIGN **17**

        SAMPLE **17**

    INSTRUMENTATION **17**

        PROCEDURE **18**

        TREATMENT OF DATA **18**

    REFERENCES **19**

193. Critique this Statement of the Problem for a research proposal:

> Research has shown that there is a strong correlation between motivation to read and reading achievement. Special education students are often lacking this motivation that they so desperately need.

194. Critique these definitions:

<u>Attitude</u>   A feeling or notion, formulated or preconceived about a certain subject, topic or idea. The attitude one harbors toward a specific subject for example, could significantly influence his external behavior with regard to that subject. In this study a researcher designed questionnaire was used to measure respondents' feelings and beliefs as negative, positive or indifferent towards reading.

<u>Motivation</u>   The act of providing an incentive or a reason for doing something (Guthrie & Wigfield, 1997). Motivation is the feeling, the impulse, the will and the drive to do something (Rinne, 1998).

<u>Motivational Strategy</u>   A thought out process aimed to increase motivation in a certain population in a specific realm. For example, in a corporate setting, overseers might employ a strategy of assigning a certain amount of commission per successful project to increase motivation to succeed among their staff. A reading teacher would perhaps employ a strategy of creating an atmosphere conducive to reading to motivate children to read for recreation.

Reading   The act of being able to decode a written passage, comprehend its meaning and deduct meaningful information on a literal, inferential, and critical thinking level.

195.   Critique the following "Importance of the Study" section:

> In a special education setting, motivating children to read is both complex and challenging. Struggling readers have difficulty decoding text and comprehending what they are reading. Failure to succeed fosters negative self-concept issues. Marietta Castle (1994) contends that the challenge facing educators in special education is not only to help the disabled reader master the mental process involved with learning to read, but also to replace their self-defeating perceptions with feelings of success and self worth and to foster motivation. How can teachers help reading disabled students overcome their feelings of failure and spur their motivation?

> Castle (1996) asserts that teachers' expectations have a very strong effect on the self-esteem of students. Teachers send their students messages with regard to the value of reading and the possibility of success through verbal and nonverbal interactions in the classroom. Therefore, it is crucial that teachers convey positive assumptions about the likelihood of improvement to their students. Cecil (1989) found that "when teachers set high expectations in reading, poor readers were challenged and encouraged to do their best and managed to tackle tasks that seemed insurmountable." Her study, which involved personal interviews with former disabled readers, gives proof of the lasting value of high expectations. All of her subjects reported that they were able to overcome their reading difficulties because their parents and teachers believed that they had potential for growth and change (Cecil, as cited in Castle, 1994, p.160).

> Castle further asserts that students read at higher levels when they are reading material that is of interest to them, and that reading interesting material stimulates further reading. Citing different researchers, Castle notes that when instruction is built around high interest materials and activities, it allows students to explore literature that excites them, and in turn has a tremendous potential for motivating achievement and positive attitudes in low-ability students. Often, this sparks discovery of the intrinsic rewards of literacy.

> Given all the gains and rewards to be gotten when students are motivated, this study aims to seek out the methods that work best for children whose motivational issues are influencing their reading ability.

196.   Critique this "Limitations" section of a proposal:

1.   This study will be limited to special education students in elementary school. Therefore, the study cannot be generalized to special education students in high school settings.

2. The sample of this study will be limited to the teachers of two private schools. Both schools have large populations of special education students, however the results of the study will not be a complete representation of all teachers.

3. The results of the surveys and interviews may not be valid for all learning situations.

197. Critique this Research Design for a proposal:

SAMPLE

This study will be conducted to determine the strategies of a number of master teachers of special education. These teachers teach at private school, a school for regular education that also has a large special education population which is mainstreamed into the regular track for certain periods according to ability, and from the Center for Special Education. This is a self contained setting for children with severe learning disabilities. All children in the study are between the ages of 6–14. The teachers will be selected from among the teachers with whom I consult as I conduct my private reading practice.

INSTRUMENTATION

I will give teachers a two-part packet. The first part will include copies of "The Elementary Reading Attitude Survey," a questionnaire answered by the students, and a teacher's survey in which the teachers will informally assess the results of the surveys and the general attitude towards reading in her class at the start of the project. They will then fill out a survey describing the strategy they implement to encourage motivation in their students. Towards the end of the project, they will administer the survey again. They will informally asses the results and then answer a final survey question where they will discuss whether or not they were satisfied with the results and what they felt the holistic outcome of their approach was.

PROCEDURE

The initial survey will be given out at the start of this project. I will then interview the teachers to determine what their students' attitudes are and what strategies they plan to implement to increase motivation in reading. The second part of the interview will be conducted four months later. Teachers will be asked to analyze the strengths and weaknesses of their respective strategies and will evaluate the results these interventions had on the class or individual students.

TREATMENT OF DATA

I will analyze the results of these interviews qualitatively and quantitatively to determine what kinds of motivational strategies are being implemented by special education teachers today, and to determine the effect each strategy had on the population for which it was designed.

198. Critique these references:

> Beers, G.K. (1996). No time, no interest, no way! The 3 voices of literacy. <u>School Library Journal, 42</u> (3), 14–16.

> Calkins, L. (1997). Motivating readers: Five ways to nurture a lasting love of reading. <u>Instructor, 106</u>(5), 32–33.

> Carter, L. (1998). Addressing the needs of reluctant readers through sports literature. <u>Clearing House, 26</u> (2), 98–102.

> Castle, M. (1994). Promoting the disabled reader's self-esteem. <u>Reading and Writing Quarterly, 10,</u> 159–170.

> Cooper, J. (2000). <u>Literacy-helping children construct meaning.</u> New York: Houghton Mifflin.

199. Describe the differences among: Leniency Effect, Central Tendency, Rater Indecisiveness, Personal Bias, Contamination, and Observer Omission.

200. True or False: *Decontextualization or reduction*—These terms refer to the qualitative researcher taking the voluminous data collected and reducing them to patterns, categories, or themes.

Answers: 1) a; 2) c; 3) t; 4) t; 5) t; 6) t; 7) t; 8) t; 9) f; 10) t; 11) t; 12) t; 13) t; 14) t; 15) t; 16) t; 17) t; 18)f; 19) t; 20) t; 21) t; 22) t; 23) t; 24) t; 25) t; 26) t; 27) t; 28) t; 29) t; 30) d; 31) t; 32) b; 33) c; 34) a; 35) a; 36) c; 37) d; 38) b; 39) a; 40) d; 41) e; 42) Not in alphabetical order; APA capitalization rules not adhered to properly in all references; Gillet reference missing place of publication and publisher; Claprice reference should not use first name of author; 43) Introduction doesn't directly and precisely provide an overview and set the tone for the review; 44) Importance: pretty good; Questions: a) word "improve" is nebulous, b) some citations incorrect (e.g., use of 'pg' for 'p' in page); 45) Abstract only provides a purpose statement, other components missing; 46) d; 47) a; 48) c; 49) a; 50) b; 51) b; 52) c; 53) a; 54) b; 55) d; 56) a; 57) c; 58) d; 59) b; 60) d; 61) c; 62) b; 63) t; 64) f; 65) t; 66) t; 67) f; 68) t; 69) Statement of Problem needs a prefatory sentence something like "Research indicates that…" – otherwise the remaining parts are satisfactory; 70) fine; 71) Pretty good; 72) b; 73) t; 74) a; 75) a; 76) a; 77) c; 78) .85; 79) t; 80) f; 81) c; 82) When you randomize a large number of individuals for an experimental study you can be assured that both groups are comparable on a given criterion (e.g., reading achievement) because each individual had an equal chance of being selected to either the experimental or control group; 83) self-esteem will be measured by a researcher-developed Likert scale questionnaire aimed to ascertain self esteem levels where a score of 50+ indicates high levels of self esteem, a score between 35-and 49 indicates average levels, and a score under 35 indicates low levels; 84) A sample is derived from the population; 85) content, consensual, face, etc. validity and inter-rater, split-half, etc. reliability; 86) In experimental studies individuals are randomized, not so with quasi-experimental studies; 87) Impact does not infer cause and effect relationships; 88) Use three or more data collection strategies or two or more research approaches, etc.; 89) Include positively and negatively worded statements randomly distributed throughout instrument; 90) Sampling issues (e.g., effectiveness of program only assessed through self-reported student surveys); 91) c; 92) f; 93) t; 94) c; 95) a; 96) t; 97) A variable not part of your research study but may taint your research findings; 98) d; 99) t; 100) t; 101) 5; 102) t; 103) f; 104) f; 105) f; 106) t; 107) d; 108) t; 109) f; 110) t-Test; 111) abstract; 112) f; 113) b; 114) b; 115) d; 116) c ; 117) a; 118) t; 119) grounded theory; 120) when for whatever reason you could not use either a quantitative or qualitative approach to data collection or analysis; 121) f; 122) f; 123) f, it's a causal type question more associated with experimental research; 124) c; 125) b; 126) t; 127) d; 128) informed consent; 129) f, sometimes you can withhold information or mislead a participant as long as s/he is not harmed and by not doing so will influence the results or integrity of the study; 130) a;131) t; 132) interval; 133) f; 134) b; 135) t; 136) generally true, but sometimes you may want to work with an unrepresentative sample; 137) purposeful or purposive; 138) c; 139) a; 140) t; 141) t; 142) multiple baseline; 143) presentism; 144) a; 145) inferential statistics; 146) t; 147) b; 148) b; 149) a; 150) Possible answers include, among others, to further one's knowledge, to advance knowledge in the field, to discover new ways of promoting student achievement, to determine what works best, to bolster one's sense of professionalism, etc.; 151) "Slow and steady wins the race" – Accomplish a little every day – Start today- etc.; 152) c; 153) t; 154) d; 155) t; 156) "There will be a difference in the mean post test scores of Group A and Group B"; 157) t; 158) t; 159) t; 160) f, not necessarily so because a sample may be large but not representative of the larger population whereas a small sample of say ten students may indeed be representative of a population of twenty students in a particular class, especially if they were randomly selected; 161) When a population consist of several sub-groups (e.g., African-Americans, Asian-Americans, etc.) and you want a sample that is representative of each group; 162) t; 163) Administer a test to one group, rank order the scores, pair them off in two groups randomly placing the highest score in one group, the next highest in the other group until all students are placed in one of two groups; 164) Provide a form of the treatment (e.g., computers) to the control group as well as the experimental group, but of course in a different way than is being used by the experimental group; 165) t; 166) Consensual validity occurs when you as researcher ask people not taking the survey or test to judge validity on an item-by-item basis, whereas face validity involves asking people taking the test or survey to react to how valid it was. In other words consensual validity occurs before administration of survey or test and face validity occurs after the administration; 167) t; 168) f; 169) reviewing the literature; 170) t; 171) t; 172) Something like: Providing participants knowledge of results will not result in greater accuracy in spelling new words than will providing no knowledge of results; 173) Applied—undertake research to improve educational practice, Basic—understand process and to build theory; 174) f; 175) Survey is generic term for collecting data and a questionnaire is a type of survey; 176) f; 177) f; 178) Parametric statistics are used for normally distributed populations whereas nonparametric statistics are not; 179) c; 180) b; 181) b; 182) Because no causal relationships are possible in non-experimental studies and the word "effect" connotes causation; 183) d; 184) t; 185) t; 186) t; 187) t; 188) t; 189) Case studies differ subtly from ethnographic research in that case studies are written descriptively and objectively, while ethnographic accounts may contain interpretive material. Case studies are also more narrowly focused on a particular person, place, or scene. Case studies may also tend to create an idealized situation by merely using descriptive accounts. Case studies are often guided by a series of questions that the researcher tries to answer. The case study, in the end, provides an in-depth, descriptive account; 190) tendency to view participants positively or negatively. For instance, if you're observing Juan, a student who has a history of not conforming to classroom rules, you may tend to rely on his past experiences as you observe him in a new setting; 191) All elements included; 192) Fine; 193) Incomplete, no citation and no purpose statement; 194) Conceptual definitions are simplistic and unnecessary, operational definitions incomplete as well; 195) Aside from awkward wording and a more direct statement of importance, section is somewhat satisfactory; 196) Unclear and imprecise, if not inaccurate; 197) Check back to Module 3 in Part Two for details as a number of important elements are missing with each section. Also, under "Treatment of Data" use of the word "effect" is incorrect; 198) Fine; 199) See the end of Module 2 in Part Eight; 200) t.

Appendix A:
Sample IRB Application

PART I. *Researcher's Information: Name, etc.*

(a)   Name of Applicant: <u>**Name**</u>

PART II. Type of Review Requested: Exempt, Expedited, or Full

(a) Please complete the following checklist by indicating YES or NO with an X in the appropriate spaces next to each of the 10 questions below and read the information below the 10th question.

		YES	NO
1.	Will the subjects studied include any of the following: Minors (under 18 years of age) not in your class, mentally retarded, mentally disabled?	_____	x
2.	Will it be possible to associate specific inromation in your records with specific participants on the basis of name, postiion, or other identifying infomration contained in your records, by individuals *other than the researcher*?	_____	x
3.	Will persons participating or queried in this investigation be subjected to physical discomfort, pain, *or the threat* of any of these?	_____	x
4.	Will the investigation use procedures designed to induce participants to act contrary to their wishes?	_____	x
5.	Does the investigation use procedures designed to induce embarrassment, humiliation, lowered self-esteem, guilt, conflict, anger, discouragement, or other emotional reactions?	_____	x
6.	Will participants be induced to disclose information of an intimate or otherwise sensitive nature?	_____	x
7.	Will participants engage in strenuous or unaccustomed physical activity?	_____	x
8.	Will participants be deceived (actively misled) in any manner?	_____	x
9.	Will information be withheld from participants that they might reasonably expect to receive?	_____	x
10.	Will participants be exposed to any physical or psychological risks not indicated above?	_____	x

If you checked YES to ANY of the 10 questions in PART II(a) above, then your proposal application requires a FULL review.
If you checked NO to ALL of the 10 questions above, then complete PART II(b) below.

(b) COMPLETE THIS SECTION ONLY IF YOU ANSWERED "NO" TO ALL QUESTIONS IN PART II(a).
Please read each of the 5 statements below. Place an "X" in the box to the left of any of these statements that are applicable to your study

[X]   1.   The research will be conducted in established or commonly established settings, involving normal education practices. For example:

    [x]   i)   Research on regular and special educational instructional strategies;

    [x]   ii)   Research on effectiveness of instructional techniques, curricula or classroom management techniques

[X]   2.   The research involves use of educational tests (__cognitive, ___diagnostic, ___aptitude, x achievement), and the subject cannot be identified directly or through identifiers with the information.

[ ]   3.   The research involves survey or interview procedures, in which:

    [ ]   i)   Participants cannot be identified directly or through identifiers with the information;

    [ ]   ii)   A participant's responses, if known, will not place the participant at risk of criminal or civil liability, or be damaging to the participant's financial standing or employability.

☐   iii) The research does not deal with sensitive aspects of participant's own behavior (illegal conduct, drug use, sexual behavior or alcohol use);

☐   iv) The research involves survey or interview procedures with elected or appointed public officials, or candidates for public office.

☐   4.   The research involves the observation of public behavior, in which:

    ☐   i)   The participants cannot be identified directly or through identifiers;

    ☐   ii)   The observations recorded about an individual could not put the participant at risk of criinal or civil liability or be damaging to the participant's financial standing or employability;

    ☐   iii)   The research does not deal with sensitive aspects of the participant's behavior (illegal conduct, drug use, sexual behavoir, or use of alcohol).

☐   5.   The research involves collection or study of existing data, documents, records, pathological specimens or diagnostic specimens, or which:

    ☐   i)   The sources are publicly available; or

    ☐   ii)   The information is recorded such that the participant cannot be identified directly or indirectly through identifiers

If you MARKED ANY of the 5 items/subitems in PART II(b) above, then your proposal application requires an EXPEDITED review. Please mark an "X" in the box to the right of *EXPEDITED* in PART II(c) below.

(c)   *Based on your responses to PART II(a) and PART II(b) (if applicable), please mark an "X" in the box adjacent to the type of review you are requesting:*

       EXEMPT ☐   *EXPEDITED* ☒   *FULL* ☐

PART III. Proposal Application for EXPEDITED OR FULL review:

Complete this section ONLY IF you are requesting Expedited or Full Review of your proposal.

a)   **Primary Researcher's Name:**   Name

b)   **Researcher's Department:**   Name

c)   **Faculty Advisor's Name (if researcher is a student):**   Name

d)   **Project Title:**   *Direct Instruction vs A Combination of Incidental Teaching & Direct Instruction in the Development of Language in Toddlers on the Autistic Spectrum*

e)   **Type of review Requested (Expedited or Full):**   Expedited

f)   **Background:**

Currently, research is being conducted on various approaches used to educate children on the Autistic Spectrum. Two popular approaches that are frequently utilized are incidental teaching and direct instruction. Incidental teaching is a method in which a naturalized approach is practiced to increase skills in the various developmental domains. Direct instruction is a structured approach that simplifies skills in order to meet the needs of each child. Each of these two contrasting methods is believed to be effective in teaching children with Autism.

Autism is a pervasive developmental disorder that is often accompanied by various difficulties in the area of language. Although some of these children do acquire language, generalization of these skills may still prove challenging for them.

Studies have indicated that both incidental teaching and direct instruction increase language ability in children with Autism. However, recent studies are attempting to determine which approach is more effective in enabling the children to generalize the skills that they have acquired. Future research should be conducted in this area; therefore, the research project being presented will analyze each of the aforementioned interventions: direct instruction versus a combination of incidental teaching and direct instruction. This study will enable researchers to obtain new knowledge and/or awareness of the effectiveness of these approaches.

g) **What is your hypothesis/research question?**

Direct Instruction vs incidental teaching & direct instruction: Which approach is more effective in the development of receptive and expressive language in children on the Autistic Spectrum?

h) **Recruitment of participants:**

The sample will include 18 toddlers in the classrooms of the researcher, attending Challenge Early Intervention Center located in Brooklyn. The children range between the ages of 2–3 years and were each diagnosed along the various points on the Autistic Spectrum. Parents of the children will each receive a parental consent form (Appendix A), which will state that the study being conducted is voluntary. The consent form will describe study being conducted and its purpose. The parents of the participants will also be informed of their option to withdraw their child from the study at any time. A comparison study will be utilized to determine which intervention increases language in children in this population. Children will be randomly assigned into two groups, an experimental group and a control group. The experimental group will continue to receive their daily sessions of direct instruction in addition to 15 minutes per day of incidental teaching, which is currently not incorporated in their classroom routine. The control group will continue to receive their daily session of direct instruction.

i) **Methodology:**

Children participating in this study will each be evaluated using the language portion of the Developmental Assessment for Young Children (DAYC) in combination with the Developmental Observation Checklist System (DOCS). The assessments will be administered twice over a three-month period; an initial evaluation will be conducted prior to beginning the study, and a 2nd evaluation will be administered upon completion of the study. The assessments will provide developmental ages in the area of language for each child. Throughout the study, the participants in the control group will continue to receive their daily sessions of 1:1 direct instruction. Data will be collected trial by trial on correct and incorrect responses using a system of pluses and minuses from which a percentage of correct responses can be determined. The scores will then be transferred onto graphs where they will be monitored over the three-month period. The participants in the experimental group will partake in 15 minutes per day of incidental teaching. They will engage in activities including singing songs, reading books, and labeling flashcards. Data will be collected anecdotally on spontaneous receptive and/or expressive responses. The number of correct responses will be recorded throughout the session. The total number of correct spontaneous responses at the end of each session will be logged. The data collection for each approach will serve as an effective tool in determining which intervention is more suitable for the participants involved. At the end of the three-month period, each of the children will be reevaluated using the DAYC and DOCS to determine the progress made over the course of the study. The children's developmental ages for each assessment will be compared proving which approach resulted in greater gains in the area of language.

j) **Informed consent:**

The researcher will receive the consent of the parents via a consent form that they will be required to sign (Appendix A).

k) **You and your faculty research advisor must sign below on the hard copy of this application that is to be mailed to the College.**

*As stated in the text, format for this IRB application was adapted from www.daemen.edu.

Appendix B:
Sample Parental Consent Form

Date

Dear Parent,

I am a graduate student in the Master's in a Special Education Program at X College. I am working on a thesis, which involves the development of receptive and expressive language in children diagnosed with Autism/Pervasive Developmental Disorder (PDD). I am writing to request your permission to allow your child, _____, to participate in a research study designed to promote receptive and expressive language skills. I, Name, Senior Instructor, have considered selecting your child to participate in this study. Your child will engage in 15 minutes per day of one-to-one incidental teaching activities, including songs, books, and flash cards for a period of three months. The one-to-one session would be provided at Howard Early Childhood Center, located at _____ during your child's two-hour class. Please remember that your child's participation is voluntary and that he/she is not required to take part in the study. You, the parent, can withdraw your child's participation at any time from this research project without penalty or prejudice. Your child's name will be kept in strict confidence.

If you agree to grant permission for your child to participate in this study, please check off the "yes" box below. If you would like to have your child exempt from this study, please check off the "no" box below.

Yes _____   No _____

Thank you for your time.

Sincerely,

Name

Appendix C:
Sample Research Proposal

Contents

Importance of Study.....................4
Statement of Problem....................5
Research Question.......................5
Definition of Terms.....................5
Limitations of Study....................6
Related Research........................7
  Introduction........................7
  What is Sugar?......................7
  Difference Between Table Sugar (Sucrose) and Sugars Released in the Body by Complex Carbohydrates.....8
  History of Scientific Studies.......9
  Studies of Impact of Sugar on Specific Behaviors of Children.....10
    Attention........................10
    Motor Activity...................11
    Aggression.......................13
    Irritability.....................13
  Factors That May Influence Sugar's Impact on Children's Behavior.....14
    Age of Children..................14
    Behavioral History of Children...16
    Food Consumed with Sugar.........17
  Mechanisms by which Sugar Influences Behavior.....18
    Carbohydrate Ingestion with Sugar.....19
Methodology.............................20
  Sample..............................20
  Instrumentation.....................20
  Procedure...........................21

IMPACT OF SUGAR ON CHILDREN'S BEHAVIOR

Research Proposal

Name

College
Date

*Thanks again to Evelyn Schachner for her stellar work and permission to use her work.

Sugar on Behavior 4

Importance of Study

Consumption of sugar in the United States has escalated to astronomic proportions in recent years. In 1999, the average American teenage boy ate at least 109 pounds of sugar per year (Center for Science in the Public Interest, 2000) and derived 9% of his caloric intake from soft drinks alone (Jacobson, 1999). Even toddlers are fed sugar-laden beverages. About one-fifth of the nation's one- and two-year olds were reported to drink soda in 2001 (Schlosser, 2001).

There has been a corresponding increase in hyperactivity and other behavioral problems among America's schoolchildren. Up to 7% of the school-age population is estimated to suffer from Attention Deficit/Hyperactivity Disorder (American Psychiatric Association, 2000).

Anecdotal and empirical evidence from several investigations suggest that sugar may affect children's behavior (Crook 1980; Rapp, 1978). Other reports, however, do not support these claims (Ferguson, Stoddart, & Simeon, 1986; Rosen, et al., 1988; Wolraich, et al., 1994).

The sharp rise in the nation's sugar consumption paralleled by the heightened prevalence of childhood behavioral disorders and the lack of firm conclusions from sugar-behavior studies demonstrate the need for further investigation of the influence of sugar on children's behavior. Dissemination of accurate information regarding the sugar-behavior connection can have practical dietary implications for parents and educators. In this study, the researcher will survey parents and health professionals to evaluate the impact of sugar on children's behavior.

Sugar on Behavior 3

Data Analysis.................................22

References.....................................23

Appendixes..................................26
Appendix A..............................26
Appendix B..............................30
Appendix C..............................33
Appendix D..............................34
Appendix E..............................35

Sugar on Behavior 5

Statement of Problem

Research provides conflicting evidence regarding the impact of sugar on children's behavior. Conclusions of previous studies that examined behavioral effects of sugar range from the view that sugar adversely affects behavior (Crook 1980; Rapp, 1978) to the assertion that sugar has no significant effect on behavior (Ferguson, et al., 1986; Rosen, et al., 1988; Wolraich, et al., 1994) to the affirmation that sugar produces salutary effects on behavior (Behar, Rapoport, Adams, Berg, & Cornblath, 1984). This study will attempt to ascertain impacts, if any, of sugar on children's behavior via surveys of parents, allergists, and nutritionists.

Research Question

How does sugar impact children's behavior?

Definition of Terms

1- Attention Deficit /Hyperactivity Disorder (AD/HD):

A persistent pattern of inattention and/or hyperactivity-impulsivity that is more frequently displayed and more severe than is typically observed in individuals at a comparable level of development. In addition, the following criteria apply:

a. Some hyperactive-impulsive or inattentive symptoms that cause impairment must have been present before the age of 7 years.

b. Some impairment from the symptoms must be present in at least two settings (e.g., at home, at school, or at work).

c. There must be clear evidence of interference with developmentally appropriate social, academic, or occupational functioning.

Sugar on Behavior 6

d. The disturbance does not occur exclusively during the course of a Pervasive Developmental Disorder, Schizophrenia, or other Psychotic Disorder and is not better accounted for by another mental disorder.

(American Psychiatric Association, 2000)

2- Behavior:

Five problematic behaviors will be assessed by researcher-developed, part multiple-choice and part open-ended questionnaires that will be distributed to parents and health professionals. Following are the behaviors, with observable manifestations of each:

a. Irritability- impatience, unobliging, crankiness, moodiness, complaining, frustration

b. Aggressiveness- anger, hitting, feet stomping, throwing things

c. Inattentiveness- inability to focus, dreaminess, forgetfulness, distractibility, failure to complete tasks

d. Overactivity- increased motor activity, inability to remain at one activity for a reasonable amount of time, engagement in physically dangerous activities

e. Tiredness- sluggishness, sleepiness

Limitations of Study

1. Since this study is qualitative in nature, no generalization will be possible.

2. The sample of parents and health professionals in this study will be small. It is possible, then, that the responses offered by the sample will not reflect the view of the larger population.

Related Research

Introduction

It is commonly believed that refined sugar encourages inattentive and hyperactive behavior in children. Since scientific validation of this claim would cause Americans to eliminate this possible health hazard from their diets and would also consequently cause major losses for the sugar industry, much effort has been devoted to the field of sugar-behavior research. For over three-quarters of a century, experimenters have been studying the impact of sugar on behavior in children (Shannon, 1922). Investigations have been trying to determine whether, and how, sugar impacts behavior and to identify the factors that might play a role in such effects. Numerous studies with differing methodologic approaches have been conducted to ascertain sugar's impact on attention, motor activity, aggression, and irritability among various subgroups of children. Some researchers have also suggested possible causes of sugar's influence on children's behavior.

What is Sugar?

Sugar is a type of carbohydrate. Carbohydrates can be either simple, short-chain carbohydrates or complex, long-chain carbohydrates. All sugars are simple, short chain carbohydrates. Complex carbohydrates, like starches, are made up of long chains of glucose molecules. The body can break down a complex carbohydrate into glucose, the smallest unit of sugar (Hoffer & Walker, 1996).

Difference Between Table Sugar (Sucrose) and Sugars Released in the Body by Complex Carbohydrates

The body requires glucose as an energy source for brain activity. The body can obtain glucose from complex carbohydrates or from table sugar (Hoffer & Walker, 1996). Obtaining glucose from complex carbohydrates is better for the body for two reasons. Firstly, the complex carbohydrates must be broken down by the body in order to be converted to glucose, and the glucose is therefore released slowly into the bloodstream, producing a slight, as opposed to dramatic, insulin response (Conners, 1989). Secondly, the glucose derived from complex carbohydrates is released into the bloodstream together with other nutrients from the carbohydrates. These nutrients from the carbohydrates help the body metabolize the sugar (Hoffer & Walker, 1996).

Table sugar is a form of sucrose. Sucrose is derived from the manufactured processing of vegetable and fruit products such as sugar cane and beets (Conners, 1989). During the refinement process, a synthetic form of sugar, sucrose, is formed, which no longer contains the vitamins of the original beets or sugar cane. When sucrose is absorbed by the body, other nutrients are not present to help metabolize the sugar (Hoffer & Walker, 1996).

Sucrose is also absorbed quickly into the bloodstream. Sucrose is composed of two molecules, one of fructose and one of glucose. The body can derive the glucose by the simple task of splitting the sucrose molecules. Since the glucose from sucrose molecules is obtained quickly, the glucose is released rapidly into the bloodstream and produces a strong insulin reaction (Conners, 1989). Because of its rapid release into the

Sugar on Behavior 9

bloodstream, not in conjunction with other nutrients, sucrose can be harmful to the body (Hoffer & Walker, 1996).

Nearly all of the sugar studies discussed below investigated possible behavioral impacts of sucrose, the most popular form of sugar. Aspartame and saccharin are sugar substitutes that were used for placebos in blind sugar challenge studies.

History of Scientific Studies

Scientists began investigating possible behavioral effects of sugar as early as 1922 (Shannon, 1922). A report published in 1929 described the results of a reduced sugar diet given to a hyperactive 12-year-old boy to relieve his problematic behaviors (Seham & Seham).

Subsequent research began to more firmly establish a connection between problematic behaviors and allergy to various foods, including sugar. In a comprehensive report on the symptoms of food allergy observed in his patients, Rowe (1931) specified several behaviors he found to be induced by allergic foods in sensitive individuals. These allergy-induced behaviors included drowsiness, difficulty concentrating, irritability, and fatigue and were triggered most commonly by wheat, eggs, and milk. In the same report, Rowe mentioned the allergic sensitivity to cane sugar of one patient.

In 1947, in his description of the tension-fatigue syndrome, Randolph attributed children's irritability, fatigue, and inattentiveness to allergenic foods such as wheat and corn. Randolph noted that frequently, corn sugars will cause more immediate allergic reactions than corn starch or whole corn. In 1954, Speer reported restlessness, irritability, and fatigue in children resulting from their allergy to milk, corn, wheat and eggs.

Sugar on Behavior 10

Since then, the research describing the influence of sugar on children's behavior has greatly increased. Controlled studies have been conducted and anecdotal data have been obtained to ascertain sugar's impact on both normal and disturbed children's behavior under varied conditions. Some investigations have supported the hypothesis that sugar adversely affects behavior while others have disagreed, stating that sugar produces either no effect, or salutary effects, on children's behavior.

Studies of Impact of Sugar on Specific Behaviors in Children

Attention

Numerous studies have evaluated the impact of sugar on children's attention. Some have found that sugar causes increased inattention in children (Crook, 1975; Goldman, Lerman, Contois, & Udall, 1986; Prinz & Riddle, 1986; Wolraich, Stumbo, Milich, Chenard, & Schultz, 1986), while others have reported that sugar produces no effect on attention (Behar, et al., 1984; Kruesi, et al., 1987; Mahan, et al., 1988).

Crook (1975) assessed the relationship between food allergy and learning problems in children. Crook found that nervous system symptoms, including inability to concentrate and short attention span, increased dramatically after the ingestion of sugar in 28 of the 45 children studied.

In a study involving two groups of preschool boys, one on a high-sucrose diet, and one on a low-sucrose diet, Prinz and Riddle (1986) found that the boys on the high-sucrose diet scored significantly lower on a Continuous Performance Test than the boys on the low sucrose diet, indicating poorer attention. Similarly, Goldman, et al., (1986) found a decrement in performance on a Continuous Performance Test in preschool children after the children received a sucrose challenge as compared to a placebo.

Sugar on Behavior 11

Wender and Solanto (1991) conducted a study resembling that of Goldman, et al., but included two groups of 5- to 7-year-old children: one hyperactive group and one normal group. Interestingly, in Wender and Solanto's study, inattention after ingesting sugar increased only in the hyperactive group.

Wolraich, et al. (1986) examined the relationship between dietary habits and behavioral problems in boys aged 7 to 12. Dietary records were obtained for a group of hyperactive boys and a matched control group. Several behaviors of the hyperactive boys were then evaluated. The ratio of sugar to total carbohydrates consumed was found to be significantly partially correlated with inattention of the hyperactive boys.

Behar, et al. (1984), Kruesi, et al. (1987), and Wolraich, et al. (1994) conducted double-blind sugar challenge studies with groups of boys aged 6 to 14, 2 to 6, and 6 to 10, respectively, who were considered by their parents to be behaviorally reactive to sugar. Behavioral ratings by trained observers who were blind to the conditions of the studies showed no significant effects of sugar on attentiveness. Continuous Performance Tests that were administered to the children in the study by Behar, et al. also showed no significant sugar effects.

Mahan, et al. (1988) evaluated the behavior of 3- to 10-year-old children after open sugar challenges, using the number of toys children touched per minute as an index of attention span. None of the children tested showed that sugar had any consistent effect on attention.

Motor activity

Studies that have examined the relationship between sugar consumption and children's activity levels have reported conflicting results. Some studies have found that

Sugar on Behavior 12

increased activity in children is associated with sugar consumption (Conners & Blouin, 1983; Prinz, et al., 1980; Wolraich, Stumbo, Milch, Chenard, & Schultz, 1986), while others have found either no effects (Kruesi, et al., 1987), or positive effects (Behar, et al., 1980; Ferguson, et al., 1986; Mahan, et al., 1988; Wolraich, et al., 1994), of sugar on activity.

Prinz, et al. (1980) and Wolraich, et al. (1986) conducted correlational studies with groups of hyperactive children, aged 4 to 7, and 7 to 12, respectively. Prinz, et al. had observers record restless behaviors of the children such as repetition of arm, leg, and head movements. It was found that the amount of sugar products consumed by the children was significantly related to restless behaviors. Wolraich, et al. used ankle actometers, acceleration-sensitive devices worn on the body (Colburn, Smith, Guerine, & Simmon, 1976 as cited in Behar, et al., 1984), to detect motor movement. Sugar to total carbohydrates consumed was found to be positively correlated with activity levels.

In a long-term, double-blind study, minor and gross motor movements of children hospitalized for severe behavior disorders were rated by observers after sugar and placebo challenges. Researchers noted an increase in total movement for sugar challenges as compared to placebo (Conners & Blouin, 1983).

Actometer counts and parental ratings of behavior showed no significant effect of sugar on behavior in another double-blind sugar challenge study (Kruesi, et al., 1987). Several double-blind sugar challenge studies have reported slight but significant *calming* effects in children after sugar challenges as compared with placebo (Behar, et al., 1984; Ferguson, et al., 1986; Mahan, et al., 1988; Wolraich, et al., 1994).

Sugar on Behavior 13

Aggression

Prinz, et al. (1980) reported a correlation between sugar consumption and destructive-aggressive behavior in hyperactive preschool children. Destructive-aggressive behavior was rated by observers during free-play and was defined as attempts at damaging objects in the playroom, hitting, kicking, and throwing objects.

A number of double-blind sugar challenge studies have since disputed the hypothesis that sugar influences aggressive behavior (Kruesi, et al., 1987; Mahan, et al., 1988; Wender & Solanto, 1991). These studies involved both hyperactive and normal children of various ages and found no significant effects of sugar on aggression.

Irritability

Pediatric allergists Rapp (1978) and Crook (1980) reported that sugar caused acute reactions of irritability in their patients. The allergists put their hyperactive patients on elimination diets which excluded suspect foods, including sugar. The eliminated foods were then individually reintroduced to the patients' diets and reactions were noted.

In Rapp's (1978) study, research assistants observed that a single sugar ingestion challenge test consistently caused irritability in 2 of the 24 patients tested. Crook (1980) quoted several questionnaire responses of parents of his patients which described changes in irritability following dietary elimination. A parent of a 2½-year-old girl declared: "as little as one teaspoon of sugar will cause constant crying, irritability, and tantrums. Since taking her off sugar, I feel as though someone has given me a different child" (p. 55).

A parent of a 6-year-old boy wrote: "Even a few bites of sugar, corn or eggs cause hyperactivity, nervousness…and other allergy symptoms" (Crook, 1980, p. 55). Yet another parent asserted about a 12-year-old child: "sugar, milk, chocolate, and prepared

Sugar on Behavior 14

foods containing preservatives cause him to be nervous and irritable. I used to use Ritalin. Although it did slow him down, he was still irritable, and controlling his diet helped him even more" (Crook, 1980, p. 56).

A double-blind sugar challenge study which tested the behavior of 14- to 19-year-old delinquent students did not support the claims of Rapp (1978) and Crook (1980). Experimenter ratings of mood did not interact statistically with substance (Bachorowski, et al., 1990).

Factors That May Influence Sugar's Impact on Children's Behavior

Several factors may help explain the inconsistencies in the findings of sugar-behavior studies. Among these factors are differences in age of children studied (Goldman, et al., 1986; Kaplan, et al., 1989), differences in behavioral diagnoses of children studied (Wender & Solanto, 1991), and varied types of foods consumed with sugar (Conners, 1989).

Age of Children

Research has suggested that younger children may be more sensitive than older children to food substances (Lipton, Nemeroff, & Mailman, 1979 as cited in Goldman, et al., 1986; Harley, Ray, Tomasi, et al., 1978 as cited in Kaplan, et al., 1989; Weiss, Williams, Margen, et al., 1980 as cited in Kaplan, et al., 1989). Several sugar challenge studies have therefore included two groups of children, preschool and elementary, to determine if younger children display more overt behavioral reactions to sugar than older children (Rosen, et al., 1988; Wolraich, et al., 1994).

394

Sugar on Behavior 15

Rosen, et al. (1988) tested the cognition and behavior of two groups of children after double-blind sugar and placebo challenges. One group consisted of 30 preschool children with a mean age of 5 years; the other consisted of 15 first and second grade children with a mean age of 7 years. None of the children in the study were diagnosed with behavioral disorders. All the children received equal amounts of the sweeteners. When researchers analyzed the results of cognitive tests that were administered after sugar challenges, it was found that sugar affected the preschoolers differently than it affected the elementary school children.

Wolraich, et al. (1994) conducted a double-blind sugar/placebo trial which involved one group of 25 normal preschool children, aged 3 to 5 years, and one group of 23 elementary school children, aged 6 to 10 years, who were considered by their parents to be sensitive to sugar. Participants and their families followed different diets for each of three consecutive 3-week periods. One diet was high in sucrose; the other two were low in sucrose and contained different sugar substitutes.

Researchers and parents evaluated the cognition and behavior of the children weekly. The 6- to 10- year-old children showed no cognitive or behavioral effects of sucrose. For this group, there were no significant differences among the different diets in any of the 39 behavioral and cognitive variables tested (Wolraich, et al., 1994).

Two of 31 variables tested on the preschool group showed significant effects of the sucrose diet. The preschool children's performance on a pegboard task was significantly slower during the sucrose diet. Parental ratings of the preschool children's cognition, however, were significantly *better* during the sucrose diet than during the sugar substitute diets (Wolraich, et al., 1994).

Sugar on Behavior 16

A number of sugar-behavior studies have been conducted on one group of children between the ages of 2 and 6 years but have not included a second group of older children subjected to the same conditions. Two such studies reported adverse behavioral effects of sugar in preschool children (Goldman, et al., 1986; Prinz & Riddle, 1986). Two other studies found no effects of sugar on the behavior of preschool children (Ferguson, et al., 1986; Kruesi, et al., 1987).

Behavioral History of Children

Researchers have proposed that hyperactive children may be more sensitive to the effects of sugar than normal children (Prinz, et al., 1980; Tauraso, 1983 as cited in Rosen, et al., 1988; Wender & Solanto, 1991). Two studies tested this hypothesis (Rosen, et al., 1988; Wender & Solanto, 1991).

Wender and Solanto (1991) assessed attention and aggression in a group of children with Attention Deficit Hyperactivity Disorder and in a group of aged-matched, normal children after sugar challenges. Research assistants noted no significant effect of sugar on aggression in either group of children. Scores of continuous performance tasks, however, showed an increase in inattention following sugar challenges only in the hyperactive group of children.

Rosen, et al. (1988) conducted a sugar challenge study with a group of children who were not diagnosed with Attention Deficit Disorder. To ascertain whether hyperactivity influenced the children's reactions to sugar, the researchers formed two groups of children: one scoring high, and one scoring low, on the Hyperactivity Index of the behavioral rating scale completed by teachers of the children. Researchers found no significant effects of sugar for either the high- or the low- rated children on the Hyperactivity Index.

Food Consumed with Sugar

A few studies have shown that sugar's effects on behavior differ are dependent on whether the sugar is consumed alone, together with carbohydrates, or together with protein. In one experiment involving normal and hyperactive children, Conners (1989) administered sugar and placebo challenges alone, together with carbohydrate, and together with protein breakfasts. The children's attention after placebo challenges was then compared with their attention after sugar challenges for each type of meal. In the hyperactive children, Conners reported that sugar increased inattention when eaten with carbohydrates, sugar caused no change in attention when eaten alone, and sugar improved attention when eaten with protein. In the normal children, Conners found poorer attention after sugar-carbohydrate meals than after sugar-protein meals.

Wender and Solanto (1991) assessed attention in normal and hyperactive children after sugar and placebo challenges with carbohydrate breakfasts. The hyperactive children displayed poorer attention after carbohydrate meals with sugar than after carbohydrate meals with placebo sweeteners. The normal children showed no difference between attention after carbohydrate meals with sugar and after carbohydrate meals with placebo sweeteners.

Rosen, et al. (1988) studied the behavior of normal preschool children after sugar and placebo challenges given with carbohydrate breakfasts. A small increase in activity level was reported after sugar-carbohydrate meals.

Bachorowski (1990) studied the behavior of delinquent and non-delinquent students after sucrose challenges with carbohydrate breakfasts. Results were inconsistent with those reported by Conners (1989) and Rosen, et al. (1988). Sugar consumed with carbohydrate breakfasts improved the performance of delinquents rated as more behaviorally disturbed and impaired the performance of delinquents with less pronounced behavioral problems.

Mahan, et al. (1988) tested the behavior of 5 children before and after sugar challenges given with lunch consisting of balanced amounts of carbohydrates and protein. Two of the 5 children tested showed significant increases in movement after the sugar challenge. One of the children also showed an increase in non-compliance, aggression, and distractibility.

Some studies have administered sugar challenges to children after overnight fasts to eliminate effects of carbohydrate or protein consumed with sugar (Behar, et al., 1984; Goldman, et al., 1984). Results of these studies are inconsistent. Behar, et al. noted a calming effect of sugar in children, while Goldman, et al. reported restless and distractibility in children after sugar challenges following overnight fasts.

Mechanisms by which Sugar Influences Behavior

Nutritionists, medical practitioners, and researchers have offered several explanations for behavioral changes seen in children as a result of sugar intake. Carbohydrate ingestion with sugar (Conners, 1989; Hoffer & Walker, 1996; Milich, Wolraich & Lindgren, 1986), allergy to sugar (Hoffer & Walker, 1996), and nutrient deficiency as a result of sugar ingestion (Hoffer & Walker, 1996) have been proffered as possible causes of children's behavioral reactions to sugar.

Carbohydrate Ingestion with Sugar

It has been suggested that the body's insulin response to a meal consisting of only carbohydrates causes an increase in the amount of the amino acid tryptophan in the brain (Wurtman & Wurtman, 1977). Tryptophan is essential to the production of the brain neurotransmitter serotonin. The rise in the level of tryptophan in the brain thus causes an increase in the amount of serotonin in the brain (Conners, 1989; Wurtman & Suffes, 1996; Wurtman & Wurtman, 1977). This neurotransmitter, serotonin, is used by the brain to control functions such as perception, thinking, feeling, and generalized activity (Hoffer & Walker, 1996). The increase of serotonin in the brain (caused by ingestion of carbohydrates) may possibly slow children's thought processes (Conners, 1989).

Researchers have found that when protein is consumed with sugar, the brain decreases its production of serotonin. This is because the amino acids (which make up protein) compete with the amino acid tryptophan for entrance into the brain. Because of the competition among the different types of amino acids, only small amounts of tryptophan are able to enter the brain. The reduction of tryptophan in the brain causes a decrease in the amount of serotonin in the brain (Wurtman & Wurtman, 1977). A decrease in serotonin level in the brain can cause changes in behavior (Conners, 1989; Milich, Wolraich & Lindgren, 1986).

Related Research In Progress

Methodology

Sample

The sample in this study will include parents, allergists, and nutritionists. Approximately 50 middle-class, Orthodox Jewish parents who reside in the New York Tri-State area were surveyed. To increase the response rate, the sample of parents will consist mostly of acquaintances of the researcher.

About 10 allergists and nutritionists in Rockland County, NY and vicinity who provide services to relatives or friends of the researcher might also participate in the study.

Instrumentation

To evaluate the impact of sugar on children's behavior, two questionnaires will be developed by the researcher: one for distribution to targeted parents and the other for distribution to several allergists and nutritionists. The questionnaires will consist of multiple-choice questions together with some open-ended questions. Content and consensual validity will be obtained for both questionnaires. Interrater reliability will ensure consistency of recording procedures.

The first part of the parental questionnaire will consist of a chart that lists five types of adverse behaviors and eight different types of sugared foods. On the chart, the parents are asked to rate the frequency at which each listed behavior is displayed by a sugar-reactive child as a result of the consumption of the foods. The descriptive terms 'never,' 'infrequently,' 'frequently,' and 'very often' are used to rate the frequency of the behaviors. Each parent will receive two copies of the chart, so that behaviors of two children can be recorded separately. The second part of the questionnaire is open-ended

Sugar on Behavior 21

and more detailed. It includes questions about about the nature and causes of the reactions. A sample of the parental questionnaire is included in appendix A.

The first part of the health professional questionnaire also consists of a chart listing five adverse behaviors and eight sugared foods. The allergists and nutritionists are asked to estimate the number of children they have treated that have exhibited the listed behaviors after consuming the specified sugared foods.

The second part of the questionnaire for health professionals is mostly open-ended. The health practitioners are asked for specific information concerning the children who reacted to the sugared foods and their behavioral reactions. A sample of this questionnaire is included in appendix B.

A researcher-written cover letter that briefly describes the thesis study will accompany each questionnaire. A sample of the cover letter for the parental questionnaire is included in appendix C. A sample of the cover letter for the health professional questionnaire is included in appendix D. Appendix E contains a copy of the consent form that will be included with the mailed questionnaires.

Before distributing the questionnaires, the researcher will call parents and health professionals to ask if they are willing to participate in the survey. The researcher will state that participation is voluntary and that all names will be kept confidential. If the parent/health professional agrees to participate, the researcher will give him/her the choice of answering over the phone or in writing, by mail. A phone script for calls to parents and health professionals will be developed later..

Procedure

1. The researcher will develop a questionnaire to distribute to parents.

Sugar on Behavior 22

2. The researcher will develop a questionnaire to distribute to allergists and nutritionists.

3. The researcher will formulate a list of parents who may have been willing to be surveyed. The majority of these parents were acquaintances of the researcher.

4. The researcher will phone the parents on the list to ask if they are willing to participate in the survey and if the researcher may mail them the questionnaires. The researcher will give the parents the option to answer the questions over the phone.

5. The researcher will mail questionnaires along with consent forms and addressed, stamped return envelopes to the parents who agreed to respond.

6. The researcher will formulate a list of allergists and nutritionists in the Rockland County area.

7. The researcher will phone the allergists and nutritionists to ask if they would participate in the survey and if the researcher may mail the questionnaires to them.

8. The researcher will mail questionnaires along with consent forms and addressed, stamped return envelopes to the nutritionists and allergists who agreed to respond.

9. Data from the returned questionnaires will be analyzed.

Data Analysis

Data will be analyzed using qualitative measures.

Sugar on Behavior 23

References

American Psychiatric Association. (2000). *Diagnostic and statistical manual of mental disorders* (4th ed.). Washington, DC: American Psychiatric Association.

Bachorowski, J.-A., Newman, J. P., Nichols, S. L., Gans, D. A., Harper, A. E., & Taylor, S. L. (1990). Sucrose and delinquency: Behavioral assessment. *Pediatrics, 86*(2), 244-253.

Behar, D., Rapoport, J. L., Adams, A. J., Berg, C. J., & Cornblath, M. (1984). Sugar challenge testing with children considered behaviorally "sugar reactive." *Nutrition and Behavior, 1,* 277-288.

Boris, M., & Mandel, F. S. (1993). Foods and additives are common causes of the attention deficit hyperactive disorder in children. *Annals of Allergy, 72,* 462-468.

Center for Science in the Public Interest. (2000). Sugar intake hit all-time high in 1999. *Nutrition Action Healthletter.* Retrieved from http://www.cspinet.org/new/sugar_limit.html

Conners, C. K. (1989). *Feeding the brain: How foods affect children.* New York, NY: Plenum Press.

Conners, C. K., & Blouin, A. G. (1983). Nutritional effects on behavior of children. *Journal of Psychiatric Research, 17*(2), 193-201.

Crook, W. G. (1975). Food allergy: The great masquerader. *Pediatric Clinics of North America, 22*(1), 227-234.

Crook, W. G. (1980). Can what a child eats make him dull, stupid, or hyperactive? *Journal of Learning Disabilities, 13*(5), 53-57.

Ferguson, H. B., Stoddart, C., & Simeon, J. G. (1986). Double-blind challenge studies of

Sugar on Behavior 24

behavioral and cognitive effects of sucrose-aspartame ingestion in normal children. *Nutrition Reviews, 44*(suppl), 144-150.

Goldman, J. A., Lerman, R. H., Contois, J. H., & Udall, J. N. (1986). Behavioral effects of sucrose on preschool children. *Journal of Abnormal Child Psychology, 14,* 565-577.

Gross, M. D. (1984). Effect of sucrose on hyperkinetic children. *Pediatrics, 74,* 876-878.

Hoffer, A., & Walker, M. (1996). *Putting it all together: The new orthomolecular nutrition.* New Canaan, CT: Keats Publishing.

Jacobson, M. (1998). Liquid Candy. *Nutrition Action Healthletter, 25*(1), 8.

Kruesi, M. J. P., Rapoport, J. L., Cummings, E. M., Berg, C. J., Ismond, D. R., Flament, M., et al. (1987). Effects of sugar and aspartame on aggression and activity in children. *American Journal of Psychiatry, 144,* 1487-1490.

Mahan, L. K., Chase, M., Furukawa, C. T., Sulzbacher, S., Shapiro, G. G., Pierson, W. E., et al. (1988). Sugar "allergy" and children's behavior. *Annals of Allergy, 61,* 453-458.

Milich, R., Wolraich, M., & Lindgren, S. (1986). Sugar and hyperactivity: A critical view of empirical findings. *Clinical Psychology Review, 6,* 493-513.

Prinz, R. J., & Riddle, D. B. (1986). Associations between nutrition and behavior in 5-year-old children. *Nutrition Reviews, 44*(suppl), 151-157.

Prinz, R. J., Roberts, W. A., & Hantman, E. (1980). Dietary correlates of hyperactive behavior in children. *Journal of Consulting and Clinical Psychology, 48,* 760-769.

Sugar on Behavior 25

Randolph, T. J. (1947). Allergy as a causative factor of fatigue, irritability, and behavior problems of children. *The Journal of Pediatrics, 31,* 560-572.

Rapp, D. J. (1978). Does diet affect hyperactivity? *Journal of Learning Disabilities, 11*(6), 56-62.

Rosen, L. A., Bender, M. E., Sorrell, S., Booth, S. R., McGrath, M. L., & Drabman, R. S. (1988). Effects of sugar (sucrose) on children's behavior. *Journal of Consulting and Clinical Psychology, 56,* 583-589.

Rowe, A. H. (1931). *Food allergy.* Philadelphia, PA: Lea & Febiger.

Schlosser, E. (2001). *Fast food nation: The dark side of the all-American meal.* New York, NY: Houghton Mifflin Company.

Seham, M., & Seham, G. (1929). The relation between malnutrition and nervousness. *American Journal of Diseases in Children, 37*(1), 1-38.

Shannon, W. R. (1922). Nueropathologic manifestations in infants and children as a result of anaphylactic reaction to foods contained in their dietary. *American Journal of Disorders in Children, 24,* 89-94.

Speer, F. (1954). The allergic tension-fatigue syndrome. *The Pediatric Clinics of North America, 1,* 1029-1037.

Wender, E. H., & Solanto, M. V. (1991). Effects of sugar on aggressive and inattentive behavior in children with attention deficit disorder with hyperactivity and normal children. *Pediatrics, 88,* 960-966.

Wolraich, M. L., Lindgren, S. D., Stumbo, P. J., Stegink, L. D., Appelbaum, M. I., & Kiritsy, M. C. (1994). Effects of diets high in sucrose or aspartame on the behavior and cognitive performance of children. *The New England Journal of Medicine,*

Sugar on Behavior 26

330(5), 301-307.

Wolraich, M. L., Stumbo, P. J., Milch, R., Chenard, C., & Schultz, F. (1986). Dietary characteristics of hyperactive and control boys. *Journal of the American Dietetic Association, 86,* 500-504.

Wolraich, M. L., Wilson, D. B., & White, J. W. (1995). The effect of sugar on behavior or cognition in children. *Journal of the American Medical Association, 274,* 1616-1621.

Wurtman, J. J., & Suffes, S. (1996). *The serotonin solution.* Fawcett Columbine, NY: Ballantine Books.

Wurtman, R. J., & Wurtman, J. J. (1977). *Nutrition and the brain.* New York, NY: Raven Press.

Appendixes

Appendix A: Parental Questionnaire

Form I

Please list the age and gender of each child between 2 and 16 years of age who may have overt behavioral reactions to sugar. Use a separate form for each child.

Age of child _____

Gender of child _____

Circle a letter in each box below to describe the frequency of the following reactive behaviors you believe your child displays as a result of consuming the listed foods. Circle N/A if the child never consumes a food.

Legend: N- Never   I- Infrequently   F- Frequently   V- Very often

Sugar on Behavior 28

Form II

Food	Behavior					
	Irritable (impatient, unobliging, cranky, moody, complaining, easily frustrated)	**Aggressive** (angry, hitting, feet stomping, throwing things)	**Inattentive** (unable to focus, dreamy, forgetful, distractible, fails to complete tasks	**Overactive** (increased motor activity, unable to remain at one activity for a reasonable amount of time, engages in physically dangerous activities)	**Tired** (sluggish, sleepy)	**Other** (Please describe)
Sugar-sweetened cereals	N I F V N/A	N I F V N/A	N I F V N/A	N I F V N/A	N I F V N/A	N I F V
Sweetened yogurt/ Chocolate milk	N I F V N/A	N I F V N/A	N I F V N/A	N I F V N/A	N I F V N/A	N I F V N/A
Cake/ Cookies	N I F V N/A	N I F V N/A	N I F V N/A	N I F V N/A	N I F V N/A	N I F V N/A
Candy/ Chocolate	N I F V N/A	N I F V N/A	N I F V N/A	N I F V N/A	N I F V N/A	N I F V N/A
Ices	N I F V N/A	N I F V N/A	N I F V N/A	N I F V N/A	N I F V N/A	N I F V N/A
Soda	N I F V N/A	N I F V N/A	N I F V N/A	N I F V N/A	N I F V N/A	N I F V N/A

1. Please list the age and gender of each of your children who is between 2 and 16 years of age: _____

2. In question number 1, circle the age and gender of any child who you think displays behavioral reactions to sugar.

3. If you circled the age and gender of (a) child/ren that you did not describe in the Food/Behavior chart, briefly describe the behavioral changes you see in this/these child/ren: _____

Sugar on Behavior 27

Form I

Food	Behavior					
	Irritable (impatient, unobliging, cranky, moody, complaining, easily frustrated)	**Aggressive** (angry, hitting, feet stomping, throwing things)	**Inattentive** (unable to focus, dreamy, forgetful, distractible, fails to complete tasks	**Overactive** (increased motor activity, unable to remain at one activity for a reasonable amount of time, engages in physically dangerous activities)	**Tired** (sluggish, sleepy)	**Other** (Please describe)
Sugar-sweetened cereals	N I F V N/A	N I F V N/A	N I F V N/A	N I F V N/A	N I F V N/A	N I F V N/A
Sweetened yogurt/ Chocolate milk	N I F V N/A	N I F V N/A	N I F V N/A	N I F V N/A	N I F V N/A	N I F V N/A
Cake/ Cookies	N I F V N/A	N I F V N/A	N I F V N/A	N I F V N/A	N I F V N/A	N I F V N/A
Candy/ Chocolate	N I F V N/A	N I F V N/A	N I F V N/A	N I F V N/A	N I F V N/A	N I F V N/A
Ices	N I F V N/A	N I F V N/A	N I F V N/A	N I F V N/A	N I F V N/A	N I F V N/A
Soda	N I F V N/A	N I F V N/A	N I F V N/A	N I F V N/A	N I F V N/A	N I F V N/A

Additional Copy for Second Child

Age of child _____

Gender of child _____

Circle a letter in each box below to describe the frequency of the following reactive behaviors you believe your child displays as a result of consuming the listed foods. Circle N/A if the child never consumes a food.

Legend: N- Never I- Infrequently F- Frequently V- Very often

Sugar on Behavior 30

Appendix B: Health Professional Questionnaire

Form I

Please *circle* a letter in each box below to indicate the estimated number of your clients (ages 2-16) who you believe exhibit the following behaviors after consuming the listed foods.

Legend: A- 0   B- 1-5   C- 6-15   D- 15-30   E- more than 30

Food	Behavior					
	Irritable (impatient, unobliging, cranky, moody, complaining, easily frustrated)	Aggressive (angry, hitting, feet stomping, throwing things)	Inattentive (unable to focus, dreamy, forgetful, distractible, fails to complete tasks)	Overactive (increased motor activity, unable to remain at one activity for a reasonable amount of time, engages in physically dangerous activities)	Tired (sluggish, sleepy)	Other (Please describe)
Sugar-sweetened Cereals	A B C D E	A B C D E	A B C D E	A B C D E	A B C D E	A B C D E
Fruit Juices	A B C D E	A B C D E	A B C D E	A B C D E	A B C D E	A B C D E
Cake/Cookies	A B C D E	A B C D E	A B C D E	A B C D E	A B C D E	A B C D E
Candy	A B C D E	A B C D E	A B C D E	A B C D E	A B C D E	A B C D E
Box Drinks (lemonade, fruit punch, etc.)	A B C D E	A B C D E	A B C D E	A B C D E	A B C D E	A B C D E
Ices	A B C D E	A B C D E	A B C D E	A B C D E	A B C D E	A B C D E
Soda	A B C D E	A B C D E	A B C D E	A B C D E	A B C D E	A B C D E

Sugar on Behavior 29

4. How often do your children consume sugar-sweetened *foods*?
    a. every day
    b. once a week
    c. less than once a week

5. How often do your children consume sugar-sweetened *snacks*?
    a. every day
    b. once a week
    c. less than once a week

If you have observed behavioral reactions to sugar in any of your children, please answer the following questions:

6. Were the behavioral reactions you observed immediate (within 30 minutes after consumption of the food) or delayed? _____

7. If the reactions were delayed, how long was the delay? _____

8. Do any other foods/circumstances trigger the reactions you indicated above? Please specify: _____

9. Do the behavioral reactions you described lead to problems at school? _____

10. Do you think your children are allergic to sugar? _____

11. Have you tried eliminating the sugar laden provoking foods from your child/ren's diet/s? _____

12. If yes, did behaviors improve after the foods were eliminated? _____

Comments: _____

_____

_____

_____

_____

_____

_____

_____

_____

_____

Sugar on Behavior 31

Form II

If your clients ever exhibited any behavioral reactions to the foods listed above, please answer the following questions:

1. Approximately how many of your clients are between the ages of 2 and 16? _____

2. Approximately how many of these clients, aged 2-16, have shown any adverse behavioral reactions to sugar? _____

3. In the population of children who reacted to the sweet foods, there were:

   a. significantly more boys than girls
   b. slightly more boys than girls
   c. significantly more girls than boys
   d. slightly more girls than boys
   e. an equal amount of each gender

4. In which age group were the children who were most likely to react to sugar?

   a. 2 – 4 years
   b. 5- 8 years
   c. 9- 12 years
   d. 13- 16 years

5. Did most of the children react immediately (within 30 minutes after consumption of the food) or were the reactions delayed? _____

6. If the behavioral reactions to sugar were delayed, how long were the delays? _____

7. What were the initial complaints of most of the parents of the sugar-reactive children? _____

8. Were the behavioral reactions in most children accompanied by physical symptoms (stomachache, trouble sleeping, etc.)? _____

9. Were most of the parents of the reactive children aware of the children's food sensitivities when they first came to seek treatment? _____

10. Approximately how many of the of parents of the sugar-reactive children complained of problems at school? _____

11. In your opinion, what percentage of the sugar-induced reactions were due to:

    Allergy _____
    Hypoglocemia _____
    Other (Please specify) _____
    Unknown causes _____

12. Did any other foods/circumstances trigger the behavioral reactions in the sugar-reactive children? _____
    Please specify _____

13. Do you ever recommend omitting sugar from clients' diets? _____

Sugar on Behavior 32

14. If you do, do the behaviors usually improve when foods with sugar are eliminated? _____

15. Do problems at school usually improve when sugar is eliminated from the diets of 'sugar-reactive' children? _____

16. After how long on the elimination diets do the children usually show improvement? _____

Comments: _____
_____
_____
_____
_____
_____

Sugar on Behavior 34

Appendix D: Cover Letter for Health Professional Questionnaire

Date

Dear Participant,

As per our phone conversation, I am sending you the enclosed questionnaire. I am a student in a Special Education Program at X College. I am working on a master's thesis which concerns the ways in which sugar may impact children's behavior. Your and other health professionals' answers to the enclosed questionnaire will help me evaluate behavioral changes, if any, in children after their consumption of snacks and foods containing sugar.

I understand that you have a busy schedule, and I am grateful for your taking the time to answer the questions on the enclosed forms (it should only take about ten minutes). If you could return the completed questionnaire as soon as possible, I would greatly appreciate it. Please remember that your participation is voluntary and you are not required to complete any or all items.

None of the information you submit will be disclosed to anyone. Your name will be kept in strict confidence.

If you would like to obtain a written summary of the results of this project, please contact me by mail in December of this year at ADDRESS.

Thank you very much for your assistance.

Sincerely,

Name

Sugar on Behavior 33

Appendix C: Cover Letter for Parental Questionnaire

October 2004

Dear Participant,

As per our phone conversation, I am sending you the enclosed questionnaire. I am a student in a Special Education Program at College. I am working on a thesis which concerns the ways in which sugar may impact children's behavior. Your and other parents' answers to the enclosed questionnaire will help me evaluate behavioral changes, if any, in children after their consumption of snacks and foods containing sugar.

I understand that you have a busy schedule, and I am grateful for your taking the time to answer the questions on the enclosed forms (it should only take about ten minutes). If you could return the completed questionnaire as soon as possible, I would greatly appreciate it. Please remember that your participation is voluntary and you are not required to complete any or all items.

None of the information you submit will be disclosed to anyone. Your name will be kept in strict confidence.

If you would like to obtain a written summary of the results of this project, please contact me by mail in December of this year at ADDRESS.

Thank you very much for your assistance.

Sincerely,

Sugar on Behavior 35

Name

Appendix E: Consent Form

I, _____ (Print Name), agree to participate in the research project, "Impact of Sugar on Children's Behavior," being carried out by Name. I have been informed by Name of the nature of the project. I understand that I have the right to withhold permission for the researcher to use any data gleaned from my participation.

I also understand that upon my request by mail in December of this year, the researcher will provide me with a written summary of the project's findings.

_____ | _____
Participant's Signature | Date

Appendix D: Sample Thesis

Sugar on Behavior 2

Acknowledgements

Many thanks are extended to:

✍ Dr. XXX, for his expert guidance throughout each step of this project.

✍ "Mom," who took the time to peruse each page of this thesis and offer constructive feedback, even while busy with her own graduate coursework. Thanks also for sparking my interest in the sugar-behavior connection.

✍ The helpful staff in the reference department of Finkelstein Memorial Library. The effort they expended to help me obtain research articles from libraries across New York State is much appreciated.

✍ All the participants in this study who so willingly gave of their time to answer my questions.

Sugar on Behavior 1

IMPACT OF SUGAR ON CHILDREN'S BEHAVIOR

Master's Thesis

Submitted in Partial Fulfillment of Master's Degree in Special Education

Name

College

Date

List of Figures

Figure 1: Instances of Behavioral Changes After Consumption of Sugar 28

Figure 2: Parental Reports of Reactive Behaviors 28

Figure 3: Ages of Reactive and Non-Reactive Children............................ 29

Figure 4: Genders of Children who Reportedly Reacted to Sugar 29

Figure 5: Reported Behavioral Reactions to Sugar-Sweetened Cereals............ 33

Figure 6: Reported Behavioral Reactions to Candy/Chocolate 33

Figure 7: Reported Behavioral Reactions to Sweetened Yogurt.................... 34

Figure 8: Reported Behavioral Reactions to Cake/Cookies........................ 34

Figure 9: Reported Behavioral Reactions to Ices................................ 34

Figure 10: Reported Behavioral Reactions to Soda............................... 35

Figure 11: Frequency of Children's Behavioral Reactions to Sugared Foods........ 35

Figure 12: Types of Behavioral Reactions to Sugar 36

Abstract

Research provides conflicting evidence as to whether or not sugar impacts children's behavior. A number of previous sugar-behavior studies concluded that sugar causes adverse behaviors in children. Other studies, however, refuted these claims. The present study intended to assess possible impacts of sugar on various behaviors in children. Parents and several health professionals from the New York area were surveyed regarding their children's/clients' behaviors after consumption of sugared foods. Data from survey responses were analyzed qualitatively. Approximately one third of the children described in parental questionnaires were reported to show behavior changes after sugar consumption, with irritability and overactivity being the most common reported behavioral reactions. Health professionals believed that sugar exacerbates adverse behaviors in children. Parents, pediatricians, and teachers are recommended to encourage children to eschew sugar consumption. Future research should include longitudinal studies that follow groups of children on diets differing in sugar content. Also, research should include schoolteachers as participants in studies involving children's sugar consumption.

Sugar on Behavior 6

Procedure...27
Data Analysis...27
Results..27
Chapter 4: Implications for Practice and Research.................44
Limitations of Study......................................44
Discussion/ Conclusions..................................45
Implications for Practice.................................49
Implications for Further Research.........................50
References..52
Appendixes...56
Appendix A..56
Appendix B..57
Appendix C..58
Appendix D..59
Appendix E..62
Appendix F..63

Contents

Sugar on Behavior 5

Chapter 1: Introduction..7
Importance of Study.......................................7
Statement of Problem.....................................8
Research Question..8
Definition of Terms.......................................8
Chapter 2: Related Research.....................................10
Introduction..10
What is Sugar..10
Difference Between Table Sugar (Sucrose) and Sugars Released in the Body by
Complex Carbohydrates...................................11
History of Scientific Studies..............................12
Impact of Sugar on Specific Behaviors of Children...........13
Attention...13
Motor Activity..14
Aggression...15
Irritability...16
Factors That May Influence Sugar's Impact on Children's Behavior....17
Age of Children.......................................17
Behavioral History of Children.........................18
Food Consumed with Sugar.............................19
Mechanisms by which Sugar Influences Behavior.............21
Carbohydrate Ingestion with Sugar.....................21
Allergy to Sugar......................................22
Nutrient Deficiency...................................22
Undigested Food in Intestines..........................22
Chapter 3: Methodology..25
Sample..25
Materials..25

Chapter 1: Introduction

Importance of Study

Consumption of sugar in the United States has escalated to astronomic proportions in recent years. In 1999, the average American teenage boy ate at least 109 pounds of sugar per year (Center for Science in the Public Interest, 2000) and derived 9% of his caloric intake from soft drinks alone (Jacobson, 1999). Even toddlers are fed sugar-laden beverages. About one-fifth of the nation's one- and two-year olds were reported to drink soda in 2001 (Schlosser, 2001).

There has been a corresponding increase in hyperactivity and other behavioral problems among America's schoolchildren. Teachers reported a drastic increase in hyperactivity, inattention, learning disorders, and behavioral problems in students during their 20-30 year teaching experience (Null, 1995). Up to 7% of the school-age population is estimated to suffer from Attention Deficit/Hyperactivity Disorder (American Psychiatric Association, 2000).

Anecdotal and empirical evidence from several investigations suggest that sugar may affect children's behavior (Crook 1980; Rapp, 1978). Other reports, however, do not support these claims (Ferguson, Stoddart, & Simeon, 1986; Rosen, et al., 1988; Wolraich, et al., 1994).

The sharp rise in the nation's sugar consumption paralleled by the heightened prevalence of childhood behavioral disorders and the lack of firm conclusions from sugar-behavior studies demonstrate the need for further investigation of the influence of sugar on children's behavior. Dissemination of accurate information regarding the sugar-behavior connection can have practical dietary implications for parents and educators. In

this study, the researcher surveyed parents and health professionals to evaluate how sugar may impact children's behavior.

Statement of Problem

Research provides conflicting evidence regarding sugar's impact on children's behavior. Conclusions of previous studies that examined possible behavioral effects of sugar range from the view that sugar adversely affects behavior (Crook 1980; Rapp, 1978) to the assertion that sugar has no significant effect on behavior (Ferguson, et al., 1986; Rosen, et al., 1988; Wolraich, et al., 1994) to the affirmation that sugar produces salutary effects on behavior (Behar, Rapoport, Adams, Berg, & Cornblath, 1984). This study was intended to ascertain impacts, if any, of sugar on children's behavior via surveys of parents and health professionals.

Research Question

How does sugar impact children's behavior?

Definition of Terms

1- Attention Deficit /Hyperactivity Disorder (AD/HD):

A persistent pattern of inattention and/or hyperactivity-impulsivity that is more frequently displayed and more severe than is typically observed in individuals at a comparable level of development. In addition, the following criteria apply:

a. Some hyperactive-impulsive or inattentive symptoms that cause impairment must have been present before the age of 7 years.

b. Some impairment from the symptoms must be present in at least two settings (e.g., at home, at school, or at work).

c. There must be clear evidence of interference with developmentally appropriate social, academic, or occupational functioning.

d. The disturbance does not occur exclusively during the course of a Pervasive Developmental Disorder, Schizophrenia, or other Psychotic Disorder and is not better accounted for by another mental disorder. (American Psychiatric Association, 2000)

2- Behavior:

Five problematic behaviors will be assessed by researcher-developed, part multiple-choice and part open-ended questionnaires that will be distributed to parents and health professionals. Following are the behaviors, with observable manifestations of each:

a. Irritability- impatience, unobliging, crankiness, moodiness, complaining, frustration.

b. Aggressiveness- anger, hitting, feet stomping, throwing things

c. Inattentiveness- inability to focus, dreaminess, forgetfulness, distractibility, failure to complete tasks

d. Overactivity- increased motor activity, inability to remain at one activity for a reasonable amount of time, engagement in physically dangerous activities

e. Tiredness- sluggishness, sleepiness

Chapter 2: Related Research

Introduction

It is commonly believed that refined sugar encourages inattentive and hyperactive behavior in children. Since scientific validation of this claim would cause Americans to eliminate this possible health hazard from their diets and would also consequently cause major losses for the sugar industry, much effort has been devoted to the field of sugar-behavior research. For over three-quarters of a century, experimenters have been studying the impact of sugar on behavior in children (Shannon, 1922). Investigations have been trying to determine whether, and how, sugar impacts behavior and to identify the factors that might play a role in such effects. Numerous studies with differing methodologic approaches have been conducted to ascertain sugar's impact on attention, motor activity, aggression, and irritability among various subgroups of children. Some researchers have also suggested possible causes of sugar's influence on children's behavior.

What is Sugar?

Sugar is a type of carbohydrate. Carbohydrates can be either simple, short-chain carbohydrates or complex, long-chain carbohydrates. All sugars are simple, short chain carbohydrates. Complex carbohydrates, like starches, are made up of long chains of glucose molecules. The body can break down a complex carbohydrate into glucose, the smallest unit of sugar (Hoffer & Walker, 1996).

Difference Between Table Sugar (Sucrose) and Sugars Released in the Body by Complex Carbohydrates

The body requires glucose as an energy source for brain activity. The body can obtain glucose from complex carbohydrates or from table sugar (Hoffer & Walker, 1996). Obtaining glucose from complex carbohydrates is better for the body for two reasons. Firstly, the complex carbohydrates must be broken down by the body in order to be converted to glucose, and the glucose is therefore released slowly into the bloodstream, producing a slight, as opposed to dramatic, insulin response (Conners, 1989). Secondly, the glucose derived from complex carbohydrates is released into the bloodstream together with other nutrients from the carbohydrates. These nutrients from the carbohydrates help the body metabolize the sugar (Hoffer & Walker, 1996).

Table sugar is a form of sucrose. Sucrose is derived from the manufactured processing of vegetable and fruit products such as sugar cane and beets (Conners, 1989). During the refinement process, a synthetic form of sugar, sucrose, is formed, which no longer contains the vitamins of the original beets or sugar cane. When sucrose is absorbed by the body, other nutrients are not present to help metabolize the sugar (Hoffer & Walker, 1996).

Sucrose is also absorbed quickly into the bloodstream. Sucrose is composed of two molecules, one of fructose and one of glucose. The body can derive the glucose by the simple task of splitting the sucrose molecules. Since the glucose from sucrose molecules is obtained quickly, the glucose is released rapidly into the bloodstream and produces a strong insulin reaction (Conners, 1989). Because of its rapid release into the bloodstream, not in conjunction with other nutrients, sucrose can be harmful to the body (Hoffer & Walker, 1996).

Nearly all of the sugar studies discussed below investigated possible behavioral impacts of sucrose, the most popular form of sugar. Aspartame and saccharin are sugar substitutes that were used for placebos in blind sugar challenge studies.

History of Scientific Studies

Scientists began investigating possible behavioral effects of sugar as early as 1922 (Shannon, 1922). A report published in 1929 described the results of a reduced sugar diet given to a hyperactive 12-year-old boy to relieve his problematic behaviors (Seham & Seham).

Subsequent research began to more firmly establish a connection between problematic behaviors and allergy to various foods, including sugar. In a comprehensive report on the symptoms of food allergy observed in his patients, Rowe (1931) specified several behaviors he found to be induced by allergic foods in sensitive individuals. These allergy-induced behaviors included drowsiness, difficulty concentrating, irritability, and fatigue and were triggered most commonly by wheat, eggs, and milk. In the same report, Rowe mentioned the allergic sensitivity to cane sugar of one patient.

In 1947, in his description of the tension-fatigue syndrome, Randolph attributed children's irritability, fatigue, and inattentiveness to allergenic foods such as wheat and corn. Randolph noted that frequently, corn sugars will cause more immediate allergic reactions than corn starch or whole corn. In 1954, Speer reported restlessness, irritability, and fatigue in children resulting from their allergy to milk, corn, wheat and eggs.

Since then, the research describing the influence of sugar on children's behavior has greatly increased. Controlled studies have been conducted and anecdotal data have been obtained to ascertain sugar's impact on both normal and disturbed children's behavior under varied conditions. Some investigations have supported the hypothesis

Wolraich, et al. (1986) examined the relationship between dietary habits and behavioral problems in boys aged 7 to 12. Dietary records were obtained for a group of hyperactive boys and a matched control group. Several behaviors of the hyperactive boys were then evaluated. The ratio of sugar to total carbohydrates consumed was found to be significantly partially correlated with inattention of the hyperactive boys.

Behar, et al. (1984), Kruesi, et al. (1987), and Wolraich, et al. (1994) conducted double-blind sugar challenge studies with groups of boys aged 6 to 14, 2 to 6, and 6 to 10, respectively, who were considered by their parents to be behaviorally reactive to sugar. Behavioral ratings by trained observers who were blind to the conditions of the studies showed no significant effects of sugar on attentiveness. Continuous Performance Tests that were administered to the children in the study by Behar, et al. also showed no significant sugar effects.

Mahan, et al. (1988) evaluated the behavior of 3- to 10-year-old children after open sugar challenges, using the number of toys children touched per minute as an index of attention span. None of the children tested showed that sugar had any consistent effect on attention.

Motor activity

Studies that have examined the relationship between sugar consumption and children's activity levels have reported conflicting results. Some studies have found that increased activity in children is associated with sugar consumption (Conners & Blouin, 1983; Prinz, et al., 1980; Wolraich, Stumbo, Milch, Chenard, & Schultz, 1986), while others have found either no effects (Kruesi, et al al., 1987), or positive effects (Behar, et al., 1980; Ferguson, et al., 1986; Mahan, et al., 1988; Wolraich, et al., 1994), of sugar on activity.

that sugar adversely affects behavior while others have disagreed, stating that sugar produces either no effect, or salutary effects, on children's behavior.

Studies of Impact of Sugar on Specific Behaviors in Children

Attention

Numerous studies have evaluated the impact of sugar on children's attention. Some have found that sugar causes increased inattention in children (Crook, 1975; Goldman, Lerman, Contois, & Udall, 1986; Prinz & Riddle, 1986; Wolraich, Stumbo, Milich, Chenard, & Schultz, 1986), while others have reported that sugar produces no effect on attention (Behar, et al., 1984; Kruesi, et al., 1987; Mahan, et al., 1988).

Crook (1975) assessed the relationship between food allergy and learning problems in children. Crook found that nervous system symptoms, including inability to concentrate and short attention span, increased dramatically after the ingestion of sugar in 28 of the 45 children studied.

In a study involving two groups of preschool boys, one on a high-sucrose diet, and one on a low-sucrose diet, Prinz and Riddle (1986) found that the boys on the high-sucrose diet scored significantly lower on a Continuous Performance Test than the boys on the low sucrose diet, indicating poorer attention. Similarly, Goldman, et al., (1986) found a decrement in performance on a Continuous Performance Test in preschool children after the children received a sucrose challenge as compared to a placebo. Wender and Solanto (1991) conducted a study resembling that of Goldman, et al, but included two groups of 5- to 7-year-old children: one hyperactive group and one normal group. Interestingly, in Wender and Solanto's study, inattention after ingesting sugar increased only in the hyperactive group.

Sugar on Behavior 15

Prinz, et al. (1980) and Wolraich, et al. (1986) conducted correlational studies with groups of hyperactive children, aged 4 to 7, and 7 to 12, respectively. Prinz, et al. had observers record restless behaviors of the children such as repetition of arm, leg, and head movements. It was found that the amount of sugar products consumed by the children was significantly related to restless behaviors. Wolraich, et al. used ankle actometers, acceleration-sensitive devices worn on the body (Colburn, Smith, Guerine, & Simmon, 1976 as cited in Behar, et al., 1984), to detect motor movement. Sugar to total carbohydrates consumed was found to be positively correlated with activity levels.

In a long-term, double-blind study, minor and gross motor movements of children hospitalized for severe behavior disorders were rated by observers after sugar and placebo challenges. Researchers noted an increase in total movement for sugar challenges as compared to placebo (Conners & Blouin, 1983).

Actometer counts and parental ratings of behavior showed no significant effect of sugar on behavior in another double-blind sugar challenge study (Kruesi, et al., 1987). Several double-blind sugar challenge studies have reported slight but significant *calming* effects in children after sugar challenges as compared with placebo (Behar, et al., 1984; Ferguson, et al., 1986; Mahan, et al., 1988; Wolraich, et al., 1994).

Aggression

Prinz, et al. (1980) reported a correlation between sugar consumption and destructive-aggressive behavior in hyperactive preschool children. Destructive-aggressive behavior was rated by observers during free-play and was defined as attempts at damaging objects in the playroom, hitting, kicking, and throwing objects.

A number of double-blind sugar challenge studies have since disputed the hypothesis that sugar influences aggressive behavior (Kruesi, et al., 1987; Mahan, et al.,

---

Sugar on Behavior 16

1988; Wender & Solanto, 1991). These studies involved both hyperactive and normal children of various ages and found no significant effects of sugar on aggression.

Irritability

Pediatric allergists Rapp (1978) and Crook (1980) reported that sugar caused acute reactions of irritability in their patients. The allergists put their hyperactive patients on elimination diets which excluded suspect foods, including sugar. The eliminated foods were then individually reintroduced to the patients' diets and reactions were noted.

In Rapp's (1978) study, research assistants observed that a single sugar ingestion challenge test consistently caused irritability in 2 of the 24 patients tested. Crook (1980) quoted several questionnaire responses of parents of his patients which described changes in irritability following dietary elimination. A parent of a 2½-year-old girl declared: "as little as one teaspoon of sugar will cause constant crying, irritability, and tantrums. Since taking her off sugar, I feel as though someone has given me a different child" (p. 55).

A parent of a 6-year-old boy wrote: "Even a few bites of sugar, corn or eggs cause hyperactivity, nervousness....and other allergy symptoms" (Crook, 1980, p. 55). Yet another parent asserted about a 12-year-old child: "sugar, milk, chocolate, and prepared foods containing preservatives cause him to be nervous and irritable. I used to use Ritalin. Although it did slow him down, he was still irritable, and controlling his diet helped him even more" (Crook, 1980, p. 56).

A double-blind sugar challenge study which tested the behavior of 14- to 19-year-old delinquent students did not support the claims of Rapp (1978) and Crook (1980). Experimenter ratings of mood did not interact statistically with substance (Bachorowski, et al., 1990).

Sugar on Behavior 17

Factors That May Influence Sugar's Impact on Children's Behavior

Several factors may help explain the inconsistencies in the findings of sugar-behavior studies. Among these factors are differences in age of children studied (Goldman, et al., 1986; Kaplan, et al., 1989), differences in behavioral diagnoses of children studied (Wender & Solanto, 1991), and varied types of foods consumed with sugar (Conners, 1989).

Age of Children

Research has suggested that younger children may be more sensitive than older children to food substances (Lipton, Nemeroff, & Mailman, 1979 as cited in Goldman, et al., 1986; Harley, Ray, Tomasi, et al., 1978 as cited in Kaplan, et al., 1989; Weiss, Williams, Margen, et al., 1980 as cited in Kaplan, et al., 1989). Several sugar challenge studies have therefore included two groups of children, preschool and elementary, to determine if younger children display more overt behavioral reactions to sugar than older children (Rosen, et al., 1988; Wolraich, et al., 1994).

Rosen, et al. (1988) tested the cognition and behavior of two groups of children after double-blind sugar and placebo challenges. One group consisted of 30 preschool children with a mean age of 5 years; the other consisted of 15 first and second grade children with a mean age of 7 years. None of the children in the study were diagnosed with behavioral disorders. All the children received equal amounts of the sweeteners. When researchers analyzed the results of cognitive tests that were administered after sugar challenges, it was found that sugar affected the preschoolers differently than it affected the elementary school children.

Wolraich, et al. (1994) conducted a double-blind sugar/placebo trial which involved one group of 25 normal preschool children, aged 3 to 5 years, and one group of

Sugar on Behavior 18

23 elementary school children, aged 6 to 10 years, who were considered by their parents to be sensitive to sugar. Participants and their families followed different diets for each of three consecutive 3-week periods. One diet was high in sucrose; the other two were low in sucrose and contained different sugar substitutes.

Researchers and parents evaluated the cognition and behavior of the children weekly. The 6- to 10- year-old children showed no cognitive or behavioral effects of sucrose. For this group, there were no significant differences among the different diets in any of the 39 behavioral and cognitive variables tested (Wolraich, et al., 1994).

Two of 31 variables tested on the preschool group showed significant effects of the sucrose diet. The preschool children's performance on a pegboard task was significantly slower during the sucrose diet. Parental ratings of the preschool children's cognition, however, were significantly *better* during the sucrose diet than during the sugar substitute diets (Wolraich, et al., 1994).

A number of sugar-behavior studies have been conducted on one group of children between the ages of 2 and 6 years but have not included a second group of older children subjected to the same conditions. Two such studies reported adverse behavioral effects of sugar in preschool children (Goldman, et al., 1986; Prinz & Riddle, 1986). Two other studies found no effects of sugar on the behavior of preschool children (Ferguson, et al., 1986; Kruesi, et al., 1987).

Behavioral History of Children

Researchers have proposed that hyperactive children may be more sensitive to the effects of sugar than normal children (Prinz, et al., 1980; Tauraso, 1983 as cited in Rosen, et al., 1988; Wender & Solanto, 1991). Two studies tested this hypothesis (Rosen, et al., 1988; Wender & Solanto, 1991).

Wender and Solanto (1991) assessed attention and aggression in a group of children with Attention Deficit Hyperactivity Disorder and in a group of aged-matched, normal children after sugar challenges. Research assistants noted no significant effect of sugar on aggression in either group of children. Scores of continuous performance tasks, however, showed an increase in inattention following sugar challenges only in the hyperactive group of children.

Rosen, et al. (1988) conducted a sugar challenge study with a group of children who were not diagnosed with Attention Deficit Disorder. To ascertain whether hyperactivity influenced the children's reactions to sugar, the researchers formed two groups of children: one scoring high, and one scoring low, on the Hyperactivity Index of the behavioral rating scale completed by teachers of the children. Researchers found no significant effects of sugar for either the high- or the low- rated children on the Hyperactivity Index.

Food Consumed with Sugar

A few studies have shown that sugar's effects on behavior differ are dependent on whether the sugar is consumed alone, together with carbohydrates, or together with protein. In one experiment involving normal and hyperactive children, Conners (1989) administered sugar and placebo challenges alone, together with carbohydrate breakfasts, and together with protein breakfasts. The children's attention after sugar challenges was then compared with their attention after sugar challenges for each type of meal. For the hyperactive children, Conners reported that sugar increased inattention when eaten with carbohydrates, sugar caused no change in attention when eaten alone, and sugar improved attention when eaten with protein. In the normal children, Conners found poorer attention after sugar-carbohydrate meals than after sugar-protein meals. Spring, et

al. (1987) concluded that the consumption of carbohydrate-rich, protein-poor meals induced drowsiness in adults.

Wender and Solanto (1991) assessed attention in normal and hyperactive children after sugar and placebo challenges with carbohydrate breakfasts. The hyperactive children displayed poorer attention after carbohydrate meals with sugar than after carbohydrate meals with placebo sweeteners. The normal children showed no difference between attention after carbohydrate meals with sugar and after carbohydrate meals with placebo sweeteners.

Rosen, et al. (1988) studied the behavior of normal preschool children after sugar and placebo challenges given with carbohydrate breakfasts. A small increase in activity level was reported after sugar-carbohydrate meals.

Bachorowski (1990) studied the behavior of delinquent and non-delinquent students after sucrose challenges with carbohydrate breakfasts. Results were inconsistent with those reported by Conners (1989) and Rosen, et al. (1988). Sugar consumed with carbohydrate breakfasts improved the performance of delinquents rated as more behaviorally disturbed and impaired the performance of delinquents with less pronounced behavioral problems.

Mahan, et al. (1988) tested the behavior of 5 children before and after sugar challenges given with lunch consisting of balanced amounts of carbohydrates and protein. Two of the 5 children tested showed significant increases in movement after the sugar challenge. One of the children also showed an increase in non-compliance, aggression, and distractibility.

Some studies have administered sugar challenges to children after overnight fasts to eliminate effects of carbohydrate or protein consumed with sugar (Behar, et al., 1984;

Sugar on Behavior 21

Goldman, et al., 1984). Results of these studies are inconsistent. Behar, et al. noted a calming effect of sugar in children, while Goldman, et al. reported restless and distractibility in children after sugar challenges following overnight fasts.

Mechanisms by which Sugar Influences Behavior

Nutritionists, medical practitioners, and researchers have tried to explain the ways in which sugar causes behavior changes in children. Carbohydrate ingestion with sugar (Conners, 1989; Hoffer & Walker, 1996; Milich, Wolraich & Lindgren, 1986), allergy to sugar (Hoffer & Walker, 1996), nutrient deficiency as a result of sugar ingestion (Hoffer & Walker, 1996), and undigested food in intestines (Crook, 1987 as cited in Appleton, 1996) have been proffered as possible mechanisms by which sugar influences children's behavior.

Carbohydrate Ingestion with Sugar

It has been suggested that the body's insulin response to a meal consisting of only carbohydrates causes an increase in the amount of the amino acid tryptophan in the brain (Wurtman & Wurtman, 1977). Tryptophan is essential to the production of the brain neurotransmitter serotonin. The rise in the level of tryptophan in the brain thus causes an increase in the amount of serotonin in the brain (Conners, 1989; Wurtman & Suffes, 1996; Wurtman & Wurtman, 1977). This neurotransmitter, serotonin, is used by the brain to control functions such as perception, thinking, feeling, and generalized activity (Hoffer & Walker, 1996). The increase of serotonin in the brain (caused by ingestion of carbohydrates) may possibly slow children's thought processes (Conners, 1989).

Researchers have found that when protein is consumed with sugar, the brain decreases its production of serotonin. This is because the amino acids (which make up protein) compete with the amino acid tryptophan for entrance into the brain. Because of

Sugar on Behavior 22

the competition among the different types of amino acids, only small amounts of tryptophan are able to enter the brain. The reduction of tryptophan in the brain causes a decrease in the amount of serotonin in the brain (Wurtman & Wurtman, 1977). A decrease in serotonin level in the brain can cause changes in behavior (Conners, 1989; Milich, Wolraich & Lindgren, 1986).

Allergy to Sugar

Pediatricians and allergists disagree about whether behavioral reactions to foods can be considered allergic responses. Many medical experts believe that the term "allergy" strictly denotes responses of the immune system (Crook, 1977). Other authorities disagree (Crook, 1977; Hoffer & Walker, 1996; Rowe, 1972), asserting that "in addition to causing wheezing, sneezing and itching, allergy often causes manifestations involving almost any and every part of the body, including the brain and nervous system" (Crook, 1977, p. 47). Allergic reactions to sugar of the central nervous system include hyperactivity, fatigue, and irritability (Crook, 1977).

Nutrient Deficiency

Natural sources of sugar contain the vitamins and minerals necessary for its metabolism. Sucrose, or refined sugar, has been stripped of these elements. The body must therefore take nutrients from other foods or break down its own tissue in order to metabolize sugar. The nutrient deficiency created by sugar consumption can cause hyperactivity (Buchanan, 1984).

Undigested Food in Intestines

Research has shown that mice which ingested sugar had an increased amount of candida, a type of fungus, in their intestines. When people have large amounts of this fungus in their intestines, partially digested food can get from the intestines into the

Sugar on Behavior 24

Nutrient deficiency can result from sugar consumption and can cause behavior changes (Buchanan, 1984). Sugar consumption can also cause undigested food to be let into the bloodstream, which can result in hyperactivity (Crook, 1987 as cited in Appleton, 1996).

Sugar on Behavior 23

bloodstream. The undigested food can cause hyperactivity (Crook, 1987 as cited in Appleton, 1996).

Summary

Sucrose, or common table sugar, is an artificial form of sugar which has no nutritive value. The body can obtain all sugars necessary for brain activity from whole foods such as complex carbohydrates and fruit (Hoffer & Walker, 1996). Not only is sugar unnecessary for the body, but it may adversely affect children's behavior.

Since 1922, researchers have been studying possible impacts of sugar on children's behavior (Shannon, 1922). Both open and blind sugar challenge studies have been conducted, but results have been inconclusive. Some studies indicated that children become inattentive, overactive, aggressive, or irritable after sugar ingestion (Conners & Blouin, 1983; Crook, 1975; Goldman, Lerman, Contois, & Udall, 1986; Prinz & Riddle, 1986). Other studies showed that sugar had no effect on these behaviors in children (Ferguson, et al., 1986; Kruesi, et al., 1987; Rosen, et al., 1988; Wolraich, et al., 1994).

Research has suggested several factors that may influence sugar's impact on children's behavior. Some of these factors are the ages of the children (Rosen, et al., 1988; Wolraich, et al., 1994), whether or not the children are hyperactive (Prinz, et al., 1980; Tauraso, 1983 as cited in Rosen, et al., 1988; Wender & Solanto, 1991), and the types of food consumed with the sugar (Conners, 1989).

Researchers have explained a number of mechanisms by which sugar impacts children's behavior. Carbohydrate ingestion with sugar causes an increase in the production of the brain neurotransmitter serotonin. This increase in serotonin can cause behavior changes (Conners, 1989; Milich, Wolraich & Lindgren, 1986). Children's behavioral reactions to sugar may be allergic responses (Hoffer & Walker, 1996).

Chapter 3: Methodology

Sample

The sample in this study included parents and health professionals. Forty middle-class, Orthodox Jewish parents who reside in the New York Tri-State area were surveyed. To increase the response rate, the sample of parents consisted mostly of acquaintances of the researcher.

Seven health professionals who practice in Rockland County, NY, also participated in the study. The health professionals included three nutritionists, two allergists, one chiropractor/alternative medical healer, and one physician's assistant/nutritionist. Most of the health professionals were referred to the researcher by acquaintances.

Materials

To evaluate the impact of sugar on children's behavior, two questionnaires were developed by the researcher; one for distribution to targeted parents and the other for distribution to several health practitioners. The questionnaires consisted of multiple-choice questions together with some open-ended questions. Content and consensual validity was obtained for both questionnaires. Interrater reliability ensured consistency of recording procedures.

The first part of the parental questionnaire consisted of a chart which lists five types of adverse behaviors and eight different types of sugared foods. On the chart, the parents are asked to rate the frequency at which each listed behavior is displayed by a sugar-reactive child as a result of the consumption of the foods. The descriptive terms 'never,' 'infrequently,' 'frequently,' and 'very often' were used to rate the frequency of

the behaviors. Each parent received two copies of the chart, so that behaviors of two children could be recorded separately. The second part of the questionnaire was open-ended and more detailed. It included questions about about the nature and causes of the reactions. A sample of the parental questionnaire is included in appendix D.

The first part of the health professional questionnaire also consisted of a chart listing five adverse behaviors and eight sugared foods. The health professionals were asked to estimate the number of children they have treated that have exhibited the listed behaviors after consuming the specified sugared foods.

The second part of the questionnaire for health professionals was mostly open-ended. The health practitioners were asked for specific information concerning the children who reacted to the sugared foods and their behavioral reactions. A sample of this questionnaire is included in appendix F.

A researcher-written cover letter which briefly describes the thesis study accompanied each questionnaire. A sample of the cover letter for the parental questionnaire is included in appendix B. A sample of the cover letter for the health professional questionnaire is included in appendix E. Appendix C contains a copy of the consent form that will be included with the mailed questionnaires.

Before distributing the questionnaires, the researcher called parents and health professionals to ask if they are willing to participate in the survey. The researcher stated that participation is voluntary and that all names will be kept confidential. If the parent/health professional agreed to participate, the researcher gave him/her the choice of answering over the phone or in writing, by mail. Refer to appendix A for a sample of the phone script for calls to parents and health professionals.

Procedure

1. The researcher developed a questionnaire to distribute to parents.

2. The researcher developed a questionnaire to distribute to allergists and nutritionists.

3. The researcher formulated a list of parents who may have been willing to be surveyed. The majority of these parents were acquaintances of the researcher.

4. The researcher phoned the parents on the list to ask if they are willing to participate in the survey and if the researcher may mail them the questionnaires. The researcher gave the parents the option to answer the questions over the phone.

5. The researcher mailed questionnaires along with consent forms and addressed, stamped return envelopes to the parents who agreed to respond.

6. The researcher formulated a list of allergists and nutritionists in the Rockland County area.

7. The researcher phoned the allergists and nutritionists to ask if they would participate in the survey and if the researcher may mail the questionnaires to them or personally interview them.

8. The researcher mailed questionnaires along with consent forms and addressed, stamped return envelopes to the health professionals who agreed to respond.

9. Data from the returned questionnaires were analyzed.

Data Analysis

Data were analyzed using qualitative measures.

Results

This study was guided by the research question "How does sugar impact children's behavior?"

Parental Questionnaires

Approximately 75 parental questionnaires were distributed to co-workers and other acquaintances of the researcher. Forty parents responded to the questionnaire.

Children's Reactions to Sugar

Each parent answered questions about ways in which sugar may impact the behavior of his/her 2- to 16- year-old child/ren. There were a total of 118 2- to 16- year-old children in the 40 families who participated in this survey. As shown in Figure 1, 66% of these children were reported to show no behavioral reactions to the listed sugared foods. Thirty-four percent of the children were reported to display behavioral changes at least sometimes after consuming some foods.

Instances of Behavioral Changes after Consumption of Sugar

- Children who showed behavioral changes after consuming sugar
- Children who did not show behavior changes after consuming sugar

Figure 1

Parental Reports of Reactive Behaviors

Of the 40 parents who answered the questionnaire, 57% reported some degree of reactive behavior in at least one child. Forty-three percent of the parents replied that none of their children ever exhibited reactive behaviors to sugared foods. Figure 2 depicts these findings.

Parental Reports of Reactive Behaviors

- Parents Who Reported Reactive Behaviors for At Least One Child
- Parents Who Did Not Report Reactive Behaviors for their Children

Figure 2

Ages of Children

Figure 3 shows the division of children who were reported as behaviorally reactive and non-reactive to sugar, by age group.

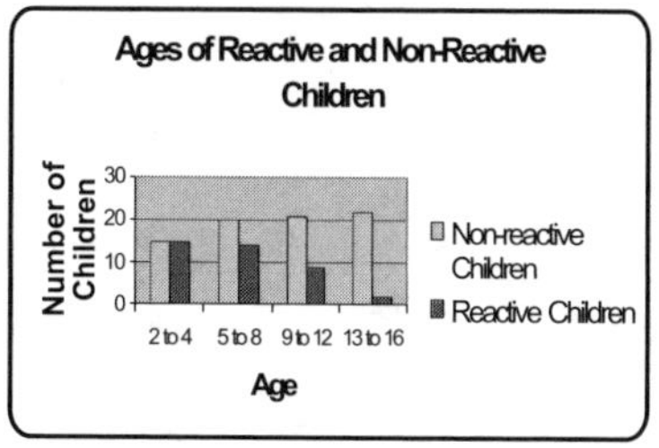

- There were an equal number of children in the 2-4 year-old age group who were reported as behaviorally sugar-reactive and non-reactive.

- As the children's ages increased from 5 to 16 years, the number of children per age group that reportedly reacted to sugar decreased.

- A mother described her 8-year-old child as inattentive and hyperactive after eating sugared foods. She commented that she had an older son with the same reactions to sugar. As a child, the boy could not withstand the peer pressure of abstaining from sugar. However, at age 16, the child was able to completely eliminate sugar from his diet, and his hyperactive behaviors ceased as a result.

Genders of Children Who Reportedly Reacted to Sugar

Of the children who reportedly reacted to sugar,

- 60% were male
- 40% were female

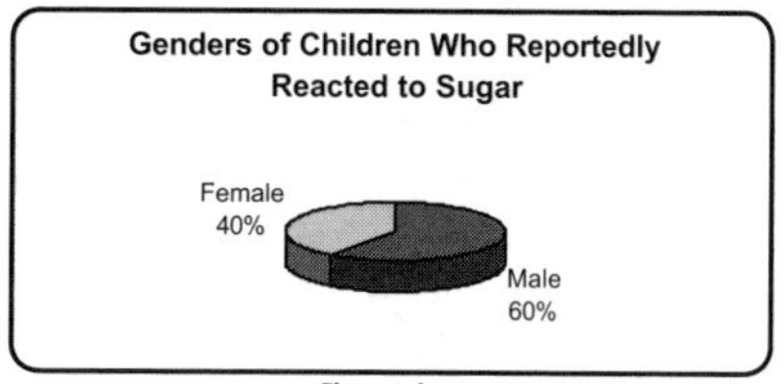

Ages of Reactive and Non-Reactive Children
(Number of Children vs. Age: 2 to 4, 5 to 8, 9 to 12, 13 to 16; legend: Non-reactive Children, Reactive Children)

Figure 3

Genders of Children Who Reportedly Reacted to Sugar
Female 40%, Male 60%

Figure 4

- A mother of 9-year-old twins, a boy and a girl, remarked that the boy shows behavioral reactions to sugared foods, while the girl does not react when she consumes the same foods.

Frequency of Consumption of Sugared Foods and Snacks

- Frequency of consumption of sugared foods and snacks was similar for children who did and did not reportedly react to sugared foods.

Elimination of Sugar

- Of the 23 parents who reported behavioral changes in their children from sugar, 43% eliminated sugar from their children's diets. *All* of these parents noticed improvement in their child/ren's negative behaviors after sugar was removed from their diets.

- Some parents commented on the drastic calming effect of sugar elimination on their children:

  - "As I eliminated as much sugar as possible from his diet I noticed how much calmer and relaxed he was."

  - "Decreased consumption of sugar makes my children calmer and in a 'sweet disposition.'"

- One mother who never correlated her children's sugar intake with negative behavior eliminated sugar from her son's diet for one month. She described her son as unfocused and inattentive. She did not notice any changes in the child's behavior after she eliminated sugar from his diet.

Immediacy of Reactions

Of the parents who noticed that their children reacted behaviorally to sugar:

Sugar on Behavior 31

- 54% reported that the reactions were immediate (within 30 minutes of sugar consumption).
- 23% reported that the reactions were delayed.
- 9% reported that the reactions were both immediate and delayed.
- 14% did not answer this question.

Of the parents who observed delayed reactions,

- Most reported reactions between 30 minutes and one hour after the children's sugar intake.
- One parent reported that if her children ate sugar at night, behavioral reactions were observed the next day.

Other Instances of Behavioral Reactions

Parents who reported behavior changes in their children after their consumption of sugared foods were asked whether any other foods or circumstances triggered the same reactions.

- 50% of the parents stated that no other foods or circumstances brought about the behavior changes their children displayed after sugar consumption.
- 36% of the parents replied that other foods or circumstances brought about the reactions they observed after their children's consumption of sweet foods.
- 14% of the parents did not answer this question.

Following are foods that parents believed to cause identical negative behavioral reactions in their children after sugar consumption:

- food coloring
- caffeine
- preservatives
- honey

Sugar on Behavior 32

- dairy
- foods high in fat

One mother commented that when her children "join in 'fun' with other siblings," she observes behavioral reactions similar to those caused by sugar.

Sugar-Induced Problems in School

When asked whether behavioral reactions to sugar caused their children to encounter problems in school,

- 74% of parents answered "no."
- 4% of parents answered "yes."
- 4% of parents answered that they didn't know.
- 17% of parents did not answer the question.

- Two parents mentioned that sugar did not pose a problem for their children in school since the schools their children attended permitted the children to bring only healthy snacks.

Allergy to Sugar

When asked whether they thought their children were allergic to sugar,

- 82% of parents answered "no."
- 9% of parents answered "yes."
- 9% of parents answered that they did not know.

Number of Sugar-Reactive Children Per Multiple-Child Family

Ten of the parents who reported behavioral reactions to sugar in their children had three or more children between the ages of 2 and 16.

- Approximately half of the children in each of these families displayed behavioral reactions to sugar.

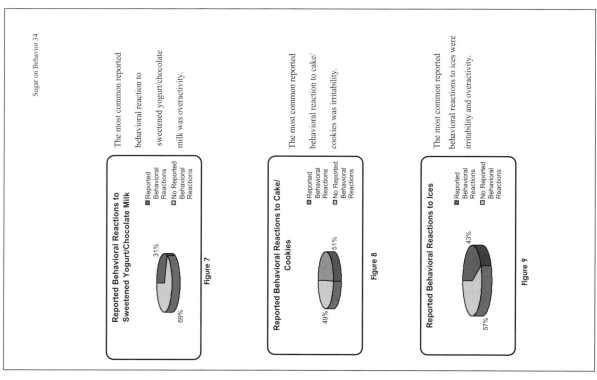

The most common reported behavioral reaction to sweetened yogurt/chocolate milk was overactivity.

Reported Behavioral Reactions to Sweetened Yogurt/Chocolate Milk

Figure 7

The most common reported behavioral reaction to cake/cookies was irritability.

Reported Behavioral Reactions to Cake/Cookies

Figure 8

The most common reported behavioral reactions to ices were irritability and overactivity.

Reported Behavioral Reactions to Ices

Figure 9

Reported Behavioral Reactions to Sugared Foods of Children Believed to be Sugar-Reactive

Charts describing reactions of children who reacted at least sometimes to some foods were analyzed to determine the frequency of reactions to each food. For each food listed on the questionnaires, parents answered whether they observed each of five different behavioral reactions never, infrequently, frequently, or very often. The responses of reactions to a food that were infrequent, frequent, and very often were added to attain the total number of reactions to that food. The total number of reactions was then compared with the number of reports of no reactions to that food. (If a child showed all five behavioral reactions to a food, this counted as five responses of reaction to that food. If a child showed only two behavioral reactions to a food, this counted as two responses of reaction and three responses of no reaction.) The number of reports of behavioral reactions to each food is presented below as a percentage.

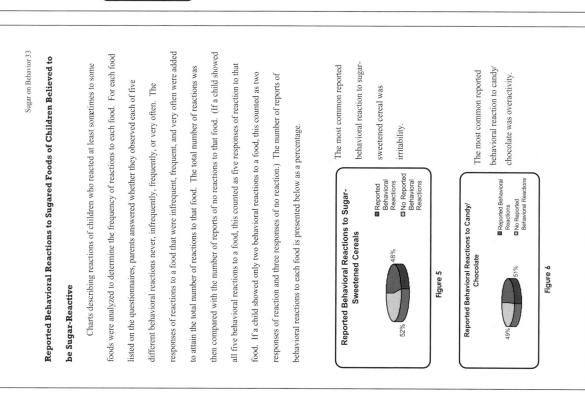

The most common reported behavioral reaction to sugar-sweetened cereal was irritability.

Reported Behavioral Reactions to Sugar-Sweetened Cereals

Figure 5

The most common reported behavioral reaction to candy/chocolate was overactivity.

Reported Behavioral Reactions to Candy/Chocolate

Figure 6

Reported Behavioral Reactions to Soda

■ Reported Behavioral Reactions
☐ No Reported Behavioral Reactions

49%   51%

Figure 10

The most common reported behavioral reaction to soda was irritability.

Sugar Consumed Alone/Sugar Consumed with Other Foods

- Three parents observed that sugar eaten on an empty stomach exacerbates behavioral reactions.

- Two parents noted that pure sugar snacks, such as candy, ices, and soda cause more pronounced behavioral reactions than sugar snacks which are mixed with other foods, such as cake, cookies, or sweet cereals.

- Four parents pointed out that protein foods consumed with sugar balance out sugar effects.

Frequency of All Children's Behavioral Reactions to Sugared Food In General

All reactions to sugared foods that were reported as infrequent were added to find the total number of infrequent reactions. The total numbers of reactions that were reported frequent and very often were also calculated. The total numbers of reports of each frequency are presented in

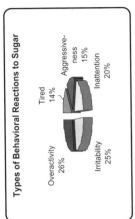

Frequency of Children's Behavioral Reactions to Sugared Food

Very Often 5%
Frequent 29%
Infrequent 66%

Figure 11

Figure 11 as percentages of total reported reactions.

Types of Behavioral Reactions to Sugar

Reports of each behavioral reaction that were infrequent, frequent, and very often were added to attain the total number of reports of the behavioral reaction. The numbers are presented in Figure 12 as percentages.

Types of Behavioral Reactions to Sugar

Tired 14%
Aggressiveness 15%
Inattention 20%
Irritability 25%
Overactivity 26%

Figure 12

Parent's descriptions of their children's behavior after sugar ingestion mainly concerned the two most frequent reactions, overactivity and irritability.

Parents described their children's overactivity after they consumed sugared foods:

- "he looks like he's running on adrenalin…like there are super-springs in him."

- "they…run and jump on my furniture."

- "[they become] more energetic and hyper."

One parent told of her children's irritable dispositions after they ate foods with sugar:

- "Both children become difficult to reason with. They only want to watch TV.".

One mother who indicated that her child became overactive after sugar consumption remarked that she believed her child became more excited *about* eating the food than *from* it.

Sugar on Behavior 37

Surveys of Health Professionals

Seven health professionals participated in this study. Three were nutritionists by profession, one was a chiropractor, one was a physician's assistant and nutritionist who specialized in orthomolecular medicine, and two were allergists. Two of the nutritionists, the chiropractor, and one allergist completed questionnaires. The third nutritionist and the second allergist were interviewed by phone, and the PA/nutritionist was interviewed in person.

Children's Behaviors as a Result of Sugar Consumption

One nutritionist indicated that her clients' most common behavioral reactions to sugar were tiredness and irritability. Another nutritionist wrote that the most common behavioral reactions of her clients were inattention and irritability. The third nutritionist could not comment about behavioral reactions specifically to sugar since she recommends that her clients eliminate multiple foods from their diets at once. The chiropractor observed only inattention and overactivity in his clients. The PA's clients' main behavioral reaction to sugar was hyperactivity.

Both allergists replied that they did not treat children who were sensitive to sugar. They maintained that the term "allergy" refers to an immunological response of the body to a foreign substance. A change in behavior, they felt, may result from sensitivity, but not allergy, to a food. They therefore could not offer information regarding behavioral reactions to sugar.

Behavioral Reactions to Specific Sugared Foods

One nutritionist reported found that the foods which most frequently caused behavioral reactions, in decreasing order of frequency, were cake/cookies, cereals, soda, and candy. The second nutritionist reported the same four foods, in the reverse order, to

Sugar on Behavior 38

cause the most frequent behavioral reactions. The chiropractor did not note any differences in reaction among the various types of sweet foods. The PA explained that fiber and protein slow digestion of food, and therefore mitigate behavioral effects when they are eaten with sugar.

Genders of Sugar Responders

The two nutritionists who completed the questionnaires found that there were an equal amount of girls and boys who reacted to sugared foods. The chiropractor noted that of his clients who reacted to sugared foods, there were significantly more boys than girls.

Ages of Sugar Responders

One nutritionist and the PA indicated that children of different age groups were equally as likely to react to sugar. Another nutritionist wrote that children in the 5-8-year age group were most likely to react to sugar. The chiropractor wrote that children between the ages of 5 and 12 were most likely to react to sugar.

Immediacy of Reactions

Table 1 shows the responses of several health professionals to the question of whether the behavioral reactions of their clients to sugar were immediate or delayed. Reactions that occurred within 30 minutes of sugar ingestion were considered immediate.

Health Professional	Immediacy of Clients' Reactions to Sugared Foods
Nutritionist 1	Fluctuated with age/size of patient Up to 24 hours after sugar consumption
Nutritionist 2	Immediate
Chiropractor	Immediate and delayed. When delayed, one hour after sugar ingestion.
Physician's Assistant/Nutritionist	Overactivity observed immediately. Tiredness at times observed one hour later.

Table 1

Initial Complaints of Parents

The surveyed health professionals wrote that initial complaints of parents when they came to seek treatment for their children included concerns that their children were overactive, unfocused, easily distractible, weepy, impulsive, uncontrollable, oppositional, and aggressive.

Physical Symptoms that Accompanied Sugar Sensitivity

The health professionals mentioned that the children's behavioral reactions to sugar were often accompanied by physical symptoms such as abdominal pain and eczema.

Parents' Awareness of Children's Sugar Sensitivities

The health professionals noted that the children's parents were not aware of the children's sugar sensitivities when they first came to seek treatment.

Problems at School

The health professionals reported that most parents of sugar-reactive children complained about their children's problems at school.

Causes of Reactions

The health professionals proffered several possible reasons for sugar's effect on children's behavior. Following are possible causes they identified.

- Allergy/Sensitivity to Sugar Due to Overconsumption - When a person consumes an excessive amount of a food, the body will become sensitive to that food and can begin to respond to it in a negative way. There was disagreement among the health professionals as to whether the term "allergy" can be used to describe behavioral reactions to sugar. The two allergists maintained that only immunological responses of the body are considered allergic reactions. Responses of other systems of the body, they believed, should be labeled "sensitivities." One nutritionist wrote that some of her clients were allergic to sugar. Other nutritionists explained that just as the immune system can react allergically to the ingestion of a food by producing a skin rash, so can the brain react to sugared foods by bringing about changes in behavior. Though they are uncertain of whether the term "allergy" can be applied, behavioral reactions are "observable clinical responses."

- Insulin Response - There is normally one teaspoon of sugar in a person's bloodstream at any given time. When someone ingests, for example, six teaspoons of table sugar in a sweet snack, the sugar travels directly into the blood and the body must then produce a large amount of insulin to "normalize" the blood sugar level. This insulin reaction can cause the blood

Sugar on Behavior 41

sugar level in the body to drop drastically, producing a hypoglycemic effect and resulting in behavior changes.

- Changes in Levels of Brain Neurotransmitters - Sugar ingestion can increase levels of certain neurotransmitters in the brain and thereby affect behavior.

- Vitamin Deficiency - Digestion of sucrose depletes the body of vital nutrients, including B-vitamins, chromium, magnesium, and calcium. Deficiency of these nutrients can cause negative behaviors. Calcium and magnesium, for instance, can have a calming effect on people (Null, 2000).

One nutritionist commented: "Sugar is a drug...There is always a reaction to its consumption. We don't always see it immediately..."

Other Foods/ Circumstances that Triggered Similar Behavioral Reactions

The foods that health professionals found to cause similar behavioral reactions to sugar included:

- White flour
- Wheat gluten
- Dairy
- Food coloring
- Artificial flavoring

The circumstances which reportedly triggered behavioral reactions similar to those caused by sugar were:

- Presence of allergens
- Anxiety

Sugar on Behavior 42

Sugar Elimination

The PA/nutritionist, chiropractor, all three nutritionists reported that they very often or always recommend that their clients avoid sugar. The PA mentioned that he advises his clients to eliminate all forms of sugar from their diets, including honey, fruit juice, and cane juice.

Respondents to Sugar Elimination

All the health professionals who advised their clients to eliminate sugar from their diets reported that the behaviors usually improved after sugar elimination. One nutritionist found that behaviors of her clients always improved with sugar elimination.

The PA/nutritionist reported that he treats about 1-2 children per month who have Attention Deficit/Hyperactivity Disorder. He always recommends that the children eliminate sugar, along with wheat and diary, from their diets. He found that after dietary elimination, about half of the patients showed marked behavioral improvement and no longer needed to take medication for hyperactivity.

Problems in School

All the health professionals who advised their clients to eliminate sugar reported that the children's problems in school usually improved after sugar elimination. One nutritionist found that her clients' problems at school always improved with sugar elimination.

Time until Improvement is Noticed

The health professionals were asked to tell after how long on elimination diets the children showed improvement. The responses were:

- 24 hours
- 1 week

Sugar on Behavior 44

Chapter 4: Implications for Practice and Research

Limitations of Study

1. Since this study was qualitative in nature, no generalization was possible.

2. Controlled experiments were not conducted in this study. Therefore, cause-and-effect relationships between sugar and behavior could not be determined.

3. The sample of parents and health professionals in this study was small. It is possible, then, that the responses offered by the sample did not reflect the view of the larger population.

4. Researcher bias may have played a role in sample selection. The researcher may have chosen to survey several parents because she suspected their children reacted to sugar.

5. Parents may not have been adequately aware of the sugared foods their children ate and if the children's behaviors were related to the consumption of those foods.

6. Parents may have reported spurious behavior changes after sugar elimination due to expectancy effects.

7. Parents may have misinterpreted some questions on the questionnaires, resulting in inaccurate reports.

8. Parents may have incorrectly estimated the frequency of their children's behavioral reactions to sugared foods. Health professionals may have incorrectly estimated the number of their clients who reacted to sugared foods.

Sugar on Behavior 43

- 1 day to 1 month
- 4-7 days
- Weeks to months

Discussion/ Conclusions

Research Question

How does sugar impact children's behavior?

Possible Explanations for Differences in Findings of Previous Research Compared to Present Study

Sugar Sensitivity

Many studies which involved eliminating sugar from children's diets (for up to several weeks) have found that sugar does not affect children's behavior (Ferguson, et al., 1986; Rosen, et al., 1988; Wolraich, et al., 1994). A possible explanation for the discrepancy between the findings of those studies and the present study is that some children may be sensitive to sugar, while others may not be affected at all by sweet foods. In many of the sugar challenge studies which found that sugar does not affect behavior, children were selected at random to participate in the studies. The selected children, therefore, may not have been sensitive to sugared foods, and hence did not react with behavior changes.

Some of the parents who took part in this study were asked to participate because the researcher suspected that a child of theirs may react to sugared foods. A larger percentage of the children, therefore, were reported to react behaviorally to sugar.

One may contend that some parents erroneously attribute all of their children's misbehavior to sugar consumption. However, results of this study showed that parents who answered questions regarding three or more of their children reported only half of the children as "sugar-reactive." This fact demonstrates that parents did not label

children "sugar-reactive" without reason, but rather used discretion in describing some children as reactive to sugar and others as non-reactive.

Presence of Observers

In many research studies, trained observers or research assistants recorded children's behaviors after sugar challenges. The children may not have displayed certain behaviors, e.g. complaining, hitting, etc. due to the presence of unfamiliar people. In this study, parents commented about behaviors they noticed in their children at home. Since children act more naturally in their homes when only family members are present, parents may have detected reactive behaviors that wouldn't be seen by research observers.

Length of Observation Time

Parents also responded to the questions in the questionnaire based on their experiences over the course of several years. Reactive behavior changes may be far less noticeable when a food is consumed only once as part of a challenge study. Other circumstances may also negate effects of one-time sugar intake, such as if other foods were eaten with sugar, fatigue, etc.

False Placebos

Experimental studies used artificial sweeteners such as aspartame and saccharin in foods given to the control groups (Bachorowski, 1990; Behar, et al., 1984; Ferguson, et al., 1986; Gross, 1984; Kruesi, et al., 1987; Wolraich, et al., 1994). These sugar substitutes contain chemicals and artificial substances and can cause behavioral change (Spring, et al., 1987). Children in the control groups may have had behavioral reactions to the artificial "placebo" foods and perhaps therefore no differences in behavior were noted between the children on the control and sucrose diets.

Ages of Children

In this study, the younger the child, the more likely he/she was to show behavioral reactions to sugar. This finding was in accordance with previous research which has suggested that younger children may be more sensitive than older children to food substances (Lipton, Nemeroff, & Mailman, 1979 as cited in Goldman, et al., 1986; Harley, Ray, Tomasi, et al., 1978 as cited in Kaplan, et al., 1989; Weiss, Williams, Margen, et al., 1980 as cited in Kaplan, et al., 1989).

In addition to the possibility that young children may be more easily affected by sugared foods than older children, it may also be more difficult for young children to avoid sugared foods. A child of 14, for example, who is sensitive to sweet foods may be better able than a 6-year-old child to withstand peer pressure to eat sugared foods because of his/her awareness of the repercussions he/she may face as a result.

Differences in Responses to Sweet Foods

The foods which received the most responses of children's behavioral reaction were Candy/Chocolate, Cake/Cookies, Soda, and Sugar-Sweetened Cereals. Cake, cookies, and sugar-sweetened cereals are foods which contain large amounts of sugar and carbohydrate. Conners (1989) found that sugar eaten with carbohydrates increased inattention in children. The combination of carbohydrate and sugar in cake, cookies, and cereals may have caused behavioral reactions.

Cake, cookies, and cereals, usually made with white flour, are high glycemic foods, or foods which travel quickly into the bloodstream after they are eaten. The insulin response to pastries and cereals may exaggerate the sugar effects. Wheat flour also contains gluten, which is a highly allergenic food. Children who consume pastries and sugared cereals may react to the gluten in the food as well as to the sugar.

In addition, children usually consume cereal in the morning, after an overnight fast. As several parents reported, effects of sugar are exacerbated when sugar is eaten on an empty stomach.

Soda may have caused behavioral reactions in many children because it is a liquid, which is ingested more quickly and in greater quantity than a solid food. The sudden rise of blood sugar caused by the quick ingestion of the sugared drink produces an increased insulin response. Additionally, the caffeine in soda may also have been responsible for some of the behavior changes.

The two food groups which parents reported to cause the least amount of behavioral reactions were ices and sweetened yogurt/chocolate milk. Ices may have caused less behavior changes than other sugared foods since they are usually eaten slowly and in small quantities. Sweetened yogurt and chocolate milk may have caused few behavioral reactions because they are protein foods. The PA and several parents in this study believed that protein foods balance effects of sugar. Findings of a study by Conners (1989) bolsters the opinion that protein counters sugar effects.

Possible Reason for Parents' Lack of Noting Behavioral Effects of Sugar

Some parents may not have correlated their children's consumption of sugar with adverse behaviors simply because their children always consume sugared foods. They therefore can not compare their children's behavior after sugar consumption to their behavior after eating totally sugar-free meals. Parents may have become accustomed to their children's overactive or inattentive behaviors. They regard such behaviors as normal for their children and do not associate the behaviors with overindulgence in sugared foods.

Sugar on Behavior 49

Conclusion

Refined sugar has been labeled "the most ubiquitous and the most unrecognized toxin to which humankind is exposed" (Buchanan, 1984, p. 1328). Though nutritionists and orthomolecular medical practitioners caution against the intake of sugar, parents disregard these warnings and continue to feed sugar-laden foods to their unknowing children. These children then become plagued with allergic reactions, hypoglycemic conditions, and nutrient deficiencies. Many of these children suffer from hyperactivity, aggression, or inattention, and some are even medicated to relieve their adverse behaviors. Scores of children are constantly irritable or fatigued and encounter behavior and academic problems at home and in school. Yet parents still feed their children sugar for breakfast and teachers still hand out candy for good work.

This study confirms the contention that sugared foods can impact children's behavior. Parents and health professionals reported that many children display irritability, overactivity, aggression, inattention, and tiredness after ingesting sugared foods. To reduce these negative behaviors, parents would be well advised to eliminate refined sugar from their children's diets. As Hoffer and Walker (1996) believe, "Pure sucrose should be barred from human use and converted into alcohol as fuel for automobiles" (p. 87). Parents might then find their children more relaxed and easily managed, while teachers might see their students more alert, focused, and calm.

Implications for Practice

Parents should carefully monitor their children's intake of refined sugar. As previous research has shown, refined sugar has no nutritive value. Children's nutrition will not suffer because of a lack of refined sugar. Children can obtain all necessary sugars from fruit and other whole foods. Parents should be especially vigilant in making

Sugar on Behavior 50

certain their hyperactive children do not consume sugars. Even a slight amount of sugar on occasion may produce acute behavioral responses in these children.

Pediatricians should be aware of sugar-behavior effects. Before recommending medication for children with behavioral problems, pediatricians should first advise parents to have their children avoid sugared foods.

Teachers should also understand how sugar can impact children's behavior. They should encourage their students to bring wholesome snacks to school. Teachers should also replace the candy they distribute to students as rewards with non-food prizes or snacks which do not contain sugar.

Implications for Further Research

In this study, parents completed sugar-behavior questionnaires as soon as they received them. It may be that some participant parents never really paid attention to their children's behavior following sugar consumption. These parents' reports might have been more accurate had they observed their children's behavior for some time before completing the questionnaires. One mother in this study who completed the questionnaire several weeks after receiving it commented that before receiving the questionnaire, she didn't notice any sugar-behavior effects in her children. After reading the questionnaire and paying closer attention to the foods her children ate, she noticed two instances of possible behavioral reactions to sugar in one child. Researchers in future studies should suggest that parents read the questionnaires and then wait a few weeks before answering the questions.

Three parents in this study remarked that eating sugar on an empty stomach exacerbates their children's reactions. In future studies, all parents should be asked whether their children only react to sugared foods when they are eaten on an empty stomach.

Two parents in this study who were teachers by profession mentioned that their students became restless and hyperactive after consuming sugared snacks during their recess break. One previous study surveyed teachers to assess their opinions of the role of food allergy on children's behavior in school. Teachers pointed to sugar as the food which most commonly induced learning and behavioral problems in their students. Negative behaviors they noted included inattentiveness, sluggishness, irritability, and aggressiveness (McLoughlin & Nall, 1988). Additional studies need to be conducted to ascertain teachers' views as to whether, and how, sugar impacts children's behavior at school.

Sugar-behavior research to date mainly consists of studies in which children's diets were manipulated. Researchers used control and experimental groups or within subject crossover designs. The studies were mostly of short duration, lasting from a few hours to several weeks. It would be interesting to see results of a longitudinal study, which would follow two groups of children, one on a high-sucrose and one on a low-sucrose diet, over a number of years. A longitudinal sugar-behavior study might produce more authentic and accurate results than a short-term, dietary manipulation test.

Future studies might eliminate not only refined sugar, but also natural forms of sugar, such as honey and fruit juice, from children's diets. A greater percentage of children with hyperactivity or other behavioral problems may show improvement in behavior on this more restricted diet.

References

American Psychiatric Association. (2000). *Diagnostic and statistical manual of mental disorders* (4th ed.). Washington, DC: American Psychiatric Association.

Appleton, N. (1996). *Lick the sugar habit.* Garden City, Park, NY: Avery Publishing Group.

Bachorowski, J.-A., Newman, J. P., Nichols, S. L., Gans, D. A., Harper, A. E., & Taylor, S. L. (1990). Sucrose and delinquency: Behavioral assessment. *Pediatrics, 86*(2), 244-253.

Behar, D., Rapoport, J. L., Adams, A. J., Berg, C. J., & Cornblath, M. (1984). Sugar challenge testing with children considered behaviorally "sugar reactive." *Nutrition and Behavior, 1,* 277-288.

Boris, M., & Mandel, F. S. (1993). Foods and additives are common causes of the attention deficit hyperactive disorder in children. *Annals of Allergy, 72,* 462-468.

Buchanan, S.R. (1984). The most ubiquitous toxin. *American Psychologist, 11,* 1327-1328.

Center for Science in the Public Interest. (2000). Sugar intake hit all-time high in 1999. *Nutrition Action Healthletter.* Retrieved from http://www.cspinet.org/new/sugar_limit.html

Conners, C. K. (1989). *Feeding the brain: How foods affect children.* New York, NY: Plenum Press.

Conners, C. K., & Blouin, A. G. (1983). Nutritional effects on behavior of children. *Journal of Psychiatric Research, 17*(2), 193-201.

Sugar on Behavior 53

Crook, W. G. (1975). Food allergy: The great masquerader. *Pediatric Clinics of North America, 22*(1), 227-234.

Crook, W. G. (1977). *Can your child read? Is he hyperactive?* Jackson, TN: Professional Books.

Crook, W. G. (1980). Can what a child eats make him dull, stupid, or hyperactive? *Journal of Learning Disabilities, 13*(5), 53-57.

Ferguson, H. B., Stoddart, C., & Simeon, J. G. (1986). Double-blind challenge studies of behavioral and cognitive effects of sucrose-aspartame ingestion in normal children. *Nutrition Reviews, 44*(suppl), 144-150.

Goldman, J. A., Lerman, R. H., Contois, J. H., & Udall, J. N. (1986). Behavioral effects of sucrose on preschool children. *Journal of Abnormal Child Psychology, 14,* 565-577.

Gross, M. D. (1984). Effect of sucrose on hyperkinetic children. *Pediatrics, 74,* 876-878.

Hoffer, A., & Walker, M. (1996). *Putting it all together: The new orthomolecular nutrition.* New Canaan, CT: Keats Publishing.

Jacobson, M. (1998). Liquid Candy. *Nutrition Action Healthletter, 25*(1), 8.

Kruesi, M. J. P., Rapoport, J. L., Cummings, E. M., Berg, C. J., Ismond, D. R., Flament, M., et al. (1987). Effects of sugar and aspartame on aggression and activity in children. *American Journal of Psychiatry, 144,* 1487-1490.

Mahan, L. K., Chase, M., Furukawa, C. T., Sulzbacher, S., Shapiro, G. G., Pierson, W. E., et al. (1988). Sugar "allergy" and children's behavior. *Annals of Allergy, 61,* 453-458.

McLoughlin, J. A., & Nall, M. (1988). Teacher opinion of the role of food allergy on school behavior and achievement. *Annals of Allergy, 61,* 89-91.

Sugar on Behavior 54

Milich, R., Wolraich, M., & Lindgren, S. (1986). Sugar and hyperactivity: A critical view of empirical findings. *Clinical Psychology Review, 6,* 493-513.

Null, G. (1995). *Nutrition and the mind.* New York, NY: Four Walls Eight Windows.

Null, G. (2000). *The food-mood-body connection: Nutrition-based and environmental approaches to mental health and physical wellbeing.* New York, NY: Seven Stories Press.

Prinz, R. J., & Riddle, D. B. (1986). Associations between nutrition and behavior in 5-year-old children. *Nutrition Reviews, 44*(suppl), 151-157.

Prinz, R. J., Roberts, W. A., & Hantman, E. (1980). Dietary correlates of hyperactive behavior in children. *Journal of Consulting and Clinical Psychology, 48,* 760-769.

Randolph, T. J. (1947). Allergy as a causative factor of fatigue, irritability, and behavior problems of children. *The Journal of Pediatrics, 31,* 560-572.

Rapp, D. J. (1978). Does diet affect hyperactivity? *Journal of Learning Disabilities, 11*(6), 56-62.

Rosen, L. A., Bender, M. E., Sorrell, S., Booth, S. R., McGrath, M. L., & Drabman, R. S. (1988). Effects of sugar (sucrose) on children's behavior. *Journal of Consulting and Clinical Psychology, 56,* 583-589.

Rowe, A. H. (1931). *Food allergy.* Philadelphia, PA: Lea & Febiger.

Rowe, A. H. (1972). *Food allergy: Its manifestations and control and the elimination diets.* Springfield, IL: Charles C Thomas.

Schlosser, E. (2001). *Fast food nation: The dark side of the all-American meal.* New York, NY: Houghton Mifflin Company.

Seham, M., & Seham, G. (1929). The relation between malnutrition and nervousness. *American Journal of Diseases in Children, 37*(1), 1-38.

Appendixes

Appendix A: Phone Script for Calls to Potential Participants

"Hello. This is Name. I am doing a survey for a thesis I am writing. This survey will help me learn the impact sugar may have on children's behavior. To gather data about this topic, I composed a questionnaire."

"Would you be willing to answer some questions on the phone or in writing? It should take no longer than ten minutes to answer the questions. Participation in this study is voluntary, and you are not required to answer any or all questions. If you decline, I will respect your decision."

If the response is negative, the researcher will say, "Thank you anyway. Have a good day."

If the response is positive: "Thanks for helping me out. All respondents' names will be kept confidential."

"Would you like to answer the questions over the phone now, at a later time, or should I mail a questionnaire to you?"

If the party answers "now," the researcher will state: "Completing the survey implies consent to participate in the study. You can obtain a summary of the results of the study in December of this year by mailing a request to the researcher at 18 Cameo Ridge Rd. Monsey, NY 10952." The researcher will then proceed to ask the questions.

If the party wants the questionnaire mailed, say, "You'll receive the questionnaire in the mail in a couple of days."

At the end of the conversation, the researcher will say: "Thank you very much for your participation. It was/will be a great help."

Shannon, W. R. (1922). Nueropathologic manifestations in infants and children as a result of anaphylactic reaction to foods contained in their dietary. *American Journal of Disorders in Children, 24,* 89-94.

Speer, F. (1954). The allergic tension-fatigue syndrome. *The Pediatric Clinics of North America, 1,* 1029-1037.

Spring, B., Chiodo, J., & Bowen, D. J. (1987). Carbohydrates, tryptophan, and behavior: A methodological review. *Psychological Bulletin, 102,* 234-256.

Wender, E. H., & Solanto, M. V. (1991). Effects of sugar on aggressive and inattentive behavior in children with attention deficit disorder with hyperactivity and normal children. *Pediatrics, 88,* 960-966.

Wolraich, M. L., Lindgren, S. D., Stumbo, P. J., Stegink, L. D., Appelbaum, M. I., & Kiritsy, M. C. (1994). Effects of diets high in sucrose or aspartame on the behavior and cognitive performance of children. *The New England Journal of Medicine, 33(5),* 301-307.

Wolraich, M. L., Stumbo, P. J., Milch, R., Chenard, C., & Schultz, F. (1986). Dietary characteristics of hyperactive and control boys. *Journal of the American Dietetic Association, 86,* 500-504.

Wolraich, M. L., Wilson, D. B., & White, J. W. (1995). The effect of sugar on behavior or cognition in children. *Journal of the American Medical Association, 274,* 1616-1621.

Wurtman, J. J., & Suffes, S. (1996). *The serotonin solution.* Fawcett Columbine, NY: Ballantine Books.

Wurtman, R. J., & Wurtman, J. J. (1977). *Nutrition and the brain.* New York, NY: Raven Press.

Sugar on Behavior 58

Appendix C: Consent Form

I, _____ (Print Name), agree to participate in the research project, "Impact of Sugar on Children's Behavior," being carried out by Name. I have been informed by Name of the nature of the project. I understand that I have the right to withhold permission for the researcher to use any data gleaned from my participation.

I also understand that upon my request by mail in December of this year, the researcher will provide me with a written summary of the project's findings.

_____   _____
Participant's Signature   Date

Sugar on Behavior 57

Appendix B: Cover Letter for Parental Questionnaire

October 2004

Dear Participant,

As per our phone conversation, I am sending you the enclosed questionnaire. I am a student in a Special Education Program at College. I am working on a thesis which concerns the ways in which sugar may impact children's behavior. Your and other parents' answers to the enclosed questionnaire will help me evaluate behavioral changes, if any, in children after their consumption of snacks and foods containing sugar.

I understand that you have a busy schedule, and I am grateful for your taking the time to answer the questions on the enclosed forms (it should only take about ten minutes). If you could return the completed questionnaire as soon as possible, I would greatly appreciate it. Please remember that your participation is voluntary and you are not required to complete any or all items.

None of the information you submit will be disclosed to anyone. Your name will be kept in strict confidence.

If you would like to obtain a written summary of the results of this project, please contact me by mail in December of this year at 18 Cameo Ridge Road, Monsey, NY 10952.

Thank you very much for your assistance.

Sincerely,

Name

Appendix D: Parental Questionnaire

Form I

Please list the age and gender of each child between 2 and 16 years of age who may have overt behavioral reactions to sugar.
Use a separate form for each child.

Age of child _____

Gender of child _____

Circle a letter in each box below to describe the frequency of the following reactive behaviors you believe your child displays as a result of consuming the listed foods. **Circle N/A if the child never consumes a food.**

Legend: N- Never   I- Infrequently   F- Frequently   V- Very often

Food	Behavior					
	Irritable (impatient, unobliging, cranky, moody, complaining, easily frustrated)	**Aggressive** (angry, hitting, feet stomping, throwing things)	**Inattentive** (unable to focus, dreamy, forgetful, distractible, fails to complete tasks)	**Overactive** (increased motor activity, unable to remain at one activity for a reasonable amount of time, engages in physically dangerous activities)	**Tired** (sluggish, sleepy)	**Other** (Please describe) _____
Sugar-sweetened cereals	N I F V N/A	N I F V N/A	N I F V N/A	N I F V N/A	N I F V N/A	N I F V N/A
Sweetened yogurt/ Chocolate milk	N I F V N/A	N I F V N/A	N I F V N/A	N I F V N/A	N I F V N/A	N I F V N/A
Cake/ Cookies	N I F V N/A	N I F V N/A	N I F V N/A	N I F V N/A	N I F V N/A	N I F V N/A
Candy/ Chocolate	N I F V N/A	N I F V N/A	N I F V N/A	N I F V N/A	N I F V N/A	N I F V N/A
Ices	N I F V N/A	N I F V N/A	N I F V N/A	N I F V N/A	N I F V N/A	N I F V N/A
Soda	N I F V N/A	N I F V N/A	N I F V N/A	N I F V N/A	N I F V N/A	N I F V N/A

Sugar on Behavior 59

Form I

Additional Copy for Second Child

Age of child _____

Gender of child _____

Circle a letter in each box below to describe the frequency of the following reactive behaviors you believe your child displays as a result of consuming the listed foods. **Circle N/A if the child never consumes a food.**

Legend: N- Never   I- Infrequently   F- Frequently   V- Very often

Food	Behavior					
	Irritable (impatient, unobliging, cranky, moody, complaining, easily frustrated)	**Aggressive** (angry, hitting, feet stomping, throwing things)	**Inattentive** (unable to focus, dreamy, forgetful, distractible, fails to complete tasks)	**Overactive** (increased motor activity, unable to remain at one activity for a reasonable amount of time, engages in physically dangerous activities)	**Tired** (sluggish, sleepy)	**Other** (Please describe) _____
Sugar-sweetened cereals	N I F V N/A	N I F V N/A	N I F V N/A	N I F V N/A	N I F V N/A	N I F V N/A
Sweetened yogurt/ Chocolate milk	N I F V N/A	N I F V N/A	N I F V N/A	N I F V N/A	N I F V N/A	N I F V N/A
Cake/ Cookies	N I F V N/A	N I F V N/A	N I F V N/A	N I F V N/A	N I F V N/A	N I F V N/A
Candy/ Chocolate	N I F V N/A	N I F V N/A	N I F V N/A	N I F V N/A	N I F V N/A	N I F V N/A
Ices	N I F V N/A	N I F V N/A	N I F V N/A	N I F V N/A	N I F V N/A	N I F V N/A
Soda	N I F V N/A	N I F V N/A	N I F V N/A	N I F V N/A	N I F V N/A	N I F V N/A

Sugar on Behavior 60

Form II

1. Please list the age and gender of each of your children who is between 2 and 16 years of age: _____

2. In question number 1, circle the age and gender of any child who you think displays behavioral reactions to sugar.

3. If you circled the age and gender of (a) child/ren that you did not describe in the Food/Behavior chart, briefly describe the behavioral changes you see in this/these child/ren: _____

4. How often do your children consume sugar-sweetened *foods*?
   a. every day
   b. once a week
   c. less than once a week

5. How often do your children consume sugar-sweetened *snacks*?
   a. every day
   b. once a week
   c. less than once a week

If you have observed behavioral reactions to sugar in any of your children, please answer the following questions:

6. Were the behavioral reactions you observed immediate (within 30 minutes after consumption of the food) or delayed? _____

7. If the reactions were delayed, how long was the delay? _____

8. Do any other foods/circumstances trigger the reactions you indicated above? Please specify: _____

9. Do the behavioral reactions you described lead to problems at school? _____

10. Do you think your children are allergic to sugar? _____

11. Have you tried eliminating the sugar laden provoking foods from your children's diet/s? _____

12. If yes, did behaviors improve after the foods were eliminated? _____

Comments: _____

_____

_____

_____

_____

Appendix E: Cover Letter for Health Professional Questionnaire

October 2004

Dear Participant,

As per our phone conversation, I am sending you the enclosed questionnaire. I am a student in a Special Education Program at College. I am working on a master's thesis which concerns the ways in which sugar may impact children's behavior. Your and other health professionals' answers to the enclosed questionnaire will help me evaluate behavioral changes, if any, in children after their consumption of snacks and foods containing sugar.

I understand that you have a busy schedule, and I am grateful for your taking the time to answer the questions on the enclosed forms (it should only take about ten minutes). If you could return the completed questionnaire as soon as possible, I would greatly appreciate it. Please remember that your participation is voluntary and you are not required to complete any or all items.

None of the information you submit will be disclosed to anyone. Your name will be kept in strict confidence.

If you would like to obtain a written summary of the results of this project, please contact me by mail in December of this year at 18 Cameo Ridge Road, Monsey, NY 10952.

Thank you very much for your assistance.

Sincerely,

Name

Form II

Sugar on Behavior 64

If your clients ever exhibited any behavioral reactions to the foods listed above, please answer the following questions:

1. Approximately how many of your clients are between the ages of 2 and 16? _____

2. Approximately how many of these clients, aged 2-16, have shown any adverse behavioral reactions to sugar? _____

3. In the population of children who reacted to the sweet foods, there were:

a. significantly more boys than girls
b. slightly more boys than girls
c. significantly more girls than boys
d. slightly more girls than boys
e. an equal amount of each gender

4. In which age group were the children who were most likely to react to sugar?

a. 2 – 4 years
b. 5 - 8 years
c. 9 - 12 years
d. 13 - 16 years

5. Did most of the children react immediately (within 30 minutes after consumption of the food) or were the reactions delayed? _____

6. If the behavioral reactions to sugar were delayed, how long were the delays? _____

7. What were the initial complaints of most of the parents of the sugar-reactive children? _____

8. Were the behavioral reactions in most children accompanied by physical symptoms (stomachache, trouble sleeping, etc.)? _____

9. Were most of the parents of the reactive children aware of the children's food sensitivities when they first came to seek treatment? _____

10. Approximately how many of the of parents of the sugar-reactive children complained of problems at school? _____

11. In your opinion, what percentage of the sugar-induced reactions were due to:

Allergy _____
Hypoglocemia _____
Other (Please specify) _____
Unknown causes _____

Appendix F: Health Professional Questionnaire

Sugar on Behavior 63

Form I

Please *circle* a letter in each box below to indicate the estimated number of your clients (ages 2-16) who you believe exhibit the following behaviors after consuming the listed foods.

Legend: A- 0   B- 1-5   C- 6-15   D- 15-30   E- more than 30

Food	Behavior					
	Irritable (impatient, unobliging, cranky, moody, complaining, easily frustrated)	Aggressive (angry, hitting, feet stomping, throwing things)	Inattentive (unable to focus, dreamy, forgetful, distractible, fails to complete tasks)	Overactive (increased motor activity, unable to remain at one activity for a reasonable amount of time, engages in physically dangerous activities)	Tired (sluggish, sleepy)	Other (Please describe)
Sugar-sweetened Cereals	A B C D E	A B C D E	A B C D E	A B C D E	A B C D E	A B C D E
Fruit Juices	A B C D E	A B C D E	A B C D E	A B C D E	A B C D E	A B C D E
Cake/Cookies	A B C D E	A B C D E	A B C D E	A B C D E	A B C D E	A B C D E
Candy	A B C D E	A B C D E	A B C D E	A B C D E	A B C D E	A B C D E
Box Drinks (lemonade, fruit punch, etc.)	A B C D E	A B C D E	A B C D E	A B C D E	A B C D E	A B C D E
Ices	A B C D E	A B C D E	A B C D E	A B C D E	A B C D E	A B C D E
Soda	A B C D E	A B C D E	A B C D E	A B C D E	A B C D E	A B C D E

Sugar on Behavior 65

12. Did any other foods/circumstances trigger the behavioral reactions in the sugar-reactive children? _____

Please specify _____

_____

_____

13. Do you ever recommend omitting sugar from clients' diets? _____

14. If you do, do the behaviors usually improve when foods with sugar are eliminated? _____

15. Do problems at school usually improve when sugar is eliminated from the diets of 'sugar-reactive'

children? _____

16. After how long on the elimination diets do the children usually show improvement? _____

_____

Comments: _____

_____

_____

_____

_____

_____

Index

A

abstract, 308–312
action research, 55–58
American Educational Research Association (AERA), 22
analytic procedures, 258–264
ANCOVA (analysis of covariance), 129
APA style, 300–307

C

case study research, 174
chi square test, 246–251
conclusions/discussion, 289
correlation research, 156–159

D

data analysis
    interpretation of, 285–288
    qualitative, 257–264
    quantitative, 221–256
data collection, 181–219
descriptive research, 152–155
design
    broadly, 123–151
    data collection, 181–219
    interrupted time series design, 130
    non-equivalent control group, 128
    one-group pretest/post test, 127
    pretest only control group design, 130
    pretest/post test control group, 130
    qualitative, 167–180
    quantitative, 151–166
    single measurement, 126
    static-group comparison, 127
    unassessed treatment, 124–125

E

EBSCO, 32–35
education research
    broadly, 39–58
    steps of, 55–58
ERIC, 32–35
ethics, 20–26
ethnographic research, 171
evaluating the thesis, 319
examining test data, 210–213

F

formulating hypotheses, 94–100
future research, 281–296

G

group comparison research, 160–166
group focuses, 205–209

H

historical research, 168
hypotheses, 94–100

I

implications for practice/research, 281–296
INGENTA, 32–35
Institutional Review Board, 20–22, 381–384
instruments, 214
intelligent consumer of research, 321–324
interpreting data, 285–288
interrupted time series design, 130
interviews and group focuses, 205–209
introduction of thesis, 75
IRB, See Institutional Review Board

L

Likert scale, 182–187, 225
limitations, 282–284
literature review, 101–122

M

Mann-Whitney U-Test, 242–245
mean, 225–226
non-equivalent control group design, 128

O

observation, 153, 188–204
one-group Pretest/Post test design, 127

P

parental consent form, 385–386
percentage, 225–226
portfolios, 213
pretest only control group design, 130
pretest/post test control group design, 130
proposal, 59–67
Publication Manual of the American Psychological Association (APA), See APA

Q

qualitative data analysis, 257–264
qualitative research design, 167–180
quantitative data analysis, 221–256
quantitative research design, 151
questionnaires, 182–187

R

reliability of instruments, 214–219
research design, 123–151
research in education, 39–58
research preparation, 1–27
    ethics and, 19–26
    stress, 2
    time management, 10–13
    writing suggestions, 14–18
research proposal, 387–406
research questions, 88–93

results, presentation of, 266–280
review of the literature, 27–38
rubrics
    evaluating research articles, 104–109, 112
    literature review, 120
    proposal, 66

S

sample IRB application, 381–384
sample thesis, 407–440
school profile data, 212
scientific method, 51–52
selecting a topic/title, 76–87
sign test 238–241
single measurement design, 126
SPSS (Statistical Product and Service Solutions), 252–256
standard deviation, 225–226
static-group comparison design, 127
statistical analyses, 222–251
STATPAK (Statistical Packages), 129, 227, 252–256
surveys, 152

T

test data, 210–213
time management, 10–13
topic search/selection, 27–38, 76–87
t-Test, 234–237

U

unassessed treatment design, 124–125

V

validity/reliability of instruments, 214–216

W

writing the thesis, 68–74, 298–301

About the Author

Jeffrey Glanz currently serves as Dean of Graduate Programs and Chair of the Department of Education at Wagner College in Staten Island, New York. Prior to arriving at Wagner, he served as executive assistant to the president of Kean University in Union, New Jersey. Dr. Glanz held faculty status as a tenured professor in the Department of Instruction and Educational Leadership at Kean University's College of Education. He was named Graduate Teacher of the Year in 1999 by the Student Graduate Association and was also that year's recipient of the Presidential Award for Outstanding Scholarship. He served as an administrator and teacher in the New York City public schools for 20 years. Dr. Glanz has authored, co-authored, and co-edited 20 books and has over 35 peer-reviewed article publications. With Christopher-Gordon he previously published *Educational Supervision: Perspectives, Issues, ad Controversies*, *Relax for Success: An Educator's Guide to Stress Management*, and the 2nd edition of *Action Research: An Educational Leader's Guide to School Improvement*. Consult his web site for additional information: http://www.wagner.edu/faculty/users/jglanz/web/